IMPERIAL
MARRIAGE

Other books by the authors

MIRABEL CECIL
Heroines in Love
A Kind of Prospero: Sebastian Walker, 1942–1991

HUGH CECIL
Salisbury: The Man and His Policies (ed. with Robert Blake)
The Flower of Battle: How Britain Wrote the Great War

HUGH AND MIRABEL CECIL
Clever Hearts: A Biography of Desmond and Molly MacCarthy

Violet Cecil as a young woman. Drawing by Mortimer Menpes
in Cape Town, 1900

IMPERIAL MARRIAGE

An Edwardian War and Peace

HUGH

AND

MIRABEL CECIL

JOHN MURRAY
Albemarle Street, London

Endpapers: (*front*) The east front of Hatfield House, 1901; (*back*) Great Wigsell, Kent, 1918

First published in 2002
by John Murray (Publishers) Ltd,
50 Albemarle Street, London W1S 4BD

A catalogue record for this book is available from the British Library

ISBN 0-7195-6043 8

Typeset in Monotype Bembo 11.5/13.5
by Servis Filmsetting Ltd, Manchester

Printed and bound in Great Britain by
Butler and Tanner Ltd
Frome and London

For Hannah Cranborne,
companion in the Hatfield House archives,
and for Richard Davies,
whose family lived at Great Wigsell.

Contents

Acknowledgements

IMPERIAL MARRIAGE BEGAN with a house – Great Wigsell Manor, near Hawkhurst in Kent, which, from 1906, belonged to Edward and Violet Cecil; Violet restored it from dereliction and lived there for more than half a century. It was sold by her grandson to the Davies family; we owe a great deal to the help and hospitality, over many years, of the late Mrs Barbara Davies and her sons Glen and Richard. Much about Wigsell was preserved as it had been in Violet's day. This remarkable house, created by a remarkable woman, evoked the vanished era before the Great War of 1914–18 and drew us into investigating the story of her life and her family. During the 1920s, a little girl called Joscelyn Verney, now Mrs Joscelyn Thorne, lived at Wigsell, which was let to her parents and we acknowledge her help in describing it to us as it was then.

The other house central to this story, Edward Cecil's birthplace and the scene of his happy boyhood, is Hatfield House, Hertfordshire, home of the 6th Marquess and Marchioness of Salisbury. To them we are indebted for family information, for permission to use the Cecil papers in the Hatfield archive, for reading the manuscript and for generous hospitality. We also thank their cousin, Lady Anne Brewis, for her recollections.

Hatfield's Librarian and Archivist, Robin Harcourt Williams, has been called without exaggeration 'a prince amongst archivists'. Unfailingly concise and generous in advice, he has been assiduous in searching out information, however arcane, and details which flesh out the past.

The Hardinge family, Edward and Violet Cecil's descendants through their daughter Helen, have been generous with their time, their memories and photographs; we thank them for permission to quote from Violet and Helen's published and unpublished writings and for the use of family photograph albums. In particular, we would like to thank Violet's surviving granddaughter, the Hon. Lady Murray; and also Lady Murray's nephews, the Lord Hardinge of Penshurst and the Hon. Hugh Hardinge; her brother-in-law, Sir John Johnston, his daughter Joanna Johnston, the Hon. Charles Hardinge and the Dowager Lady Hardinge. Anthony Maxse, Violet's great-nephew, kindly gave permission to quote from the letters of Violet's family.

André and Marcel Wormser, the sons of Georges Clemenceau's *Chef de Cabinet*, discussed the vital influence of the statesman on Violet and her family, and organised a memorable visit to the Clemenceau Museum in Paris with Clemenceau's great-niece, Mme Lise Devinat.

Our lengthy research into the papers of Edward and Violet Cecil and of her second husband, Lord Milner, at the Bodleian Library, Oxford, was enormously lightened by the generous hospitality and the extensive library of Roy Foster, Carroll Professor of Irish History at the University of Oxford and Fellow of Hertford College.

Of Violet's friends, Iverach McDonald, who knew her well over the last twenty years of her life, has given us a penetrating picture of her; as has John Grigg, who took over from her the editorship of the *National Review*.

We are grateful to Kenneth Rose, author of *The Later Cecils*, who stimulated our investigations into Edward Cecil's life. On Edward's Egyptian career we have benefited from David Pryce-Jones's extensive knowledge of the region and the period; John de Havilland lent us Mafeking material; The Earl Haig kindly gave permission to use his father's 1898 Sudan letters. We are grateful to Jacky Hughes, especially over E.B. Iwan-Müller's diaries; to Timothy Palmer; to Professor Richard Dawkins and to Michael Burden, at New College, Oxford; and to Sir Edward Hulse.

We are particularly grateful to Colin Harris at the Modern Papers Reading Room, the Bodleian Library, Oxford, for his interest and help; and to Richard Childs, the County Archivist, and Alison McCann, at the West Sussex Record Office, Chichester; Mrs P. Judd, the Assistant Librarian at Pembroke College, Cambridge; Jane Hogan, the Archivist of Durham University Library; the staff of the Brenthurst Library, Johannesburg, especially Diana Madden, the Librarian; Sandra Rowolt of the Cory library, Rhodes University, Grahamstown; and Geoffrey Phillips, the Curator of Mafikeng Museum, who maintains on a shoestring this key historical collection.

We would like to thank the following institutions for permission to quote material: the Bodleian Library and the Warden and Fellows of New College, Oxford (Milner papers); the British Museum; the Brenthurst Library; the Cory Library; the National Library of Scotland; the National Trust and A.P. Watt & Son (Rudyard and Carrie Kipling).

We thank Anthony and Antoinette Oppenheimer for their hospitality in South Africa and for absorbing trips to Boer War battlefields; Graham Viney, for help with the architecture and society of Cape Colony; and Alta Kriel, the Curator of Groote Schuur.

Over the history of the Mafeking siege we were helped by the unrivalled knowledge and understanding of Tim Jeal and Brian Willan. Tim Couzens gave much background on South African history, as did Bill Nasson, Fransjohan Pretorius and André Wessels; Thomas Pakenham's stimulating book awoke our interest in the Boer War.

Our thanks are due to our agent Georgina Capel; to Jenny Moores for secretarial help; to Christine Groom for typing the drafts of this book; and to the editorial and production staff of John Murray.

Every effort has been made to locate current holders of copyright in text and illustrations; we apologise for any omissions and would welcome information so that amendments can be made in future editions.

Finally we thank Dervla Murphy for her invaluable editorial advice.

EDWARD CECIL'S SUDAN CAMPAIGNS, 1896 & 1898

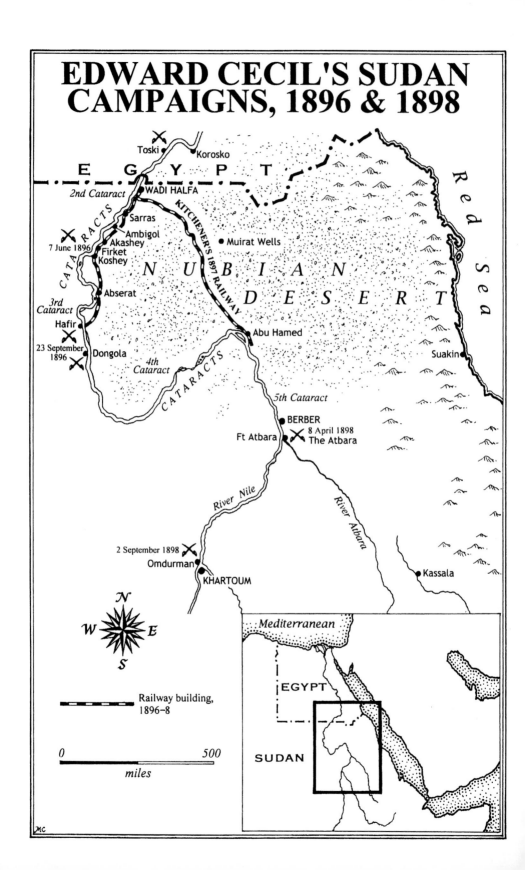

Toski

Korosko

E G Y P T

2nd Cataract

WADI HALFA

Sarras

Ambigol

Akashey

7 June 1896

Firket

Koshey

Muirat Wells

N U B I A N

D E S E R T

Abserat

3rd Cataract

Hafir

23 September 1896

Dongola

4th Cataract

CATARACTS

Abu Hamed

Suakin

5th Cataract

BERBER

Ft Atbara

8 April 1898

The Atbara

River Nile

River Atbara

2 September 1898

Omdurman

KHARTOUM

Kassala

Red Sea

KITCHENER'S 1897 RAILWAY

CATARACTS

N
W E
S

Railway building, 1896–8

0   500
miles

Mediterranean

EGYPT

SUDAN

MC

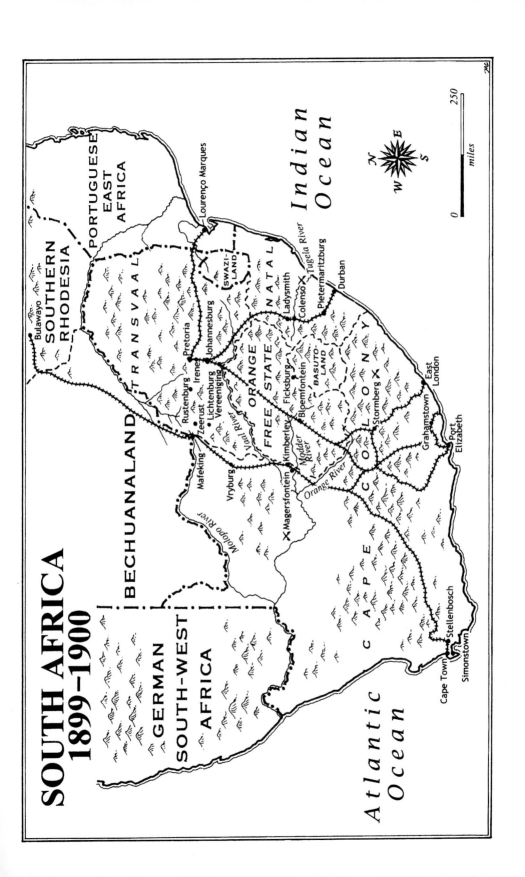

SOUTH AFRICA 1899–1900

GERMAN SOUTH-WEST AFRICA

BECHUANALAND

SOUTHERN RHODESIA

PORTUGUESE EAST AFRICA

TRANSVAAL

SWAZILAND

NATAL

ORANGE FREE STATE

BASUTOLAND

CAPE COLONY

Bulawayo

Lourenço Marques

Pretoria
Irene
Rustenburg
Zeerust
Lichtenburg
Johannesburg
Vereeniging

Ladysmith
Colenso
Pietermaritzburg
Durban

Ficksburg
Kimberley
Bloemfontein
Stormberg
East London

Magersfontein
Mafeking
Vryburg

Grahamstown
Port Elizabeth

Cape Town
Simonstown
Stellenbosch

Moppo River
Vaal River
Modder River
Orange River
Tugela River

Indian Ocean

Atlantic Ocean

miles
0   250

The Cecils, the Maxses and the Hardinges

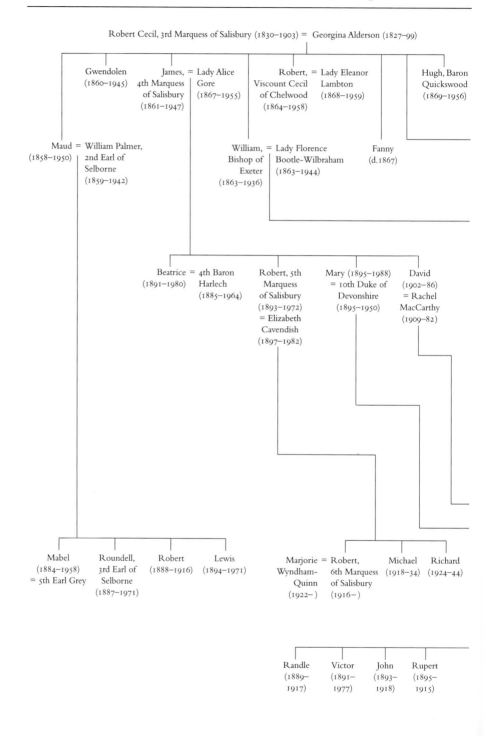

Robert Cecil, 3rd Marquess of Salisbury (1830–1903) = Georgina Alderson (1827–99)

Gwendolen (1860–1945)

James, 4th Marquess of Salisbury (1861–1947) = Lady Alice Gore (1867–1955)

Robert, Viscount Cecil of Chelwood (1864–1958) = Lady Eleanor Lambton (1868–1959)

Hugh, Baron Quickswood (1869–1956)

Maud (1858–1950) = William Palmer, 2nd Earl of Selborne (1859–1942)

William, Bishop of Exeter (1863–1936) = Lady Florence Bootle-Wilbraham (1863–1944)

Fanny (d. 1867)

Beatrice (1891–1980) = 4th Baron Harlech (1885–1964)

Robert, 5th Marquess of Salisbury (1893–1972) = Elizabeth Cavendish (1897–1982)

Mary (1895–1988) = 10th Duke of Devonshire (1895–1950)

David (1902–86) = Rachel MacCarthy (1909–82)

Mabel (1884–1958) = 5th Earl Grey

Roundell, 3rd Earl of Selborne (1887–1971)

Robert (1888–1916)

Lewis (1894–1971)

Marjorie Wyndham-Quinn (1922–) = Robert, 6th Marquess of Salisbury (1916–)

Michael (1918–34)

Richard (1924–44)

Randle (1889–1917)

Victor (1891–1977)

John (1893–1918)

Rupert (1895–1915)

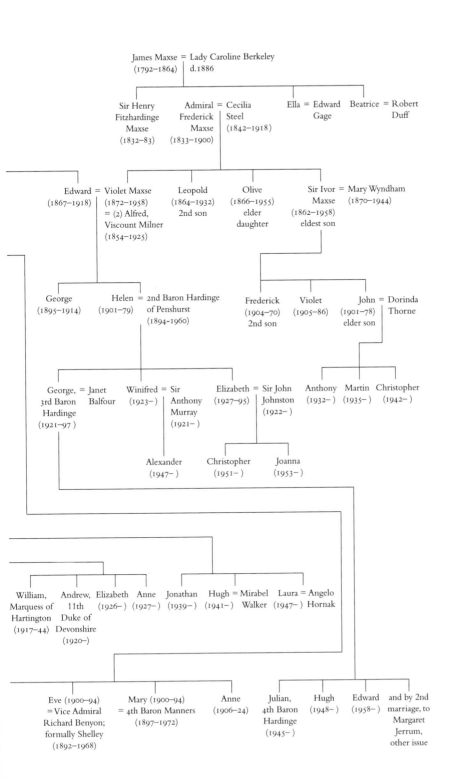

James Maxse = Lady Caroline Berkeley
(1792–1864) | d.1886

Sir Henry Fitzhardinge Maxse (1832–83)

Admiral = Cecilia Steel
Frederick | Maxse (1842–1918)
(1833–1900)

Ella = Edward Gage

Beatrice = Robert Duff

Edward = Violet Maxse
(1867–1918) | (1872–1958)
= (2) Alfred, Viscount Milner (1854–1925)

Leopold (1864–1932) 2nd son

Olive (1866–1955) elder daughter

Sir Ivor = Mary Wyndham
Maxse | (1870–1944)
(1862–1958) eldest son

George (1895–1914)

Helen = 2nd Baron Hardinge
(1901–79) | of Penshurst (1894–1960)

Frederick (1904–70) 2nd son

Violet (1905–86)

John = Dorinda
(1901–78) | Thorne
elder son

George, = Janet
3rd Baron | Balfour
Hardinge
(1921–97)

Winifred = Sir
(1923–) | Anthony Murray (1921–)

Elizabeth = Sir John
(1927–95) | Johnston (1922–)

Anthony (1932–)

Martin (1935–)

Christopher (1942–)

Alexander (1947–)

Christopher (1951–)

Joanna (1953–)

William, Marquess of Hartington (1917–44)

Andrew, 11th Duke of Devonshire (1920–)

Elizabeth (1926–)

Anne (1927–)

Jonathan (1939–)

Hugh = Mirabel
(1941–) | Walker

Laura = Angelo
(1947–) | Hornak

Eve (1900–94)
= Vice Admiral Richard Benyon; formally Shelley (1892–1968)

Mary (1900–94)
= 4th Baron Manners (1897–1972)

Anne (1906–24)

Julian, 4th Baron Hardinge (1945–)

Hugh (1948–)

Edward (1958–)

and by 2nd marriage, to Margaret Jerrum, other issue

Prologue

CERTAIN LIVES EPITOMISE their period. The three central figures of this book, Lord Edward Cecil (1867–1918), his wife, Violet *née* Maxse (1872–1958) and Alfred Milner (1854–1925) with whom she fell in love, epitomised theirs. This was a time when Britain's overseas Empire was at its apogee and when the English aristocracy in their great houses enjoyed a last ebullient flowering before the Parliament Act of 1911 struck a blow at their constitutional authority as a ruling class. It was a time, too, when the professional classes came to dominate the political scene: men like Alfred Milner adopted, as though by natural succession, much of the style and bearing of the aristocracy, a veritable *noblesse de la robe*.

Lord Edward Cecil's father, the 3rd Marquess of Salisbury, was Foreign Secretary and Prime Minister during the period of England's greatest imperial expansion. The Cecils' magnificent Jacobean country seat, Hatfield, was a powerhouse of English politics, where the great men of the day met and the issues of Empire, diplomacy and the constitution were the daily fare of family debates.

Edward himself, a brave imperial soldier, fought in Africa, notably during the Boer War, that conflict where the tactical superiority of the Boers on the veld challenged Britain's traditional military organisation. His experience there mirrored his country's triumphs and humiliations.

Alfred Milner, born into a family as impecunious as the Cecils' was grand, overcame the setbacks of his father's professional failure and his mother's early death to reach, via Oxford University and outstanding work as a civil servant, the lonely eminence of South African High Commissioner. There, at the Cape and in Johannesburg, he tried unsuccessfully for eight years, against Boer opposition, to shape the destiny of the Empire. Years later, in December 1916, he gained great power over Britain's fortunes once more, as a member of Lloyd George's select executive War Cabinet; and afterwards as a plenipotentiary, thrashing out the terms of the Treaty of Versailles.

At the Cape, during the Boer war, Violet, young, attractive, brimming with eagerness for life, came to believe that her destiny and Milner's were inseparable; and so they were. Much of the story of her marriage to Edward, despite quintessentially English features, recalls Tolstoy's *War and Peace*: the aristocratic setting, the conflicts of temperament and religious feeling, the impact of wars, the sporting life. Violet shared Natasha Rostov's *élan vital*, good looks and resilience; her father, the eccentric, valiant Admiral Maxse, might have been a model for Prince Bolkonski, while Edward had something of Pierre Bezhukov's spiritual yearning, of Count Andrew Bolkonski's sense of honour and moral contempt, and of Nicholas Rostov's weakness for gambling; Olive Maxse, Violet's pretty elder sister, just like Natasha's sweet and catlike cousin Sonya, lacked that essential vitality which makes people plunge into life. Petya Rostov and George Cecil, Violet's son, boys in a men's world, shared the same tragic fate in war.

To Violet, Edward and Alfred, the Empire was a cause to live by. Edward spent his later years administering the finances of Egypt, where he held high office and wore himself out struggling steadfastly for his principles. In his modest and capable way he embodied the remarkable spirit of the British Empire as much as Alfred Milner, ennobled as Viscount Milner in 1901, and one of the most lauded heroes of Empire. Neither the imperial statesman who died covered with honours and was given memorials in Canterbury Cathedral and his Oxford college, nor the imperial soldier who died little noticed in a remote Swiss sanatorium, is greatly remembered today. Milner features in history books as a cold, racist functionary who provoked the Boer war and was idolised by a clique of idealistic young imperialists, while Edward is forgotten, save for some clever, facetious vignettes of Egyptian life, occasionally read. The Empire they served is discredited. Violet, who survived them both by many decades, lives on only in a long-out-of-print memoir and in the recollections of relations and friends, as a redoubtable woman, still vigorous in old age.

These three lives, courageous, poignant, dramatic and humorous by turn, are redolent of an age separated from ours by less than a century – and yet seeming a whole world away, along with the vanished glories of imperial Britain.

The northern approach to Hatfield House

Lord Edward Cecil aged 7, dressed as Queen Elizabeth I's Lord Chamberlain, for the children's fancy dress ball at Hatfield House, New Year, 1874

CHAPTER ONE

A Hatfield Childhood

'The main thing inculcated as early as possible was that every child was responsible for his own thoughts and actions.'

Lord Robert Cecil's autobiography, *All the Way*

WHEN THE twenty-two-year-old Violet Maxse first met her husband-to-be's family at Hatfield House in April 1894, she found that 'The Cecils are a particularly attractive family – they have been brought up in a very curious way and have all proved the truth of their father's theory which is that everyone should be left very nearly alone. They have an immense sense of humour – are deadly keen about politics and are, I suppose, on the whole the most religious family in England.' Violet's description of the vigorous, idiosyncratic and influential family of the 3rd Marquess and Marchioness of Salisbury into which she married a few weeks later left out one other characteristic – their devotion to one another. The Cecils were clannish in two senses of the word: throughout their lives the seven brothers and sisters preferred each other's company to any other, and their family on both their father's and their mother's sides was extensive. Edward Cecil, Violet's fiancé, was brought up with innumerable cousins. When Benjamin Disraeli arrived for the first time to see his political colleague at Hatfield, one of his strongest impressions of the household was being confronted 'with a great many little boys of various families'. At any moment large numbers of aunts, uncles and cousins, the 'collaterals' as they were collectively known, would be staying in the west wing, while the Salisburys and their children occupied the east wing. Aunts Pooey and Blosset, sisters-in-law Fluffy and Nelly, cousins Miss Baffy and Luly flit through the pages of family correspondence as they flitted through the rooms of the great house throughout Edward's childhood.

His upbringing was one of contrast: besides the formality predictable in an aristocratic house of that period, a wholly unexpected, vibrant informality emanated from his parents. His father Robert, the 3rd Marquess of Salisbury, was determined to compensate for the lovelessness of his own boyhood, and, like his wife, Georgina, preferred to have the children around them as much as possible even when he had risen to be Foreign Secretary and then Prime Minister. The children were free to come to luncheon with knees begrimed from climbing trees in the shrubbery and without washing their hands, wrote a cousin, Blanche Dugdale; as far as Lady Salisbury was concerned, 'children could be as noisy, as dirty, and as objectionable as nature had made them, without fear of criticism'.

Once, Edward and his little brother Hugh jumped into his mother's carriage, to ride with her. 'Two boys tumbled into the carriage, bareheaded, dressed in blue suits and red sashes. Both were completely covered from head to heel in earth, both were talking at the top of their voices. No one was listening, their mother cast an eye on them and said "I suppose you have been down a rabbit hole"' – a remark which might have come from Lewis Carroll, another frequent visitor during this period, when he was creating the *Alice in Wonderland* books; he found the family atmosphere wonderfully sympathetic, with its high tone and eccentric logic. He enjoyed photographing the children and playing word games with them, watching their Christmas parties and reading his stories aloud to them in the evenings.

Hatfield House itself also presented a contrast between the imposing and the scruffy. Completed in 1611, it was a magnificent setting for entertaining, which throughout Edward's boyhood was on a grand scale. In summer there were garden parties, in winter shooting weekends, with dances and lavish dinners; and weekend parties all year round. Yet the elements of hygiene were often ignored: a probably apocryphal story is told to this day of a nest of little rats found dead in the Prime Minister's bed one morning, having suffocated under the weight of the soundly sleeping statesman. Rats and mice scurried through the corridors and up the staircases. While immaculate footmen, the upper echelons accoutred in the family livery of blue edged with silver, with white-gloved hands, opened doors, waited at table and carried messages, and ladies' maids, trim in white caps and black uniforms, attended to their mistresses, an additional army of unkempt figures, some from the estate, cleaned the house, not always conscientiously. Sooty-faced muscular men heaved coal and lugged

Lord Edward Cecil's father in 1861, before
he became 3rd Marquess of Salisbury

wood for the fires lit daily in the main rooms and bedrooms, clatter-
ing up and down backstairs and filling the air with the stench of
unwashed feet and well-worn clothes. The dozen or more maids who
lived in the house had salubrious rooms on the top floor, leading off
the nursery passage where Edward and his siblings slept; as many male
servants slept in the basement. At a still lower level were damp and
lightless holes where odd-job men were housed, but such arrangements were unknown to Lady Salisbury, for they were at the discre-
tion of the Steward, who like the Housekeeper lived in the state
befitting his position and had the power of hiring and firing the
household staff. Nor did she concern herself with petty pilfering; the
voluminous skirts of the cleaning staff as they left the house might
hide a half-finished ham or other delicacy. Lord and Lady Salisbury
took a pragmatic view of small irregularities. 'You can't prevent these
things,' said Lord Salisbury. 'If you keep too tight a rein on the household your guests suffer. I have a limit, beyond that I don't allow the
expenditure to rise.'

Hatfield House, in reality a palace, and its estate of fifteen hundred
acres, was a microcosm. Everything needed was within its compass –

from the dairy to the stables, from the Home Farm to a forcing house
for pineapples, from a cricket ground and a 'Real Tennis' court to a
small golf course. It was – is still – a house where history seems to
reverberate from its very fabric. Some of the history was real, some
bogus, added for atmosphere. Queen Elizabeth spent part of her girlhood there and learnt of her accession to the throne while she was
sitting under an oak in the vast park; Edward and his brothers and
sisters played in the branches of that oak. The policies and decisions
of such monarchs – especially over religion – were discussed and
debated by the Cecil family, as Edward's brother Bob, next to him in
age, described: the learned Librarian at Hatfield had an especial admiration for the Tudors and 'frequently talked of them as if he had
known them personally. Indeed, when he referred to "The King",
that meant Henry VIII. To me he talked of my Elizabethan ancestors
and their attitude to Christianity' as he prepared the twelve-year-old
for confirmation.

In the rooms where Edward grew up these same monarchs,
Lancastrian, Tudor and Stuart, gazed down upon him, alongside
family ancestors. Hatfield's uniquely beautiful collection of
Elizabethan and Jacobean portraits was a reminder not only of his
family's glory at that time, but also of the continuity of history within
the great house. In the Marble Hall, which the family used as a dining
room, for instance, the delicate sad features of Mary Queen of Scots,
framed with a lace ruff as pale as her face, gazed out of the canvas; here
too were the altogether more vibrant portraits of Queen Elizabeth
herself, one especially fascinating to a child, the *Rainbow Portrait*, in
which the Queen's fabulous costume is embroidered with eyes and
ears, and a sinuous pearl snake winds up her gorgeous left sleeve. The
eyes and ears of the state, the snake full of wisdom, the rainbow and
the motto in the background – *Non sine sole iris* (no rainbow without
the sun) – were equally symbolic.

The pageantry of Britain's greatness and adventures across the globe
was embodied in the banners hanging from the gallery, and Russian
helmets captured in the Crimea, and, in the Armoury, Hertfordshire
Militia swords and a fine collection of Renaissance armour. The date
inscribed above, 1588, was a spurious touch of chivalry added by
Edward's grandfather, the 2nd Marquess, to convey the impression
that his forebears had participated in the glorious defeat of the Spanish
Armada. In fact, he bought armour wholesale in the mid-nineteenth
century when the craze for everything 'Jacobean' and baronial was at

its height. As a boy Edward enjoyed dressing up in this formidable gear.

His father, the 3rd Marquess, though traditionalist and Conservative, was fascinated by the latest inventions of science and technology. While his government was out of office, he liked nothing better than to retreat down a little staircase leading from his study to the laboratory he had fitted up in the basement and there to experiment with chemistry and, above all, with domestic electricity. The Marble Hall was his testing ground. He had a bulky 'Jablokhoff' arc lamp hung in the centre over the diners, shedding a vibrating and unflattering glare to which the ladies, in their evening gowns and jewellery, objected until Lord Salisbury removed this monstrosity. He hung rows of unshaded Swan Edison incandescent lamps in the library and gallery, powered by electricity generated at the saw mills in the park; the supply was capricious, so that lights either blinked violently or were extinguished, leaving the house in darkness. Once naked wires overheating caused a fire in the library; 'it was not a fire of much violence,' wrote Lady Frances Balfour (mother of Blanche Dugdale):

> the stout old beams saw to that . . . with perfect coolness and great interest his Lordship headed his family and such Balfours as were present, in shying cushions taken from the couches and sofas up into the ceiling and by what today seems like a miracle, extinguishing successfully the little fire coursing above. Everybody laughing and applauding the successful, and still more the unsuccessful actors in the unique fire brigade, . . . I stood by her Ladyship who with a lighted hand-candle held at the slope, looked on with voluble interest.

Edward, born on 12 July 1867, had been six months old when his father inherited the title. The new Lord Salisbury's fortune at once changed: from being a family outcast following what was deemed to be an unsuitable marriage eleven years previously, and having to make money by prolific political and literary journalism, he became one of England's richest landowners. He moved with his young family into the ancestral seat of Hatfield, twenty-four miles from London. Now Hatfield and the Cecils enjoyed a pinnacle of power and prestige that they had not known since the time of King James I. This coincided with the period of England's greatest ever influence and domination in world affairs. In an age where imperial policies were discussed and settled in such aristocratic establishments as much as in the royal residences or Whitehall itself, this was the heart of the British Empire,

*Georgina Salisbury, Edward's mother, in 1867, the year of his birth: 'impervious
to fatigue . . . the buoyant confidence of her outlook upon life' sustained
Lord Salisbury throughout his long career*

and during the thirty-five years until his death in 1903, Lord Salisbury
was a leader of its course, as Secretary of State for India, Foreign
Secretary and, in four governments between 1885 and 1902, Prime
Minister.

In his career he was supported unwaveringly by his wife. Georgina
Salisbury had given birth to her eight children over a period of ten
years: Edward's two sisters, Maud, born in 1858, Gwendolen, born
1860, and four brothers, James, who as heir took the courtesy title of
Viscount Cranborne, born 1861, William, born 1863, Robert, born
1864 and Hugh born in 1869; another sister, Fanny, died aged just over
a year in 1867, when Georgina was six months pregnant with Edward.
His mother always 'thought that her agony of sorrow had reacted on

the child that was coming'; that is how she explained Edward's volatility, and although both parents scrupulously avoided favouritism in the family, she possibly compensated for having, as she thought, been the involuntary cause of Edward's stormy temperament by showing a particular affection for him, which was reciprocated by his own affectionate nature.

The children acquired arcane nursery nicknames which stayed with them all their lives. Hugh, later a distinguished parliamentary orator, was called 'Linky', on account, it seems, of his large chimpanzee-like ears, suggesting the 'missing link' between man and ape. William, who became a bishop and was the most markedly spiritual of all that religious family, was known as 'Fish': he was always thought to be – and was – an 'odd fish'. Edward, mysteriously, was 'Nigs'. James and Robert were fortunate to get away with the conventional 'Jem' (pronounced Jim) and 'Bob'. Gwendolen's pretty name was replaced by 'Tim' or 'Titi'. Only Maud was called by her own name.

The personalities of his father and mother permeated Edward's childhood. His father's bouts of melancholia amounted to depression – in part the result of his unhappy boyhood, in part temperamental – and were passed on in good measure to his sons, including Edward. Georgina, a woman of abounding energy, did much to counteract this. 'Robert could never have done anything if he had not married Georgie,' one of her sisters commented. 'She put him on the rails and drove him.' It was an exaggeration, for Salisbury was a man of powerful character and intellect; but she certainly gave him the confidence he needed to enter politics. She and her husband were of one mind, though physically very different: she, small and bustling, bright-eyed, downright in manner; he, tall, massively built, often silent, with no 'small talk', but witty and eloquent when he did speak.

The pessimistic Salisbury expected little of human nature; he believed, too, that most change was for the worse, and could seldom be reversed, only mitigated. However, in addition to the antidote of Lady Salisbury's warmth and ebullience, as he grew older he also derived an inner serenity from his deeply held Christian faith. One of the most important elements in his relationship with his wife had always been their passionate adherence to High Anglicanism. To understand them and their children, the nature of their faith must also be understood: they believed the Anglican Church was a pure and reformed part of the true, sacramental, universal Catholic church, closer than Roman Catholicism to early Christianity, because purged of medieval superstition; their faith was free of the sentimental or morbid elements which has given Victorian Protestantism a bad name ever since. Nor was their outlook speculative or broad church: on many points of religion they were open-minded, but about the fundamentals of their faith there was no argument.

This was the creed they imparted to their children who, when little, were taught elementary theology by their mother. Salisbury never lectured them on their moral duty. If consulted, he would only point out the various alternative choices and leave them to decide. This was good for developing their sense of responsibility but put a heavy moral burden on them.

They learnt about religion in the course of endless conversations about the Church, and from daily services in the family chapel where life at Hatfield began each morning before breakfast. The living of Hatfield being in the gift of the family, one of the curates attached to the parish frequently conducted family prayers. These were no mumbled, rushed proceedings uttered by rote. All members of the family participated fully, though characteristically, as their children grew up, the Salisburys did not compel them to attend the services. Believing so profoundly in individual freedom of choice, which he extended to a degree enlightened for its day to his children, their father thought that their presence in chapel was a decision for them to make. They came to look on attendance as a privilege.

Significantly, one of the first improvements that the Salisburys had made when they came to Hatfield had been to dignify and embellish the chapel. Its magnificent stained-glass window had miraculously survived a fire in 1835 which had burnt down almost the entire wing. Kneeling on a hassock embroidered with the family arms, elbows resting on the carved oak pews his parents had commissioned from a leading firm of church furnishers, Edward could gaze at the highly coloured – in every sense – Old Testament scenes which leave such a vivid impression on all who worship in the little chapel: the grisly head of Goliath, held aloft on the broad blade of David's sword, David himself, an elegant little figure in pink, with golden curls; the infant Moses found in the bulrushes, with a crowd of solicitous females around him and in the distance the artist's view of the buildings of Egypt; a clean-limbed Naaman emerging from the water after his leprosy cure; a pallid and sinewy Samson lying helpless in Delilah's power; and Jonah in the mouth of a hideous whale.

The Anglican service book used in the chapel was similar to the

Roman missal in its daily commemoration of one or more saints and martyrs. On Edward's birthday, St John Gualbert's day, they remembered the martyrs Nabor and Felix. The gospel for that day promulgated the hardest of all Christian doctrines – to love your enemies and persecutors.

After morning chapel, when the last blessing had been given by the curate with outstretched arms, Lady Salisbury would rise from her knees, full skirts rustling, and lead the way to the Armoury, a long arcaded room linking one wing of the house to the other. Here the chef, in white toque and checked trousers, would be waiting, writing-pad in hand, with the day's menus. She gave him only cursory attention, being more interested in talking to her family. As the daylight streamed in, the armoured figures of knights, their faces hidden with grotesque visors which so terrified the children in the dark, now gleamed cheerfully, the sunlight glinting off their highly polished cuirasses. The family moved on towards the Marble Hall, on the left, where breakfast was laid either at the main table or on a series of smaller round tables, depending on how many were staying at the house. People helped themselves at the sideboard and sat where they pleased.

Edward and his brothers and sisters grew up on the top, nursery floor: as a baby he slept in the night nursery, a simple, cheerful room, indistinguishable from any other Victorian nursery except for its romantic views down the grassy drive, where he could see visitors in their carriages sweeping along a broad avenue up through the south gate to the door of the house. Edward's crib was alongside 'Nanna', in her iron bedstead, trimmed with a chintz valance to match the curtains. The painted walls of panelled wood were hung with a few family photographs. At night the room was lit by candles in brass candlesticks and the flickering flames of the coal fire, reflected on the brightly polished brass coal-scuttle. The baby's bath was placed on a stand in front of the fire, towel airing on the fender. Nanna herself bathed in a hip bath similarly placed on the Brussels carpet, before the fire. There were only two fixed baths in the whole of that vast house.

As Edward grew older, he spent more time next door in the day nursery, the Ivy Room, where he ate his meals or did lessons at the circular mahogany table. Some food was prepared in the little nursery kitchen next door, and carried in on japanned trays by the nursemaid; other meals came up from the main kitchens, by which time they were barely warm, and never hot. The coal scuttles and basket of logs were replenished by the footman whose domain was the nursery floor. The day nursery was hung with prints of various heroes in gilt and maple frames, such as the Duke of Wellington, who had been a close friend of Lord Salisbury's mother, and Dick Whittington – images forever stamped in the children's memories. The room was cosy, as nurseries should be, but not luxurious. The children curled up on chintz- or green damask-covered chairs absorbed in their picture books, or sprawled with them on the hearthrug; but with such excitable and energetic children peace cannot have reigned long.

In 1869, when Georgina's last child, Hugh, was born, he joined the two-year-old Edward in the night nursery; Edward by now occupied a larger cot. Eventually, both boys had their own bedrooms, further along the nursery corridor. Their parents' rooms, on the ground floor, were reached by the poplar staircase. The walls at the top of the stairs and on the nursery landing were covered with black-and-white cartoons from *Punch* and other journals, including images of Lord Salisbury, a delight to caricaturists because of his size and his beard, tremendous even for those days when men's faces were customarily hirsute. These were a fascinating study for the young Cecil children as they dawdled upstairs to bed, candles in hand. Many of the other politicians lampooned in these drawings had been guests at Hatfield House, including Salisbury's erstwhile foe, Disraeli.

Life at Hatfield alternated with visits to the Salisburys' town house at 20 Arlington Street, off Piccadilly, to their other seat, Cranborne Manor in Dorset, and most enjoyably, with holidays during the parliamentary recess, to the house they built on the cliffs above Dieppe, in northern France. Châlet Cecil, as it was modestly known, was a house of arresting ugliness and, if accounts by the family and their guests are any guide, of a discomfort only the British aristocracy would endure in the name of holidays. But the children and their parents adored their weeks on the cliffs and beaches of Dieppe; they loved the strong salt wind that blew across the sea, adding an edge of danger to their bathing with their *baigneur* Auguste; they loved the picnics and excursions into the forests, the bicycle expeditions, and above all, they enjoyed the transformation that came over their mother. From being the harassed and overtired wife of a leading public figure running the household at Hatfield or organising political entertaining in London, she became once more their relaxed and happy mama enjoying the sea air and the bathing in all weathers in the company she loved most – her family.

Châlet Cecil was simply furnished with handsome carved armoires, lined with pale coloured silk, in the bedrooms and comfortable chairs in the drawing room. When the wind blew – the house was nicknamed the Temple of the Four Winds – the wooden shutters were closed, the *calorifique* stove was lit with the attendant characteristic smell of paraffin, and the family sang round the piano and played cards or complicated word games.

Although a complete household moved there, chef, servants and all, still the life was comparatively simple, not least because communications with England were largely restricted to telegrams. There was the usual attendant pack of relations; and, in addition, a succession of tutors for the children. All the family spoke French and some German, and Georgina encouraged the children to share her pleasure in contemporary French literature of a 'suitable nature'.

Back at home, as Edward grew up, his life at Hatfield shifted from the top-floor nurseries to downstairs, where the children participated far more in the daily life of the house than was conventional in the aristocracy: the Salisburys encouraged their children to be heard as well as seen.

Until they went to Eton at thirteen, Edward and his brothers were taught at home, where they were also given the free rein of the Library, at the end of the Long Gallery on the first floor. Here, as well as the classics, they could browse through more unusual works, such as Lord Salisbury's unique collection of pamphlets on the French Revolution and the latest French novels bought by Lady Salisbury. As was the custom then, Edward's two sisters, Maud and Gwendolen, never went to school but were taught at home. In addition, the house itself and its visitors were an education in history, religion and politics.

The main lesson instilled into all the children was the concept of service, public and private, which, although idealistic, was expressed in practical, down-to-earth terms. Their privileged birth and status brought attendant obligations, first to their family, especially to the lonely or bereaved, then to their tenants, their Queen, their country and the Empire beyond the British Isles. 'We were taught to recognise the old tradition, coming down, perhaps, from feudal times, that we enjoyed these advantages in exchange for a duty to serve our country and our fellow-men to the best of our power.' These obligations formed the underlying philosophy of Edward Cecil's life.

CHAPTER TWO

Youth

As a boy, Edward was the most high-spirited of the children. Jem, with pale, refined good looks, felt the weight of his future inheritance, and an oppressive sense of guilt at never attaining the high Christian standards to which he aspired. The next brother, William, 'Fish', with his golden-red curls and angelic features, already showed the unselfconscious eccentricity for which he became famous all his life. Bob, very tall, was excitable and argumentative, 'born with two grievances and a right', as his mother said; the youngest, Hugh, 'Linky', was intellectual, with a shrill voice and a hilariously precocious turn of phrase – as, for example, when he accused his nanny of Pelagian heresy. All were robustly hypochondriacal.

'*Il n'y a que des hommes dans cette famille-là,*' remarked a French visitor to Hatfield. The eldest of the family, Maud, was as forthright and opinioned as any of her brothers; Gwendolen, profound and passionate in argument, was obsessive in her devotion to causes. Neither cared how she dressed. For all the diversity of their characters, the Cecils' world was inward-looking, self-contained with its own tribal solidarity, and united by their religious and political creeds. Much of the children's education derived from star visitors such as Benjamin Disraeli and Lewis Carroll, and from vehement political discussions round the dining table. Lord Salisbury's conversation included religion, literature, science, political ideas and history and fervent debates between members of the family always ensued. Salisbury never spoke down to his children; he expressed himself clearly and simply, but they still had to strain to keep up. Given their father's powerful personality, there were times when, despite his care not to stifle independence of thought, they deferred too much to him. Some of the children read relatively little, preferring absorbing expositions of the contents of books to ploughing through the works themselves.

In September 1880 came Edward's first break from his adored mother, his loving family circle and the fascinating process of learning from his father. At the age of thirteen he was sent to Eton to board, as were all the Cecil boys, despite their father's loathing of the school where he had been bullied and coerced into doing the older boys' work for them. Edward's fate was less hard: unlike his father's, his home life at Hatfield was happy and secure, which gave him confidence with the other boys. His brother Robert, who was captain of the house, stayed on for a while to keep an eye on him and to start him off in the arcane ways of public-school life. Naturally Edward missed home: indeed, for many years he was homesick whenever he went away; but his high spirits and popularity got him through. He enjoyed games, cricket in the summer, football in the winter, and rowing; he joined in the life of the house, and studied after a fashion, without distinction. Few Etonians worked hard, save very ambitious boys like George Curzon, the future Viceroy of India, several years his senior. Even fewer wished to be seen working. The emphasis was on 'character' and no 'side', not on 'sapping up for trials' (working hard for exams). Edward exerted himself as little as any.

Despite the usual grumbles about school life, such as being given over-liberal doses of cod-liver oil by 'M'Dame', the house matron, Edward's letters home were bright. 'I am known as the untidiest boy at my tutor's,' he announced cheerfully. This was to be a lifelong characteristic. Like all the boys he relied on supplies from home to supplement school fare; when they were late, loud was his lament. 'Do send a hamper I am starving . . . I have got no hamper this week.' He asked for other necessities such as 'some candles . . . as my tutor's candles are not much good to work by and burn quickly. Please send more the next hamper.'

As might be expected, he was happiest during the holidays at home, rabbit hunting, or skating when the pond froze over, or joining in excitements such as his brother Jem's coming of age. Edward was already used to lavish entertaining at Hatfield, especially at the tenants' Christmas dinner in the Marble Hall when one of the sons was a principal speaker, and where Salisbury never failed to give a witty speech. One of the first grand events Edward had attended was at the age of seven in 1874, when the New Year ball for the young people, 'the Juvenile Ball', was in Elizabethan dress. Jem, aged thirteen, was his ancestor Robert Cecil, Earl of Salisbury, Queen Elizabeth's minister; Maud was the Queen herself; Edward was the Lord Chamberlain in a

*The New Year ball at Hatfield, 1874. Edward and his
brothers and sisters in Elizabethan dress superimposed on a
photograph of the Long Gallery:* (left to right) *Gwendolen,*

Maud (as Queen Elizabeth), Bob, Jem (as his ancestor the 1st Earl of Salisbury), William (as Sir Walter Raleigh), Hugh and Edward (as Lord Chamberlain)

fetching and elaborate costume; and Hugh, aged six, was the poet Spenser.

Jem's coming of age celebrations in October 1882 eclipsed all of these. The house was *en fête* for days, every bedroom packed with relations and their servants. George Curzon, then aged twenty-three, described the 'princely' entertainment, the hundreds of tenants, children and the needy fed throughout days of festivities, everyone congratulating the young Lord Cranborne, who thanked them with 'innumerable modest and appropriate speeches'. A special train from London carried at least '150 swells' for the ball; that evening 1,000–1,200 people were catered for, the menu including 240 quarts of soup *jardinière*, 10 peacocks and as many boiled tongues, 60 partridges, 50 pheasants, nougats, brioches, jellies and *chartreuses* among the desserts, and even in the small hours a hot supper was served – 6 quarts of consommé, lamb cutlets and pheasants, to sustain the remaining dancers. By day there were sports and every kind of entertainment for the children of the estate and the town, and that evening there was a county ball with fireworks and toasts, speeches and dancing, ending about 5 a.m.

Dinner next evening for 350–400 people began with 100 quarts of *julienne* soup; the fish course included turbot with lobster sauce (6 dishes) and codfish with oyster sauce (6 dishes); there were 50 pheasants, 60 partridges, 30 chickens and 10 hares; 8 dishes each of venison, turkey, roast beef; and then plum puddings, jellies, pastries, 20 apple tarts, as well as cheese, celery, two dozen large cakes, and fruit, nuts and raisins. At the end of the evening's dancing, supper was served to twice as many people, a cold collation this time, including 20 galatines, 12 raised pies, 10 blancmanges and 40 jellies.

The scale of the Salisburys' entertaining at this period has to be read to be believed. Shooting parties were particularly elaborate: one to which minor royalty was invited, held every year, went on for days. In December 1883 the guests of honour were the Duke and Duchess of Albany: on the first evening, thirty-six sat down to dinner at round tables in the Marble Hall, with a band playing in the gallery during dinner, and dancing in the Long Gallery afterwards; on another evening, nearly 1,000 people danced in the Winter Dining Room and the Long Gallery, with supper in the Marble Hall and the summer drawing-room. The dancing went on until four in the morning.

Similar numbers, and more, were habitual at the Salisburys' London house in Arlington Street, where enormous political dinners and

Edward at about the age when he went to Eton

evening parties, nicknamed 'packs' by the children, were given. The elaborate menus were printed in French, on elegant crested cards edged with blue, the family colour.

Children who were old enough to join in were expected to contribute to the parties at Hatfield, where the County had to be entertained, in Edward's case the shooting parties in particular, for he loved shooting.

To broaden their circle of acquaintances and their understanding of the political world, Georgina Salisbury encouraged her children to take part in Society. They did not particularly reciprocate her enthusiasm. One of Edward's favourite haunts at Hatfield became the billiard room, with its twelve-foot table by Thurston's, suppliers of the finest slate top tables, lit by a large gas lamp with eighteen shaded burners. It was a haven for the young people to let off steam with wild games after formal dinners, which could seem interminable, with the County to the right and relations to the left of them.

The whole family enjoyed escaping to the Châlet Cecil in summer, where entertainments were arranged according to the weather rather than social duties. Just after Edward left Eton, in 1883, a young Frenchman, M. Coppini, went there as tutor. He captured with the fresh eye of a foreigner the household's unique character. He realised that the impeccable courtesy of Lord Salisbury – his Lordship would always make a point of showing Coppini into a room in front of him – was a useful cloak for his indifference as to his presence. Lady Salisbury, also extremely courteous, would talk to him for exactly five minutes, and then suddenly stop, 'pulling out the plank from beneath [his] feet', and leaving Coppini 'crumpled by this profound indifference'.

But far from being a paternal despot in the traditional mould, as he expected, Lord Salisbury, '*le père, est aussi gai que les enfants, qui sont comme de jeunes fous*' – unselfconscious and overflowing with vivacity. Lady Salisbury was '*pétillante d'intelligence*'. Besides the seven children were Lady Salisbury's sister, Aunt Pooey, the maiden aunt – '*la tante classique anglaise*' – which became a family phrase thereafter, and Maud's fiancé, Viscount Wolmer, the first in-law to augment the close-knit circle of brothers and sisters. Willy Wolmer, soon to be 2nd Earl of Selborne, was serious and hard-working, destined to achieve eminence as an imperial administrator. To Coppini, who 'could read his soul in his limpid, azure gaze', he was '*le type anglais dans toute sa splendeur*'. Coppini was also struck that though Willy was the heir of the Lord Chancellor in Gladstone's Government, the Tory leader, Lord Salisbury, raised no objection to his daughter's marriage to the son of a Whig minister. The fact was that by now the aristocracy, Whig (Liberal) and Tory, were closing ranks; three years hence, Willy Wolmer had become a close ally of the Tories in Parliament in opposition to Home Rule for Ireland.

Edward was now expected to take up a profession, as were all his brothers. Jem, the eldest, went in for politics; Robert read for the Bar and became a successful barrister; William entered the Church; Hugh also entered Parliament, and Edward chose the Army. This was not a career which had appealed to his father: 'I detest all soldiering beyond measure. As far as taste goes I would sooner be at the treadmill,' Salisbury had told his own father. Edward, however, was attracted to the military life. At a time when Britain's empire stretched from Vancouver to Mandalay and from Auckland to the West Indies, the Army was an enticing challenge to England's youth, who were dazzled by the tales of imperial adventure. He was fired by the romantic exploits of General Gordon, whose supposed betrayal by Mr Gladstone's Government led to his death at Khartoum in 1885; this had enraged Jem and Gwendolen, who was always moved to tears by tales of bravery, and they even sent a professional lecturer round the country to denounce Gladstone. Edward watched their campaign with ardour. He had a theatrical streak, too, which went with an enjoyment of dressing-up − one of the Army's great attractions in those days, when the glamorous uniforms were used shamelessly in recruiting. Edward was a fine-looking young man, certainly a more martial figure than his somewhat cerebral-looking brothers.

To gain an officer's commission in the Army, Edward had to pass an exam into the Royal Military Academy at Sandhurst. Although, he reported to his mother, he was happy working hard for the Sandhurst exam, his standard of what constituted hard work was an Etonian one. He lacked maturity and self-discipline, the exam unnerved him and he failed. Another route was found for him, a commission in the Militia Battalion of the Bedfordshire Regiment, in which Jem was an officer. The historian Edward Gibbon once claimed that his few months' service in the local Militia had helped him to understand the nature of the Roman army, but that was a credit to his imagination: there was little real soldiering about this curious survival from more feudal days, locally drafted and for local defence only. However, the Duke of Cambridge, Commander-in-Chief of the Army, promised Lord Salisbury that Edward would be found a place in the Grenadier Guards in a year or two, going straight in as an officer.

His Militia duties were few, and he went to Germany to study the language and the nature of the army. He arrived in Hanover in October 1885 with his dog, Spot, his inseparable companion − later to play a heroic part in saving Hatfield House from fire, by barking to alert the sleeping household. He found lodgings where, in preference to the lumpy bed, he slung a hammock across the room. This, along with the dog, and the young Englishman's insistence on bathing − the landlord kept removing the bath from the room so his children could be washed − caused some consternation in the household.

In Hanover Edward dined with General Schroetter, commanding the 10th Artillery Brigade, 'rather a jolly old boy', in the company of five other generals, but he tried, he told his mother, to avoid Society 'which is here, as elsewhere *entre nous* a terrible bore, though interesting in the same way as the zoological gardens is.' At one party the formal German practice of being presented to every lady in the room took, he complained, 'five and twenty minutes hard introducing and gave me a stiff neck from repeated bows'.

Later he moved to Berlin, where he witnessed a student duel, was presented to the Emperor and Empress, and dined informally with

Prince Bismarck. He was 'in a blue funk' about going: the evening began at the early hour of six o'clock when the Prince appeared, in uniform, not from any overweening attachment to it, but to save having to change into it each time the Emperor summoned him, which could be several times a day. Then seventy years old, Bismarck looked his age, but his bearing was as imposing as ever, and his voice strong. He, Princess Bismarck and their boisterous, unappealing son, Herbert, reverently toasted Edward's father in champagne. After dinner Bismarck solemnly puffed at a porcelain pipe three feet long, produced ready-filled from a rack.

When he returned to England later that year, Edward found the family circle augmented by the engagement of Jem to Alice Gore, daughter of the Earl of Arran. Alice's parents had died young, and she, her two sisters, Mabell and Esther, and her brother had been brought up by their grandmother in a household of unexampled lugubriousness. Despite her exposure to Victorian evangelical religion at its gloomiest, Alice's was a buoyant, life-enhancing character of great patience and humour. In 1887 she embarked on what was to be a marriage of sixty happy years, balancing Jem's introverted shyness and moods of anxiety as surely as Georgina Salisbury balanced the melancholy of her husband.

On her marriage, Alice was expected to merge into the Cecil household, as was Violet when she married Edward. They did not have houses of their own. Alice was, however, glad to be part of such a secure, loving and interesting family, then at its height as a political centre. Lord Salisbury had entered his second term of office as Prime Minister, and Jem was MP for Darwen in Lancashire.

Edward and his sister-in-law, both nineteen, soon forged a strong friendship. She recalled him as

> a magnificent looking creature, six foot four tall, and very fair, bubbling over with good spirits and already the brilliant talker that he was to the end of his life. He was just my age, one month older, and was either deputed by his mother, or moved by his own kind heart, to look after me.
>
> Jem was very busy, and I had hardly found my feet in that large family and we used to go off to the old Smoking room at the north east corner of the house where he would talk and talk and talk uninterruptedly of all things both in heaven and earth; there was no limit to his mind or to his reading. Absolutely undisciplined, it ranged over any subject that interested him and one could have said anything to him without fear of misunderstanding.

She was particularly struck by his being 'even then deeply religious though in fact it did not control his life much in those days; but he had, I think, from the beginning Spiritual Vision, and never lost it.' She also understood the volatility of young Edward's nature: 'He was a mass of moods, stormy, with violent attacks of temper which often passed almost before they had begun, but which made him difficult to deal with. Added to this was a touch of Drama in his composition, which was never far distant. He was intensely affectionate, passionately fond of and believing in his family, who at the bottom were the one and only standard, notwithstanding that in so many ways he differed from them.'

The bond between Edward and Alice strengthened as the years went by, long after Alice had found her feet as Jem's wife and had become the 4th Marchioness of Salisbury and mother to four children.

This was the age when, after lengthy dinners, men savoured plump cigars. Not at Hatfield: Lord Salisbury's dislike of smoking was such that it was allowed in only one uncomfortable room in the house. Lewis Carroll spent two consecutive New Year's Eves there; after the New Year had been seen in and the main household had gone to bed he 'sat up till about one with the gentlemen in the smoking-room as usual in former visits'. Lord Salisbury obviously thought that those who indulged in it would best not do so in comfort, for even when a new smoking room was made on the ground floor, its uncomfortable furniture was covered in what was known as 'American cloth', oiled cloth stamped to imitate leather, with oak spittoons with tops of crimson velvet.

Salisbury, once resigned to his son becoming a soldier, flung himself into finding the right regiment, even asking advice, something he had a reputation for never doing: 'My father has been learning the Army List by heart,' Bob told Edward, '. . . and discusses the question at every dinner party he goes to – my mother does the same and they will shortly be acquainted with the history of every regiment in the service.'

Edward did not want to become 'a ballroom soldier' or to be regarded as such. The Cavalry, socially the most élite branch of the Army, was considered, and the Guards, the most select infantry brigade: 'As regards "moral health" the family, I believe, think the guards are the fastest,' Hugh told him, '. . . but I don't think the family attach much weight to it . . . The only thing that matters is success

FOREIGN OFFICE

S stands for Salisbury;
In speeches important
He's certain to utter
Some phrase that he oughtn't.

*A cartoon of Lord Salisbury, c. 1900, by F. Carruthers Gould. Salisbury
sometimes alarmed his colleagues by his 'blazing indiscretions'*

and if I were you I should decide in favour of what the most compe-
tent military critics say is the most sure road to it.'

From the point of view of ambition, the Cavalry had nothing
against it – as the composition of the First World War High Command
was to show. Expense, however, may possibly have counted with Lord
Salisbury for, though generous, he disliked unnecessary extravagance
and Edward, a younger son, had only a small income. The Guards regiments were hardly for poor officers – long spells in London, spare time
taken up in fashionable pursuits, costly uniforms on which even the
buttons were hand carved. But the Cavalry was the most expensive of
all: the uniforms were even more elaborate and there were horses to
maintain. Finally, in April 1887, Edward's name appeared in the
official *London Gazette* as holding the commission of 2nd Lieutenant
in the Grenadier Guards.

The Grenadiers were, and still are, a regiment of powerful tradition proud of their *esprit de corps*. Their exploits resounded through British military history, associated with engagements such as Waterloo (where Wellington's alleged command 'Up Guards and at 'em!' became immortal). Recruits to the ranks had to be at least six feet tall, and their towering appearance was augmented by great black bearskins.

When Edward joined the regiment, life for officers was not hard: Guard duty started late in the morning, followed by a huge breakfast, and apart from inspecting a few sentries and marching them off, there was little for the officers to do until dinner at the Guards' Club. Cards followed: whist, or more often nap, poker, loo or baccarat. Many officers, including Edward, were tempted in the excitement of play to raise their bid. At 10.55 p.m. those on night guard duty turned out for two hours each until 5 a.m. They moved quarters every six months – from their barracks to the Tower of London, to Windsor, and then back to barracks again. During the summer came camp and manoeuvres.

Pay was low – not much above £90 a year for a subaltern and a £70 supplement while on duty in London or Windsor – and was mostly immediately absorbed by regimental life. Although Edward found diversions, the theatre and some society events during the Season, he was bored. This was *not* why he had joined the Army. He was becoming the 'ballroom soldier' he had dreaded – and a smoking, drinking, gambling one at that.

He was elected to a dining club, the Beefsteak, and rapidly gained a reputation as a wit and raconteur. At the club, in a mock-baronial room off Leicester Square, members sat at one large table; there was no pecking order, so members talked to whoever they were next to, however young or eminent.

Edward hoped, like many a young Guardee, for the moment when his battalion would be warned for service overseas. In that age of Empire, when Britain had lately celebrated Queen Victoria's Golden Jubilee, a world of excitement and opportunity stretched ahead for merchants, missionaries, administrators – and soldiers. When would the Grenadiers be out there, delivering the time-honoured 'black eye' to Britain's enemies? When would Edward's turn come?

CHAPTER THREE

Violet Maxse

Violet maxse, Edward's future wife, was born on 1 February 1872, into a family as stormy and strife-ridden as the Cecils' was harmonious. Her grandmother, Lady Caroline Berkeley, came from the ancient aristocratic line of the Earls of Berkeley, which stretched back far beyond the Cecils' Tudor peerage to the reign of King Henry II. It was their seat, Berkeley Castle, which had resounded with the horrible shrieks of King Edward II being impaled with a hot poker one night in 1327, though the family had no part in this atrocity.

There was nothing *fin-de-race* about the nineteenth-century Berkeleys. They were mostly soldiers or sailors or active in public life. Lady Caroline was a slim, handsome woman who rode until an advanced age. Tough and down to earth, she was also clever, and like most of her children and grandchildren, literary; she enjoyed Latin authors. One of her brothers, George, as a young man, wrote romantic fiction; in 1836, when one romance, *Berkeley Castle*, was offensively reviewed, he assaulted the paper's publisher and fought a duel with the reviewer.

Violet's unusual family name originated in Northamptonshire; the Maxses had owned estates for generations in Essex, and Violet's grandfather, James Maxse, had branched into overseas commerce. Her father, Frederick Maxse, although preoccupied with farming, politics and field sports, was no conventional country squire. He was hot-blooded in battle, politics and love. Small and wiry, he had a great curiosity about people and places, the arts and public affairs. His energy and zest for life won him many friends as well as critics. At nineteen, as a naval lieutenant, he became a hero of the Crimean war, as aide-de-camp to Lord Raglan carrying despatches through enemy lines. By the age of twenty-two he was a Captain commanding the *HMS Ariel*, reputed to be the smartest corvette in the Navy.

His disgust at the callous treatment of ordinary seamen and at the incompetence of aristocratic commanders turned him, despite his origins, into a radical, at war with hierarchy and privilege. Violet recalled, 'He never got over the Duchess of Cleveland – his mother's most intimate friend – saying to him one day, in the presence of her doctor: "Captain Maxse, do you shake hands with your doctor?"'

He retired from active service at the age of thirty-four, though he continued up the naval ladder to become an Admiral in his early forties. In 1868 he stood for Parliament as a radical Liberal candidate. Well known for his idiosyncratic pamphlets and eloquence, he was an extreme supporter of constitutional and education reform – to the extent that his friend, the statesman Joseph Chamberlain, a Liberal radical reformer himself, told him: 'It is a comfort to think, when I am accused of being a fanatic, that there is somebody more irreconcilable still.' The Admiral could not be relied on, however, to support every radical cause: for example, he was a passionate defender of blood sports, capital punishment and a strong Navy. He infuriated the mainstream Liberal Party organisation in 1885 by accusing the Liberal Government of betraying General Gordon in the Sudan and by opposing the Irish Home Rule policy of the Liberal leader, Gladstone; that year, alongside his radical friend Joseph Chamberlain, he left the party, in protest.

Voters did not know what to make of him and he was never elected to Parliament. Both his Whig and his Tory critics judged him a class traitor, on account of his attacks on privilege and the Anglican Church, but the more amiable pronounced him 'mad', citing his vegetarianism and abhorrence of alcohol. However, his courage and integrity were respected, and he made and kept close friends all his life. To him, sticking to what you believed was all-important, more important even than family ties. The novelist and fellow-radical George Meredith immortalised the Admiral in *Beauchamp's Career* (1876), charting the political and amorous progress of young Captain Nevil Beauchamp. Nevil was a close portrait of Frederick Maxse: obsessive, quixotic, maddening, but also romantic and honourable – a Cavalier, as one character observes, fighting for Roundhead causes.

Frederick Maxse was twenty-nine when one day, in a London park, he espied a beautiful woman, with lazy, voluptuous looks. Impulsive and passionate as he was, he followed her back to her home. Violet later described her as 'like Titian's "*Vierge au lapin*". A perfect type of dark haired, fair skinned Italian.' Cissie (Cecilia) Steel was in fact

*Violet's mother, Cissie Maxse, in the 1860s in the flower
of her beauty. Violet inherited her expressive eyes
and slender figure but not her indolence*

English, the nineteen-year-old daughter of General Steel, formerly of the Indian Army. The family lived in London with estates in Cumberland. Frederick laid siege to her and soon afterwards they were married – a hasty beginning, copied with similarly unfortunate results by Violet thirty-two years later.

Frederick and Cissie settled in a village outside Southampton, at Holly Hill. A succession of children followed: Ivor was born in 1862, Leo in 1864, Olive in 1866 and, finally, after another child had died, Violet. It should have been a happy household, for Frederick and Cissie were sociable and clever; neither was conventional, they both enjoyed the arts and making friends with artists and writers, and were devoted to their children. This was not enough, however. Violet later said of her parents that it was a wonder they stayed together so long.

Frederick, like so many of his family, was restless, impatient and fierce-tempered. He hated not to get his way. He craved adventure, physical feats, riding and sailing. He always felt happiest at sea, and frequently sailed his yacht to France, the country he loved. George Meredith, a regular sailing companion, recalled Frederick (in the guise of Nevil Beauchamp) 'clad cap-à-pie in tarpaulin' at the tiller, 'where he seemed in his element, facing the spray and cunningly calculating to get wind and tide in his favour', his craft 'dipping and straining, with every inch of sail set'.

Cissie Maxse, by contrast, had no interest in such pursuits. Her husband tried to reconcile himself to her world of parties and drawing rooms: 'Her métier is Society,' he told his mother. 'When I see her in it, so popular and in such complete enjoyment of it, and behaviour (especially considering her looks) irreproachable (she has not the slightest inclination for intrigue) – I feel it is folly on my part to lament her line of life.' He was prepared for his beautiful wife to enjoy herself, since 'the more she has of Society (so long as my independence is, as far as it can be, recognised) the better for me and the less worry for me and the better for Society when she is such a cheerful bird.'

But, he admitted, 'her placid temperament is the very antithesis of ours'. The undomesticated Cissie was entirely dependent on her household to provide her with a routine. Once when her maid left her, she proved incapable of interviewing a new one or of getting herself up and dressed before lunchtime. Frederick was distracted: 'Never was such forlorn irredeemable helplessness embodied in any human creature as it is in her – I often think what would become of my children were I to die. There is no note of mistress or mother in the household. She adores her babies, pets them, fondles them, thinks of them, but as they grow is not equal to the responsibility their growth involves.'

For all his radicalism Frederick was old-fashioned about women, who, he felt, had little right to independence. Cissie, despite her languor, was far from submissive. She met his explosions of wrath with peevishness and inertia. He became like an exasperated parent rather than a husband: 'She deserves compassion on account of her passive organisation – torpid I should have said,' he complained to his mother, 'but with my quick nervous sensibility, I too deserve some.'

He admitted that sometimes she had reason to be vexed. He was horrified when his sister Beatrice took her to the Derby, then left her almost all day alone in their carriage, 'flanked by prostitutes and stared at by men'.

Although sociable, Cissie was lethargic as a hostess: 'My wife lacks the energy to invite people . . . I represent her as Host and Executive – I do not think any one has ever dined or lunched with me except by my own invitation. She is glad to see people if someone will take the trouble to ask, and make all the arrangements for them,' Frederick told his mother.

Lady Caroline wrote, when it was plain that matters were reaching a crisis,

> I have put up with Cissie's temper and insolence for years without com-plaining . . . hoping that she would make up for her cussedness to me and mine, in some way or other, by rendering herself pleasing in her home to you. When she was here, last December, her conversation was made up of sneers at you and all whom I love. I never met with such rudeness from anyone before. Then why am I to be exposed to this? . . . I hope you will show her this letter . . .

Eventually in 1877, when Violet was five, Cissie and Frederick Maxse concluded that their life together was intolerable. As there were no grounds for divorce under the laws of the time, Cissie settled in London, which, free from onerous domestic obligations, suited her. She lived on the Admiral's allowance of £600 a year, in a small but attractive terraced house in Alexander Square, Kensington. Living on her own, she had to guard her reputation carefully to avoid social ostracism. Later, the Admiral secretly set a detective on his wife's trail, hoping perhaps to find grounds for a complete break through divorce,

*Admiral Maxse, c. 1874, with Olive, Leo and Violet
(in the arms of her nurse Emma, to whom she was devoted)*

but Cissie Maxse was either innocent or very circumspect and the detective found nothing, to the Admiral's annoyance.

Only one of her four children remained with her: Violet, whom she looked after with the invaluable support of a nurse, Emma Annett. Emma belonged to that vanished breed of educated, highly intelligent, unmarried women who often took over most of the nurturing and education of the children of the aristocracy. Behind most powerful politicians and Society hostesses there was a devoted 'nanna'.

Violet called her parents' separation the greatest misfortune of her life: 'the division . . . the never hearing them talk to each other, the differing views about our lives they often held, all these were a terrible burden to us.' At a time when such arrangements were rare, it made the Maxse children feel conspicuous: Ivor and Leo were in their teens and Olive was eleven – vulnerable ages. From her early childhood, Violet's pretty china-doll features also seemed to bear a challenging and not absolutely amiable expression. It seems she quickly became attuned to the idea of struggle.

At least the breakdown of their parents' marriage intensified the bond of affection between the children. They were always loyal to one another. Her brothers were to make particularly loving and stable marriages, as though resolved to avoid their father's mistake; but Violet's first marriage was destined to echo that of her parents. With all of them save Olive, the troubled upbringing seems also to have toughened them and reinforced their independence of outlook. Ivor, Leo and Violet were boldly self-confident like their father, though the extent to which they sometimes felt resentful or threatened bespoke a certain insecurity. Both parents were devoted to them. When she was ten, Violet moved to her father's house and it became more of a struggle to see enough of her mother, but, already very determined, she managed this despite her parents' mutual mistrust and dislike.

Cissie's circle included celebrated artistic figures, such as James McNeill Whistler, Walter Sickert, Edward Burne-Jones and Frederic Leighton, with whom Violet became friends. Cissie went to the Grosvenor Gallery, the Mecca of aesthetes, and was also an avid theatregoer. Among her playwright friends was Oscar Wilde, who used to enthral Violet or make her laugh with stories he told in his bizarre and inimitable style. Music was important to Cissie, too, whether at concerts, at the Covent Garden opera, or performances at Leighton House by Neruda or Joachim. Both Violet and Olive received music lessons from an early age.

From time to time, the Admiral let Violet and her mother have the use of 'Coachie', his coachman, Mr White, who would take them in a one-horse Victoria carriage into Hyde Park, to see fashionable Londoners parading themselves. 'There were splendid turn-outs, with magnificent horses, beautiful carriages and very smart liveries worn by immaculate coachmen and footmen,' Violet remembered.

The great moment was the advent of the Princess of Wales [later Queen Alexandra] for whom an alley-way was cleared so that she could drive at a spanking pace down the middle of the road . . . Out great moment, my mother's and mine, was when she recognised my mother among the

Violet, aged 12, with violin

throng and returned her bow with a smile, which she never failed to do. The Princess did not stay long in the Park, and when she left, my mother, who was unconventionality in person, allowed me to climb on the box and drive her for the rest of the afternoon.

With her father Violet led a very different life. They stayed regularly at his mother's rural, secluded home, Effingham Hall in Surrey, near Dorking, then a quiet picturesque market town. Lady Caroline's house, surrounded by its estate of 900 acres, was a plain classical manor, the rugged and romantic setting reminiscent of *Wuthering Heights* and exciting riding country for the Maxse children. To them, their grandmother seemed straight out of the eighteenth century when she talked of her glamorous youth or dispensed her somewhat brutal opinions; she told Leo of a recent sporting tragedy in which 'a silly little boy' had been mistaken for a rabbit and shot. 'No short-sighted man ought to shoot,' she concluded bluntly.

While married, she had lived on the grand level of the Georgian aristocracy, with lavish entertainment, a renowned cook and many well-connected guests. Now a widow, she retained something of her old grandeur. Violet remembered asking her why she always took three servants with her for a day in London.

'I take the cook to cook my lunch . . . And my maid to carry my bag and my parcels.'

'What do you take the footman for, Grandmama?' I asked.

Lady Caroline looked at me with mixed amazement and scorn as she answered: 'And who would take our tickets?' I never forgot her face. It expressed the fact that she thought I was mentally deficient.

In the country, Lady Caroline started a school for her employees' children to save them a two-mile trek every morning and evening. Such paternalism, which was shared by Violet's future family, the Cecils, was the other side of the coin to the caste exclusiveness deplored by Frederick Maxse. The role of country gentry and aristocracy as local rulers and benefactors had been diminishing during the course of the century. In 1888 an act passed under Lord Salisbury's Conservative Government removed finally from the squirearchy their traditional control over the counties, and replaced them with the newly instituted County Councils. Caroline Maxse, who died in 1886, had long lamented the measures that preceded the assault on aristocratic rule, such as the secret ballot and graduated income tax. Violet herself, in her old age in the mid-twentieth century, became as much of an anachronism as her grandmother had seemed to her at the end of the nineteenth century.

Frederick Maxse inherited half his mother's estate, and immediately set about building a house on it, which was to be Violet's favourite home, at Dunley Hill, near Dorking. The Admiral had become a squire and an ally of the Tories.

When Violet was fifteen her father took her and her sister Olive with their governess to live in Paris to finish their education. The two years Violet spent here instilled in her a lifelong affection for French culture, its theatre, music, fashions and, above all, paintings and sculpture. She found the atmosphere of Paris deeply sympathetic, largely because she absorbed it from her father and his great friend, the politician Georges Clemenceau, two vital, cultivated, worldly but idealistic men of strong political opinions.

Paris in the late nineteenth century was the cultural capital of the world. Creativity was in its air: it was the seed bed for Proust's great novel, published two decades later; it witnessed the blossoming of writers from Maupassant to Zola and Huysmans, the Impressionist painters such as Clemenceau's friend Claude Monet, the poetry of Mallarmé and Verlaine and the music of Debussy, Saint-Saëns, Massenet and Franck.

France was a modern democratic republic, but its economy, despite Paris's supremacy in *haute couture* and luxury goods, lagged behind those of Britain and Germany. Paradoxically, this made for a richer quality of life, as Violet observed: artists and bohemians, the flower of that free and vibrant society, could live in Paris with a certain style on small means. The working class still bore traces of its thrifty peasant roots and consisted largely of artisans in thousands of small workshops, whose wives extracted value from every sou, which in turn raised the standards of even humble eating places where poorer Bohemia congregated. 'The greatest advantage that a Frenchman has over an Englishman is that he has a French wife,' pronounced Georges Clemenceau. This impressed Violet, for whom these standards became crucially important.

Now she acquired a style of her own, distinctive and chic, which was to single her out for the rest of her life. She started to have her clothes made with the inimitable Parisian cut; there was something French, too, about her gift for enjoying herself and giving others a good time, and in the combination of cynicism and idealism with which she approached the world.

The two sisters were in Paris to acquire the accomplishments considered desirable in young women of their class, without becoming too professional or dowdy and intellectual for the sake of 'Cultcha', as their brother put it. Violet continued to learn the violin, and took dancing and French lessons; their father read to them, guiding them through English and French literature. Violet's main occupation was learning to draw with Mme Noëmi Guillaume at a studio on the Quai, a few streets away from their flat in the Boulevard St Germain on the Left Bank. Violet was not a natural artist, and never acquired a good technique, but she learnt to appreciate painting and sculpture and cultivated friends within the artistic world.

Her first meeting with Edgar Degas at his studio among a jumble of ramshackle buildings was memorable. When the Admiral and Violet rang the bell, Degas's fierce, shaggy head poked out of a window announcing that everyone was out. They persuaded him to

let them in, and Violet was spellbound by his pastels of the ballet. She
was impressed by his apparent admiration – so unlike their own
painter friends such as Whistler – for every great artist *except* himself.
She told her mother: 'He is a wonderful man . . . He addressed his
conversation to me . . . I was so taken back by his eloquence that I
could say nothing.' Unfortunately when, greatly daring, they invited
him to dinner, that flow of eloquence dried up; it was now his turn
to say nothing, and the evening was a failure.

Violet relished expeditions to the theatre, particularly the Comédie
Française, as much for the spectacle of the audience – the women in
elaborate gowns and embroidered evening cloaks, the men bearded
and top-hatted, in white tie and tails – as for the performances themselves. She saw classic plays and light and serious modern pieces,
dealing with contemporary manners, by such playwrights as Eugène
Labiche, Alexandre Dumas *Fils* and Emile Augier. The Comédie
Française was hardly ahead of its time in challenging orthodox
opinion. Yet for a young girl like Violet, these 'problem plays', dealing
with adultery or love triangles in bourgeois society, seemed audacious
and entirely new. Afterwards, in her room, she would pretend to be
the actors, silently mouthing the lines of Sarah Bernhardt, for
instance, lest anyone should guess what she was doing.

Her delicately pretty sister Olive was dedicated to music. It might
have been better for her if she had continued indefinitely in Paris
happily studying the piano. Languid like her mother and lacking the
vigour that had been so generously bestowed on Violet and her
brothers, Olive was doomed to an ineffective life; but at this time she
practised all day and in the evenings swept Violet and their father off
to the opera or to concerts, as Violet described.

> We arrive home to find Olive fussing because her dress has not come and
> it is half past seven – she starts at a quarter to eight.
>   'Good gracious! Violet, how on earth can you be ready?' 'Me?' 'Yes!!'
> 'I'm not going.' 'Yes you are, cut along,' – and, darling mother, I stripped,
> washed, changed everything, dressed in my pink dress and was ready in a
> quarter of an hour and did my hair too.'

Violet was always to retain this ability to transform her appearance at
a moment's notice into something chic and presentable.

Violet's mother, in the long, inconsequential letters that fluttered
from her pen, was enthralled by 'the darling's' Parisian life. In London a
girl of Violet's background would not have been free to make her own

discoveries or to discuss 'daring' subjects: 'It is curious to me to see that the opera and French Artists are suitable for you because it is Paris! Nothing of the kind was considered correct for you here. What rot all such opinions are – not worth considering – or troubling about – except that they are the cause of very serious trouble and I see no end to it!'

Cissie Maxse sent reports of her life in London, including her adventures with her artistic and musical friends: Sir Arthur Sullivan giving her tickets for the last Philharmonic concert of the season; James McNeill Whistler's 'at home' to display his latest pictures; or, particularly diverting, the exploits of her eccentric hanger-on, Mortimer Menpes, an ambitious Australian artist of minor talent, who worked indefatigably to keep himself in the public eye and to become an R.A. Menpes's slight reputation suffered momentary damage when he quarrelled publicly with Whistler, but, unabashed, he continued to tout for custom with rich heiresses and to advertise his portraits of celebrities in the newspapers. He even tried to learn horsemanship so that he could be seen riding in Rotten Row by grandees such as the Prince of Wales. Menpes was to crop up again in Violet's life a decade later during the Boer War. Now he accompanied Cissie Maxse to the latest exhibition while she treated him as a kind of pet clown, describing how:

> Menpes spends all his time trying to impress people – and is moulding them by various means – the critics he invites to dinner and in order that they shall be thoroughly influenced, he has sent his wife and maidservant to South Kensington, to have a source of instruction in the culinary art! When he calls on brother artists and others, he is followed or attended by a very small Boy in Buttons, carrying an umbrella!! You can imagine the picture! I am told it is singularly impressive!

The letters between Cissie Maxse and her daughter do not suggest a protective mother and a dependent child. Quite the reverse; it was Cissie, full of endearments, and craving entertainment and affection, who begged for small Parisian luxuries – a *fichu*: 'I am wanting another badly – could you not manage Le Grand's in the Rue St Honoré?'; pink lawn or zephyr from Bon Marché suitable for underclothing; *parfums solidifiés* to put inside a bracelet or brooch to exude scent at hot crowded functions; and delicacies – 'It does one good to see pretty dainty arrangements [of chocolates] out of Paris – somehow one never does . . .'

*Violet in the Bois de Boulogne, Paris, 1888, with her father (*right*) and their lifelong friend, Georges Clemenceau, the politician-writer whose combination of worldliness and idealism profoundly affected her*

Violet's letters, on the other hand, brimmed with the latest excitements, including the inevitable trip up the brand-new Eiffel Tower in May 1889. Like the Cecil children in the spheres of politics and current affairs, the Maxse children were encouraged to an unusual extent to deliver their opinions articulately and boldly – a habit Violet never lost. She was anxious to amuse her demanding and often lonely mother, whose choice of bohemian circles partly resulted from being too short of money to sally frequently into grand Society.

Much of the Maxses' life in Paris revolved round the Admiral's friend Georges Clemenceau. He would become one of the most magnetic influences in Violet's life: 'He was vital to a degree, swifter in thought, wittier in talk, more unexpected in what he said, than anyone I ever knew.' He had been a part of the Maxses' circle at her father's London house since she was a small child. When they met him again in Paris, he was in his mid-forties, dark, vivid, with flashing eyes. Both as a journalist and as a politician he was feared for his merciless hounding of fellow politicians in the name of radical republicanism. Although he and the Admiral differed on some matters, such as imperialism, to which Clemenceau was opposed, they were natural companions. They both believed in political emancipation through education, and both loved the countryside and its sports, especially shooting. Often pale from overwork as a journalist and author, Clemenceau nevertheless retained the aspect of a countryman, with his stocky peasant physique, thick eyebrows and heavy moustache. Putting his horse through its paces at daybreak in the Bois de Boulogne, he looked, in his gaiters and battered felt hat, every inch a farmer. At later, more fashionable hours, the Admiral and Violet often accompanied him in the Bois wearing top hats and dashing riding gear. Violet, like all fashion-conscious girls, knew how becoming was her well-cut habit to a slim figure and graceful seat on a horse.

Both Clemenceau and Admiral Maxse were men who took risks and showed cool courage. Clemenceau was more than once involved in a duel; and as Mayor of Montemartre from 1870 to 1871, during the siege of Paris by the Prussian Army and the revolutionary period of the Commune, he had handled tense confrontations with calm and panache. Both men enjoyed the arts and literature – Clemenceau being a devotee of the Impressionists. His lifelong friendship with Claude Monet began in the mid-1860s, when Clemenceau was a medical student, and culminated in his goading Monet to finish the *grandes décorations* in 1924, and persuading the Government to install them at the Orangerie in Paris. It is in part due to Clemenceau's zeal that we are able to enjoy so freely today Monet's great sequence of canvases and his immortal water-lilies.

Above all, Clemenceau and Frederick Maxse were fascinated by their fellow humans, both preferring the friendship of close companions to fashionable parties. Clemenceau was not a man to be impressed by rank or reputation.

He often took Violet and Olive to the opera, and was an invaluable guide to the theatre, 'a superb and ruthless critic', leading them behind the scenes to meet the actors. He stimulated, too, Violet's interest in another sort of drama – of French politics.Scandals and weakness had undermined public confidence in government. A new star had risen: the magnetic populist General Boulanger. Clemenceau soon came to regret his initial support of the handsome, blond-bearded Boulanger, darling of the crowds, when '*not' brav' général*' emerged as a potential dictator, a new Louis Napoleon, backed by the Right. By 1889, when Boulanger seemed certain to be elected by an overwhelming vote to lead the country at the head of a 'Boulangist' party, Clemenceau was his implacable enemy. Violet, riding with him in the Bois one morning, was shocked, and excited, to hear cries of '*A bas Clemenceau!*' It was Boulanger, however, who fell from grace, strangely losing his nerve in the face of his likely victory and fleeing the country; later he blew out his brains.

The Maxses returned to England late in 1889 to move into their new house. When Violet next saw Clemenceau on her return to Paris four years later, his political reputation was temporarily damaged by association with the Panama Scandal, and he had had to fight a duel (in which neither man was hurt) to defend his honour. He had been defeated in an election and was out of politics. Estranged for some years from his American wife, he lived with his daughter Thérèse. The Admiral found Violet a *pension de famille* across the street from him; from April to July that year, 1893, she worked long hours at the celebrated Julian's studio, and nearly every evening after dinner would cross the road to see them. To Clemenceau she was no longer simply the charming adjunct of her father – between them now a lifelong bond of friendship was established. It endured throughout the years of his championship of the victimised Jewish officer, Dreyfus, in the notorious 'Dreyfus Case' at the turn of the century, and of his two prime ministerships – years in which his true greatness was recognised, culminating with the First World War when 'the Tiger' as he was called, became the saviour of France.

CHAPTER FOUR

Violet in Society

IN ENGLAND the Admiral's new family home, Dunley Hill near
Dorking, was an expression of his more settled view of life. He had
chosen his architects with care: Ernest George and Peto of Maddox
Street, Mayfair, to whom Edwin Lutyens was to be articled, designed
for him a late Victorian gentleman's residence, part of a working farm,
brick-built with a tiled roof, and topped with a little tower. The
chimney stacks and gables gave it a 'Jacobean' character, while its
louvred shutters and verandah had a colonial air, not unlike the houses
around Cape Town which Violet was to get to know so well during
the Boer War.

Dunley Hill was neither grand nor particularly beautiful, but like
everything the Admiral concerned himself with, it had character. A
spacious porch led into a high-ceilinged hall with long windows and a
gallery. The rooms beyond included a library and a conservatory. There
were six main bedrooms; the children and servants slept in the attics.
Most rooms were painted white or had chintz-patterned wallpapers.
There was only one bathroom in the house – but what a bathroom! It
boasted the very latest splendid and elaborate shower, so beloved in that
era of modish plumbing, the work of George Jennings, Sanitary
Engineers, with various sprays coming from all round. The most
modern electric lighting was installed. A key feature in that horse-
loving household was the coach house and stables, with a graceful
clock-tower and equipped with every efficient device, including
sleighs for snowy weather, which could be substituted for wheels on
the carriages; remote Dunley might be, but the Admiral intended to
entertain neighbours and London friends. His home reflected an age
of abundant servants, with its housemaids' rooms, butler's pantry,
housekeeper's room and polishing room. As the Admiral's creation, its
design was emphatically masculine, and it was not especially luxurious;

the kitchen, as so often in those days, was a fair way from the dining room, so that the food rarely arrived piping hot.

The garden, with its greenhouse, where brightly coloured calceolarias and lobelias were reared for 'planting out' in traditional Victorian fashion, was tended by a head gardener, an under-gardener, a boy and an 'odd man', their weekly wages ranging from £1.8 shillings down to just 7 shillings – the very low general level being one reason why so many farm workers were moving to the towns. The faithful 'Coachie' continued to look after the horses until he finally retired, when the Admiral gave him a plot of land; as a man of property, Coachie, who had previously been wont to mouth sentiments as revolutionary as his master's, became a conservative of the most reactionary hue.

One great attraction of Dunley Hill was its dramatic position 600 feet above sea level, with unspoilt views for miles around; this was partly because water was available only by sinking deep wells which few people in the past had been able to afford. The 300-acre estate on heavy clay soil was unsuitable for wheat which, from the 1880s, was on the decline owing to competition from cheaper grain from the New World. Instead the Admiral reared stock. Even so, and despite stringent economies, the farm lost more than £150 annually. This was part of the general malaise which afflicted British agriculture until the Second World War. Unprotected by tariffs, backward-looking in techniques through lack of incentive, and with landowners subjected to high death duties after 1894, farmers were giving up, and in many parts of England rural trades were in decline and land was going out of cultivation. All the while the Admiral's capital was diminishing: he enjoyed speculating in property and business, never very successfully, and was generous to his friends and family.

Despite the permanent shadow cast over the Maxse children by their parents' separation, Violet always looked back on these years of her girlhood as idyllic and tried, in a sense, to replicate the atmosphere of Dunley when she acquired her own house sixteen years later. The Dunley visitors' book records guests from the world of politics and the arts. Two neighbours, especial friends, were quintessentially of that confident period: the writer George Meredith, aesthete, iconoclast and preacher of an enticingly optimistic philosophy of life; and the fashionable Maria Theresa Earle, whose book *Pot-pourri from a Surrey Garden* had made her famous, describing how she had transformed a commonplace arrangement of flower beds and lawns in her garden

*Theatricals at Dunley, 1891: Violet as an
eighteenth-century French heroine*

into an arcadia of exquisite colour and design. The Admiral was among her devotees, and so was Violet, for Mrs Earle combined a romantic belief, typical of her time and class, that life could be shaped into a paradise, with the hard-headed practical understanding of how best to go about it. She taught Violet the useful lesson of how to make a little money go a long way. An entertaining gossip, warm-hearted and flattering, she was also a valuable confidante.

Amateur theatricals were a highlight of the house parties, using one end of the hall as a stage. In 1890, on her eighteenth birthday, Violet took the female lead in F. Anstey's *Vice Versa* and Olive played the incidental music; red morocco-bound books record two elaborate productions in October 1891. Violet starred as a young French girl in one, and as 'Rose' in the other, 'The Rosebud of Stinging Nettle Farm', with Ivor playing the farmer.

Violet always loved opportunities for dressing up, whether for theatricals, for hunting or for daily life. Sometimes she got carried away. Ivor passed on to her an aunt's critical remark that Violet should be careful in English social circles not to wear costumes that were too unconventional and go about calling herself 'Tosca' (Puccini's heroine, who lived for her art): 'Do not start the notion that you are "fast". You and I don't care one jot for their opinions but we must recognise that it is most essential, especially so for you and Olive (who go about alone) to avoid having these sort of things said, even by idiots.' Clemenceau was more worried at the effect unorthodox clothes might have on her dress sense: '*Les excentricités vous vont; je ne vous les conseille pas.*'

This terse lesson she took to heart. The sartorial influence of Paris was deep and her scorn for bad dressing was always withering. As bridesmaids for a cousin's marriage, she told Ivor,

> Olive and I are going to figure in the most hideous hats that have been seen since the Conquest. Figure to yourself a dead white silk hat (think of our poor complexions) with a beaded brim turned up <u>all round</u> . . . and an enormous white bow and spray of white heather at the back to finish it off . . . poor me!

The first big family celebration at Dunley was the wedding of Violet's brother Leo to Kitty Lushington, on Christmas Eve 1890. Leo's wife was universally popular, intelligent and an accomplished musician, who delighted her new family with her piano playing. For the ceremony neither Leo nor his father wore the customary frock coat: the Maxses were hardly conventional churchgoers; neither religion nor correct church behaviour meant anything to them.

At twenty-six, Leo still had no profession; despite having proposed the motion at an undergraduate debating society that 'an aimless life is on the whole desirable', he was not lacking in purpose, and his arresting, eccentric personality attracted many unusual companions, from the ghost-story writer Montague James to the doomed elder son of the Prince of Wales, Eddy, Duke of Clarence. Clarence was briefly with him at Cambridge, and dazzled by his high spirits. By Leo's mid-twenties, after a tour of the world in a vain attempt to recover his health, the sleepy-eyed, solid-looking boy had become a spare young man, alert and intense. He had his father's determined, obsessional nature. All his life, Leo was a campaigner, holding fiercely-defended, controversial views which moved ever further to the Right as he grew older and were a beacon to Violet. Current affairs absorbed him and he had already become a friend of his father's ally Joseph Chamberlain, and of E.T. Cook, Editor of the influential *Pall Mall Gazette*.

Ill health thwarted his ambitions to enter Parliament but in 1893 an opportunity for a new career was offered by a family friend, Alfred Austin, whom Lord Salisbury later made Poet Laureate for his services to the Conservative Party. Austin, an indefatigable patriotic doggerel-ist, was only five feet tall and a favourite butt of satirists such as Max Beerbohm. Meredith nicknamed him 'the Admiral's Ancient' and when Austin confessed to him that he had a 'cult' for Violet, com-posed a series of ludicrous odes with which he bombarded her, pre-tending that they came from her swooning swain, Austin. These were silenced when Austin dedicated his next book of verse to Meredith.

Austin owned a monthly journal, the *National Review*, then mori-bund, which the Admiral bought from him in the hope that Leo might edit it. Leo transformed it into a lively journal of news, politi-cal criticism and analysis. Catching his enthusiasm, all the family flung themselves into the new venture. Leo and Kitty had come to live at Dunley, and in the *National Review*'s early days the writing, editing and soliciting of contributions were run from the house, unassisted by any such later inventions as motor cars, typewriters or telephones. The copy, all handwritten, and return proofs had to be sent by horse or dog-cart the four miles to and from Dorking station.

Contributors were recruited from among friends and contacts such as Meredith and Clemenceau; in due course Violet herself wrote regu-larly. Leo proved a born editor, with his prodigious industry, wide knowledge of public affairs, talent for picking good writers and dis-cretion in protecting his sources. Radical and stimulating, the journal became largely the expression of the family's viewpoint, supporting Clemenceau's championship of Dreyfus, but also increasingly imperi-alist, and in the years leading up to and during the Great War, obses-sively anti-German. Although still a good paper, with a wide circulation, it had by then acquired a ranting edge.

When Violet was eighteen she was presented at Court and did the London Season with her mother. Cissie Maxse was in no position to give parties or elaborate *soirées* to 'launch' her, and the Admiral despised the whole business. However, Violet enjoyed her Season, from the balls and parties to which she was invited, to her presenta-tion at Court dressed in 'chilly white clothes with white ostrich feath-ers and a white tulle veil', and a train nine feet long which was the court regulation. 'We passed before the Prince of Wales – Queen

Ivor Maxse as an officer in the Sudan and the author
George Meredith, a close friend of the Maxses

Victoria only received . . . the Corps Diplomatique, high ranking ministers and other great persons.'

Graceful and musical, Violet enjoyed dancing, especially with foreigners, who did not feel inhibited, as young Englishmen did, by thinking that to dance well was 'bad form'. It was a pleasure too, for her to realise how popular and pretty her mother was, compared with those of many of her contemporaries.

In the country, Violet hunted with the local pack, the Surrey Union: 'Is there any greater pleasure than a day out in the open, on a good horse,' she asked, 'with the hounds ahead promising sport, and a bit of open country? If there is I do not know it.' She was accompanied on the field by her father or her brother Ivor. Devoted to his family, and with the same vigorous intelligence as Leo and Violet, Ivor was developing into a tough, formidable young man. In 1889 he returned to England after soldiering for seven years in far-flung parts of the Empire. He was frustrated by his life in India where he fell victim to tropical illnesses and boredom: he had seen no action and felt opportunity passing him by, as Edward Cecil was to do on joining the army. In 1891 he transferred to the Coldstream Guards.

He took Violet, with three horses between them, on a sporting tour in Gloucestershire with the Duke of Beaufort's and Lord Bathurst's hunt, the Vale of the White Horse. Violet wildly enjoyed the sport and the social life. There were balls, including a fancy-dress party – and new friendships. One was with Margot Tennant, who 'was riding a grey horse, Seagull, and was going very well. She was much better mounted than I was, but something happened to make Seagull refuse a jump which my mare took, giving Seagull a lead. Miss Tennant, afterwards, with characteristic generosity, came up to me and thanked me. I was thrilled . . .'

For Margot Tennant, the daughter of one of the Liberal Party's paymasters, an extraordinarily rich Glasgow industrialist, was at the pinnacle of fashion. Although she was neither pretty nor fine-grained, her spontaneous charm and power of enjoyment had captivated the *beau monde* and even the elderly Liberal leader, Gladstone. Her conversation combined razor-sharp *aperçus* and wild fantasy. Margot was a leading member of the 'Souls', a well-born and talented group of friends who delighted in conversation, talking as easily about metaphysics as about the arts, flirting, penning poems or playing tennis and discussing their souls – hence their nickname. They gathered at country house parties at the Tennants' house, Glen, in Scotland; Lord Desborough's at Taplow, in Berkshire; Lord Cowper's, Panshanger in Hertfordshire; and Lord Elcho's, Stanway in Gloucestershire. Staying at Glen, accompanied by Ivor, Violet made friends with another of the Souls, George Curzon, ambitious, arrogant, but also self-mocking and headed for a glittering career. He was Viceroy of India at the age of only thirty-nine in 1898.

Other 'Souls' with whom Violet became acquainted included the urbane American diplomat Harry White and his popular wife, Daisy; and the peerless but flawed politician and journalist Harry Cust, dangerous to women. Cust seems to have tried his luck with Violet, but she escaped seduction, and later watched, shocked, along with the rest of the fashionable world, when a pregnancy, a broken engagement and a shotgun marriage to a rich heiress led to his temporary ostracism.

One weekend in August 1893, at Ashridge, Lord Brownlow's Gothic Revival house in Hertfordshire, Violet made friends with one of the most attractive of the 'Souls', the brilliant Arthur Balfour, tall, willowy, liquid-eyed, a close cousin of the Cecils, now making a name for himself as a Conservative politician, the toughness of his views belied by his graceful, intimate manner and languid deportment. Balfour wrote to his great friend, Mary Elcho: 'After dinner walked up and down the terrace talking Art with Miss Maxse, whom I like', showing enough interest in Violet for Mary Elcho to wonder who she

was, as 'I therefore regard her with a sort of acid interest!' Balfour and
Violet's friendship continued when she became a cousin by marriage.
His sister-in-law, Betty Balfour, met Violet at Glen the following
month, and wrote to Kitty Maxse: 'I am always prepared to love her,
and think her one of the most original and attractive women I have
ever met. She makes me a little shy for there is a good deal of reserve
about her, and I think I should find her difficult to know well, but that
is no defect – and she is a most delightful social companion.'

When Margot Tennant came to stay with the Maxses at Dunley,
Violet and the Admiral took her on their usual Sunday walk to visit
Meredith; the gravel drive, between high hedges, to his house at Box
Hill had become a path of pilgrimage for readers inspired by his novels
and poetry. The handsome old man with his kingly, medieval looks
urged the breaking of stifling shibboleths, poured scorn on pretension
and rated women's intellects as high as men's – often higher. The forthright Margot Tennant plunged straight in, telling him of her fancy to
start a weekly paper, for which she had assembled a list of famous contributors. She hoped at least for a *succès d'éstime*. The old poet looked at
her. 'A *succès de snob* would be more likely,' he said. It was precisely
because she could have stepped from the pages of one of his novels that
he understood her only too well. Violet could not resist telling this story
in her memoir years later, by which time she had become a ferocious
critic of Margot and her husband H.H. Asquith, the Liberal Prime
Minister, for their conduct during the First World War.

The hostess at Ashridge where Violet stayed, the pious Lady
Brownlow (who nearly made Arthur Balfour 'cry with boredom'),
was the sister of 'Gerty' Pembroke, wife of Lord Pembroke. The
Pembrokes welcomed Violet at their magnificent country house,
Wilton, in Wiltshire, and on their yacht, the *Black Pearl*, on which
they invited her to cruise during the summer. From Cowes, she wrote
that she had 'lost my heart to the German Emperor. He is so handsome and has a very pleasant smile' – sentiments not destined to
endure. She, like her father, loved the life at sea. 'Think of me getting
as brown as a berry with desperately untidy hair and red hands! Not
at all attractive, but very happy.' Lady Pembroke impressed her by
wearing, with aristocratic nonchalance, a 'splendid necklace of huge
pearls, even with a seaman's jersey'. The Pembrokes were childless,
and Lord Pembroke, twenty years Violet's senior, 'constituted himself
my guardian and mentor'.

Violet attracted, as she was to do all her life, many devoted friends

The Maxse sisters, Violet and Olive, were much admired by the artist Edward Burne-Jones who sent them illustrated letters. Alongside this drawing, he wrote to Violet: 'I have praised you so heartily for throwing over the trumpery world and setting yourself to hard work . . . I think you are beautiful – and an old artist may tell a young girl that without hurt or blame.'

among men older than herself, such diverse characters as Georges Clemenceau, the Earl of Pembroke and Edward Burne-Jones. The artist Burne-Jones, who was as much taken with Olive as with Violet, wrote the two sisters many amusing illustrated letters – when Violet was about to go to the dentist, he suggested she could come and see him instead. 'I can draw teeth, come to me, I will draw them all so carefully.' The Burne-Joneses were cousins of Rudyard Kipling, whose family was later to become close friends.

There was no suggestion of impropriety with any of these friends and their encouragement meant a good deal to her. 'I felt fortified by dear Burne-Jones's blessing. Not everyone approved of me. It was an unusual thing in 1893 for a girl who need not work to do so, and Paris was believed to be a sink of iniquity instead of what it was – and is – a place where people respect and understand work.'

It was now that Violet made the acquaintance, though as yet no more than that, of the man, eighteen years her senior, who was ultimately to be the greatest influence on her life – Alfred Milner. Ambitious and hard-working, Alfred was well on the path to an outstanding career as a civil servant and statesman. When younger he had been handsome;

Olive Maxse, to whom he had a sentimental attachment,
was a favourite model for Burne-Jones's drawings

in 1892, at the age of thirty-eight, his years of toil at official papers had narrowed his close-set eyes, lined his brow and given a dog-like determined set to his lean jaws. However, he kept his tall, slender figure and the controlled vitality in his conversation and demeanour was attractive. He was increasingly known to be a man of power and of mystery. Even when people had doubts about his views, as they often did during his controversial career, they were readily drawn to him by his kind and confidential manner when they came to know him.

Alfred Milner had learnt self-reliance at an early age. He knew what it was to work things out for himself and to trust his own intellect, which was formidable. He enjoyed the company of women and a busy social life but allowed neither to distract him from his work in serving the Empire, in which he believed with an almost visionary faith. 'I have nothing to fear in a life the first condition of which is celibacy,' he had written in his diary, eleven years before. 'One cannot be every-thing. I am a poor man and must choose between public usefulness and private happiness. I choose the former, or rather I choose to strive for it. Besides could private happiness be mine in any case?'

Born into a professional family which had fallen on hard times, he had had an unusual upbringing divided between Germany and England; he was at home in both countries, as Violet was in France and in England. He was a quarter German, through his grandmother, the daughter of a German government official. His father was the son of a wine merchant from Manchester, who had settled in Germany. Alfred's mother, Mary, was English, the daughter of a successful soldier and civil servant. She married an Anglo-Irish officer, was widowed young and went to live on her limited means in Germany. There she fell in love with a medical student, Charles Milner, twenty years her junior, who was tutor to her two sons. Alfred, the only son of her second marriage, was born on 23 March 1854, and spent most of his earliest years in Tübingen, twenty miles from Frankfurt, until, at the age of six, he moved with the family to London where Dr Milner attempted to practise medicine. He did not prosper; after six years the Milners returned to Germany, where Alfred's father took a lowly, ill-paid post at the University of Tübingen.

Dr Milner's lack of focus and industry was more than compensated for by young Alfred's resolution: the boy now relearnt German and threw himself into his schooling at the Tübingen Gymnasium with a concentration of purpose he was to show all his life. Weekday school work went from 7 a.m. to 4 p.m., followed by gymnastics and early bed. He was brought up as an only child after his much older half-brothers had left home and gone to India and China. He made many friends, whose ardent young faces gaze out from the family photo-graph album preserved from this period. Already there was something of the future statesman in the unflinching composure with which the youthful Alfred regarded the camera. He had acquired the high seri-ousness of purpose that was the hallmark of his politics.

The town of Tübingen itself was an education, with its fine med-ieval and renaissance buildings and its tradition of humanistic scholar-ship, science and poetry. Alfred became an avid reader, as he was to remain all his life, fond of opera and theatre and an admirer of ancient architecture. On walks with his father in the nearby hills, he deve-loped a romantic affinity with natural beauty and an enthusiasm for outdoor exercise. These happy childhood years ended when he was only fifteen with the death of his mother after a long illness: this was

Alfred Milner in 1867, aged 13, at Tübingen,
Germany, where his family were living

a devastating blow for Alfred and his family. Although his father was
a good companion and teacher to him, it was Mary Milner, reserved
but affectionate and intelligent, who had been the unwavering
influence in her youngest son's life. Wishing him to be brought up as
an Englishman – he was an English citizen, despite his place of birth
– and reluctant to leave him in the charge of his unpractical father, she
had arranged before she died for Alfred to return to England under
the care of her brother. And so, having been a model German schoolboy, he became in turn an exemplary English pupil, as a day boy at
King's College School, London. He lost all traces of his German
accent save a slurring of his 'th's which stayed with him all his life.

The emotional void left by his mother's death and his loneliness as an
adolescent were long-lasting. Despite an affectionate nature, he became
emotionally reserved. He was always fond of his father, and came to love

Alfred c. 1871, in England

his father's second wife, a German, and to get along with his step-family; but he never ceased to miss his mother and the secure domestic life that ended with her death. For several years he lived in London in the charge of an alcoholic cousin, Marianne Malcolm. Still in his teens, he had to cope alone with the painful situation. She died in 1885.

By strenuous effort, in 1872, the year of Violet's birth, Alfred, at the age of eighteen, sat and won a scholarship to Balliol College, Oxford. It was the most prestigious open scholarship offered by the university. There is a poignant description of the announcement of his triumph in the hall full of waiting candidates from Eton, Winchester and other public schools: when Alfred's name was announced, last, there was a silence for, unlike the other boys, he had no crowd of friends. Then the silence was broken by a resounding 'Yahoo!' from the one who had come with him and who now, singing and dancing, whirled him out of the college and round the streets of Oxford.

At Balliol Alfred achieved a remarkable success, winning all but one of the prizes for which he entered. He graduated with a double First in 'Mods and Greats' (Classics and Philosophy) and shortly afterwards New College recognised his brilliance by electing him to an open Fellowship.

Debates with his fellow-undergraduates had awoken Alfred's fascination with public affairs – especially the increasingly powerful British Empire which seemed to offer limitless opportunities for one small island to shape the destinies of the world. He formed a lifelong ideal of a greater Britain, united into one immensely strong force with her colonies and dominions, by language, political beliefs and economic interests, leading the world forward to peace and progress. It was a racialist ideal, even if, for him, 'race' was less a matter of blood or colour than of values, traditions and culture. On his first job abroad in Egypt, for example, he was very far from being contemptuous of the Egyptians, whom he felt would soon be fit for self-government.

Searching for a path towards serving his ideal, Alfred tried and rejected the Bar, journalism and Parliament. An early defeat as a Liberal candidate in a by-election was his first significant set-back, and the experience left him with an intense dislike of democratic politics which, in his view, put able men at the mercy of a wayward and ill-informed electorate.

The young Alfred's romantic and aesthetic side, which owed much to his German education, led him to brood on whether the greatness to which he aspired did not lie in being in a 'condition of intellectual and spiritual all-aliveness' rather than in the more prosaic path he had chosen: 'Throw up the dull business of life, which chokes the soul; and blunts the intellect,' he urged himself, when in this mood, 'and live at Florence, Venice, at Athens – anywhere the combination of Beautiful Nature, Noble Art and Great Architecture forces you to live at the top of your powers. Ah me! Shall I ever do it, before it is too late?' He wondered whether, if his political hopes failed, he should turn to writing: 'to record my most intimate experience of life, so that all I have felt at times with such feverish intensity about the life of man and his mysterious destiny, may be something more than as breath upon glass, vanished as soon as seen.'

For several years he was secretary to George Joachim (later Viscount) Goschen, a former Liberal who in 1887 served as Chancellor of the Exchequer in Lord Salisbury's Conservative Government. In 1889, on Goschen's recommendation, Alfred went to Egypt as Director-General of Accounts. Under Cromer, the head of the British administration, he rose to a controlling position as Under-Secretary for Finance, thrilled by the speed with which prosperity and social improvement seemed possible in Egypt through adroit financial reform. He hurried up the ladder of promotion, returning in 1892 to London, where he had been appointed Chairman of the Board of the Inland Revenue, with magnificent offices in Somerset House.

His much-acclaimed book, *England in Egypt*, was a eulogy of Britain's achievement there and in the Empire. Winston Churchill, a few years later, praised it as 'more than a book. The words rang like a trumpet call which rallies the soldiers after the parapets are stormed, and summons them to complete the victory.'

It was in Egypt, too, that Alfred first fell wholeheartedly in love. Late in 1891, when Margot Tennant visited Cairo, they saw each other constantly. He proposed to her – but was rejected. Until then he had felt that he was incapable 'of that single and enduring love, which could alone make marriage desirable in a life so busy and full of interest as mine'. After she turned him down he believed, once more, that celibacy – or at least non-attachment – was to be his fate, aware that he was not rich enough to support a wife and family. He relied on what he earned and his shrewd investments. He wondered about his future happiness: 'that I shall for long live an intenser life that is certain. Will it also be a more useful, a more unselfish, a nobler one – that is the only important question. And God only knows what will be the answer.'

The answer was years in coming for this courteous, ambitious and high-minded man, who made an impression on many women as being marked out for eminence but who, a friend to many, seemed to hold back from emotional involvement. 'Why are all the nicest women out of tune with the world, or the world out of tune with them?' he wrote in his diary. 'It is pleasant to find that one is sympathetic & consoling – but I wish they would not need my sympathy – though I like giving it.'

He had come to know Admiral Maxse and his family through mutual political acquaintances such as Joseph Chamberlain, the powerful Birmingham radical who, indignant at Gladstone's Irish Home Rule policy, had switched, like Goschen, from the Liberals to alliance with Lord Salisbury's Conservative Government. Chamberlain was shortly to be the dominant figure in British imperialism. Socially Alfred and Violet frequently encountered one another. But it would be another seven years before circumstances more momentous than his work at the Inland Revenue and more threatening than the balls and parties of the London Season, or the clever games and poetry-making of the Souls brought him and Violet irrevocably together.

CHAPTER FIVE

Gambling and Love

AT THE END of July 1890, Lord Wolseley, the newly appointed Commander-in-Chief of the British forces in Ireland, had invited Edward Cecil to be his aide-de-camp. Georgina Salisbury had secured this post for him, as she arranged most of her sons' professions. She was a great admirer of Wolseley, a clever and innovative soldier who was heading a strong movement to bring the British Army up to date. Wolseley, for his part, felt that having young men of high social status on his staff increased his own. Edward's duties 'would be more social than military'. He would get only his quarters and a horse, and various small allowances, in addition to his regimental pay. 'I hope you mean to go through the Staff College,' Wolseley wrote. 'If so, you will have plenty of time for study in Dublin.' Unfortunately, things did not work out like that: over the next four years in Ireland, Edward had time aplenty, but it was not spent in study.

On 2 October, Edward joined Wolseley and his entourage on a rough sea crossing. 'Young Cecil was ill, but he does not mind being ill, he says. The first man I ever heard say so,' Wolseley reported to his wife. Their reception at Kingstown (now Dun Laoghaire) was a precedent of things to come. As they drew up to the pier it 'seemed to be richly adorned with waving plumes and sword-carrying warriors of all sorts, whilst behind there was a Guard of Honour of the Royal Rifles . . . The same thing, Guard of Honour, etc. was repeated at the Railway Road Station in Dublin, where the crowd was very considerable.'

Edward would have to get used to the ceremony and the protracted official receptions given to his chief, particularly on tour: the formal entertaining in provincial garrison towns was wearisome. Edward swiftly came to realise just how unmilitary his duties were:

Lieutenant Edward Cecil, Grenadier Guards, with Lord Wolseley,
Commander-in-Chief in Ireland, to whom he was ADC

I fetch the carriage, preside at table [in other words arrange the *placement* according to rank], entertain visitors, carry coats . . . we dine out every night when I am toadied by the snobs and pitied by the gentle. I have no military duties and am told nothing. I wear a very pretty uniform . . . I have not time for sight seeing as I always go with my incubus wherever he goes . . . The wives of the officers talk about the Lords of their acquaintance and the officers make fulsome remarks about my old nightmare

Wolseley while the civilians flatter and fawn about "Lard Sarlisbury" . . .
I don't mind scoundrels, and fools I feel for, but a snob has no right to
exist . . . And now out to another dinner. So up on to my hind legs and
on with the deferential grin. Curtain please.

Wolseley, then aged fifty-seven and reaching the height of his poten-
tial, was ambitious and energetic; when he eventually succeeded the
Duke of Cambridge, who had enjoyed an interminable reign as a backward-looking Commander-in-Chief, he was at last able to blow a fresh
breeze of reform through the antiquated halls of the War Office; but that
time had not yet come. If his young ADC complained in his letters
home, so did his Chief: 'I feel I am wasting my short spell of life,'
Wolseley told his wife. He claimed to want nothing better than to die in
action defending 'what I prize most – namely, the honour and reputation of our Empire.' This posting to Ireland – then effectively a colony
ruled from both Dublin and London – at the head of an army of occupation, seemed to cheat him of that ambition. Wolseley missed his family,
who soon joined him. As far as Edward was concerned, this made things
worse. The daughter, Frances, was lent Edward's horse to ride without
his permission, and the horse had a bad back in consequence – 'rather
cool is it not?' was Edward's tight-lipped comment. At other times his
irritation at 'the Chief's female appendages' spilled over: 'they now have
caught the true Dublin twang & talk malicious small talk in a way that
makes me have a nasty taste in my mouth . . . Lady W. complains that
Mrs. Jackson is "not quite what you would call a Lady"; I look at the
kettle on the hob and wonder what it said to the Tongs about the Pot.'
Of course, that most sporting and hospitable society, the Anglo-
Irish Ascendancy, in which British officers moved, had plenty of com-
pensations and Lord Edward was much in demand by country house
hostesses. While professing not to like 'Society' – he signed one letter
to his mother 'Your-convinced-against-Society-with-a-big-S-son' –
nevertheless, he enjoyed the house parties on what were some of the
loveliest and most romantic country estates in the world.
During that time Arthur Balfour came over to Dublin as Irish
Secretary. Balfour, closer to Lord and Lady Salisbury than any other
cousin, knew Edward well. They sometimes met to play golf together
– Balfour's passion, some would say his only passion.
Ireland was then enjoying an unaccustomed spell of tranquillity.
During previous years, Gladstone, as Liberal Prime Minister, had
attempted to solve the problem of Irish nationalism and agrarian

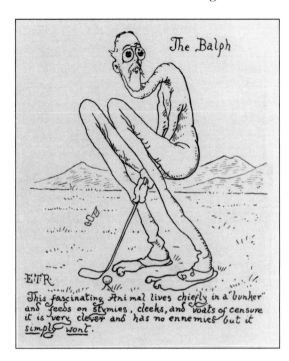

The Balph

This fascinating Animal lives chiefly in a "bunker" and feeds on stymies, cleeks, and voals of censure it is "very clever and has no ennemies but it simply wont.

E.T.R.

'The Balph.' Caricature of the golf-loving Arthur Balfour by E.T. Reed

violence, first by land reform and then by Home Rule – semi-independence – which Salisbury and its other opponents believed could not be a harmless measure of devolution, because the 'forces of fanaticism' would insist on an absolute severance from British control. Home Rule had been defeated in Parliament and Gladstone had succeeded only in driving many of the most influential members of his party into alliance with the Conservatives. Under Lord Salisbury, Arthur Balfour had punished violence and sedition severely through the Criminal Law Amendment Act – but also offered economic development for poor rural areas and, eventually, finance for Irish peasants to buy out their English landlords, which they did in great numbers. The combination was effective and the Conservatives, underestimating the strength of nationalism, hoped it would die away altogether. Gladstone returned to power in 1892 and re-introduced a Home Rule Bill, but Salisbury knew he could count on British popular support if it were thrown out by the House of Lords, as happened in 1893.

Far from giving Edward the opportunity of working towards the Staff College examination, his underemployment demoralised him. It was all too easy to slip into dissolute habits; a letter to his mama was a foreboding of the storm about to break: 'I fear I have been a dreadful fool for the last year, idle and shiftless, however, I am now going to pull up and try again.'

Soon his debts of over £1,000 (at least twenty-five times that in today's money) could not be ignored, postponed or paid without recourse to his parents. He wrote to his father, confessing. Salisbury replied:

> The sum is large – and it is a nuisance to pay it. But if it were merely a question of extravagance, I should be satisfied with expressing a hope that you would attend more carefully to the details of your expenditure. Unless you look after them more sharply, this sort of thing will be constantly happening.
>
> But what makes me say something more is the fact that this large sum has been rolled up, less by extravagance than by gambling: and that from the circumstances it is evident that you belong to the class of men who lose their self-restraint when they are at the gaming table. Of the people who game, there are two sorts – the people who are very fond of it but who are quite cool at the table, and can stop when they please – and the people who, at first at least, are not very fond of it, but who get excited at it, and lose their heads. To these last – and I am afraid you belong to them – the taste for gambling is one of the extremest danger. It may lead them anywhere . . .

This was humiliating enough; worse was Lord Salisbury's letter a month later announcing that he had paid the debt of £1,126 8s 6d: 'Please do not run me into any more large sums – for the practical result is that I am delayed in collecting the provision which I wish to make for Gwenny – now that it is probable she will not marry: and as life is uncertain I do not like to be delayed.'

A subtle man, he chose to make only this oblique condemnation, calculating, accurately, how much the implied loss to his beloved sister Gwendolen would pierce Edward's conscience. Beyond that, no word of reproach came, but his mother wrote:

> I am sure if you saw his sad wounded look when he speaks of it you would never touch a card again while you live. I earnestly trust you may have a good success in your exam. That will be the best thing you can do now. God bless you my darling – If you only knew how much we love you.
>
> Your very affn mother
> G Salisbury

Contrite, Edward wrote home emphasising his healthy, open-air life, sailing in Dublin Bay – 'I am becoming an A.I. skipper' – and promising, 'I am economising . . . I don't play cards now as I am perfectly happy without.'

The promises were accepted, the debts forgiven – until the next time. But it was hardly realistic to expect that Edward, young, popular, thirsting for action yet stuck in a position halfway 'between a private secretary and a butler (most butler)', with no one to supervise or to propose a timetable for any work he might do towards Staff College, would stay out of temptation. He remarked plaintively that his father could 'understand neither the motives nor temptations of my life'. Besides which, the prevailing attitude towards Staff College on the part of the Army generally was that officers there 'were a set of shirkers who left their regiments with a view to an idle two years at the College, to be followed by loafing and well-paid jobs in the plums of the profession,' as Count Gleichen, Edward's near-contemporary in the same regiment, later recalled. Gleichen himself was advised by a cousin in another regiment to say nothing about his cramming for the Staff College exam, 'or you will get yourself jolly well disliked!' Such attitudes were hardly an inducement to Edward to study towards that goal.

Gleichen's recollections also show that it was well-nigh impossible for a Guards officer not to be overdrawn; he himself was often hundreds of pounds in the red: 'anyhow, it never worried me, for a subaltern's views on the subject of cash are always pleasantly buoyant. After dinner, which was always a cheery feast washed down by excellent Pol Roger or Dagonet (alas! no more), we at once adjourned to cards. The play was generally pretty high, or it would be considered so nowadays.' With 'fairly stiff' gamblers, 'it was nothing unusual for fellows to bet £25 on the turn of a card or to win or lose £200 or more in a night.' Captains were supposed to keep an eye on their subalterns, like Edward, to prevent them from playing for more than they could afford. But undoubtedly the atmosphere in the mess, particularly after the quantities of champagne had been followed by brandy and soda, was conducive to forgetting that debts would one day have to be paid. Lord Wolseley saw only the tip of the iceberg: when he joined in playing cards with Edward and his cronies one evening, it was for shilling stakes only.

Besides which, it would have been assumed that Edward, the son of Lord Salisbury, the Prime Minister, was rich enough to be able to afford to gamble: not so. He was kept on a tight financial rein by his parents, and if any extra expense arose, such as an expedition he made to Tangier during this time, he had to ask them for the wherewithal.

His enjoyable but brief journey into the wilds of North Africa whetted his appetite for action: he watched the international situation eagerly. The discovery of gold in South Africa was leading to a poten-tial conflagration between British imperial and business interests on the one hand and the Boer farmers, who controlled the mining areas, on the other. Edward hoped 'we shall have a row in S. Africa' and that 'the Chief' will be sent out as 'he has promised to take me'. Eight years later, Wolseley was to remember this promise he had made to his young ADC. But now, only annual manoeuvres in England in the summer months went any way towards providing the longed-for mil-itary experience: 'I had an A.I. time . . . and quite got over the indigo blues which are chronic in this country,' Edward wrote when, all too soon, it was back to duty in Dublin.

In May 1893 he joined his parents and Gwendolen in the north of Ireland, where his father, who was fighting off Mr Gladstone's last effort to introduce Home Rule, had a rapturous reception and spoke to massed crowds. As Salisbury walked to the platform, the band played 'See the Conquering Hero Comes'. Edward often talked to Arthur Balfour about British policy in Ireland, and once attended a meeting organised by the great Irish nationalist Charles Stuart Parnell, which interested him strongly, as did Parnell's 'distinctly impressive' funeral, not long after; otherwise he had little direct experience of the world of Irish politics. But that was only right: politics were out for Edward, a soldier of the Queen.

A diversion which was to have longer-lasting significance for Edward was the arrival, in the New Year of 1894, in Dublin of Violet Maxse.

There are no more than enigmatic allusions as to any amorous entan-glement Violet may have had at this time, except for just one refer-ence, by an ambiguous initial, to someone for whom she seems to have had strong feelings. Who he was, she has left no trace. Her brother wrote to her, referring to this person, and Violet, thanking Ivor for his interest in her wellbeing, declared that she had got over him. Beyond this, nothing. The Admiral, however, was plainly sufficiently anxious about her in Paris as to prefer his pretty daughter to be somewhere more securely chaperoned. He therefore arranged for her to be invited to Dublin to stay with an old family friend, Mrs Jekyll, the sister of Mrs Theresa Earle, their Dunley neighbour. Agnes Jekyll was the wife of Colonel Herbert Jekyll, who worked for John

Morley, now in Arthur Balfour's old position as Irish Secretary. Jekyll's sister, Gertrude, was the famous garden designer.

Violet looked forward to staying in Dublin, where the Season lasted from Christmas to St Patrick's Day, in March. She arranged her 'trousseau' in Paris; the star item was an elaborate court dress with an immense train to wear at Dublin Castle, a royal court in miniature. There she soon found herself going through 'the absurd ceremony of presentation' to the Viceroy, Lord Houghton, in his court dress, with the 'Irish diamond insignia resplendent round his neck (worth £20,000 we are told) . . . He grasps your hand and kisses your right cheek. You then make your best curtsey and move on.' Violet was not overawed. 'Lord Houghton is a fine show figure. He has firmness enough to kiss a regiment of women and a good bow. He is not popular here because of his reputed stiffness, but I believe if he is properly treated, that, though not satisfactory, he could be made tolerable,' was her succinct verdict. She was amused by the rituals at Dublin Castle: 'Oh, I am a great person at Court! . . . It is all like playing at houses as one used to when one was little.'

An attractive part of the social scene was the military, the officers resplendent in their uniforms. On her first evening in Dublin Violet met Edward Cecil at dinner at the Jekylls. He was at once captivated by her, graceful in her new evening gown which set off her lissom figure, with fashionably slender waist; even her long gloves were the softest and most elegant Paris could provide. Her dark curly hair was becomingly swept up on top of her head and ornamented with fresh flowers. Altogether she was a contrast to such girls as the amiable, but plain, Frances Wolseley (she of the horse-borrowing incident) who were all too often his company at dinner. Any hopes Frances's mother, or any other of that ambitious tribe, might have harboured concerning the dashing Lord Edward, were scotched when Miss Maxse, in full Parisian chic, arrived for the Season. And what good company she was! Without being an ostensible flirt, or forward, Violet always responded to intelligent men and showed her appreciation of their company to a degree unusual in girls of her age and upbringing; like her friends among the 'Souls' she preferred discussion to small talk. Edward basked in all this, starved as he felt himself to be of stimulating female company. She came from a larger social sphere, similar to his own. 'Lord E. paid me the greatest compliment I've ever had in my life – and was sincere too – he said my talk reminded him of his father's

– don't repeat this but I can't quite keep it to myself,' she wrote delightedly to the Admiral.

Violet singled out Edward, too, as making her 'feel really at home. He is curiously unlike any Guardsman I have ever seen and we made friends quicker than anything I have yet done. I wonder if it will be lasting?' They found plenty to talk and laugh about, sending up the stiff Viceroy, discussing the theatre, which they both loved, and gossiping about mutual friends, among them Arthur Balfour, of whom he reminded her. In that small society it was possible to meet often. Edward, with time on his hands, and 'so glad to find anyone to play with', was attentive. Violet, just forward enough to be interesting, not so much as to be pushy, knew how to handle even the most daunting people. Of his chief, Wolseley, she said, 'I think I could make friends with him if I were left alone with him. He has a delightful face. Lady W. is a regular old campaigner, the girl is nice.'

She asked the formidable Lord Houghton to write an article on the Viceroyalty in Ireland for Leo's *National Review*. 'The idea pleased him chiefly, I am afraid, as a piece of impertinence.'

In Dublin Violet felt at once as if she were abroad in a foreign country and yet at home, removed from reality and yet in familiar territory. Dances, dinners and excursions filled the days and nights. Within a fortnight both her ball dresses were 'worn to a shadow' and her maid had to turn to and make her another, a copy of the Parisian confection she had had made for Court. Her gloves, which had cost her fifty francs, were worn out too. The fashionable light colours she had chosen in Paris could not be worn with dark shoes, so her pale shoes suffered and had to be constantly cleaned or replaced. 'However I am having real fun for my money,' she wrote home; her mother obligingly sent her five pounds to replenish her wardrobe. Writing to thank her, Violet had to break off her letter when luncheon guests, including Edward Cecil, arrived. 'We talked much – chiefly of politics – everybody wore a wise air of knowing more than they possibly could.' Afterwards, as the light faded and the evening drew on, 'we walked with our Guardsmen across the Phoenix Park with a delicious lemon-coloured sky over our heads and spidery looking trees all round us . . . This week we go out every night – tonight to the play. It is Lord E. Cecil's party . . . Tomorrow a dance, Wednesday a concert, Thursday a "State Ball" . . . Friday and Saturday dinner parties. Isn't it a life?'

Violet always loved meeting literary men and she enjoyed her encounters with the florid, blunt-featured Professor Mahaffy of Trinity College, 'most genial of Irishmen', to whom Edward introduced her. He liked 'good company and long sittings over great subjects . . . and he made great friends with Lord Edward, in whose conversation he delighted. "I would pawn my boots," he said, "to dine with Ned Cecil".'

And so it was that in February 1894, a month after Violet had arrived in Dublin, Edward Cecil wrote to the Admiral saying that he had asked her to marry him. Although he recognised that of course he should have consulted her father first, 'I can only assure you of my deep devotion'; he gave him his word 'as a gentleman that . . . neither she nor you shall regret what has occurred . . . the feelings which her beauty, her mind and her cleverness have produced in me are not of a transient character.' He concluded this letter, at once romantic and proper, with a characteristic note: 'I am not a suitable husband for her in any way, but I don't think anyone else is either.'

As for Violet's hostess, poor Aggie Jekyll scarcely knew how to begin in writing to the Admiral. She eventually took the plunge: 'I feel very frightened at writing to you . . . Yesterday afternoon he came and saw her whilst I was out, and when I came back he told me that she had accepted him subject to your consent. She is quite certain about it and very happy.' She stressed Violet's good sense – she is 'so very high-minded about these things' – and Edward's reputation:

> They all speak warmly of him in the regiment and he is I am sure, a gentleman in the very best sense of the word, delightful to talk to, and knowing and caring about all sorts of out of the way things.
>
> Please believe that I should have written to you before to consult your wishes if I had realised that he had so far succeeded in gaining her affection, but one is so unaccustomed nowadays to this good old-fashioned way of two people falling simply and frankly in love with each other and asking no-one's advice or opinion and Violet seems perfectly happy and absolutely confident. She has such good judgement that one can't treat her like an inexperienced girl.

The anxious hostess and the young lovers did not have long to wait for the Admiral's response. Cordial letters came from him by return of post: 'I am convinced of the sincerity of your attachment to my daughter,' he told Edward, hoping that his family would welcome Violet.

The Salisburys were the next hurdle. Edward's recent financial difficulties might have made them wonder whether he was yet able to take a wife. Besides, Georgina, a famously possessive mother, perhaps would not take kindly to a prospective daughter-in-law whom she had never met. Edward canvassed his brothers and sisters-in-law on the subject of Violet, 'one of the most charming people in the world . . . Ask Betty Balfour about her and do Old Boy do your best for me,' he asked Bob. They were all encouraging, to Edward's relief. 'Violet and I love you for your kind wishes,' he wrote to Nelly, 'I only wish I could as well deserve happiness as Bob . . . We are very happy but very anxious as to how Mama will act. Admiral Maxse gave his consent in writing tonight. I am sure she is far too good for me and I can't now believe my luck. I am sure she will love you as I have my dear sister. I can only say I will do my very hardest to make her happy in the greatest and truest sense of the word.'

His mother's letter to him was full of spontaneous affection: 'As long as you are happy I have no doubt we shall think your choice a charming one . . . when you can so far master your ecstasies as to descend to details we should like to know all about your "Violet" . . . And now may God bless you and make you always as happy as you are now.'

His father, characteristically, offered sound advice, a note of caution, and emphasised the financial aspects of the match. He had heard nothing but good about Miss M. He knew little about her – but that little was all to her advantage – and less of her relations, 'but you are quite right in thinking that their characters are a matter of infinitely less importance than hers. You are not going to marry them.'

Money was more of a problem. Salisbury prepared to settle £1,000 a year on him, as he had done on his brothers when they married. Edward would therefore have to weigh up whether he would be able to make a go of marriage on £1,200 a year:

> The more you love and admire her, the more careful you ought to be not to expose yourself, and therefore her, to a trial which you are not able to face. It is a mere question of your own personal character and self-control. For many years of my married life I had much less: and I do not think I was less happy than I have been since I was richer. Plenty of people in our rank of life have had similar experiences. But it will require a certain amount of restrained effort, and of contempt for the opinion of other people. Given those conditions and if the lady answers to your description of her I have no doubt that your marriage will make you a better and happier man.

His future wife, too, would have a crucial part to play in all this, Salisbury added, 'as she has not had, as I understand, a wealthy life up to this time, she will not have to put up with too sharp a contrast in her way of life.' He urged Edward to try once more for Staff College to help push along his career.

Violet had £400 a year of her own; even so, their income would not be large. Edward was not free from debt, and his father had once more to settle his bills of well over £1,000.

Then there was the question of religion, or rather Violet's lack of it: 'She has been brought up a heathen I hear – I even doubt if she has been baptised!' Georgina wrote to Nelly. However, 'All the rest I like – it will be good for Nigs to have a clever wife and one accustomed to take care of expense and I hope he will convert her . . . I am sure she will be "all Hatfield" in a year and I am quite happy,' his mother concluded. Both parents reckoned that a steady wife and domestic stability would do Edward good, as well as making him happy – as it had made them.

The possibility remains, however, that the swiftness with which Violet became engaged to Edward was on the rebound from her mysterious entanglement, about which we know so tantalisingly little.

At the end of March, when their engagement was announced, the many letters of congratulation showed what true friends both Edward and Violet had across a broad spectrum of writers, artists, politicians and the nobility. To Violet, Lord Pembroke wrote: 'It is a delicious family (I think) to marry into. Such a large wholesome free life about it – in spite of orthodoxy. You'll find it rather like going into a nice public school when you go among them.'

Clemenceau wrote to his old friend the Admiral, '*S'il y a une femme capable d'agir sur le compagnon de sa vie, je crois que c'est Violette.*'

Violet was invited to meet the Salisburys at their sombre town house in Arlington Street, behind the Ritz Hotel. Even for the dauntless Violet the occasion was intimidating. She passed through the great iron gates into the forecourt and as she drew up at the door a liveried footman emerged to show her into the gloomy hall.

The first appearance of His Lordship was unforgettable: he came into the dining room, 'a grim room with no ornaments to take your mind off the food set before you; the windows are opposite the door through which he came. His size was at first sight overwhelming – indeed even those people who lived with him never quite got accustomed to it.' His physical size was equalled by the magnitude of his personality – not because he conveyed his opinions forcibly, quite the opposite: 'He might be said to govern by wit. Certain it was that while he never took anyone to task or upbraided them, his opinion was conveyed indirectly by *bon mots* that bit in – never unkindly – but with an acid of their own,' as Violet was to find out when she was drawn further into her family circle, which would orbit round her parents-in-law.

Visiting Hatfield House was 'the next memorable day'. To Violet, the spell of the house was immediate and lasting. She and Edward had the place to themselves, as the family was in London; they wandered round its magnificent formal rooms, and Edward also showed her the rooms on the top floor where he had been brought up. An elegant phaeton and pair was brought round from the stables, and Edward drove, with an outrider to open gates, through the park and down to the vineyard. This romantic spot had long since ceased to be connected with growing vines. It was a landscape fashioned entirely from yew: entered through a wall of yew, within were arched branches forming a roof along a long green avenue, with walls like a fortress, with towers and battlements cut on top. In the centre, the grass sloped down to the river Lea, the deep green of the yew reflected in its waters; the screech of peacocks completed the romantically melancholy atmosphere.

Apart from this intimate interlude, the period of their engagement was not easy for either Edward or Violet: he had to be away on duty a good deal – a pattern that was to repeat itself throughout their married life. Aware of the dangers of a soldier's life to marriage, he wrote to Arthur Balfour that he did not want to drag a wife from 'one petty colonial appointment to another'.

Violet found her introduction to the Salisburys, and to the circle of brothers, sisters and cousins who would constitute her new family, perhaps more alarming than she had anticipated in the dreamy Dublin days when she and Edward were falling in love. Welcoming though they were, the absence of religious faith of any kind in Violet would, it was plain, be a problem in a household so energetic in its religious observances. The strength of their devoutness can be illustrated by what Nelly Cecil wrote to her fiancé Bob during their engagement a few years previously: 'The most lasting bond between you and me is that we agree on religion. I don't think I could have perfect confidence in anyone who differed very much from me on that.'

Edward's religion went deep, and from the beginning Violet's lack of faith was an unbridgeable difference between them. At Hatfield her absence from the chapel services was conspicuous, as this glimpse shows: 'Violet attended chapel in the gallery,' Frances Balfour wrote on 14 May, 'looking very like a framed saint with light through her hair.' In other words she stood in the gallery above the chapel, looking down on it, thus attending but not participating fully or taking Communion. 'She looks ill, and has been so, and Tim[Gwendolen] thinks the whole religious question is a great trouble to her. Niggs' appearance is due to the collection of his debts prior to his Father paying for them. He has already paid £2,000, £1,500 of this being baccarat. A good deal of what I have heard does not increase my love, or rather does increase my hatred, to[wards] the Guards.'

Betty Balfour wrote that 'Violet seems to have told Nigs she did not mind going to church as a mere form if he wished it, whereupon much to his Mother's admiration he is reported to have answered "By God you shall not go for such a reason".'

'In the meantime Violet is taking Nigs the round of her social friends . . . Nigs rather surprised at the number of intimate men friends she has, but in no ways objects.' When they lunched with Betty and Gerald Balfour and were asked about their plans, '"I discuss nothing", said Nigs, "I agree with everybody and then rush up to my room, lock the door and smoke a pipe". From this I gathered that the family circle had produced a few trying moments,' Betty concluded.

Nor could Violet look to her mother for the support needed by young women on the verge of matrimony. Cissie, ever languid, left the shopping and dress-fittings, letter-writing and thanking for gifts to Violet; Ivor organised the wedding ceremony, with advice from Lord Hugh on religious questions. For respite from all these arrangements Violet went again on the Pembrokes' yacht, the *Black Pearl*, the month before her marriage and benefited from their company and the sea air.

At least the betrothal was not long: Violet was to be a traditional June bride. On the 18th – Waterloo Day, as Violet, who always liked to remember such anniversaries, noted with pleasure – she was escorted up the aisle of St Saviour's Church, Pont Street, Kensington, on the Admiral's arm. It was a cold, wet day, almost like winter, but the church was full of scented flowers from Hatfield, and 'crammed full with all sorts and conditions of men and women . . . Fish married them, and he was said to look handsome and holy in his beard. Aunt

Georgie said he looked like John the Baptist.' Appropriately, the author of *Salome*, Oscar Wilde, 'might be seen under the pulpit,' wrote Betty Balfour, who noticed altogether

> Eight poets scattered about the congregation. Amongst them George Meredith leaning on a stick and looking patriarchal and affected. When I came out I said to Aunt Georgie 'What a mixed set!'
> 'Yes,' she said, 'dear Violet has made an extraordinary number of friends amongst all classes of interesting people'. When I made the same remark to my mother she answered, 'Yes. It is always the way with the Salisburys. They are broader than anyone I know in the way of mixing everybody.'

The newly-married Margot Tennant, now Mrs H.H. Asquith, made her presence felt, as usual. She went straight to the family pew, 'Arthur [Balfour] behind her. Lady Londonderry behind him. The latter indignant at Margot's position, and Margot jealous of her mono-polising Arthur.' After the service, during the signing of the register, 'Margot also went to the vestry, as I thought to get introduced to Uncle Robert but I believe this was not accomplished' – as it was not likely to have been.

Equally characteristically, 'All the Cecil family came in late. Aunt Georgie looked much moved. Uncle Robert, as Mother said, "Saying his prayers so simply as if no-one else was there." Mr & Mrs Maxse sat in the same pew with a daughter between them. One felt the pain-fulness of this situation,' Betty wrote, noting 'separation' in the margin. 'However all parties behaved well and Mrs Maxse went to the house afterwards which I had been told was not to be.'

Betty was impressed by the groom, who 'shouted out the most military "I will" I ever heard and looked far happier than most bridegrooms'. The register was signed by the four parents and Lord William Cecil, Arthur Balfour and Lord Selborne for the bridegroom, with George Meredith, John Morley, Joseph Chamberlain and H.H. Asquith signing for the bride. Neither Morley or Asquith had ever spoken to Salisbury before. Morley's presence did not please Lady Salisbury, who said she nearly left the church when she saw 'that atheist Morley' standing by the bride.

Afterwards, the handsome couple, he so tall and imposing in his uniform, smiling down at the the slender figure of his bride, who was as pale as the bouquet of stephanotis and gardenia she carried, walked down the aisle to Hubert Parry's music, the composer and his family being guests at the wedding. The reception afterwards was at the

Admiral's house in Hans Place, nearby, where the poet and political agitator Wilfred Scawen Blunt found himself in uncomfortable proximity to Lord Salisbury who had rejoiced at his imprisonment a few years earlier for stirring up sedition in Ireland.

From Paris Clemenceau had sent his regrets; in the last letter he addressed to Violet as a single woman he wondered, 'What will Lady Edward Cecil make of Violet Maxse? We shall see. When I was a child, I imagined a "Lady" as a very imposing person, who had swallowed a piano of which one saw the keys every time she opened her mouth. She had feathers on her head. A little negro carried her train. I hope you are not going to present yourself before me in such an *équipage.*'

On the contrary, the young Lady Edward Cecil who drove off that afternoon to her honeymoon presented a rather vulnerable spectacle, albeit an elegant one, in her new going-away clothes. They had borrowed Maud and Willy's house, Blackmoor, in Hampshire, a favourite of Edward's, but not especially sympathetic for a honeymoon: baronial and medieval in inspiration, with a mighty fireplace in the hall, flanked by inglenooks where Willy's father, the first Lord Selborne, an illustrious lawgiver, sat and pondered on the British Constitution. Its tall rooms were dim with stained glass, and sombrely decorated in dark greens and blues and bronzes; its wallpapers were deeply embossed, and its plumbing nobly planned. No doubt Maud saw to it that flowers from the garden were arranged in the house, and fruit from the hot-houses appeared on the table, but years later Edward recalled jokingly how they had to send off to the Admiral for extra rations owing to the frightfulness of the cook, 'an aged cinder-sifter or something of that sort who was out of a job . . . I have put down half Violet's nasty tempers to her incautiously eating pie made by that old harridan. It soured her for life.'

CHAPTER SIX

Married Life

FOR THE FIRST four years of their married life, Violet and Edward had no home of their own, but joined the family at Hatfield and Arlington Street. This had its advantages and its disadvantages. The reigning spirit was always Georgina Salisbury: 'She was so keen to have us all around her and so disappointed when we went anywhere else that nearly everyone gave way to her.' It was not always easy to be her daughter-in-law: she now had four – Alice Cranborne, Nelly, Florence – 'Fluffy', wife of Lord William – and Violet. Of the four, only Violet had had any independence between 'coming out' and getting married: the other three had been fresh from the schoolroom, and fitted willy-nilly into the family circle. Bob and Nelly had, at least, taken the radical step of buying their own house in London. Violet found that 'the Cecils lived at Hatfield as a family, going away of necessity for work, or occasionally for social duty, but always returning home, with marriage making very little difference to their way of life.'

But Violet had tasted some freedom in Paris, and she found it more difficult than the others to fit in. Besides, Georgina's overbearing tendency seems to have intensified during these last years of her life as the cancer which was to kill her began to gain a hold.

Only six weeks after Edward and Violet's marriage, Frances Balfour recorded the following little interchange at Hatfield:

> Aunt Georgie has been in extraordinarily good mind and there has not been the symptom of a ruffle till last night when George Meredith's new novel★ came up. Aunt Georgie announced it was missing, and asked who had it.

★ This was *Lord Ormont and His Aminta*; a dramatic tale of a nobleman, Lord Ormont, who marries Aminta, forty years his junior. His haughty sister, Lady Constance, refuses to believe Aminta is his lawful wife, and indeed he will not present her publicly as such: eventually Aminta puts an end to her humiliating position and elopes with a childhood sweetheart. Ormont dies after forgiving them, and Aminta is free to marry again.

Uncle Robert: 'I have it.'

'Oh, you wicked man. It's very bad for you. You shouldn't read it.'

Uncle Robert: 'I'm trying hard to read it, but it's not my style.'

Aunt Georgie to Violet . . .: 'You'll see he'll say such cutting things about it. It's the most improper disgusting book I've ever read.' Violet then began very quietly and calmly to defend it, and then of course Aunt Georgie got more and more violent in her abuse. Finally Violet said: 'Well it's intensely interesting to me because Lord Ormont's sister is my grandmother, and it's exactly like her.'

'You were blest in your grandmother then, that's all I can say', retorted her Ladyship with a snort. Violet was not the least put out . . . and merely smiled amiably.

The time would come when the smile wore thin.

When the family gathered at weekends, they habitually sat down thirteen or fourteen to dinner, without any guests. Besides the Salisburys were Maud and Willy Selborne, the four married sons and their spouses, and Gwendolen and Hugh, neither of whom ever married. That other lifelong bachelor Arthur Balfour was nearly always there, too, and often his brothers Gerald and Eustace and their wives, Frances and Betty.

Lady Salisbury's generous invitations meant the house was often full to capacity at weekends. Once, her husband asked how they could be accommodated and was told 'someone might sleep in the bathroom'. 'That is what she calls a quiet Sunday!' he said resignedly. (There were still only two bathrooms at Hatfield, although more were installed shortly thereafter.)

Sunday was of course 'observed': a day apart, for rest and devotions – and games. As Frances Balfour put it: 'The Anglican Church was the beautiful fibre and essence of many an English home in this period. The Parish Church lay under the shadow of Hatfield . . . and it always seems to me an integral part of the web of life.'

Communion was at 8 a.m., then a lengthy and substantial breakfast was followed by Matins at 11 a.m. for the whole household, including the servants, the guests and their servants, conducted by Lord William. Afterwards, there might be cricket in the park, watched by the ladies of the house, or, in winter, long walks: 'The day closed with Evensong in the Chapel, where the westering sun streamed in and lighted the east window with its many coloured glories.' On long summer evenings guests could then go out and walk or play golf on the little course that had been created in the park.

The talk was enthralling and non-stop. After the servants had left the dining-room at the end of dinner, came uninhibited political discussion, but not of the sort that Violet was used to.

> They were all brilliant at scoring off their opponents and their jokes were first class, but they did not want to find out what they thought nor very much what other people thought, they were not getting down to the roots of things or trying to. They knew what they thought on fundamentals. Their excellent brains were full of interest . . . but they were certain that they had the key to all essentials and that this lay in the Anglican Church.

Family group at Hatfield, 1896, outside the door into the Armoury. Front row, left to right: *Alice Cranborne, Gwendolen Cecil, Florence Cecil, Violet Cecil;* back row, left to right: *Maud and Willy Selborne, Hugh Cecil, William Cecil (in mortar board), Jem Cranborne, Lord and Lady Salisbury, Edward Cecil (wearing a sixteenth-century helmet), Nelly and Bob Cecil*

They tried, affectionately, to open Violet's eyes to God, concerned, for her sake, at her starting on married life and having a family without knowledge of Him. They did not hound her, but their strength of feeling is expressed a few years later in a letter Gwendolen wrote to Violet describing her relief after Alice had recovered from a nearly fatal illness:

It was as if I felt His arms around me, almost heard His voice, realised His tenderness, His sympathy even with my earthliness and blindness. Forgive me, Violet, I resolved long ago not to bother you with religion till God himself should have chosen his own time and spoken to you . . . and I already feel that perhaps it is presumptuous to have said anything and not have left it in God's hands, but I do love you and want to help.

Violet was not converted, and although she tried as best she could to conform with the outward practice of religion, she disliked the Cecils' Anglicanism for another reason, the effect she thought it had on their appreciation of art, especially the new and experimental, as she later wrote:

> As for musicians, [Lord Salisbury] would have consigned them to the lower circles of the infernal regions, for music was positively painful to him. 'There's a dreadful man called Brahms,' he said, describing a sad evening at some musical function he had had to go to, 'I think him the worst'.
>
> . . . He was very much affected by Lady Salisbury who thought the arts, especially music, demoralising. This strong bias came from the fact that both Salisburys believed that there was a better object than art for work and devotion: religion; they had no need of any other anodyne, or of any other help to bear life, than the Church afforded, other devotions seemed to them quite unworthy in comparison with the Service to which they gave themselves. What the arts bring to life they thought they already had in something far more inspiring.

It must be remembered that Lord Salisbury, who had a wicked sense of humour, would have enjoyed teasing his artistic daughter-in-law with his irreverence towards art. But there is no doubt that Violet felt herself more of an outsider because her passionate attachment to literature and music, sculpture and painting, was not shared by her new family. She had been profoundly influenced by the Aesthetic Movement, at its height in the 1880s and 1890s, which saw art as the guiding light of society. Salisbury, according to her account, positively 'despised everyone who likes pictures or music and any other literature other than that which he, with a clerical and fastidious but not always certain taste, admired.'

Once Violet asked Arthur Balfour about this; he put the matter briefly: 'My dear, my uncle thinks that any one who likes music is a fool or a liar.' But, Violet objected, Salisbury hardly thought his nephew Balfour a fool. 'The answer came quick: "Well then he thinks I am a liar."'

'Lord Salisbury never aired these views,' Violet continued, 'he was much too courteous – and he never aired any views at all – but nevertheless one was profoundly conscious of his permanent scepticism.

The Armoury

"Hatfield," he said, the first time I saw him "is Gaza, the capital of Philistia", and so it was.'

The effect, Violet noted, was withering: 'Never was so free a life, but somehow even to the most determined, it became impossible to talk with admiration of anything to do with the beautiful side of life or worship any hero, however great or however long departed.'

The Cecils would perhaps have put the opposite view: that without a love and worship of God, the highest creative efforts of His creation, man, could not be of transcendent value. To take but one example, Bob Cecil was later repelled by Rupert Brooke's much-quoted 1914 poem, 'The Soldier', because of its assertion of patriotism beyond the grave – 'an English heaven': 'Two thousand years of Christianity, and we can't do better than that!' he exclaimed.

Although the size of Hatfield House meant that all the extended

family and their servants could have their own quarters – Violet and
Edward's were on the top floor, where he had grown up – there was
not much privacy in this arrangement. If Violet wanted to entertain
her own friends, or if her family visited, it was difficult to enjoy their
company in a secluded sitting or dining room.

Violet's first Christmas as a married woman was utterly different
from her previous year, unmarried, in Paris. The lively city streets, her
pension life and art classes, and Clemenceau's New Year greeting, '*Que
Titien vous sourie, que Rembrandt vous prenne par la main et vous conduise
d'un pas sûr, dans la voie des hautes félicités. Et puis soyez jeune longtemps,*'
all seemed far from Hatfield House and her new family. Lady Salisbury
loved to surround herself with her increasing number of grandchildren – the eldest was Maud's ten-year-old daughter Mabel, whose
brothers were Roundell, aged seven, and Robert, aged six; Maud's last
child Lewis, 'Luly', was still a baby. Alice Cranborne's eldest daughter, Beatrice, was three, and the star of this particular Christmas was
her enchanting little brother, the two-and-a-half-year-old Robert,
'Bobbety', the heir. Fluffy's children were Randle, five, Victor, four,
and twelve-months-old Jack. They made 'a fine family piece', clus-
tered round their grandmother, who stood with her husband at the
end of the Armoury where the huge Christmas tree, its candles the
only lights, shed its sparkling glow down the length of the black-and-
white marble floor. The household, the maids in their black uniforms
and white caps, the men in their livery, were joined by the choir boys
from the church in surplices and white ruffs, for carol singing.

This was the moment of peace before the scarlet lanterns with their
mysterious red glow held by the armoured knights were lit down the
Armoury, and Lady Salisbury distributed presents to each member of
the household and the outdoor staff.

'Christmas Day saw a good deal of church-going,' Violet wrote,
'and an early lunch, for the nurses went down to the housekeeper's
room, and the nursery maids to the servants' hall for their Christmas
dinner.' There was, even on that day, a hierarchy in the servants' ranks.
After Evensong the four curates came to dinner, 'one, so to speak, to
each daughter-in-law'.

The celebrations went on until the New Year. Outdoors there was
skating on the pond, but Violet did not skate – she was pregnant. The
baby, due in September, was to be born at Arlington Street, which,
though a cheerless house, had the advantage of being central. As her
pregnancy progressed she was pushed about in a bath chair to take the

Violet and the baby George

air and often met friends with whom to pass the time in Green Park nearby.

'Yesterday I dined with Violet Cecil . . . and that queer old father of hers,' Arthur Balfour wrote on 4 September. 'Poor dear, she by no means appreciates the privilege of becoming a mother, and as the fêted moment approaches she likes the prospect less and less. She seemed pretty well all the same.'

A few days later Violet's son was born. After the birth, difficult as he was a very large baby, he was constantly sick, and started losing weight. A hasty baptism was arranged at Arlington Street. Edward, summoned from the barracks, arrived in full uniform at the same time as the curate in his surplice. The baby was too ill to be taken off his nurse's knee, and was baptised using a washbasin from the bedroom. During the anxious days that followed, the baby's health gradually stabilised, and soon a proper christening ceremony for George Edward Cecil was held in the chapel at Hatfield. Lord Hugh Cecil was godfather, and gave his nephew a magnificent silver cross. There was a christening tea party, which the usual excited crowd of children attended.

Violet took long to recover; she and Edward embarked on a tour of Italy that autumn. While she was in Rome the Admiral wrote that her nurse, Emma, had died. Violet was grief-stricken: 'Emma had been all in all to us in childhood . . . the best woman I have ever known, tender, loving, faithful, unselfish and with an infinite refinement of mind and heart . . . all my childhood seemed gone with her.' To the end of her life in her dreams she would call for Emma.

In the summer of 1895, the Liberal Government, led by Lord Rosebery, had resigned after a defeat in Parliament. The Queen sum-moned Lord Salisbury to form a government and in the election that followed the Conservatives, with their Liberal Unionist allies, who had rebelled against the Liberal Party because of its Irish Home Rule policy, scored an overwhelming victory. Lord Salisbury, as before, took the offices of both Prime Minister and Foreign Secretary. On the Continent, his experienced and balanced approach to foreign policy was immediately welcomed, but in England, among the more dynamic imperialist element in politics, he was soon regarded as too cautious and insufficiently aggressive in promoting national prestige – for example, by his young Under-secretary for Foreign Affairs, George Curzon, who 'always wants me to talk to Russia as if I had five thousand men at my back and I have not,' Salisbury complained.

This 'New Imperialist' element was led by Joseph Chamberlain, the most powerful Liberal Unionist in Parliament. In forming his govern-ment Salisbury recognised his importance, and Chamberlain, a radical and a patriot, chose the Colonial Office as offering the most scope for his vision – of Britain as a progressive commercial world power, her close-knit Empire underpinned with an expanding infrastructure of schools, hospitals, railways, deep-water harbours and all the wonders of modern engineering. Perceiving the decline of Britain's mid-Victorian commercial supremacy, he feared the rivalry of continental powers, particularly Germany. Chamberlain's vision was shared by men like Alfred Milner and the writer Rudyard Kipling, when he spoke of 'the white man's burden' of spreading Western civilized stan-dards, interspersing this with solemn warnings about backsliding and lack of dedication. The British public loved Kipling's verse and the jingoistic celebrations of Queen Victoria's 1887 Golden Jubilee, the music-hall chauvinism and news of fresh conquests of African terri-tory – Nyasaland, Uganda, Zululand, Matabeleland. But Kipling was right to be worried for the future of his vision: when it came down to it, the public did not care to pay the price – higher taxes, tariff duties, expanded armed forces – for this very long-term plan; and indeed it was unrealistic of the imperial visionaries to have expected unqualified enthusiasm for an indefinite period. For the time being, however, in the last decade of the nineteenth century, that mood held. It was not the mood of Lord Salisbury, an old man, pessimistic and sceptical, detached from this and other modern movements. He saw rather 'the sea covered with white horses' – the prospect of a fearful European war should the prevalent build-up of weaponry and armies and diplomatic rivalry be allowed to run out of control.

When Edward and Violet returned to England at the end of 1895, they found Hatfield buzzing with preparations for a great ball in January. The Salisburys' house party of twenty-five guests, nearly all with a maid or valet apiece, included Queen Victoria's daughter, Princess Christian of Schleswig-Holstein. Even such grand festivities could not, however, be allowed to interfere with Lord Salisbury's work at the centre of world affairs. In South Africa tension was mounting. The German Emperor, Wilhelm II, had sent a telegram congratulating President Kruger of the Transvaal for thwarting an unauthorised attack, 'the Jameson Raid', on his country. The raid was led by British subjects. Violet was present on the night before the Hatfield ball, when Lord Salisbury learnt the extent of the Kaiser's hostility. A message in an official red box was brought to the dinner table. He read it and scribbled a reply to the Foreign Office.

'What was the message?' asked one of the guests beside him.

'The German Emperor is landing a hundred and fifty marines at Delagoa Bay in Portuguese East Africa.'

'What was your answer?'

'Send gunboats.'

Fortunately, the Portuguese refused to let any German troops cross their territory to assist President Kruger, or the naval squadron would have gone into action and Britain would have been at war with Germany. Soon afterwards Salisbury was dealing with a new crisis in north Africa, and this time Edward was in the thick of the fighting.

CHAPTER SEVEN

The Sudan

THE SALISBURYS, finding their much-loved Châlet Cecil too cold, had moved to Beaulieu-sur-Mer in the South of France. Here they built a stone house, La Bastide, high up on the wooded hillside with a magnificent view of the coastline. This was the heyday of the French Riviera, which the English made peculiarly their own discovery. For much of the year there were few visitors, but in spring the *beau monde* and royalties from all over Europe migrated there, as Violet described in 1896, when she and Edward were staying at La Bastide and the graceless Prince of Wales came to lunch.

> He hardly speaks and rarely smiles. His equerry said he must be enjoying himself as he stayed an hour longer than he meant to. He sent for me after lunch to talk to him (we sat out on the terrace). I never worked so hard or with so little result in my life . . . he shut his left eye – the right one is permanently closed, and left me to do the talking. We were sitting in front of all the others and I was conscious of the entertainment we were affording them as I grew more and more desperate.

This was typical of the Cecils' attitude to the Prince, whom they thought ill-mannered and flashy; the dislike was mutual.

At La Bastide a telegram came for Edward from Sir Herbert Kitchener, the Sirdar (Commander-in-Chief of the Egyptian Army), inviting him on to his staff as one of his ADCs for the forthcoming campaign in the Sudan. Lord Wolseley had honoured his promise to get Edward a taste of military action.

'Active Service at last!' he exclaimed delightedly. Knowing that it had long been his heart's desire, his mother put a stoical face on her son going so far overseas. He returned with Violet to England at once. During his long absence she and George were to stay mostly with her father and Olive at Dunley.

★

The campaign in northern Sudan was prompted by the Ethiopians' recent severe defeat of the Italian army at Adowa. It was feared that the white man's prestige had been so much damaged in the region that there would be a general attack by the Africans on the European would-be colonists; a show of strength was needed.

Since 1885 the British public had been clamouring for action against the Dervish army of the Muslim spiritual leader, the Mahdi, after it overthrew the small Anglo-Egyptian force holding Khartoum, killed the commander, General Gordon, and forced the Egyptian government to withdraw from the Sudan, which had formerly been Egypt's vassal. There was a constant danger that the Mahdi and his successors, with their army of hardy, passionately religious Dervish warriors, would overwhelm Egypt itself.

Britain's direct involvement with Egypt had begun in 1882, when British forces moved in to protect commercial and imperial interests before soon taking responsibility for Egypt and its chaotic financial affairs. The British established a colonial-style domination over a land ruled by a nominally independent head of state, the Khedive, and his ministry, under Turkish suzerainty. The Khedive's government was now controlled by the British Agent, Lord Cromer, and his staff. Senior officers of the Egyptian Army were British and its successive Commanders-in-Chief trained it rigorously to defend the country.

At first, this Anglo-Egyptian Army had made a poor showing. To avoid military service, many peasants had even blinded themselves with 'Dead Sea fruit' – a kind of poisonous nightshade. Soon, however, led and trained to a high pitch of efficiency by British officers, they made tough and steady soldiers, though unlike the dashing black Sudanese troops also recruited by the British, not keen on hand-to-hand fighting. In 1889 and 1891 Egyptian soldiers beat off attempted invasions by the Dervishes.

Under the Mahdi's successor, the Khalifa, the Sudanese Islamic regime had declined in moral fervour since its founder's great victories. Much-publicised accounts by Europeans who had escaped from captivity there after many years were full of the corruption and lust of the Muslim rulers; hangings and torture, it was said, were daily occurrences. Much of this was propaganda, though mismanagement, and favouritism of certain tribes and families, were deep grievances, aggravated by famine. Many of the Sudanese tribes had turned against the Khalifa and the pressures to strike against this 'disgraceful tyranny' and regain the Sudan were mounting.

Herbert Kitchener as Sirdar of the
Egyptian Army

Slatin Pasha, in Sudanese dress

Lord Salisbury, as Foreign Secretary, was responsible for relations with Egypt, as it was not a colony. On 12 March 1896, after an appeal by the Italians for a show of force, he and his Cabinet authorised an attack by Anglo-Egyptian forces against the Dervishes in the northern Sudan.

The Sirdar, Kitchener, in charge of the operation, was a rising star of Empire, both controversial and complex. Lord Cromer, the Agent, had mixed feelings about the decision to strike against the Dervishes and about Kitchener himself, who had never commanded a large army in battle, and was compulsively secretive. Many thought him impetuous and bloodthirsty, for his manner could be rough and harsh, and his pronouncements, like his appearance, intimidating. This was deceptive: he was an engineer by training, cautious, methodical and parsimonious. His determination to keep costs to the minimum was central to his strategy. 'His principle,' Edward wrote later, 'is to cut everything until real friction occurs. The result is wonderful.' Kitchener was sure that the Dervishes could be beaten at a low cost.

Edward worked at close quarters with Kitchener over the follow-ing months at the start of a relationship between them which spanned the next twenty years. It suited Kitchener to have Edward on his staff; he was anxious to keep in not only with the Prime Minister but also with Alice Cranborne, whom he had already cultivated as a confidante. One of Edward's duties was to send weekly reports on Kitchener's progress directly to Lord Salisbury.

Edward's pay was ten shillings a day: 'They can't say I rob the Egyptian government. I consider I am dirt cheap at the price.' He arrived in Cairo in mid-April and was given less than two days to hire servants, buy horses and acquire his kit, including tarboosh – his Egyptian Army headgear – fly whisk, pepsin tablets to cope with 'gyppy tummy', and folding chair and table. Owing to Kitchener's notorious secretiveness, there was only rumour and speculation about the forthcoming campaign: that they would conquer the whole Sudan that year; or that they would just take the enemy strongholds at Berber and Dongola; the war might be over in a few months – or perhaps it would take five years. As Edward said, 'Really nobody knows.'

On 22 April he embarked on the Nile in a boat 'like a nice penny steamer', bound for Kitchener's headquarters at Wadi Halfa, 700 miles south, just inside the Sudanese border. It was as if he and fellow-officers had their own yacht. They were exhilarated by the voyage through fertile country on either side of the river, glimpsed through gaps between the sandhills. The climate was 'by far the nicest' Edward had ever experienced, and he had seldom before had such a feeling of physical well-being, despite the monotonous fare: lukewarm boiled Nile water, potted beef and sardines. He tried to teach himself Arabic (he never spoke it well). At Luxor they stopped and, led by a drunken guide, visited the ancient ruins at Karnak by moonlight.

On 29 April they reached Halfa on the east bank, where Edward now met some of the men who were to be his close companions during the campaign: Leslie Rundle, the Adjutant-General, brawny, direct in manner, with a broad, frank countenance; Major Count Gleichen, a Grenadier, of the War Office Intelligence Department, who was there to report on Kitchener's doings and ate with headquarters staff; and the Austrian soldier of fortune and Assistant-General of Military Intelligence, Baron Rudolf von Slatin, 'Slatin Pasha', famous for his adventures as a prisoner of the Mahdi, described in his memoir, *Fire and Sword in the Soudan*. He and Edward shared a house in Halfa. They rode out to explore the traces of the old town defences, mud walls and bastions; beyond stretched a flat plain and, across the river, the rolling yellow sands of the desert. Their mess was luxurious, and to Edward's dismay they wore evening dress at dinner. Thinking it all 'rather rot', but feeling dirty beside these immaculate figures in white, he ordered an outfit from the master tailor of the Staffordshire Regiment, stationed nearby.

The heat was intense – 113 degrees in the shade on one afternoon; many went down with dysentery. Hearing reports that the fighting had gone well at Akashey, further up the river, Edward longed for something to do: 'I am pining away for work, quite a new sensation for me.'

Early in May, he joined Kitchener at Sarras, the railhead, further south, travelling through a rough and desolate country of black tumbled rocks, and innumerable *khors* (dry watercourses) but no water apart from occasional glimpses of the Nile, and seldom any vegetation. Returning with Edward to Halfa, Kitchener at last made his aims clear: to take his troops and equipment up the Nile in barges and steamers commandeered from Thomas Cook & Son, and via the old Sudan railway which was to be extended south down the line of the river from its southern railhead. Soon the Anglo-Egyptian force would move headquarters to Akashey for about a month, while the railway was being built to reach it; then they would strike first at the Dervish base on the east bank of the Nile, at Firket, and afterwards at the provincial capital, Dongola. If a full conquest of the Sudan were later authorised, Kitchener's ambitious long-term project, which he did not now divulge, was to build a railway 230 miles across the desert – a short cut to enable troops from Cairo to penetrate into the heart of the Sudan, a thousand miles in a mere eleven days. Edward was impressed by the chief engineers, such as Percy Girouard, the fabled and indominatable Canadian, scarlet-faced and cheerful, with an eyeglass and a fondness for whiskey, whose efforts were to be chiefly responsible for the success of the railway enterprise.

Kitchener and his senior officers were encouraged by their victory at Akashey, where the Dervishes had seemed half-hearted, though their powder, as the expression went, was still good. Edward found 'The Staff are really quite A.1 . . . All on Christian name terms, they all laugh at routine yet keep everything straight and are all fond of one another.' Kitchener was harried by messages from the War Office and Edward sympathised: 'They are worrying him at home about the merest details such as why a sergeant has not been applied for in the proper way etc. Worrying a man on a campaign is simply monstrous . . . However all this shall be known at home by the proper people,' he added, intending to tell his father. When Kitchener saw the reports

Edward now posted to Lord Salisbury, he thought them understated. He wrote to Edward a model of what he thought should be sent, 'which would,' Edward said, 'have made the most hardened ink-slinger of the *Daily Mail* blush.' Edward ignored his advice.

Edward at first found Kitchener 'quite the most agreeable man I know and his accounts of government here very interesting and amusing. He . . . has much of the oriental and the tease-cat in him. He is very grim in his mind but nice and very fond of nature [i.e. affectionate]; he has also the gold gift of the gods, a sense of humour.' He did not confide in Edward, however, or any of his staff.

Kitchener was neat and clean, and expected others to be, but his office 'was a sea of papers lying on tables, chairs . . . [and] the floor. No one but himself knew where any particular paper or subject was kept or could find anything.' He would rise soon after dawn and make an inspection. Nothing escaped his notice, even if he were officially engaged in looking at something else. He usually worked for three hours before breakfast, and then without a break, save lunch, until six, when he relaxed over a gin or vermouth and soda; he worked again before dinner and Edward often noticed his light burning late. What struck Edward particularly was his grasp of detail in every department of the Egyptian Army.

The Sudanese country, so wild, merciless and desolate, was exciting. Two war correspondents returned from a trip across the desert told Edward of finding, beside the bones of a Dervish, an old British Army rifle taken years before, its wooden stock bleached white by the sun but still usable: it was like something out of Rider Haggard's recent thriller, *King Solomon's Mines*.

Soon Edward himself joined an expedition, this time to Ambigol, passing through tortuous, steep-sided gorges. They slept (very well) on the ground under the stars, and ate gazelle and freshwater turtle. Inexplicably there was no sign of the Dervishes anywhere, but the unpopularity of the Khalifa's government was widespread. One of Edward's companions on this journey was Count Gleichen, whose role as an informer for the War Office infuriated the secretive Kitchener, 'as with his masterful character he intended that this should be "a one man show"'. Gleichen irritated Edward, too: his mountain of baggage was 'a sight for the blind and death for 2 camels', and he purloined Edward's own 'luxury camel', bred for speed and responsiveness, and used it for heavy loads like the lower-grade 'baggage brutes'. During the campaign, Edward concluded that camels were too easily decimated by disease or over-loading to serve a modern army and only good for sniffing out water in the desert.

When they reached Ambigol, the temperature was 150 degrees in the shade. Edward's hands became scorched and when Gleichen fell ill he was unsympathetic: 'An awful spectacle. Perspires through his sword belt, face colour of tomato; will drink beer and spirits.' Gleichen put Edward's irritation down to his being homesick. 'I am not,' retorted Edward, 'I am Gleich sick!' This so effectively silenced poor Gleichen that Edward felt penitent, but it did not last: 'G will make me die of heat apoplexy.'

The Dervishes had to be dislodged from their strongholds before the whole province could be conquered and the railway, which was advancing at the rate of a mile a day, could be properly protected. Edward's first taste of action was at the battle of Firket, on 7 June. He did not feel frightened, just excited, when the bullets started to fly, but afraid that his jumpiness might be mistaken for fear. Kitchener's chosen vantage point from which to direct the battle looked down on the Nile Valley, the fertile grassy plain, with a fringe of palms along the river and the town; Edward could see from the big one-storey houses, arranged round courts like Roman villas, and from traces of previous cultivation, how rich the country must once have been. Now, under Dervish rule, it was barren and neglected. He was impressed by the orderliness of the black and Egyptian forces advancing coolly under fire – 'so regularly that it looked like a Hyde Park Field Day'. Although they far outnumbered the enemy, they were attacking, without cover, a strongly-held position.

This first battle came as a revelation to Edward. The toughness and courage of their enemies was impressive. After it was all over, he saw one of them, shot through both legs and arms and back, near the spine, sitting up and talking with little sign of distress. Numbers of the Dervish prisoners were shot summarily when locals came forward with evidence that they had committed atrocities. Edward, aware of concern in England about the humanity of the campaign, justified this action: 'I feel sure that if people from home could see what sort of brutes they are and what they have done they would not talk such rot.' However, Kitchener's Second-in-Command, Colonel Hunter, managed to shock him with the view, probably tongue-in-cheek, that all the Dervish prisoners should have been shot, and that Britain's national honour would have been better served by the deaths of a few more white soldiers in the battle.

Young Sudanese woman

The opinions of the Sudanese troops on matters of honour also came as a revelation to Edward. In one bizarre incident, a man, fighting furiously against a Dervish, killed him, making 'rather too sure of him for civilised warfare'. He then asked permission to bury him, 'because he is my father, a very bad man always raiding and plundering', but performed his filial duty perfunctorily, covering the body with just enough stones and leaving one arm protruding.

In all Edward's astringent diary, 'Lord Teddy's journal or a fool's record' as he nicknamed it, there was hardly a word of criticism for either the Egyptians or the Sudanese, only wonderment or occasional exasperation. For the most part he was full of praise, especially for the black Africans. On his travels he lost his heart briefly to a graceful Berberine girl, naked except for a small red kerchief, and 'presented her with the most valuable gift I could think of, to wit six different coloured bottles. She was awfully pleased and gave me some milk and dates, all the people chaffing her obviously about her conquest.'

After the victory at Firket, Kitchener established his headquarters for many weeks at Koshey, further south, waiting for the completion of the railway, which, under his orders, was being built at a record rate so that supplies and troops could be brought up to the railhead there;

and waiting also for new steamers to be constructed on the neighbouring stretch of river, to avoid impassable rapids further downstream.

The camp at Koshey was on the east bank of the Nile in a dense jungle of thorns and palms and flanked by a dry watercourse running back into the hills – a desolate spot which was to be the scene of great discomfort, tension and tragedy, and where, Edward recorded late in July, 'we have had bad luck and no fun'.

At first, however, he was well content, for the Sudanese soldiers built each of the staff a spacious hut, or *tukul*, eighteen feet in diameter and seven feet high, thatched with leaves. His own was right above the water, and was fanned by whatever cooler breezes blew off it. The Nile, however, was the main conduit for an enemy more deadly than any Dervish – cholera.

Edward had heard the first intimations of an outbreak in Alexandria when he was at Halfa in mid-May. By the 26th it had reached Cairo. Hopes that the epidemic would fade away were dashed when it was reported further upstream at Aswan, then Korosko. One of the Anglo-Egyptian battalions was afflicted. It was the first time within memory that it had ever been so far up river, carried by those employed in Nile traffic who spread the illness by washing their clothes, or defecating, in the water. Inexorably infecting each stop along the river in turn, it reached Koshey by 15 July. Edward, who had been constantly plagued by lesser diseases, was already in bed with a feverish attack, which was less dangerous but reduced him to skin and bone, his legs as thin as his brother Hugh's, he said, a tongue like the Brazilian flag, and his trousers hanging in folds. However, he escaped cholera, which was claiming a dozen victims a day. The labourers and engineers of the railway battalion contracted the disease through bathing, despite police being posted on the river banks to stop people doing so. To Kitchener's relief, the river was rising, giving him hope that the armed steamers, essential for the campaign, could be brought up the cataracts.

Cholera carried off many good men, such as the heroic Bimbashi Fenwick, described later by Winston Churchill as 'twice a VC without a gazette'. Typhoid, sunstroke and jaundice, which were a constant threat, killed others Edward knew, such as Bimbashi Trask, one of the most capable surgeons: 'We buried Trask at 7.30 by candlelight Rundle reading a short funeral service. Very awful and sad but matters go on just as if nothing had happened it must be so. I shall never forget that service but His Will be done and in a way the splendid words of the service made me feel braver and steadier.'

Added to these tragedies were the merciless heat and fearful storms with 'devils', whirling tornadoes loaded with baking hot sand, as Edward witnessed: 'Suddenly the clouds began to cover the sky the mountains were blotted out by dust storms. It began by being a devil day and one most magnificent one over two hundred feet high which made the stones leap 10 or 12 feet in the air. Luckily it struck nothing for nothing could have stood against it. The heat from it was like the heat of a furnace.' On 24 July a tempest blew down Kitchener's tent, and he narrowly escaped being brained by the heavy poles. In Edward's *tukul*, the air was so dusty that he could not see to the other side.

More catastrophic still were the rainstorms, which turned the whole place into a swamp, sweeping away miles of track which had just been laid, or driving boats on to rocks. Edward was sent out repeatedly to supervise repairs: 'We paddled about in greatcoats driving in pegs and holding on to poles . . . about 4 broad streams descended from the hills and we had an exciting time turning them so as not to sweep down the tents.'

In such circumstances everybody's nerves were frayed – one of Kitchener's servants murdered another after a particularly vicious storm which left mud over everything. Slatin Pasha infuriated Edward: 'He is so trying, he said why did you not gallop about with fever, it is the way to get rid of it; ass. With temperature 104 1/2, or 105, you can't see, much less gallop, and besides you would fall off your horse if you tried, besides dying and a few other things. The Pasha is an idiot.'

All of them cursed the war correspondents for their inaccurate reporting, drunkenness and opportunism, particularly the overbearing Bennet Burleigh of the *Daily Telegraph*, who had years of experience in the Sudan and whose foul language so offended Rundle that once he threw him out of his tent. But worst of all were Kitchener's fearsome moods. When plans went wrong he blamed everyone on his staff, including Edward, who could see nonetheless that Kitchener possessed, like nobody else, the power to make the impossible happen:

> Most people think that dynamite is the only agency which will remove a large rock with celerity, but they are wrong. There was a large rock between here and Akashey on the track of the railway, and it was said to need 3 days' steady blasting to remove it, but when the Sirdar had been

there for 1/2 an hour that rock did not exist, it had come to be a mere pebble easily got round, could be carted away on a wheelbarrow.

Again, when twelve miles of rail near Sarras were washed away by storms towards the end of August:

The railway across the khors hung in festoons like a decoration of the streets abroad. This the engineers wanted to take to pieces, build up the embankment and then to lay the line. Sirdar however did it this way. First he built a series of Towers of stones all along under the railway and propped it up levelled it by <u>eye</u> and then filled it up with earth and tightened the fish plates etc. and succeeded in mending 12 miles or more of railway in 6 days a perfectly unheard of performance. Girouard said it would take a month to do . . . but the Sirdar is going to risk it and as it is him it will come off if it were anyone else it would not.

The price to pay for this engineering genius was Kitchener's fury when he was thwarted; then he became impossible, cursing, threatening to break or court-martial everyone in sight.

Regret to say K's temper has really become awful bit all our heads off. Told me because I slept too much I would never get on and other cheering remarks. I am afraid he is very much worried by time. Why they, I mean generals, don't go off their heads beats me but the result is I am very uncomfortable I feel my withers are unwrung as I have begged for anything to do etc. but he is now <u>froid</u> for some reason and snubs my head off very good for me I expect my tongue has got me into the mess as usual I called him the great white Czar the other day or something and he has heard it.

Disasters brought by the weather, including severe damage to one of the new boats, and the continual postponement of their launching, exacerbated Kitchener's rage; so did the bad publicity attending Colonel Hunter's so-called 'death march' to Abserat from Koshey on 27 August, en route for the final offensive at Dongola, when eight men died of exhaustion and 200 had to be carried in on camels. Hunter was bold enough to blame Kitchener for ordering him to take a fatal short cut across desert. Edward, taking Kitchener's side, condemned Hunter, with his dour demeanour, bulging forehead and lugubrious moustache, as 'a real live Cromwellian, brutal, cruel, licentious, religious, brave, able, blunt, cunning, all genuine too' – a somewhat exaggerated picture, but many years' hard campaigning in the Sudan had certainly trained Hunter out of many frailties and sensitivities.

On 11 September the low-pressure cylinder of the fast, new, armed Nile boat, which was to be one of the principal terror weapons against the Dervish army, blew up. So did Kitchener, knowing that he would be blamed for having got the boat cheap. He retired, Achilles-like, to his tent.

Fifteen thousand soldiers and a flotilla of armed steamers were gathered for the final push. Coming upstream, one of the boats, *Teb*, became stuck. Another, the *Tamai*, tried to pull her round, but only ripped open her bottom. 'K at his worst simply odious, not to me personally but to everyone, bitter savage childishly unreasonable. In point of fact worried out of his life.'

The next day Edward was at his duties during a battle at Hafir, where the gunboats and field artillery shelled Dervish positions and killed some 200, who appeared in boats to attack them. That night the Dervishes made a tactical withdrawal, later removing most of their forces from Dongola as well. With only 5,500 troops, they knew they had no hope of beating the Egyptian force. Although victory was imminent, Kitchener remained on edge. Only when Dongola was finally taken, on 23 September, in an atmosphere of anti-climax for those who had wanted a bloody reckoning, did his spirits revive. 'I hope that the time of my deliverance draweth nigh,' wrote Edward a few days later. 'I like Egypt very very much but K's temper has ruined my fun for the last three weeks and I only want to get away from him.'

Kitchener and his staff remained in the area to set up an army advanced base. Edward and Leslie Rundle became friends and rode together, discussing marriage from a soldier's point of view; and concluding that as a rule it was a mistake for a serving soldier to be married. Edward's time away from Violet on the Dongola campaign and the years that followed were difficult for both. After just two years of marriage, with a small child and only slender means, they were out of touch for months on end, he in acute danger from disease as much as from the enemy. They eagerly awaited each other's news, but he himself did not always have time to write and her letters were often held up for weeks.

During the second week in October Edward was on his way home. Like most people who had been through the ordeal of that campaign, he was worn out and imagined, hypersensitively, that Kitchener had not recognised his services. But on return he found that Kitchener had mentioned him in his dispatches on the battles of Firket and Hafir and saw that he was rewarded with the rank of Brevet-Major, Dongola

Boats on the Nile

medal with two clasps and the 4th class of the Medjidie. Later he came to realise the extent of Kitchener's difficulties and the reasons for his nerve storms – one serious failure and neither the War Office nor Cromer would have lifted a finger to save him: there was a powerful anti-Kitchener faction in the Army; and Kitchener could never afford to be ill in spite of chronic stomach trouble. Edward's admiration for the boldness and imagination of his vision was restored.

CHAPTER EIGHT

'The Apotheosis of Empire'

WHILE EDWARD WAS away with his regiment, as he frequently was, Violet was often on her own with his family. For a while, early in 1897, the household in Arlington Street was predominantly male, as Lady Salisbury was staying at Beaulieu, accompanied by Nelly Cecil. Bob, then thirty-three years old, was making his way as a junior barrister; Violet described him as 'the strangest-looking creature . . . with a head like Savonarola on a body almost deformed by a round back.' Missing Nelly, he found Violet's company intensely irritating, and in his letters let off steam about her social manner, particularly her moments of aesthetic uplift when she pushed 'her poetical stop': 'I always like Violet alone. And I nearly always dislike her in society. I think it is the competitive air about her conversation in society which is so tiresome. She treats the whole thing as a kind of game in which it is her business to be more brilliant and to attract more attention than others.'

To him it seemed as if she craved excitement. When bored, she felt ill and out of temper. Bob, who found Society 'wearisome', was embarrassed when she tried to get him and others of the family to accompany her on social occasions and then was hurt by their refusal: 'I think it is that side of V., her childish worldliness and materialism which makes me a little irritated by her poetical stop when she has it on. It does not sound quite in tune by itself, but compared to her more real self it makes a moral discord.'

Once Bob started to become irritated with Violet, it seemed almost as though he could not stop: everything about her grated on his nerves, from her questioning Lord Salisbury about topics of the day – which seemed to her quite a natural way of making conversation at dinner, but which only served to increase the already profound taci-turnity of the Prime Minister and drove him into his study – even to her bathwater: 'There's Violet's bath again. The number of baths she takes is positively appalling. I hear them running at all hours – sometimes they wake me in the middle of the night.' 'Poor V,' he reflected. 'I am a brute to her internally. I hope I don't show it much. She is devoted to that stupid Nigs and he has gone away for months without hope of communicating and I do find fault with her manners – it is no more.'

It was an intimidating household, and an intimidating house, with little of the domestic about it, giving 'one the impression of camping out in a Public office', the rooms converted to be lived in, and beyond the high-ceilinged, formal rooms the family inhabited were still more, empty and echoing, the furniture under wraps, awaiting entertainments of an impersonal nature. Dinners were long and rich; in Lady Salisbury's absence, ordering from the chef fell to Bob, who did not know how the tricksy little French dishes would turn out, and in any case preferred plain 'roast or boiled'. Nicknaming the chef 'Chaumette', after a notorious poisoner, Bob recalled his pleasure in 'crossing out an Entrée of Foie Gras and writing lamb cutlets instead!' When he could, he handed the duty over to Violet, whose knowledge of French cuisine improved that aspect of dinner at least. But conversation with the Cecils could be treacherous; in addition to Lord Salisbury, who saw no need to speak, and the edgy Bob, Hugh, Violet's youngest brother-in-law, had an insatiable appetite for religious controversy and would debate minutiae of Church education, ignoring what were, to her, more interesting metaphysical questions about death or art such as might be discussed among the Souls, that pinnacle of Society about whom she was so enthusiastic – over-enthusiastic in the sceptical eyes of her in-laws. The spectacle of the twenty-eight-year-old Lord Hugh, tall and gaunt, all elbows and Adam's apple, working himself into a passion about 'the Cowper Temple clause', made her feel very distant from his family and their religion. 'It is curious to see, how, even with intellectual people like the Cecils . . . the Ceremonial, Doctrine and such aspects of the Church have swallowed up religion,' Violet concluded.

Apart from her London and Dunley life, Violet was invited to house parties at Panshanger, Mells, Taplow and Esher Place, the new home of Edgar and Helen Vincent. The handsome Sir Edgar, later Lord D'Abernon, financier and successful diplomat, was statuesque and sensual, looking, as a friend said, 'like Jupiter in a Turkish bath'. His wife Helen, herself a goddess in appearance, had to put up with her husband's Jupiter-like lunges at any attractive woman who came his way. Violet joined a cycling party organised by the Vincents round Touraine, but Edgar was kept in Constantinople on Ottoman Bank business, and they missed the spectacle of him perspiring magnificently up the French hills.

The climax of Violet's year was joining the Cecil family on a stand at Whitehall to watch Victoria's Diamond Jubilee celebrations for her sixty years as Queen, masterminded by the Colonial Secretary, Joseph Chamberlain, a charismatic public figure with his monocle and orchid buttonhole. Representatives of all the peoples of Victoria's Empire processed, with her, through London. This was followed the next day by a naval review.

It was, as Violet said, an apotheosis of the monarch herself, and of the British Empire. Of that Empire, Alfred Milner – Sir Alfred since 1895 – was one of the most important personages, appointed Governor of Cape Colony and High Commissioner in South Africa, where he sailed in April 1897 at the age of forty-two.

Over the previous five years Violet had met him with the Souls, and he had dined at the Admiral's house in 1896, taking Violet into dinner and thus spending a large part of the evening with her. Fellow-guests on that occasion included one who was to pursue Alfred to South Africa, much to Violet's annoyance later on – his close friend Mrs Richard Chamberlain, 'Mrs Dick', the wife of Joseph Chamberlain's brother. Violet and Alfred had also been house-guests at Lord Rothschild's home at Tring in October 1896, when they had enjoyed walking *tête-à-tête* through the rainy Buckinghamshire countryside.

In London Alfred had a bachelor set of rooms in St James's but he entertained at a favourite restaurant, Dieudonné's, nearby. There he enjoyed seeing his old Balliol friends, among whom he had been something of an idol, as well as guests such as Violet and Edward. When he came home on periodic leave from South Africa these dinners continued.

Although dedicated to his work, Alfred had a secret life, which today the press might have pounced on and exposed, but which in those days was far easier to conceal. His trysts were with Cécile D (her full name is unrevealed in his diary), who was that stereotypical late Victorian figure, the kept mistress. Alfred set her up in various houses in South London, and with her this austere, high-minded toiler for Britain and the Empire spent some of his precious free days on seaside, river and bicycling holidays. It was on a hot July day in 1895, when he was staying with her at Great Marlow on the Thames, that he learned that he had been rewarded with the KCB for his work on Death Duties at the Treasury. Alfred's resolution to be celibate, after Margot Tennant turned down his proposal, meant only abstention from marriage.

The mission to Ethiopia which Edward Cecil joined in March 1897 was to secure a guarantee of the Emperor's friendship with Britain during the reconquest of the Sudan. The diplomat Rennell Rodd, Counsellor to the Agent at Cairo, was leader, with Reginald Wingate as second-in-command; Edward was responsible for ordnance. His old acquaintance Count Gleichen was in charge of intelligence and water. A huge, elderly officer, Captain Speedy, had been chosen for his knowledge of Ethiopia, but this was out of date and he seemed drawn to the worst kind of drinking companions: 'the old fool knows nothing,' Edward complained. The unfortunate Captain Swayne, a sapper and transport officer, also claimed local knowledge, but in Edward's view mismanaged his job and caused mutiny among the camel men and carriers: 'He really ought to be stuffed; we shall never find a specimen like him . . . It is his hideous incompetence and bad

Rennell Rodd's mission to Menelik, 1897. Edward is seated on ground, right; behind, seated left to right: Swayne, Wingate, Rodd, Gleichen and Speedy

'A terrible catastrophe' on the
Ethiopian Mission, 1897,
drawn by Count Gleichen,
who credited Captain Swayne,
not Edward, with rescuing the
silver that fell with the camel

advice that led us into half the errors we have made. We found camp, naturally, on marsh with filthy water,' he wrote angrily on 9 April.

As before, Edward kept a detailed log. The landscape of Ethiopia delighted him, such as the route from Worabili to Shala leading over

> upland pastures dotted with spinneys like the richest English parks. . . . The vegetation is so varied and rich it is impossible to describe . . . The cactus and olive, wild vine grow from the rich undergrowth of English covert. The birds and insects are dazzling. The smell of the cedars and wild roses, the singing of innumerable birds, the magnificent panoramas and the exquisite woodland glades are beyond idea.

When a camel fell over a cliff carrying the silver they had brought as a present for Menelik, Edward averted disaster by climbing down to investigate, and finding the precious goods. A month later the Emperor, with 'a nice but rather ferocious smile', accepted these gifts and a phonograph. His queen, to whom they also presented presents, 'was so covered up that a pair of bright eyes was all we saw . . . The room was crammed with boys (slaves really) etc.; one or two eunuchs waited round the throne. She had horrible lap dogs.' The mission was a complete success.

Edward was relieved when the expedition at last came to an end, but adventure was now in his blood, and 'except to see Violet and my people,' he confessed, 'I don't feel anxious to go back to dull old England.' He did not have long to stay there. No sooner were he and Violet settled in a temporary home at Windsor than his battalion was sent off to Gibraltar, as a 'punishment' for some misdemeanour. It was certainly a punishment for Violet: the little house where they lived with George, his nurse Clear, Spender the maid and Cross, Edward's valet, was squalid, though with beautiful views over the Mediterranean, and there was no social life outside the Grenadiers.

Then in January 1898 Kitchener, who was preparing for the final stage of the reconquest of the Sudan, summoned Edward to Egyptian Army service again to join his staff as ADC. Ivor Maxse, who was himself forging a successful career in the Army, had urged Edward to build on his earlier success with Kitchener in the Sudan; it did not do to be forgotten.

Violet went with Edward to Cairo. George, with his nurse, was sent back to England. This, Violet's first trip to Egypt, was her happiest. After Edward had departed for Kitchener's headquarters in the Sudan, she set off to Aswan at the invitation of the able Under-secretary for Finance in Egypt, Clinton Dawkins, and his wife Loulie, who were going on an inspection trip up the Nile. Intimate friends of Alfred Milner, they urged Violet to write to him when they did. He answered her letter gratefully while on his official travels as South African High Commissioner, from his 'present exile' in Maseru, Basutoland, a region he loved for its sublime mountainous landscape.

When Violet returned to England that summer, she heard the news that her old friend Edward Burne-Jones was dead. She went to stay in Somerset with another friend of his, Frances Horner, and her husband at Mells, their Tudor manor house, always a haven when Edward was abroad and Violet wanted to escape from the Anglican debates at Hatfield. This was a meeting place for the Souls and for important political figures of different opinions, which, under that roof, were never allowed to come between them. That August of 1898 Frances and Violet talked of their dear Burne-Jones, and waited apprehensively for news of Edward in the Sudan.

In April, he had been at Kitchener's side at the first important victory of 1898, the battle of the Atbara, when Mahmoud, the powerful young son of the Khalifa, was defeated and captured at his stronghold. The climax of the campaign was the Battle of Omdurman on 2 September, when the Dervish forces were decisively vanquished: 11,000 Dervishes lay dead on the field; Khartoum was retaken; General Gordon was avenged, though the Khalifa escaped. As he entered the city with Edward and fellow officers and found the place where Gordon had fallen, Kitchener was moved to tears. He was approached by a pathetic figure, an ancient gardener who had worked all his life there; now he feared the British would dismiss him. Edward noticed that Kitchener spoke to him kindly, as he usually did to humble people.

The Egyptian and British flags were hoisted side-by-side over the city, to show that from now on the Sudan would be a British responsibility as well as an Egyptian one. In fact the British, to the anger of Egyptian nationalists, ruled it almost exclusively. To prevent the continued worship of the Mahdi's memory, his mighty tomb was demolished and his bones dug up and thrown into the Nile. Kitchener was rumoured, falsely, to be making a drinking cup out of his skull. Pockets of Dervish resistance remained, but Kitchener considered these a less urgent matter than a new emergency to the south.

After the battle, Edward joined an Anglo-Egyptian force of two 600-strong battalions of Sudanese troops, a company of Cameron Highlanders and a mountain gun battery going further up the river in four steamers, led by Kitchener in the *Dal*. The expedition was bound for Fashoda where a small French force was reported to have arrived, under Commandant Marchand, all the way from French West Africa, to stake a claim to the Upper Nile. Kitchener, as Governor-General of the Sudan, intended to insist that the French should recognise Anglo-Egyptian control of that territory.

The river regions the boats now reached abounded with hippopotamuses and crocodiles; the local people were the tall, ebony-skinned Dinka and Shilluk. On its way south, the force shelled and plundered a Dervish fort. The weather was oppressive, with rainstorms. The confrontation with the French took place on 19 September.

Kitchener had warned them that he was on his way. The first sight of them was in a small boat flying the French flag – Senegalese oarsmen in red jerseys and an officer in spotless white uniform. These accompanied the Anglo-Egyptian force to their little fort at Fashoda, five miles away. Here two more French officers were waiting; Edward received them and led them to Kitchener, on the upper deck of the *Dal*. Bitterly, the French accepted the situation: they were few, running short of food, and they did not want to embroil their country in a war. Together Marchand and Kitchener drank the wine produced by the

French, and the Egyptian flag, not the British – a diplomatic gesture – was hoisted over the fort. Later, Marchand received a letter from Kitchener, laying down the conditions the French were to observe. This was not, however, the end of the matter. Britain and France came almost to the brink of war. It was a salutary crisis, however, for it forced them to settle their many colonial differences and this, as it happened, paved the way to the *entente* with France of 1904.

The British soldiers present at Fashoda admired young Marchand and his small band of companions for their courage and enterprise in penetrating miles through uncharted regions to this lonely spot far up the Nile – doing so, too, with perfect military discipline, immaculate dress and bottles of excellent wine.

Lady Salisbury wrote to Violet that Edward and Kitchener 'have gone up the Nile – how far no one knows. We can hear nothing of them till they come back to Khartoum as they have no post or telegraph. It is very mysterious but I suppose we must trust the Sirdar!'

It remained mysterious. Kitchener had peremptorily packed the British war correspondents off from Omdurman to Cairo and home to keep them away from this top-secret affair. Kitchener chose Edward to carry his dispatches back to England, with their news of the victory at Omdurman and its aftermath. On his arrival he was a hero. Gwendolen Cecil wrote,

> He enjoys the proud position of being the first man from Fashoda to reach England . . . One incident in that journey was 300 miles on the desert railway by night going forty miles an hour clinging to a baggage wagon which was the only vehicle obtainable. As he finished by a journey of 48 hours from Trieste on end, it was a little trying though gratifying to find Hatfield in a state of martial enthusiasm and the whole village turned out with band and torchlight procession . . . However he took it like an angel and made them a nice little speech, and my mother was immensely pleased and to the surprise of her brutal sons on the verge of tears the whole evening.

The Sudan campaign was of profound significance to Edward. Having to take responsibility in the thick of action made him grow up; he was now a soldier to be reckoned with. Kitchener alarmed him, as he did other officers, but he could not intimidate him. Edward was mentioned again in despatches for the Atbara and Omdurman battles, and awarded the DSO for his services. Most important, he had acquired a taste for Egypt and the vast, exhilarating wilderness of the Sudan.

His soldiering, however, was about to take him into a new theatre altogether. Once again Lord Wolseley kept his promise. In the summer of 1899 he recommended Edward as a Special Forces officer to Colonel Robert Baden-Powell, to help him raise a frontier protection force and reinforce strategic points in the Cape Colony, South Africa.

The bookplate designed for Violet by Edward Burne-Jones who died in August 1898, from a sketchbook in Wigsell Library

CHAPTER NINE

The South African Crisis

WHEN EDWARD AND Violet disembarked from the mail steamer *Dunottar Castle* at Cape Docks on 26 July 1899, after two weeks at sea, to begin Edward's latest military adventure, they can have had no idea that South Africa, and the tumultuous months they were to spend in it, would alter the course of the rest of their lives. Indeed, it was hard for them to know what to expect. They had little understanding of the country itself, the complexities of the many-sided conflict, or the antagonists' preparedness for war; nor indeed were they certain whether there would be a war at all.

The crisis into which they were plunged was the outcome of a century-long conflict in that rich and disputed land of mountain, grassland and desert between the two white peoples who colonised it: the British, occupying Cape Colony and Natal, and the Boers, descendants of seventeenth-century Dutch migrants to the Cape who had largely moved north to escape British rule in 1834. There they had formed their own republics in the Orange Free State and the Transvaal. The Boers, picturesque frontier farmers who had pitted themselves against the wilderness and the black African tribes, were organised into primitive democracies in their two states. Dominant among their characteristics were an exclusive racial tyranny over the Bantu Africans, to whom they denied civil rights, an antiquated seventeenth-century Protestant faith which underwrote their bigotry and a desire to be left to their own devices.

Quarrels between these hardy Bible-reading farmers and horse-men, with their beards and wide-brimmed hide hats, and the British administrators and traders they hated, turned on Britain's long-term plans to control the whole Southern African region and above all, from the late 1880s, the fabulously rich gold-bearing area of the Transvaal at the Witwatersrand, which was in Boer hands. British imperialists looked on the independence of the Boers, whom they had repeatedly defended against African attacks, as an anomaly and a nuisance. Particularly intransigent towards the British were the Boers of the Transvaal – known as the South African Republic – who had won a small war against them in 1881, humiliatingly defeating them at the Battle of Majuba Hill. But the British believed reason and progress must win soon. They operated according to a doctrine of British supremacy in the region, which the Boers, despite grudging acknowledgement, continually tried to overthrow. The Transvaal Boers, rich from their new-found gold, became increasingly confident about standing up for their separate existence. For them, however, the gold was a two-edged sword: it brought the new threat that the largely British miners and businessmen who had poured into the Transvaal to exploit it would use their numbers and economic leverage to take control of the country. Under their President, Paul Kruger, a tough, elderly patriarch of impressive ugliness, the Boers therefore denied political rights to these 'Uitlanders', as they called them, while the terms on which they mined and employed native labour were dictated by 'Oom Paul' Kruger's government.

In 1895 a group of Uitlanders in the city of Johannesburg plotted to take over the mines and government by force. It was agreed, with the unofficial connivance of the British Colonial Secretary, Joseph Chamberlain, that mounted Cape troops led by Dr Leander Starr Jameson should ride from British Protectorate territory at Pitsani on the Transvaal border to help the rebels. The moving spirit was the powerful British diamond magnate and Cape politician, Cecil Rhodes.

The raid was a fiasco: the revolt collapsed and Jameson and his force were intercepted by the Boers and led off into disgraceful captivity. In the aftermath of the 'Jameson Raid', which had provoked the German Kaiser's notorious telegram of support to President Kruger, pressure groups in South Africa and in Britain campaigned fiercely for Uitlander rights, accusing the Boers of trying to oust the British from South Africa. Kruger's government multiplied defence-spending fourfold, and equipped their citizen army with modern Mauser rifles. In 1898 Kruger won the presidential elections once again, confirming the popularity of his stand against Britain.

Joseph Chamberlain's determination to take a tough line with the Boers had been his reason, in 1897, for choosing Alfred Milner as South African High Commissioner and Governor of the Cape. He knew that Alfred was not only one of the best brains in government service, but also exceptionally tenacious. Alfred's passionate belief in the British imperial mission fitted with Chamberlain's own: to bring the whole region of South Africa under British control and make it an immensely wealthy country on a par with the United States. This was clearly incompatible with Boer independence.

Alfred was the man on the spot, the expert, and whatever he decided, the British Government was bound to follow. At first he was confident that Kruger's support would collapse in the Transvaal and

Alfred Milner as High Commissioner in South Africa in Cape Town at the time of the Boer War

the Uitlanders, under the pressure of events, would gain their rights at last; but after Kruger's re-election he grew alarmed by the spread of the President's popularity among the large number of Boers still inhabiting Cape Colony, undermining Britain's control over her own territory and jeopardising her supremacy in South Africa. Alfred disliked the ordinary run of politicians, especially in the Cape Colony and Natal where he found many in the elected governments far too accommodating to Kruger. He felt desperately isolated – outside his immediate loyal entourage there was nobody out there with whom he could discuss the situation.

Although in many respects liberal and progressive, Alfred was fundamentally an autocrat. He became convinced that unless strong action were taken, the Uitlanders and Cape British might well give up their British protectors and throw in their lot with the Boers. Because he was confident that the Boers would back down, or if foolish enough to hold out, would be easily defeated in a war, his negotiations to gain Uitlander rights and assert British supremacy became uncompromising. Meanwhile Kruger's government made a military alliance with the Boers of the other independent republic, the Orange Free State. With neither side trusting the other, Alfred worked hard to present the British public with an unassailable case for his policy as the crisis of mid-1899 headed towards war.

By the end of the summer he could have accepted a settlement with the Boers which would effectively have met the wishes of the Uitlanders. However, the solution of their grievances had been a lever, rather than the main object, of his diplomatic campaign for British supremacy – achievable in his view only by the complete submission of the Transvaal. Backed by the British mine-owning 'gold bugs', such as Alfred Beit and Percy Fitzpatrick, who resented Boer tariffs and controls over labour and mining supplies, Alfred persuaded Joseph Chamberlain in late August to reject the Boer offers and demand more concessions. To back this up he asked for a 10,000-troop reinforcement to the existing British garrison. The Cabinet agreed, convinced by Alfred and the press, which had largely supported him.

Alfred firmly believed that the Boers would wriggle out of any undertaking they made and that he was therefore justified in pushing them to the brink of war. What he did not expect was that the Boers would take years to defeat, and this would irreparably damage Britain's reputation for invincibility.

Lord Salisbury, still Foreign Secretary as well as Prime Minister, did not consider South African affairs to be a Foreign Officer matter and had left them to Joseph Chamberlain as Colonial Secretary: 'Never jog a man's elbow,' was his dictum. Salisbury's view of colonial business-men and political bosses, based on his travels as a young man, had taught him to trust neither the Uitlanders nor the Cape politicians; he suspected the mine-owners of putting their selfish interests first, and regarded Alfred's views as 'too heated' on their behalf. Salisbury had an equally low view of the Boers, however, and in the end, fearing for the prestige and authority of the British Empire, he accepted that Alfred's tough line was probably for the best; but for a long time he believed that the object of Alfred's policy was not to seize territory or gold-mines. Although in principle Alfred might have agreed with him, in effect economic control of the whole region meant just that.

Salisbury was distracted during this crisis: his wife's health had been bad for many months. Cancer was finally diagnosed. Salisbury watched for any signs of recovery, his hopes rising with every remis-sion and falling when the disease resumed its inexorable course. It was a period of deepening anxiety for the family at Hatfield.

Edward had more confidence than his father that Britain had a just cause in South Africa. Many soldiers like himself wished to 'avenge Majuba' as they had 'avenged Gordon' in the Sudan. When he and Violet sailed for the Cape, leaving behind four-year-old George, they assumed, like most, that even if there were a war it would soon be over.

On the voyage out, Edward had plenty of time to get to know Colonel Robert Baden-Powell, his chief for the next months; one would emerge from their time in Africa as an imperial hero, the other thoroughly disenchanted. In appearance, character and ambition, the two were very different types of soldier: 'B-P', spruce in all circum-stances, was every inch the professional soldier who had been driven upwards by his own ambition and was going to continue to rise; B-P loved military appurtenances, uniforms and, indeed, dressing up gen-erally (his entertainments in fancy dress at Mafeking, whether on the stage or at the weekly sports, were to become legendary). A cavalry-man, Baden-Powell, now forty-two, had served in India, Zululand, the Ashanti expedition in West Africa and Matabeleland in Southern Rhodesia, making a speciality of gathering intelligence through scouting and reconnaissance, on which he wrote a book.

Compare this erect, natty little man, with his neatly trimmed mous-tache and jaunty whistle, with the tall, stooping figure of Edward

Cecil, whose very moustache seemed to emphasise the melancholy cast of his face, belied, in fact, by his quick sense of humour. He had inherited his family's insouciance as to dress and punctuality and unlike 'B-P', to whom all detail of uniform and accoutrements mattered, was little concerned with the outward show.

Despite the lack of natural sympathy between them, as professional soldiers both would consider it their duty, using all their powers of self-control and self-discipline, to work together in the trying months to come. Upon arrival, Edward's immediate task was to provision and equip the up-country force which B-P was raising. This was a new sort of infantry, Mounted Infantry, using horses to carry men and rifles quickly to the action rather than for the outdated cavalry charge.

Cape Town, dominated by the mighty mass of Table Mountain, was regarded as the most attractive town in the British Empire: 'The beautiful sweep of the bay, the towering crags behind and the romantic pinnacles which rise on either side, make a landscape that no one who has seen it can forget . . . A nobler site for a city and a naval stronghold than that of the capital of South Africa, can hardly be imagined,' wrote a recent visitor, the eminent jurist Lord Bryce.

When Edward and Violet arrived, however, it was the winter season and the rain fell in torrents on the Sunday after their arrival: it burst the sewers and fire engines had to pump out the cellars; the city centre was inundated and worshippers arriving at the city's chief Anglican church, St George's, found the street outside like a river in full flood. On Long Street, close to the Parliament, a tram was derailed by the deluge.

Apart from these natural obstacles human impediments, especially the obstruction of Sir William Butler, the British Commander-in-Chief at the Cape, labelled a 'pro-Boer' by Edward, made his work at times seem insuperable, 'rather like some of the mythological punishments, for it consists in trying to extract stores, clothing etc. from a recalcitrant general of Boer tendencies, who being a clever Irishman is almost as successful as Parnell in obstructing Government policy. The friction is what you may imagine with officers pouring in by every mail [boat] anxious to get to their work up country and absolutely stumped and handcuffed in Cape Town!' Violet wrote.

This 'recalcitrant general' Butler, who was, Edward wrote, 'almost openly' against Alfred Milner, was recalled to England shortly. Even so, men like B-P and Edward had little support from the home government which, owing to the War Office's grossly inadequate

Ben Weil in Mafeking, 1900

expenditure on intelligence, had no real idea of their enemy's strength. This was to become all too dramatically apparent once the war began. The elected Cape government, too, was hostile to military prepara- tions. Its Prime Minister, W.P. Schreiner, was at best neutral over the struggles with Kruger, disregarding Alfred's pleas and the demands of local communities at Mafeking and Kimberley for assistance in their defence, and allowing the continued export of rifles to the Boer republics.

But Edward had one decisive meeting during these early frustrating weeks, which was materially to affect the course of the war. Ben Weil was one of several enterprising sons of an East End small businessman who had started trading in South Africa, and had virtually the monop- oly of providing supplies and equipment from the coast up-country. Now the canny Weil and the increasingly frustrated young Army officer took a chance, and Edward's gambling habit, which had so often got him into trouble, came into its own. From the Weil brothers he ordered £500,000 worth of stock, giving no more than his own signed promissory note, without any higher authority (which in the present climate he knew would take too long to apply for and might never be given), and Ben Weil agreed to supply British troops up-country. He, too, gambled on the honourable word of Lord Salisbury's son.

Many months later, in a dimly-lit bomb-proof shelter beneath his store in Mafeking during the worst of the siege, Ben Weil recounted the story to Reuter's correspondent:

> Lord Edward Cecil . . . expressed himself most anxious to put down at Mafeking and Bulawayo equipment, food and fodder for a certain number of men without any delay . . . His Lordship took the responsibility of ordering these stocks entirely upon himself remarking 'There is no time for delay, I place this order with you without the authority of my superiors. I may have to pay for it myself, but I will take the responsibility on my own shoulders, as I consider that delay will be dangerous.' Fortunately, I immediately executed the order and the goods were dispatched with all possible speed to Rhodesia and Mafeking. Later on His Lordship arrived in Mafeking and consulted with me with the result that again without authority, as far as I know, he took over large supplies of grain and forage which I had already laid down here in anticipation of the outbreak of war. For as a commercial man and a contractor, I did not require any further cue to cause me to lay down the very heavy stocks, which have proved so beneficial to this garrison. Though not actually asked to do so by His Lordship, the indirect, vulgarly speaking, 'tip', was taken.

Owing to inside information he had received, Weil had already bought large stocks of fodder, grain, clothing and equipment, enabling him to meet Edward's demands. He was emphatic that without Edward's foresight, the British soldiers in Mafeking would have been without kit or equipment suitable for modern South African warfare. As Edward, with characteristic modesty, declined to have his name mentioned in the report which Reuter's correspondent sent out of the besieged town, the world never heard one of the main reasons why the little town of Mafeking was enabled to endure for so long and thus attain its heroic status.

When they arrived at Cape Town, the Cecils found an invitation from Sir Alfred Milner to stay at Government House. 'You will find a rather weary crowd for we have all been working for many weeks much harder than any body can work without breaking down somewhere. But I can promise you a hearty welcome all the same.'

Violet and Edward had last seen Alfred during his leave in Britain during the previous winter. In December, dining with the Queen at

Windsor Castle, he sat next to Edward, and he had spent a night at Hatfield to talk to Lord Salisbury about South Africa. At dinner there, Violet was his companion. The next day Alfred had left that chaste household for a very different meeting in South London – with his mistress Cécile. The simple happiness of a few days' incognito cycle tour of rural Hampshire they took together was interrupted briefly by his trip to town for a magnificent farewell dinner for George Curzon, who was off to take up his post as Viceroy of India. Violet was also a guest.

Before Alfred himself left England for South Africa, early in 1899, he entertained Violet at Dieudonné's with many other friends, admirers of his ideas and achievements such as Clinton and Loulie Dawkins and the Liberal lawyer-politician Richard Burdon Haldane, and several Souls – D.D. and Alfred Lyttelton, Frances Horner, Willie and Etty Grenfell. 'It was a cheerful party and they all stayed late. After they left, I sat up working for some time,' Alfred recorded in a typical diary entry.

Alfred was no more short of feminine friendship in Cape Colony than in London – with the novelist of Cape Society, Miss Dorothea Fairbridge, for example. Their companionship was strictly intellectual, whatever the emotional undercurrents for her.

Meeting Alfred afresh, in this new context as powerful imperial Proconsul, guiding events at the Cape on the brink of war, Violet was bowled over. She immediately put him on a pedestal from which, as far as she was concerned, he was never to step down: 'Seeing so much of Sir Alfred has been delightful. I am immensely impressed by him; he seems to me to have grown bigger on very fine lines. He has kept his gentleness and charm and width of view and to them has added a firmness and a certainty of purpose which seem to me very unusual,' she wrote on 14 August.

'His gentleness and charm' were reserved for the few out there. In public he seemed severe and impersonal. Violet's old friend, the artist Mortimer Menpes, who arrived in South Africa at this time seeking work, described being ushered in by an ADC to His Excellency's study at Government House where he was to paint him.

A tall figure rose up from an enormous desk where he had been writing. This cold, quiet, sedate figure in the chilly, icy Government room somehow filled me with a sense of awe, and seemed even more unsympathetic than the caricatures in the ante-room. The great room with its hundreds of books that lined the walls; the bare tall windows where the light

Government House and the gardens where Alfred and Violet enjoyed peaceful interludes during the crisis. Table Mountain is in the background

shone in garishly; the very papers that littered the desk – all were cold and bluey in colour, and even the delicious peeps of sunlight and green trees that one caught through the windows only served to accentuate the dreariness of the interior. The Governor himself was cool in colour; his thin scholarly face looked like the finest ivory browned with age; his hair was of a silvery colour; his eyes had a glint of steel; his clothing was sad, without a touch of warmth; his very manner was cool, courtly and polite. When the ADC left us I felt that I also must freeze. Yet there was a touch of sympathy in Sir Alfred himself . . . When he smiled the change was extraordinary. It transformed the whole face, and made it sweet and gentle.

The very feminine Violet was certainly able to pierce Alfred's masculine defences. As well as being attracted to him, she admired and respected him, being herself an ardent imperialist. She sympathised with his isolation; six weeks after she arrived, she wrote to her brother Leo:

> I wish Milner had a less heroic fight to make. Three and a half month's crisis – telegrams all day, up at seven and generally not to bed until 2, an hour's ride or walk the only change – some days he is in the house altogether. He is well, alert and cheerful, absolutely fearless for himself – realizing his strong and his weak points, knowing that he holds British South Africa for the moment absolutely behind him, which has never happened before and will not happen again for many years.

The situation between Britain and the Boer republics was now reaching the peak of its crisis – and with it the crisis of Alfred's career. In the end it was the Boers who issued an ultimatum to Britain and who were the first to attack when it expired. To Alfred, a total victory was crucial for British prestige, and his master plan of imperial expansion. If today that plan looks little better than arrant robbery, we must think ourselves back into the age. Apart from China, all the leading nations were expansionist, including the United States and Japan. Britain's European critics during the Boer War, such as the Dutch, themselves had large foreign empires. The Boers, also, had been conspicuously land-hungry. Britain's record as a colonial power was far from blameless, but in Africa it was better than that of the Germans or the Belgians, or of the Boers, for that matter, who treated their black servants as little better than slaves. At the core of Alfred's outlook was his deep belief in British culture and institutions, and the conviction that spreading her superior standards of fair government and her advanced technology must bring great benefits to the colonised countries. For him and his fellow-administrators the empire was a cause to be served selflessly, demanding the utmost of their ability, and conferring not bondage but enlightened rule.

Britain's nineteenth-century domestic achievement was self-evident to her people at the time – certainly to the Cecils. Even now it seems impressive: the magnificent literature, the superb engineering, the massive social change and political progress gained with a minimum of violent unrest; and the fostering of a creative and enterprising individuality, even in an age of increasing mass-production and standardisation. Logically, from that perspective, Britain had much to offer a wider world as an imperial power.

Politically, Alfred did not fit in to a conventional mould, nor crave the limelight. He was progressive, though a Conservative insofar as he shared that party's views on empire; but unlike his close ally, the British Colonial Secretary, Chamberlain, who 'loved the roar of the multitude and . . . could always say "I have never feared the English democracy,"' Alfred disliked modern parliamentary democracy. He believed, with his friend Rudyard Kipling, that democratic politics interfered with the serious business of ruling; though, unlike Kipling, he was not a populist promoter of Empire. He operated best behind the scenes as an outstanding administrator who worked unsparingly to achieve smooth-running government of the highest standard. Unfortunately he regarded all but the smallest compromises as defeat and failure: doing a 'deal' with the Boers was out of the question. Some have attributed this to the German element in his education, emphasising his thoroughness and dislike of half-measures.

His 'liberalism' did not include the nineteenth-century liberal idea of national self-determination which must, in his view, give way to the higher claims of the British Empire. But despite calling himself 'a British race patriot', and being unquestionably a white supremacist, he cannot be convicted of the worst colour prejudice. Wherever he went on visits round the country, he always took care to listen to the African point of view, such as that of the Barolong Chief Wessels at Mafeking. In 1897 he told his friend H.H. Asquith that he considered the blacks had been 'scandalously used'. By being prepared to ignore their needs, he continued (he used the ironic phrase, 'to dish the nigger'), Boer and Briton could, he knew, reach common agreement; but that was not the basis on which he wished to operate, and he tried, after his fashion and without success, to shift entrenched Boer attitudes. In 1910, he, among others, was upset when a Liberal Government led by Asquith accepted a constitution for the Union of South Africa, which, to placate Boer prejudice, doomed to extinction the limited voting rights of black people.

Inevitably there was an element of self-deception in Alfred's racial altruism; for British influence to grow, as Alfred hoped, there had to be numerous British settlers to counterbalance the Boers, and many Africans would be expelled from their lands. But he cannot be likened to the diamond magnate Cecil Rhodes who, though an imperial idealist, was also a political adventurer of a more dubious kind. Yet without Rhodes, it is hard to imagine that Britain's South African dream, espoused by Alfred, would ever have gained impetus. Alfred's supporters included many mine-owners and businessmen such as Percy Fitzpatrick whose interests were mercenary.

Alfred inspired his staff at Government House with devoted loyalty. Now Violet came to know them well. Annie, wife of the Military Secretary, Major Hanbury-Williams, was one of the few women in that preponderantly masculine household; warm and spirited, she shocked many by publicly kissing a black child, with Alfred's approval. She 'received for Sir Alfred', as Violet put it, acting as his hostess. Government House was a curious mixture of official and familiar: it ran like a small version of the Court of St James's, with reminders everywhere of the great Queen-Empress at home – from the actual image of the crown, in gilded wood atop the portraits in the reception rooms, on the writing paper, on the metal lamps outside, on the servants' livery, to the ritual of the receptions, at which everyone had to stand as long as His Excellency was present, or until he gave the order not to; and to the National Anthem which the orchestra struck up in the ballroom gallery. At dinner, the ADCs wore black evening coats faced with scarlet silk and a loyal toast was drunk to the Queen. The invincible might of the empire represented in the icily formal figure of His Excellency the Governor was impressed on visitors.

On the other hand, in this relatively new society, where ceremony played little part, Alfred could relax in what free time he had in the company of his entourage, riding with his secretary, the devoted Osmund ('Ozzy') Walrond, or his ADCs, the dashing Lord Belgrave, 'Bend'or', soon to inherit the dukedom of Westminster, and the sporting Captain Chester-Master, who was Master of the local hounds. The butler, Brockwell, had been Alfred Milner's manservant in England. Thus it was a peculiarly English and insular household, typical of so many throughout the Empire.

'I do so long to see you and tell you about this funny half-Dutch half-English place. It is very pretty but colonial and provincial and I should think when there is no crisis, dull,' Edward wrote home. He was referring to the centre of Cape Town itself, but the description could equally apply to Government House: a charming, white-washed low building, it is unpretentious, 'an English gentleman's country house of moderate size clad in colonial guise,' as one architectural historian described it. Its Regency veranda and porticoed loggia are elegant interpretations of the *stoep*, traditional to South African houses. Its formal gardens, with box-edged flower beds, give way to more expansive grounds; just a step across a dividing path are the fascinating Company Gardens, planted by the Dutch settlers partly as a practical exercise to see what vegetables would grow in that climate, full of magnificent trees and exotic birds. In these shady walks Violet and Alfred often strolled in the peace of the evening after 'dreary and weary' days of crisis and war.

Inside Government House, however, the formality was oppressive. Combining the worst pomp of Buckingham Palace with second-rate department-store furniture and a hefty amount of trophies – mounted game, relics of Zulu wars and mediocre oil portraits – it was neither cosy nor even particularly domestic. It was at least comfortable; and the good-natured Annie Hanbury-Williams did her best to humanise life there with balls and parties, where the orchestra played and the young ADCs could mix with Cape society, reinforced by visitors from Europe.

Alfred himself had little interest in such socialising beyond 'duty' entertaining; he felt more at ease in his study, with its masculine furniture and the leather reading chair with its brass bookstand where he worked, hour upon hour. This single-mindedness, the steady light from his study shining through the small hours of the night, this overwhelming sense of the steady flame of the Empire burning, this unshakeable sense of high imperial mission, impressed Violet deeply: Alfred seemed the only man who could concentrate single-mindedly and govern as the crisis deepened into war. This was reinforced by the purposeful ambience at Government House, a command centre full of idealism and of hard work. Violet had no reason to change her opinion of her hero during the subsequent years of war.

Alfred's calmness was commented upon by many in contrast to the jittery atmosphere at the Cape; yet his diary and his letters to a few intimates, as Violet became, reveal a more emotional side, which was to emerge in the difficult months ahead.

After a muddled, hectic three weeks in Cape Town, Edward and Violet departed, 'much to my regret' Alfred wrote, after a short walk round the garden with her before she left for Kimberley, the key diamond mining town and railway stop. The rail journey north took two days. They stayed at the invitation of Cecil Rhodes at the Sanatorium Hotel which he had provisioned. Through his position as head of de Beers, the pre-eminent diamond company, Kimberley, the chief source of diamonds, was effectively his kingdom. This was to be the start of Violet's debt of hospitality to Rhodes, which alleviated her life greatly during the war.

Violet had met Rhodes soon after her arrival in South Africa, when Annie Hanbury-Williams took her to lunch at his Cape Town home, Groote Schuur. Rhodes was notoriously awkward with women, but Violet got on well with him:

> A carelessly put together large man with a top-knot of brown hair, turning grey, and a complexion that gave notice of the heart trouble that killed him three years later. He had a face you could not look away from, with the blue eyes of a seer, and the mouth of a Roman Emperor. He had a curious voice that ran up and down the scale and a very individual way of expressing himself. No other man of great intellectual power can ever have had a smaller vocabulary, and he would repeat the same thing again and again – 'I give you this thought,' he would say, and the thought, badly expressed in words of one syllable, was always worth attending to.

Violet had intended to stay for some time with Edward while he assisted the Colonel Commanding, Baden-Powell, in setting up a defence force, the Protectorate Regiment, and co-ordinating supplies. But she trod on a hatpin, running it deep into her foot, and had to remain where she was, at Kimberley, while Edward went on to Bulawayo in Rhodesia, and then to his eventual destination, Mafeking. From Kimberley Violet wrote a letter to Alfred, on 22 August, the tone of which shows the easy terms which they already enjoyed and how much her mind was in tune with his. She was lucky to be in comfortable quarters and good air,

> but <u>furious</u> at being away from all news and I ache to know how you are and what you feel like and what is going on. It is like being put on prison rations after a merry life at the Savoy to be suddenly so far away. Mrs Hanbury [Williams] and the Colonel have both written but what is the good of a letter, I want to see and hear and feel. Feeling is everything – and I want to be cheerful at lunch and depressed at dinner according to the news and atmosphere and to have sleepless nights if I chooze [*sic*] because everyone is worried, or . . . go to bed and think about my passage home because everything is going so well that the

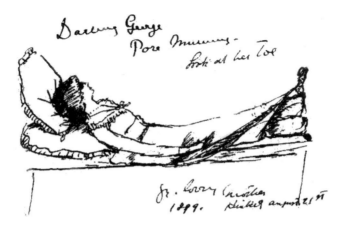

Drawing attached to a letter by Violet to George
describing her 'hatpin' accident at Kimberley

crisis will be over in a fortnight — is this very feminine? I claim the right of being so until I get Civil Rights, by which I don't mean politeness — when I have a vote I will cut my hair off and be reasonable for the rest of my life and not care what happens to my friends, who they marry or what they do — however that is all far off in the 20th Century and first now . . . I wish you all good things and your own way about South Africa because you have found the straight way through this latter day labyrinth.

When Violet was well enough to move, she returned to Cape Town, to escape the siege at Kimberley which would be certain if war broke out. At Government House 'after two nights in the train — such a train! being dead lame with my bad toe and only able to wear a stocking, I was pitchforked into a lunch party before I could turn round — only at least when I got there, I was next to Milner!'

CHAPTER TEN

Groote Schuur

'LADY E. CECIL today returned from Kimberley in time for lunch and staying here,' Alfred noted in his diary on Wednesday, 30 August 1899. Violet returned to stay in the pretty bedroom at Government House she and Edward had shared earlier, with a weaver bird making its elaborate nest outside the window overlooking the garden, where she and Alfred would stroll before dinner in the cool of the evening – not, of course, completely alone: somewhere almost out of sight, there was always a security officer keeping an eye open for possible attackers. Nonetheless, the regular *tête-à-têtes* and riding excursions, often three or four times a week, of His Excellency and the pretty wife of an officer, almost conferred on Violet a special status.

Foremost in their conversation was of course the coming crisis: 'the days grow more exciting,' Alfred recorded as rumours of Boer preparations flooded in. Thousands of British troops from India were on their way to bolster the garrison force in Cape Colony. Crowds of refugee families of Uitlanders, British and European miners from the Witwatersrand gold-field in the Transvaal (the 'Rand'), poured in from Johannesburg. Many men were said to have faces bleeding from the Boers' whips as they were herded into the trains.

Violet joined the Rand Relief Committee, set up to deal with these dispossessed families. They were numerous: every woman seemed to have ten children under twelve years old and a baby on the way. She noted that they were unused to relief, being quite self-reliant and the women often wage-earners. At the end of October, she reckoned there were 75,000 refugees in Cape Town, effectively doubling the city's population. By then she was helping with the Committee's appeal for British funds.

On 11 October the Boer republics of the Orange Free State and the Transvaal declared war, following the expiry of President Kruger's

*Cecil Rhodes drawn by Mortimer
Menpes and presented by him to
Alfred Milner*

ultimatum to the British to cease their ever-mounting demands or
face invasion of their colony. They expected to be joined by the Boer
subjects of Britain in the Cape. By seizing the initiative they hoped to
drive the British forces into the sea.

Violet, undecided whether to go back to England, had been
waiting on events just before the war, when she was invited by Cecil
Rhodes to stay on at his house, Groote Schuur, along with her friend
Cecily Bentinck, whose husband Lord Charles Bentinck was serving
with Edward at Mafeking. Rhodes, realising the danger from Boer
attack, was off to see to the defence of his mines in Kimberley: 'I want
you to take care of my house until I come back, and if you don't stay,'
he told Violet and Cecily, seeing hesitation in their faces, 'I shall think
you are two very small-minded women.'

'This little scene took place outside the front door at Groote Schuur
while he was walking down the steps to his Cape cart. He shook
hands. "Now remember, I want to find you both here when I come
back," and with that he climbed into his Cape cart, Old John Cloete,
his black coachman, whipped up, and they were off.'

In due course the Boer armies besieged Ladysmith in Natal, base
of the main British garrison, Mafeking, and Kimberley, where
Rhodes now found himself immured. He telegraphed Violet and

Cecily, asking them again to stay on at Groote Schuur. Violet was delighted to do so; she felt very much at home. Rhodes's taste, so unexpected in such a man as 'the Colossus', was sympathetic to her. She was always alive to the effort which concealed effort, and to the harmony of a house with its gardens and, in this case, of the whole with its stupendous natural setting in a vast park on the side of Table Mountain.

Violet often felt homesick and missed little George sorely. She was also hundreds of miles from Edward in Mafeking – now, as far as she could tell from the unreliable news, in hourly danger from fighting or fever. Nevertheless, much was comfortingly familiar even in these exotic surroundings: the chintz covers of the chairs where they sat on the *stoep* outside having tea, the Sheffield plate tea service itself, with its immense teapot necessary for Rhodes's legendary hospitality, and the two-tier ebony tea-table laden with very English delicacies, scones with jam and cream, and sponge cakes. Rhodes had rejected plans sent out from England by the notable garden designer, Gertrude Jekyll, as 'too fussy', considering the great sweep of blue hydrangeas more in proportion to the mountain behind. However, he had laid out much of the grounds like an English country house garden, with a rose walk and a pergola and well-tended lawns sweeping into the distance. When Violet and Cecily Bentinck were photographed there in their patterned muslin dresses, they could have been in a country house at home, but for the stone pines in the background and the dim outline of Table Mountain beyond.

Closest to home of all, the house's architect, Herbert Baker, was fresh from the offices of Ernest George, the architect at Dunley. Despite their different settings and vastly different budgets, the two houses shared a simplicity and comfortable masculinity. Rhodes, like Admiral Maxse, was a strong-minded man with decided tastes, who knew what he wanted and obtained it with little reference to feminine aesthetic. Groote Schuur is not a palace. It is spacious, solid and hospitable; the collaboration of Rhodes and his architect created a fusion of South African vernacular with Arts and Crafts which makes it one of the most distinguished and distinctive houses in that country. What now seems so appropriate was then *demodé*, and they were regarded askance for reviving the traditional 'Cape Dutch' style. Great Wigsell, the manor house in Kent, which Violet was to restore a few years later, had many characteristics in common with Groote Schuur.

One of the unexpected things about Mr Rhodes was his taste [she wrote]. It was perfect. He took a lot of trouble about making the rooms at Groote Schuur look their best. I have seen him walk about for an hour with a blue Delft pot under his arm trying it first here and then there, and the best evidence of his taste was that he did not overload his rooms, and had no pictures or decoration in them but what might have been bought by people of moderate means. I believe he had spent a fortune building Groote Schuur but there was no particular feel of money about the house. It was just beautiful and very simple.

In the morning, after breakfast, Violet sat on the *stoep* to devour longed-for letters from home; in the evening, when the sun's last rays brushed the slopes of Table Mountain with pink, she and Cecily would compare notes of their days, as the African night fell swiftly, the pale blue of the great horseshoe of hydrangeas being the last to disappear into the inky night, and even the black-and-white stripes of the zebras which roamed beneath the stone pines beyond, extinguished from sight.

This was to be Violet's home for the next nine months: tumultuous months, unlike any that had come before or would come again – of joy in her awakening feelings for Alfred; of anxiety for Edward besieged in Mafeking; of sorrow at the death of friends; and of excitement at being at the centre of events played out upon a vast stage of the Empire, in a war which would change it profoundly.

Apart from his natural hospitality, it suited Rhodes to have wives of two aristocratic officers, one the daughter-in-law of the English Prime Minister, as house guests, along with visits from the flower of the British Army – wounded officers whom they invited to stay, to be nursed or to recuperate. Cape Town was crammed with visitors, refugees, soldiers awaiting orders to go to war, or sent back wounded, and their wives and relations. Violet never ceased to be thankful for the haven offered her by Rhodes, away from the tension of war: 'It is a most amusing house to stay in, being the only real Liberty Hall I have ever come across. You get up when you like, breakfast when you like, lunch at any time between 1 and 2.30, no one cares whether you are there to meals or whether you are alive or dead, you have your own pony to ride and your own Cape cart and pair which you order when you please.'

Violet's pony, a grey, was called Naughty Boy, although, as she wrote to George, he was very good, and only started when the lion cub, which Rhodes kept in a cage, frightened him as they passed by. During Violet's sojourn the cub grew from a little bundle of claws and

Violet in the garden at Groote Schuur

fluff whom the men played with, into a handsome beast. 'One day I know he will break his chain and I shall find him in my bedroom. What shall I do?'

Riding was Violet's favourite pastime, as in England: 'Rhodes owns one side of Table Mountain and the drives and rides all about his place are lovely.' Cecily often joined her on her rides with Alfred and his staff, galloping across the Cape Flats, not, as now, covered with shanty dwellings, but wide open sands, with the distant roar of the waves of Table

Bay sounding in their ears. Alfred frequently brought over guests from Government House, like the dashing General Pole-Carew, 'Polly Carew', to meet up with the two ladies at Rondebosch, and ride through the grounds of Groote Schuur and on to the racecourse. Very occasionally, Violet and the young men of his entourage persuaded His Excellency to join them for a day out with the hounds, hunting for jackal.

Indoors, there were the treasures of Rhodes's outstanding library to enjoy: the handsome room, where his leather-bound books were arranged alphabetically, had a large stone fireplace, characteristic of the scale of the house, to warm it on wet days. The billiard room, too, was magnificent and the energetic games here provided an outlet for the pent-up energies of young officers. But it was the back *stoep*, cleverly accoutred by Rhodes and Herbert Baker as an outdoor room, which, as so often in South African houses, was the social centre of Groote Schuur. It could be a smoking room because of its open aspect, a sitting room, cool in the heat of the day, peaceful in the evenings with the noises of the African night beyond the pool of lamplight.

Groote Schuur became the focus of all that was amusing and fashionable in the early, disastrous, days of the Boer War, and Cecily and Violet, excellent chaperones for each other, the magnet for all who passed through the Cape, from Europe or on leave from the fighting. They made a memorable pair: 'I often, or rather always, think of my two dear hostesses of Groote Schuur and should like to settle down after this and live with them somewhere in the country in some splendid and lovely place to be managed by them,' wrote one friend, George Peel, when he was back in England. The strain of the war gave an edge to the zest of their life there. They half-longed for, half-dreaded, news from the front; but in the meantime, they relished their position as friends and confidants of so many – Hedworth Lambton, for example, the naval hero of the hour, and his soldier brother, Billy, siblings of Nelly Cecil; Billy remembered the *stoep* and its company with longing after being invalided back to England. They undoubtedly flirted with some of them, such as Colonel (soon to be General) C.P. Ridley, whose name Violet was at pains to suppress in the correspondence she quoted at length fifty years later in her memoirs.

One of the most attractive young ADCs at Government House was 'Bend'or', Lord Belgrave, next in line to the Duke of Westminster, his grandfather: 'South Africa was full of his aunts, two of whom had come out with one of the voluntary hospitals,' Violet recalled, and he 'adopted a number of others, including Lady Charles Bentinck and myself, and he always began his letters to us "Dearest Aunts", which added to the confusion of the South Africans, who were muddled enough about the English titles of their visitors and how to address them in that informal country.'

Violet wrote to Olive at the end of December 1899:

Our principal event has been the Duke of Westminster's death, which Bend'or only heard on the 27th – five days late – so blocked are the telegraph wires. Poor boy, he is very unhappy about . . . the bewilderment of such a tremendous load being put upon him while he is still a baby – he is not yet of age. If ever there was a fortunate youth it surely is Bend'or. Handsome, intelligent, with one of the most delicious characters I have ever known in anyone, with great charm – a good sportsman – a good companion. I don't think I ever knew a boy who was better fitted out for life's journey. I love him dearly as I think everybody must. His spirits have helped Cissy [Cecily] and me through many a depressed day. He is truly born with a golden spoon in his mouth and no drawbacks as I can see – though I think he may be going to make a foolish marriage – that was why he was sent here. I am afraid his grandfather being dead he may be unmanageable.

Her fears were to prove true. Bend'or's life was to be littered with failed marriages.

'Our wounded – Claude Willoughby and Count Gleichen,' she continued, 'have gone up to Modder . . . I got very fond of Count Gleichen. In spite of a certain obstinacy, he is a dear good fellow – one *does* get to know people here!' Gleichen wrote from the front: 'I have the greatest admiration for both you two ladies, your pluck and cheeriness under circumstances which would have made most women curl up and cry . . . that sprig of myrtle you gave me, too, I shall keep for ever.' Later, in his memoirs, he said he would always be grateful for being able to recuperate there from what he described as shell shock. He had had a narrow escape – at the battle of Modder River a bullet had gone through his neck, just missing his spine.

From the same battlefield, H.A. Gwynne, the energetic Reuter's correspondent, told Violet: 'Groote Schuur appears now like a dim misty vision of something like Paradise.'

As Groote Schuur was only a short drive by Cape cart from Government House in the centre of town, Violet could easily visit Alfred for lunch or a walk in the garden after tea. They met at the very outbreak of war, 11 October, despite it being a 'day of fearful rush', as he put it, and almost daily between 19 and 29 October. Although he tried to conceal it he was often in poor spirits, and pessimistic about the war.

'It is no exaggeration to say that, while I was in South Africa I literally lived on my letters,' Violet recalled later. 'In these days of air travel, of wireless, or telephone communication, people can have no idea of what the post used to mean . . . True, we had telegrams, but, at four shillings a word, this was not usable except for the briefest message, and . . . we relied upon letters. These took eighteen days to come, and only arrived weekly with our English newspapers.' Violet's post-bag revealed England in a jingoistic mood, individuals and institutions alike seized with a desire to tug Kruger's beard. 'The war fever here is at its height,' wrote Herbert Paul, the Liberal politician and writer. 'The clergy are preaching that the Lord is the God of battles (though for Kruger to invoke his name is blasphemy) and the Stock Exchange is unanimous.'

Frederick Maxse had expressed the general incredulity at Kruger's ultimatum: 'Was there ever anything so audacious? *The Times* truly enough said that Napoleon in the meridian of his glory would hardly have dictated such a summons. Bible belief is responsible for much in the Boer conduct: "The Lord will justify his People" etc. etc.' This gave way to amazement that the Boers, 'a mere mob of irregulars', having threatened the might of the British Empire, 'should have contended as well as it had, against trained troops.' Then came stupefied exasperation with the British High Command. 'Are we fools? Or have we lost our capacity and courage?' the Admiral expostulated after the capture of a British armoured train and with it the young Winston Churchill: 'It seems that Mafeking is sustaining the honour of the army – and Kimberley.' As Christmas approached, and things got even worse, the Admiral had the grace to admit, 'Their ultimatum does not now seem as idiotic as it appeared at the time.'

The war had started badly for the British: their troops failed to make headway and the Boers scored many small victories; there was also an apparently interminable delay in the British expeditionary force's arrival under General Sir Redvers Buller. Then because of the weather, 'When the transports were just coming and every man was worth a hundred, the SE wind raged for five days and they couldn't get in [to the Cape docks],' Alfred told a friend, 'and I used to lie awake at night hearing this d----d wind amongst the trees.' He was also worried by the uncertain loyalty of the Cape, extensive areas of which had large Boer populations with no liking for their British rulers.

The longed-for arrival of General Buller with reinforcements in late October was greeted with cheers and with profound relief by Violet, for 'he takes the weight off Milner'. Yet Buller was under no illusions that the British army was properly prepared for war. Violet met the stout, reassuring-looking General at lunch with Alfred on 6 November, when he talked incessantly from one o'clock until five: 'Buller was solidly determined that all will go well because Tommy Atkins "takes knocks better than any other man in the world". But he had no doubt that "if we do pull it off it will be one of the narrowest shaves on record,"' she told Gwendolen.

Buller had decided to split his force three ways: one part to Kimberley, another to Bloemfontein, the Orange Free State capital, and a third, led by himself, to relieve Ladysmith. Almost at once these troops were dogged by inadequate transport, military intelligence and training. They were fighting a well-armed enemy on unfamiliar terrain.

When General Lord Methuen pushed forward to Kimberley, he scored only a qualified victory at Modder River on 28 November, the Boers narrowly managing to save their guns from the British. Seventy-one British soldiers died, including a son of Violet's friend Maria Theresa Earle. Lady Helen Vincent wrote from England telling Violet of the Earles' distress – 'There are days when the web of life seems spun of greyest darkest colour and today is one of them' – and that everyone was in a state of suspense: 'We devour every telegram and listen to every rumour – and I am afraid criticise every movement, though less from captiousness than from anxiety.'

'Black Week', 10-17 December, followed, with three major British defeats – at Stormberg, near the Basutoland border, General Gatacre's force lost 100 killed and 600 surrendered, with two guns. At Magersfontein, near Kimberley, nearly 1,000 men, including many of the Highland Brigade, with their commander General Andrew Wauchope, were mown down by Boers firing from concealed positions; the General was buried on the veldt as the pipers played the yearning air, *Lochaber No More* – a romantic ceremony which could not conceal the humiliation. Even worse came at Colenso, near Ladysmith, on 15 December when Buller's troops tried to dislodge part of the besieging force. The Boers poured withering fire into the ranks of the Dublin Fusiliers, while twelve British guns were lost to the enemy. Buller, having warned the British Government of the Army's inadequacies, was castigated for its failures.

'Thus we are punished for the obtuseness of our superiors,' wrote Admiral Maxse. 'Has Milner any explanation for the extraordinary ignorance we were in, regarding Boer armaments and war prepara-

Billy Lambton convalescing at Groote Schuur, 1900

tion?' In a few weeks the Admiral came out to the Cape and asked Milner for himself.

Violet's mother wrote of

'a terrible week of gloom and darkness in London . . . and still Ladysmith, Kimberley and Mafeking are surrounded . . . It seems interminable . . . London will be empty after tomorrow for everyone wants to get out of it for Xmas and every place will be shut up which will add to the hideous gloom . . . no one goes to the theatres or buys anything more than necessities.

Britain rallied, however; Queen Victoria reminded her Court with words that became famous: 'We are not interested in the possibilities of defeat. They do not exist in this household.'

The army volunteer movement sprang into life as in Napoleon's day. Hundreds of young city clerks joined the City Imperial Volunteers to go out to South Africa in slouch hats and puttees;

prosperous country squires gathered their tenants into mounted units of the Imperial Yeomanry. Rudyard Kipling, bard of the Empire, stirred the young men of England to action and the general public to pay for blankets and boots, with his rousing doggerel put to music, 'The Absent-Minded Beggar'. Despite a robust core of country gentry and their retainers, the Yeomanry, as one friend of Violet's told her, seemed to accept everyone who applied, regardless of age or infirmities, to the derision of the regular Army: 'There is a comic, sorry sight to be seen every morning in front of Knightsbridge Barrack . . . Anaemic looking London Yeomanry trying to hold on to their horses with their thin little bodies and pale little faces looking anxious and keen. There is something of the Opera Bouffe about the Yeomanry part of the business.'

The public took heart from the decision to replace Buller as Commander-in-Chief with Lord Roberts, who was much loved by the soldiers and had captured the affection of the whole nation, all the more so after the heroic death of his only son attempting to save the guns at Colenso. Small and dapper, with a long record of victories, he seemed more human than the formidable Kitchener, who accompanied him to South Africa as Chief of Staff. Everything, it was believed, would come right when 'Bobs' arrived. For the moment, though, all was in suspense.

As for Alfred Milner, the stormy weather at the year's end, the wind still raging from the south-east, matched his inner agitation, however calm a face he showed to the world. He worked harder than ever, but he was stunned by the frustration of his policy, having assumed that the Boers would be quickly defeated.

For comfort he turned to his women friends. He wrote to his mistress, Cécile, far away in London. He saw Violet constantly throughout December: they met one day in three, including New Year's Eve, when she and Cecily Bentinck joined the guests at his dinner party at Government House. Afterwards he lay awake, listening to revellers celebrating the new century by firing their guns, heedless, it seemed to him, of their country's crisis.

CHAPTER ELEVEN

Mafeking

O N 3 OCTOBER 1899, after a 300-mile rail journey through the thorny mimosa and scrub of Bechuanaland, Edward Cecil had arrived in Mafeking. He would not shake its red dust off his boots for eight months.

The dreary little town – Mafeking means 'place among the boulders' – felt fresh in the evening air when he alighted from the train. The sinking sun glinted on the corrugated iron roofs and the shadows softened their new brick walls. Mafeking stood hardly higher than the surrounding plain and was but three-quarters of a mile square; shanties outnumbered houses, and no building, save the railway station and a convent, had more than one storey. The featureless landscape dotted with scrub was relieved only to the east, where faraway ridges of higher ground glowed purple. The view was to become imprinted on Edward's mind over the coming months, as he scanned and re-scanned it for signs of enemy activity or for the longed-for relieving forces. He was still suffering from the after-effects of the fever he had contracted in Rhodesia. A nurse acquaintance of Violet, who had come to the town to offer her services, had been on the train with him and administered 'Cocoa Wine', a tonic she swore by; he took it with relish before reporting to Baden-Powell at his headquarters in Dixon's Hotel.

At least the town was well supplied with hotels, bars and stores; it had its Town Hall, Court House and Market Square; prominent buildings were the Victoria Hospital, the Standard Bank of South Africa, the church, the gaol and Messrs Weil's store, now bulging with merchandise, one of the best-stocked retail outlets outside Cape Town. Leading citizens included the Mayor, the Town Clerk, the Resident Magistrate and the indispensable Ben Weil, owner of the least uncomfortable house in town, where he was soon to use grain bags from his shop to construct an elaborate bomb-proof shelter.

The siege defences, frantically constructed along a perimeter of nearly six miles, enclosed not only Mafeking itself but also a laager for the 600 white women and children, who were urged to take refuge there from enemy fire. There was a native village of 'Kaffir huts', the 'Stadt', with a refugee camp outside it, and a 'location' housing 500 'coloureds' of mixed descent half a mile south of the town. One of the most prominent landmarks, and a key to the town's protection, was a modest eminence, known as 'Cannon Kopje'. From a few aspects the enemy could look down upon their opponents; otherwise there was little advantage on either side, though such small dips and gradual rises as there were could make all the difference between cover and exposure to fire, as British soldiers in Flanders fifteen years later were also to realise.

Edward found the streets and hotels full of recently-arrived soldiers of the garrison: the Bechuanaland Border Police and newly-formed Protectorate Regiment. War correspondents from the various British and South African papers were also conspicuous, deep in conversation and their drinks: Edward would come to know them well as he briefed them at Baden-Powell's behest over the months ahead. The food, at first, was good: better, one observer commented, than in Cape Town's celebrated Mount Nelson Hotel.

The little town was a-buzz with rumours of an imminent attack by thousands of formidably armed Boers, although sporting types said it would be no more dangerous than a season's hunting, playing down the numbers to calm a potentially hysterical population of 1,500 whites and 7,000 black Africans. The Africans included refugees from the mines of Johannesburg: 'Fingoes' (Mfengu of the Eastern province) and 'Shangaans' (Shangana of the Northern Transvaal), but most were local, the Barolongs, with a high proportion of literate, mission-educated individuals. Baden-Powell intended to use them as part of the defensive force.

On 11 October, Edward, as Chief Staff Officer, prepared and posted up Baden-Powell's terse announcement:

War has been declared by the Boers against us from 6.0 p.m., to-day. The duty of the force here is to be ready to withstand any attack, but not, for the present to act on the aggressive across the border . . . The Boers talk of attacking Mafeking to-morrow afternoon. It is probable they will come in two or three columns, probably about five thousand or six thousand strong and try and surround the town. It is only necessary for us to inflict a good blow on them and send them back again – hence it is necessary to lie low and reserve our fire till there is a good crowd of them to fire into and then to let them have it . . . The Boers will never come on and storm a position. They cannot possibly, in or even near the place, if everyone sticks to his post and shoots straight.

By order Edward Cecil (Major) C.S.O.

The whole nature of the coming siege was encapsulated in this notice, starting with expectation of attack. With about 1,050 rifles at their disposal, the British – and the 400-odd armed native contingent who were officially only defending their own homes – were no match in the field for the Boers, of whom there were initially 7,700, under General Cronje; even after Cronje moved to the Transvaal, taking 2,000 men with him on 19 November, followed by subsequent reductions of the Boer force, the garrison was too weak to break the siege without outside aid. However, the defences had been constructed to keep the Boers from overwhelming the town. So it was a question of sitting it out.

British weakness under fire was soon demonstrated on 14 October. A small force of defenders going to the aid of the garrison's pride, an armoured train, were engaged for four hours against superior numbers of enemy, with no prospect of further support, and only just escaped defeat.

Baden-Powell's emphasis that every man must be on the alert at all times had to be maintained for the next eight months of siege: townspeople who failed to observe martial law would not be protected by the military. The unpaid Town Guard, recruited from white and Indian males aged sixteen to seventy capable of bearing arms, was an important part of the defence force. Baden-Powell fostered the whole town's sense of involvement. He organised the making of gunpowder, fuses and even a simple gun, issuing postage stamps and bank notes and making up for the garrison's inferior firepower by ingenious methods of outwitting the enemy, using dummy men in trenches, for example. Rigorous in his attention to detail, he seemed never to sleep, moving noiselessly about the town at night.

Astutely, he treated the Boer enemy with respect whenever possible and kept in regular touch with them. He thanked them for helping to carry the British dead off the battlefield; he gratefully acknowledged the Boer General Snyman's kindness in sending a list of wounded prisoners-of-war and looking after them. Equally, too, he insisted that the enemy keep the laws of war, pointing out to Snyman in January 1900 that the recent Boer shelling of the women's and children's camp and firing on a flag of truce were an abuse of the rules of 'civilised warfare'. When a shell fragment disembowelled a little African boy herding cattle, so that he died four hours later, Baden-Powell informed General Cronje that he was holding him personally responsible.

Edward added his voice, stating officially that if the Boers continued to commit atrocities, he would shoot any prisoner that came into his hands, even at the expense of his own reputation. He was responsible for drawing up the General Orders which were posted in the town almost daily, and received hundreds of neatly-pencilled instructions on small pages torn out from Baden-Powell's pocketbook. As one journalist afterwards observed, his work was ceaseless: 'as C.S.O. he came in for both the external fights and the internal discords. He smoothed down quarrels, dispensed justice, alloyed "siege fever" in all its intermittent phases, and in fact performed the tasks of ten men with unfailing courtesy and inexhaustible patience.'

In his acclaimed history of the Boer War, Thomas Pakenham suggests that Edward deliberately put himself in the jaws of death at Mafeking because of his wretched marriage to Violet and his awareness of her love for Alfred Milner; that he was a sort of self-appointed Uriah the Hittite, out for 'Death and Glory. The Last Stand.' Edward's attitude amounted to 'a moral surrender', Pakenham concluded.

This is a travesty: Edward's bravery was matched by a determined cheerfulness. Edward Ross witnessed him in November, enjoying one of the Sunday cricket matches, between the motley Town Guard and the armoured train's crew. Several months later, hearing Edward entertaining diners with hilarious stories, Ross contemplated selling them to a newspaper; while the Chief Staff Clerk, James Shimwell, observed the way Edward, at a dinner for the staff and the postal clerks, was 'very amusing in giving his daily experiences during the siege and very soon put us all at our ease'. Had he wished for suicide, he had endless opportunities. He preferred to do his duty, and far from morally surrendering, showed great resource.

Years later, when his marriage was really going badly, Edward told Violet he wished he had died before ever involving her in his troubled life. At Mafeking, however, his morale held up – despite his missing Violet and also his mother whom he knew to be mortally ill, and despite chronic bad health from the start of the siege. This he disguised, when he could, as 'lumbago . . . nothing serious'. 'Please don't tell anyone as they might make a mountain out of a molehill,' he told Ben

From Violet's album: 'Nigs telling stories . . .' Edward wore a black armband in mourning for his mother. To his right sits Baden-Powell

Weil, refusing a dinner invitation. 'If you would say that I don't think I ought to dine out until I am quite fit it would be very kind . . . forgive me but you know what I should like to do and what I have to do.'

On 9 December he was officially reported too ill with a fever to carry out the duties of CSO, which were taken over by a fellow-officer. Edward's repeated illness when CSO taxed the patience of Baden-Powell who complained in his notes that Edward was 'pretty well useless' at running the Cadet Corps. Baden-Powell's jauntiness jarred on Edward and the Colonel was aware of it; he must have been annoyed, too, by Edward's tendency to speak his own mind; but, in keeping with Baden-Powell's stress on working together and Edward's Guards' training, these differences did not surface openly. Years later Baden-Powell preferred to forget them.

During the siege Edward's special gifts of tact and social awareness were indispensable for conveying orders, however unpopular, especially during the last desperate weeks of the siege. Unlike many fellow-officers he was at pains to get on with a wide cross-section of both the garrison and the town. A story he told afterwards was of being approached by a man asking whether he could give him a divorce. As he had no power to do this, Edward persuaded the couple to stay married.

He was often called on to mediate between the military authorities and Ben Weil, who was suspected (perhaps not unfairly) of creating artificial shortages to raise prices. Because of their original negotiations, Edward started at an advantage with Weil, and was regularly his guest. Sometimes he backed him up strongly, at other times he intervened to reduce tension. Learning that two junior staff officers who did not get on were invited to dine together with Ben Weil, Edward told Weil he was going to keep one of them back at work that night: 'You know how these little matters worry me so please excuse him . . . I am acting for the best though I regret having to do this.' Edward's diplomatic skill was important, too, when briefing the press, communicating with officers in the front line and receiving their reports; and his judicious outlook was an asset to the military tribunals on which he periodically served as Judge Advocate.

One of his most daunting tasks was presiding at the Court of Summary Jurisdiction, set up in November 1899 to judge the huge increase in offences under martial law connected with the siege. It sat two or three mornings a week, with senior officers and the town magistrate taking turns together as president and member. The magistrate, Charles Bell, a genial and humane man, rapidly became irritated with his military colleagues: 'Conceit, contempt . . . and an indescribable arrogance being the predominant feature of the general run of British officer occupying the higher grades of the service, when they first arrive in this country.' Edward was the exception and, at Bell's insistence, the two nearly always served together.

The court had power of summary arrest of possible spies and traitors for whom the punishment was death and confiscation of goods. Disinformation too could be a capital offence. In one case over which Edward presided, an African had endangered the town with the false intelligence that the Boers' largest gun had been withdrawn. He was sentenced to be shot. Spreading alarm and despondency was punished, too: a lawyer was imprisoned – to the outrage of his dignity – for complaining to fellow townsmen that they were being badly treated. Marauding and looting could be punished 'according to the usual usages of martial law, with death'. For theft of food, capital sentences were meted out only to persistent offenders. More common were fines, gaol or lashes.

Edward, seated left next to Bell, the town magistrate, jointly presiding over the Court of Summary Jurisdiction; Plaatje, the interpreter, stands behind them while the Barolong headman Molema (centre, in white suit) watches the proceedings; the alleged spy, in shirtsleeves, is half obscured by the uniformed figure left foreground

The court's activities, and even pictures of it, have been used by some historians to condemn Baden-Powell and his staff for inhumanity. However, if many sentences were draconian, one has to bear in mind the ever-present threat of starvation and betrayal and even of assassination. At the beginning of the siege, the Stationmaster, Quinlan, a facetious blabberer of Fenian sympathies, had been held in prolonged custody, on suspicion, among other things, of plotting to murder Edward.

Among the court officers' disagreeable duties were to see justice carried out, such as the shooting of a spy Edward and Bell had examined: 'He stood alongside the grave without the slightest sign of nervousness. Death was instantaneous. Six men fired and five bullets went into him. He must have dropped before the sixth was fired.' In all, five death sentences were passed during the siege.

The packed Court House was oppressively stuffy. 'Billingsgate was not in it for smell,' declared Shimwell, the staff clerk; outdoor sessions were preferred. Dress was informal to the point of scruffiness, which would have suited Edward. Bell sweated away in jacket and tie, the staff officers in khaki, while the Barolong chief, Molema, in a suit, kept an eye on proceedings; the lawyer de Kock wore Town Guard uniform or a working farmer's clothes and the Barolong interpreter, 23-year-old Sol Plaatje, wore a collarless suit, braces and flat cap. Plaatje, a remarkable youth who was destined to have an important career as a founder of the African Nationalist Congress, occupied an indispensable position in the court, earning five shillings a day – more than any other African interpreter, thanks to Edward's and Bell's recognition of his worth.

Edward's multifarious duties gave the lie to Thomas Pakenham's dismissive conclusion that 'Baden-Powell was able to give him a task in which he could do no great harm – looking after an improvised cadet corps'. In fact, organising the Mafeking Cadet Corps was a very small part of Edward's work. The inspiration for the Boy Scouts came from it, Baden-Powell was later to say. However, neither man could claim credit for this forerunner of the Scout movement, since the Cadet Corps of white boys, too young for full military service, already existed at Mafeking before either of them arrived. These boys, nimble messengers, orderlies and postmen, operating sometimes at great risk to their lives, were crucial to the internal communications of Mafeking.

As for external communications, 'We . . . have chiefly to exist on the fabrication concocted in the camp,' Bell wrote. 'There are a few prized liars in the place, who are experts at this sort of work . . . But in a way . . . they are useful, as giving us something to talk about and argue over. We cannot get any news less than ten days old.'

Edward read out the first official letter received from outside publicly in the Market Square, on 9 November. It gave welcome news of a British victory at Elandslaagte, near Ladysmith, nearly three weeks before. The Queen's message to her troops in South Africa wishing them 'a bright and happy New Year' arrived on 24 January.

When Edward had learned, by messenger, that their compatriots besieged in Kimberley believed that Mafeking had surrendered and its population was massacred, save for a few women and children, such demoralising reports had to be corrected. Accordingly, press despatches were sent by African runners, who risked being caught and shot by the Boers. Edward's family continued to write to him, but neither they nor Violet at the Cape had any idea whether their letters were getting through or how the siege was going. His few surviving communications to Violet were written on tiny scraps of paper smuggled out in a shoe, or on the back of another letter.

One message which reached Edward carried tragic news. On 24 November an African runner carrying a white flag managed to penetrate right up to the town's defences, before being seen. His eyes were immediately bandaged, and he was taken to Baden-Powell, to whom he handed a letter. In it, General Snyman told him of Lady Salisbury's death four days before. Violet, at the Cape, had prevailed on the military to make sure it reached her husband through the Boer leader Reitz. The Mafeking town clerk recorded, 'This little act of courtesy we all appreciated,' although Baden-Powell was furious that a runner had been allowed to get so far into the town unobserved.

Edward played a crucial part in the exchange of Lady Sarah Wilson for a Boer prisoner. Lady Sarah, the aunt of Winston Churchill, with much of his courage and penchant for self-advertisement, had been busy transmitting information to the British about the war in the Northern Cape. While seeking safety with her husband, Captain Wilson at Mafeking, she was captured by the Boers. General Snyman, determined to drive a useful bargain, demanded an exchange with Petrus Viljoen, an enterprising Cape Boer rebel, jailed in Mafeking for stealing a horse and stirring up Africans against the British. Neither Baden-Powell nor the town's civil authorities were happy about giving up so dangerous a man; but the Boers' alternative was packing Lady Sarah off to Pretoria as a spy.

Edward intervened, pointing out to Baden-Powell that it would be unseemly for an Englishwoman to be taken as a prisoner on the rough journey to Pretoria and subjected to insults and worse. In that event he personally would take the blame, for he shared the responsibility. He and Baden-Powell worked out a compromise in a letter to Snyman claiming the moral high ground: 'The war was at first, and would remain as far as Her Majesty's troops are concerned, a war between one Government and another; but you are making it one of people against people, in which women are considered as belligerents.'

The exchange was effected. Viljoen, looking unrecognisably well-washed and clean-shaven, was brought out of prison and Edward

*Lady Sarah Wilson in front of
her bunker in Mafeking*

warned him that were he ever taken again, he would be shot. Lady
Sarah crossed the British lines, cheered by the troops. Immediately
afterwards, the Boers began to shell the position, 'evidently', as one
onlooker remarked, 'wishing to let her know the dangerous place she
had come into'.

Lady Sarah threw herself into the life of Mafeking, impressing even
the somewhat misogynistic Baden-Powell, whom she joined 'rough
riding' around the defences. She later recorded her gratitude for
Edward's gallantry on her behalf: 'If Cecil had been in any other family
he would have been marked out as a genius.' She felt that he stood in
the shadow of his eminent father and brothers Robert and Hugh.

Although Edward presented a good face to the world, the
confinement, constant sniping and shelling and fear of hunger preyed
on his as on everybody's nerves. From the beginning, the British were
bombarded by the Boers' modern, high-velocity Krupps and
Armstrong guns, as well as a French Creusot monster with many nicknames, such as Black Maria, which could hurl a 94-pound shell accurately miles across the plain, well out of range, though not always out
of sight of British observers. On 17 October, the first day that the
Boer shelling began in earnest, sixty-three shells rained down on the

town where a mood of defiant nonchalance turned almost to one of levity. Edward showed the strain in getting drunk that night.

Once Edward and Bell were eating together when the 'big gun' struck a corrugated iron building nearby. A European was killed, and also an African who had come to clear the table: 'rather an unpleasant entertainment for us, just after our lunch,' Bell remarked, with the grim irony cultivated by the besieged. The shells, falling randomly in the town, killed or maimed many, including women and children, Dutch, African or British, not to mention livestock crucial to supplies.

Although, steeled by Baden-Powell's example, the garrison and citizens proved steadfast, the mania for 'souvenir hunting' could be as dangerous as the shelling itself. One man stood trial before Edward for possessing a live shell; he had hired a soldier from the Protectorate Regiment to defuse it, which he attempted while smoking. When he opened it, he was blown to bits.

Certain rituals soon became established at Mafeking: the hoisting of a red flag at dawn on Dixon's hotel was the signal for 'stand-to', when everyone was to be in a state of readiness. By February, in the orders issued by Edward, only the largest bell was sounded initially to warn of signs of the Boers' big gun being loaded. If its muzzle pointed towards the centre of the town, all bells sounded three times; if in any other direction, six times.

Stress led to drunkenness and sometimes brawls: Mr Parslow, the correspondent for the *London Daily Chronicle*, mistakenly argued with Lieutenant Murchison, a demented officer in the Protectorate Regiment, about the definition of the word 'gentleman'. The gallant lieutenant shot Parslow in the back of the head outside the door of Dixon's hotel. This was just after Murchison had been the hero of the hour for driving off a Boer attack against Cannon Kopje. Edward and other staff attended the journalist's funeral, the coffin carried by his fellow correspondents. The murder cast a blight over the town, but served as a lesson. Bar keepers were warned that they would be fined and their stock destroyed if they served drink to individuals who had clearly had too much. The indiscretions, when drunk, of a young Staff officer, Lieutenant Ronald Moncrieff, eventually landed him in gaol and earned him the contempt of Baden-Powell. Edward, knowing well the temptations young subalterns faced, stuck up for him repeatedly; this cannot have pleased Baden-Powell, who blamed the death of a young trooper on Moncrieff's incompetence.

As 1899 drew to a close, the besieged town did its best to remain cheerful, with a Christmas tree and a party for 250 children of Dutch and English origin. In Lady Sarah's dug-out, resplendent in an outsize Union Jack, she served Christmas lunch, in the company of Ben Weil, Edward, Baden-Powell, Captain FitzClarence, Lieutenant Ronny Moncrieff, her husband and other officers.

That Christmas night, the Protectorate Regiment's dinner at Dixon's Hotel was 'an exceedingly good spread. Such a sight is not often seen, Her Majesty's officers, friends of the Prince of Wales, etc., sitting down to their Christmas dinner in their flannel shirts with their sleeves turned up to their elbows, and looking generally very hot but very comfortable . . . at the same table sit two of our titled British aristocrats, viz., Lord Edward Cecil and Lady Sarah Wilson.' As on Sundays, both sides agreed not to fight over Christmas festivities.

The interruption was momentary. At 3 a.m. on Boxing Day, the press, briefed by Edward, were asked to witness an assault by the Protectorate Regiment on the Boers' strongpoint at 'Game Tree fort'. This heroic though unsuccessful action was to earn three men the VC and great honour for Mafeking in the eyes of the British public. The charge of 'C' squadron, Edward said that evening, had been absolutely the finest show he had ever seen, and it would have been the extreme pleasure of his life to lead such men.

At the burial ceremony that followed, Ross observed his tall figure as he commanded the buglers to sound the Last Post. Two squads of men stood by with reversed arms as eighteen bodies, each sewn up in white canvas, were laid in one long trench, and three officers, in coffins, in separate graves. As one was being lowered by his men, 'the rough hard voice of an old soldier, a hardened character of the world, . . . was heard to fervently ejaculate, "God bless you Captain!" Coming from such a hard adventurer it brought tears to the eyes of many onlookers.'

Edward himself was nearly a victim. On New Year's Eve, just after seven o'clock, when he was still busy at his desk in the sitting room of Dixon's Hotel, a shell burst with a deafening roar in the street outside; one fragment shattered a chimney leading down to his office and whizzed into the room, which was filled with dust and the stench of explosive. Another piece of the same shell killed the steward at a nearby club, carrying away the side of his skull as he crossed the street to Dixon's for his nightly chat. Edward Ross rushed to the office: still sitting at his desk, 'His Lordship . . . very coolly turned round saying

NOTICE.

——

SPIES.

——

THERE are in town to-day nine known spies. They are hereby warned to leave before 12 noon to-morrow or they will be apprehended.

By order,

E. H. CECIL, Major,

C. S. O.

Mafeking,
7th Oct., 1899.

he would lodge an objection, as it was not fair, he said, to shell him down the chimney. He was very much upset nevertheless, and came up to the bar to steady his nerves. I cannot describe the noise of the bursting shell, seemingly right in our midst, but it sounded as if the bowels of the earth had split asunder and the last day had arrived.'

'Shell-shock' – what would now be called 'battle fatigue' – which became a recognised phenomenon during the First World War, was not a concept accepted by medical opinion in 1900. Yet Edward and many others, who repeatedly came within inches of violent extinction from high explosive shells, were afflicted with this condition by the end of the siege.

CHAPTER TWELVE

'A Titled Female Foreman'

ON 10 JANUARY 1900, at dinner in Government House, Violet sat between Alfred Milner and Lord Kitchener, who had just arrived at the Cape with Lord Roberts. Alfred was especially glad to have her company that evening, for the debonair Bend'or, who had done so much to keep him cheerful, had just left for England to attend to his inheritance as Duke of Westminster. The arrival of the two generals gave Alfred new hope of success in this war. Turning to Violet he said: 'I feel now that I shall not be shot sitting.'

But 26 January, before the tide turned in Britain's favour, saw one of its worst defeats, the catastrophe of Spion Kop, the strategic vantage point near Ladysmith taken, then lost, by the British, whose dead lay in packed masses on that tragic hill.

From England, Violet's friend D.D. Lyttelton described the nation's mood:

> This is the first time I have ever seen the whole people feeling the same thing at once. The Jubilee was nothing to it. . . . you can feel it as you walk about the street – every man seems to be your brother and you rejoice in every tall athletic figure. Every servant, every shop girl asks you for the news. My maid was standing on the steps waiting for a paper just when news that Spion Kop was taken [by the British], got up on the posters. An old gentleman bounded up to the door seized both her hands and shook her violently, saying 'Isn't it splendid, isn't it splendid?'

The continually changing public reactions foreshadowed similar swings in the popular mood during the First World War fourteen years later. When the British gave up the defence of Spion Kop, one correspondent told Violet, 'You have no idea of the terrible depression there is today.' Although the British fortunes revived, the danger to husbands, sons and brothers remained; as much as the enemy's rifles, typhoid fever, brought on by drinking draughts of 'Château Modder' ('full of body') and other tainted river water, was claiming the lives of officers Violet knew.

Small wonder that much of the jingoism, especially among soldiers, had evaporated, giving way to gritted-teeth resolution: it was a war of attrition, Edgar Vincent wrote to Violet, 'Go through we must and will: there is no vacillation or failing here – only a grim wish to put the [Jameson] Raiders and *The Times* and *Daily Mail* and Rudyard Kipling on asses' backs in the front line.'

Lord Lansdowne, the War Minister, writing to thank Violet for sending him news of his grandson, Lord Kerry, the High Commissioner's new ADC, told her: 'Naturally no one wants to have parties or gaieties . . . everyone is busy in some way in connection with the war.' Bend'or gone, Alfred Milner's riding company were now Kerry or his secretary, Ozzy Walrond. One evening they rode over to Cecil Rhodes's cottage on the edge of the Atlantic at Muizenberg, where the architect Herbert Baker was then living. They sat on the *stoep* looking at the stars and the lovely outline of the coast towards Sea Point. Such alleviations of Alfred's anxieties were fleeting and his sense of responsibility for the war policy weighed on him. In his diary he confessed to feeling stale from the long strain.

On 15 February Kimberley was relieved and in the Sanatorium Hotel that night Rhodes threw a party where champagne flowed. On 27 February General Piet Cronje, defeated at the hard-fought battle of Paardeberg, surrendered to Lord Roberts and Kitchener with 4,000 of his men, signalling the end of large-scale engagements by Boer armies in the field, though they were far from defeated. Young enterprising commanders like de Wet began a highly effective guerrilla campaign to which the Boers were better suited. Nonetheless Roberts was able to press on rapidly to Bloemfontein, the Orange Free State capital, which was taken on 13 March: the conquest of the Boer republics was taking place in earnest. Ladysmith, too, had been relieved by General Buller on 28 February. Edward Cecil's long ordeal, however, was not yet over: Mafeking remained under siege.

For Violet and other soldiers' wives the answer to the prolonged suspense lay in helping to care for the troops. Horrified by what she saw in Cape Town and heard from visitors and correspondents about the state of the wounded, she determined to improve their conditions. The loss of life through inadequate medical care was one of the greatest disgraces of the Boer War. Altogether about 13,750 British troops died in hospitals out of 450,000 fighting during the whole war; 8,022 deaths were from enteric fever (typhoid) alone. The military authorities' attitudes towards the sick and wounded had progressed little since the Crimean War fifty years earlier, as Violet was quick to point out. At the outbreak of war the hospitals, she told her father-in-law, Lord Salisbury, lacked even necessities which should be supplied by Government. Theoretically, the medical officers in charge could requisition them from either the Government or the Red Cross. They invariably failed to do so.

There were several reasons for this negligence. One was the medical officers' lack of status: until 1898 the War Office had not even granted them equivalent rank with other officers. The Army Medical Corps tended therefore to attract only mediocre recruits and morale was low. In addition, much of their equipment was obsolete or sub-standard. Field surgery, for example, was done by old and feeble oil lamps. This intensified the suffering of the wounded, as did the ambulances which were so shaky that even a healthy man could not keep his seat in one when moving over rough terrain at speed. Medical supply outside Cape Town depended on railway or wagon transport, difficult to maintain over vast distances. Confusion became routine: a current joke was that some railway wagons containing a new consignment of nurses on their way up country had been labelled 'Remounts for the Officers'.

Such problems were compounded by inadequate sterilisation and neglect of commonsense rules of hygiene. The soldiers' attitudes, too, increased the risk of disease. To Tommy Atkins, boiling water − an added chore on a hot and dusty trek − was thought of as somehow unmanly. Kitchen utensils were sometimes washed in the same sinks as the bed-pans of typhoid sufferers. Through lack of communication, officers often sited military camps where there had already been out-breaks of the highly infectious enteric fever. In her despairing letter to Salisbury, Violet reported that a base hospital was being built 'on a flat bit of ground (the site of a condemned infirmary) in the most squalid suburb of Cape Town − Woodstock − where mules have been tethered for four months and where the water stands in the wet season now coming on. It is enough make one cry.' Her appalled observa-tion of the lack of elementary hygiene intensified her worries for Edward's well-being in Mafeking.

To Violet, as to many other observers during the war, the fresh milk shortage epitomised the negligence and obduracy of the medical authorities:

> The minutes of our local Red Cross committees are a standing condemnation of the military system. Every week comes a refusal from some medical officer of comforts urgently required. For instance everywhere they refuse fresh milk – at Nauuwpoort, we had actually bought our cows and hired our man to take care of them – when the one in charge . . . refused saying that tinned milk was better. At Bloemfontein it is worse. Enteric and wounded patients are put together with the result that the wounded patients get enteric . . . In spite of the whole country being a dairy farm the patients never get anything but tinned milk. The nurses are overworked and are getting sick – two died last week. The Red Cross store there has plenty of wine and medicine but as usual the doctors won't requisition.

This contrasted with the enlightened attitude of Edward in Mafeking, who, according to a young bank clerk, Charles James Weir, had encouraged the supply of milk and white bread to typhoid cases.

To the British soldiers' chagrin, the allegedly unwashed and primitive Boers sometimes enjoyed superior medical care. Ivor Maxse, now a Major, advancing with Roberts' forces to Bloemfontein, told Violet he had been amazed, on reaching the little town of Petrusburg, to find:

> a most excellent Field Hospital with seventeen Free State wounded and two wounded Kaffirs. I never saw anything better done than this hospital in the field, which was shown me by the *Dutch* army medical officer in charge. He brought the whole hospital here in December last from Batavia, it being a Dutch army hospital. They had everything you could think of, as our own medical officer who accompanied me said; and possessed eight wagons, thirty three mules and eight horses to carry their stuff about in . . . they actually have a portable gas machine for lighting up the operating tent so that after an action they can operate in brilliant light all night!! If badly wounded I should be better off in a Boer hospital than in a British one: and we all know it.

To Violet these conditions represented a challenge. Her contempt for the military's medical organisation was unbounded. 'Our men are dying for want of the milk and care which it would be so easy to give them,' she informed Salisbury. 'The doctors all stand by each other and the civilians who come out here to get honours are not going to make a fuss.' She blamed General Forestier-Walker, commanding at the Cape, and in charge of the lines of communications, later describing him as 'a charming man, desiring above all things a quiet life, and quiet lives were not to be had in Cape Colony in 1899.' Only outside criticism and fear of exposure by people like herself, was to improve the Cape Town hospitals at least, but the problems up country and at the fronts remained.

She exempted Doctor Leander Starr Jameson, the hero of the catastrophic Jameson raid, and a trained medic, from her criticisms of his profession. Small and bald, with a magnetic personality, Jameson joined the large group of her admirers. Now he filled her in on the unhappy conditions at Kimberley: 'The sanitary arrangements are an absolute disgrace, and the four hospitals in the town, entirely filled with enteric, are simple centres for the production of typhoid, which is becoming very rife among the inhabitants of the homes around.'

Jameson implored her to use her influence with Milner and with Salisbury. In fact, much of the trouble was down to the strategy of Lord Roberts, for whom victualling and general supply work took second place to the movement of troops and munitions. Too few staff officers were put on to organise that side of the work. Count Gleichen, who was, complained to Violet that he was expected to do the work of three and that one of his colleagues had tried to commit suicide because of the strain. In his drive to reach Bloemfontein, Roberts neglected the proper protection of transport wagons – which the Boers raided. As a result, water and food rations for each soldier were reduced. Soldiers took their water where they found it and, with their resistance low after a long march, the effects were predictably disastrous. Roberts did not ignore the state of the hospitals but they were not a priority.

Violet attempted to offer the military hospitals improvements through the British South African committee of the Red Cross, with its access to large funds, but 'The military authorities treat the Red Cross like dirt,' she told Gwendolen Cecil. As a result of her almost single-handed pressure on the none-too-dynamic committee, the Red Cross made more money available, which at least benefited the civilian hospitals.

Seeing the way she lobbied everyone who might be of help, Alfred quipped: 'What the Colony needs is a titled female foreman.' Violet, noting the 'miraculous effect' he had on morale whenever he dropped his work to travel and talk to people, persuaded him to visit hospitals. She and Cecily Bentinck founded the Field Force Fund for comforts and supplies for troops: Gwendolen gathered supplies together, piling

Violet's friend, Mortimer Menpes, who sketched war scenes and characters in South Africa during 1900

them up in the house at Arlington Street which the family described as resembling a grocery shop. Whatever Gwenny sent out was gratefully received.

There was a more frivolous sense in which the South African hospitals were contentious. 'The hospitals may be called the theatre of war,' wrote another correspondent to Hatfield House, Lady Airlie, sister of Alice Cranborne. 'I am so sorry for the wounded,' she continued ironically, referring to the skirmishes among the profusion of smart ladies who had come out to the Cape intent on adventure and were a prominent feature of life in Cape Town early in the war; many stayed on under the guise of nurses. The leading offender was the now widowed 'Mrs Dick', Mrs Richard Chamberlain, Alfred's friend. She had come to Cape Town in pursuit of him, so the tongues wagged, but had been thoroughly trounced by Violet. By March 1900, when Lord and Lady Airlie arrived in Cape Town, David Airlie being an officer in the 12th Lancers, Mrs Chamberlain's antics provided a rich seam of satisfying gossip: 'I have seen Mrs Chamberlain, and have even made her acquaintance which is perhaps less desirable . . . She entirely runs Forestier-Walker, but with Milner she has signally failed. They hardly speak now, and she says she has refused him,' Mabell Airlie wrote.

Other society women who sailed out with their families included another old friend of Alfred's, the bonny Julia Maguire (*née* Peel), who arrived two weeks after the Cecils, accompanying her husband, 'Tommy' Rochefort Maguire, a rich and clever Irish business colleague of Rhodes, and with various other members of her family, including her brother, George Peel, one of Violet's favourites at Groote Schuur, who worked alongside her on the Red Cross Committee. The Tommy Maguires went to Kimberley with Rhodes, and there they had to stay for the duration of the siege, attracting a good deal of personal publicity. After it was over, Julia's father Lord Peel, much embarrassed, ordered her home, whence she wrote warm letters to Violet about George, whom she went specially to see.

In contrast, Cape Society regarded Lady Sarah Wilson, when she eventually emerged from Mafeking, as unaffected, as well as plucky: 'Really she is splendid,' Cecily Bentinck wrote, 'so different to Julia, not a bit a heroine − saying that she had plenty of food − no horse flesh and that donkey etc was really very nice. I never saw anyone with less nonsense − and looks full of commonsense.'

The Portland Hospital at Cape Town, financed by the Duke of Portland, drew numbers of fashionable ladies ostensibly to work as nurses. Among them were the Duke's daughter-in-law Birdie Bentinck, and her friend Dosia Bagot, eager for exciting adventure, like their MP husbands, Lord Henry Cavendish Bentinck and J.F. Bagot, a retired Captain of the Grenadiers, who had both joined the Imperial Yeomanry.

Violet was at pains to differentiate between herself, the public-spirited wife of a serving regular officer, energetic on behalf of the refugees and in exposing hospital conditions, and the flibbertigibbets out for thrills on the veldt; Birdie and Dosia, she wrote,

> look as if they had dropped from the clouds and, no opportunity for heroism likely to be afforded them, are bitterly disappointed. They had visions of battlefields, but even trained nurses are not allowed to the front. Also this place is not organized enough to make a splash in, that is what Mrs Chamberlain has found to her disgust. There is no one to 'épater' which is awfully dull for those sorts of people. They hate just settling down to doing the same things that we have been doing for months!! No crowds to meet them, no national gratitude − nothing but rather a cross overworked official who wishes everyone at the bottom of the sea and says so!

Equally unacceptable to her were those women who arrived at the Cape 'without evening dress of any kind and without any "tidy" clothes'. They were at a loss when invited to tea by well-dressed South African women, or put on a crowded platform covered with flags and told to speak in favour of a war charity. Even in wartime, dressing suitably was important. When Alice Cranborne was contemplating coming out to join Jem, serving with the Bedfordshire Regiment, her sister Mabell Airlie was quite precise in advising her on her wardrobe, which should be, she said:

> about the same as Cannes, by then, and some furs. They want to be tidy, but not too smart as it looks rather vulgar. It is better to have cheap things, as they get ruined here, and not too long skirts. You want a sort of table d'hôte gown for dinner, old summer gowns would do. And I think it would be wise to take one dinner gown with a high and a low body [bodice]. This letter is rather like the answers in 'The Queen' [magazine].

Violet herself was, as always, particular about her wardrobe. Although she and Lady Charles revelled in the unconventionality of Groote Schuur, nevertheless they would never have flouted the rules so much as not to change for dinner: indeed, after long days in hospitals or on committees, to bathe and change was a relief in the evenings, not a mere formality. (The bathing arrangements at Groote Schuur were not primitive: Cecil Rhodes' marble bath with lion taps was magnificent – but it was the only one in the house. On arriving back from Kimberley, Rhodes found young Major the Hon. Billy Lambton, Nelly Cecil's brother, in his bath, 'before he even knew he was in the house'. Rhodes was quite equanimous about this, 'shook hands with him over the edge of it and seems to take him and anyone else as a matter of course,' Violet wrote.)

Mabell Airlie gave a shrewd picture of Violet at the Cape: 'Violet is a great lady here but . . . inclined to carry things with a high hand, and a little apt to annoy by trying to Juggernaut officials – who require to be tenderly dealt with . . . But what I do like about her is that I honestly don't think she has any of the petty jealousies of these other women and she is so serenely happy in her own confidence in herself, that it is quite a rest to be with her.'

Violet, confident in her reliance on and growing affection for Alfred Milner, thrived on being at the centre of things. She did not always feel serene, though she always did her best to appear so, being buffeted by anxiety for her husband at Mafeking. She said that those at home in England had more reliable information from their newspapers than they did at the Cape, where false rumours abounded. On 3 January,

Violet had heard that Edward was wounded at Mafeking: she was told no more. 'And I don't know *when* I shall know, which is the hardest part of all,' she wrote distractedly to her sister: 'I am indeed under the deep waters now, and cannot expect comfort for many weeks, for there will be no rest until this war is over. I think Milner saved my life – at least he has been everything just now and I owe him what I can never even tell him . . . I try not to think of horrors but it is very hard.'

It transpired that Edward Cecil was not wounded, but a Cecil someone else. There had been a mix-up of names. Happily for Violet, she did not hear, until after the siege, of the shell which nearly killed him in his office.

Edward's few short notes to Violet were an exercise in morale-boosting, betraying no pessimistic feelings lest the letters should fall into enemy hands:

> We are all getting on very well with very few quarrels and except we are bored to death no hardship. We have started all sorts of factorys for every kind of thing. We are even making our own matches our own money and stamps for local use . . . I was wretchedly seedy for a time dysentery fever and mental worry but now that is behind me. Tis awfully dull here, Shells are our only interest. I am alternately very glad and very sorry you are not here you would have been all in all to me but I should have trembled every time a shell went Please God it draws near its close now I will write lots but interesting matter I dare not.

Only a scrap or two reached her thereafter, sending her 'all the love in the world' (16 November) and telling her, 'we have a chicken-hearted set of Boers and barring the shells and sniping don't have a bad time and we are used to those' (February). Finally in the last month of the siege, May 1900, he scrawled: 'Dearest V., All well here and going very strong. I only long for the sight of your face. Please don't worry we are practically invincible.'

Violet had been cheered in the New Year 1900 by the arrival of her soldier brother, Ivor, with his bride of a few weeks, Mary Wyndham, youngest daughter of the Earl of Leconfield. They came, Violet wrote, 'at a time when we greatly need comfort. I feel I am here for life and my whole days are at present a pendulum between greeting friends and condoling with relations.' She had found 'being inside this crisis absorbingly interesting, but the strain too great.' Ivor went up country with the Mounted Infantry to Bloemfontein, while his wife stayed near Groote Schuur.

Later in January, Violet's father, the Admiral, arrived on the same boat as Rudyard Kipling and his wife, whom Violet already knew through Burne-Jones, Kipling's cousin. The Admiral enjoyed Kipling's company: 'he is a genuine and delightful schoolboy,' he said without irony. As they crossed the Equator, they had held a concert and sang a poem of Kipling's, set to music by another passenger, William Burdett-Coutts, the MP whose devastating report on the hospitals, published later in the year, forced the Army to face the facts honestly. The Admiral's heart beat anxiously for Violet, being 'in profound ignorance as to news. I have a dreadful vision of Violet in black!' But he found her cheerful. She took him to Government House to dine with Alfred, who impressed him deeply: 'I only wish to Heaven Milner had had more power. His influence would have been most salutary.' Although as High Commissioner – effectively Viceroy – in South Africa, Alfred had been delegated considerable powers by Joseph Chamberlain to lay down policy for the whole region, the elected governments of the Cape and Natal could be obstructive locally. Moreover, military decisions were entirely matters for the War Office and Army. Alfred could only advise and plead, he could not overrule.

Admiral Maxse, absorbed in all that he saw in this new country, and ready to talk to any he met there, took himself off on a tour, and at Kimberley encountered Lord Kitchener, who, despite Maxse's buoyant spirits, afterwards remarked somewhat ominously to Violet that her father did not look strong. The Admiral was suffering from the food: 'The British are splendid colonists but they bring two obnoxious elements, the one in their Sabbath (surpassed in gloom only by the Dutch) and the other in their bad food . . . they can hardly cook an egg let alone their vegetables which are simply steeped like dirty linen in hot water.' Like most soldiers and civilians, he had resorted to a diet of Maggi stock cubes and dry biscuits, supplemented by whatever meat he was offered.

When Bloemfontein, one of the keys to control of the region, finally surrendered to the British forces, it became British Army Headquarters, from which Lord Roberts conducted operations. The Admiral came up to see Ivor, bringing with him a flag for the Guards Brigade, stitched by Violet and Cecily, and many effusive messages were sent to Violet, urging her also to visit, especially from the gallant Major-General Pole-Carew, yet another claimant for the title 'the handsomest man in the Army' (other candidates were Generals

Hildyard and Brabazon): 'The whole blessed Guards Brigade, – and more especially the blooming Brigadier – wish to be permitted to assure you two delightful creatures of their and his extreme gratitude for the really lovely flag you have sent up – it was quite A.1 . . . It looks awfully well flying . . . on the top of a rock in our Rose Garden.' Kipling, too, was there, writing for Roberts's bi-lingual propaganda paper *The Friend*, run by British war correspondents; but the presence of non-combatants in the field was controversial and only civilians with specially issued passes were allowed up country. Ivor Maxse put the fighting man's point of view: 'Violet and Lady Charles are coming here next week – I think ladies are out of place in a military campaign – but as you know – the Admiral is here – and it was he who arranged with Lord Roberts for V and Lady C to come up on some pretence job or other. Bobs never can say "No".'

Cecily Bentinck and Violet, escorted by officer friends, travelled from Cape Town by the mail train. After two nights and a day, they met Alfred Milner's train on its way back from Bloemfontein: 'one of the charms of this country,' Violet wrote, 'is that, as there is only a single line, you can't whirl past your friends . . . you have to get to a siding and wait for them . . . I had flagged Sir Alfred's train so as to see him and get the latest news.'

At the Free State Hotel, where she and Cecily were staying in Bloemfontein, Violet was pleased to receive a note from Lord Roberts with a telegram dated a week previously, saying that Colonel Plumer and his relief force were only thirty miles from Mafeking.

There was much competition to entertain these two attractive ladies. Lord Kitchener wrote wistfully: 'The chief has just broken to me that he insists on your and Lady Charles dining with him tonight as well as coming to tea. This is perhaps as well as he has ordered me off by a 3 p.m. train. I will look in on my way to the station.' Roberts congratulated himself facetiously on thus combining military orders with pleasure: 'It was cunning of me was it not, ordering Lord Kitchener away? Now I hope I may have the pleasure of receiving Lady Charles and you at dinner today.'

On the same day, 5 April, a hospital train arrived in Bloemfontein, disgorging Birdie Bentinck and Dosia Bagot, without official passes, who had evaded detection when the train was searched further down the line. Lord Roberts, furious, ordered them to leave. They stormed and raged but he was obdurate. Violet and Cecily were also asked to go back to the Cape, and did so, as Boer attacks on the railway line

Lord and Lady Airlie, Alice Salisbury's sister and brother-in-law.
He was to die at the Battle of Diamond Hill near Pretoria in 1900

were increasing. Violet had a last vision of Dosia 'dancing up and down on the platform at Nauuwpoort lamenting that she had been too lenient with Lord Roberts!'

Such unseemly behaviour and open love affairs between Society ladies and soldiers attracted the unamused eye of Queen Victoria. Through Joseph Chamberlain, she ordered Alfred Milner to do something to discourage ladies from going to South Africa for the wrong reasons. He was dismayed at the idea of having to put his hand into 'that hornets' nest', but there was no gainsaying the Queen, and a telegram was duly published under his name, dated 10 April, deploring the increasing number of visitors to South Africa whose presence was a hindrance rather than a help.

'There was a great deal of cackle about this message,' Violet wrote on 29 April, relieved to hear from Gwendolen Cecil that Queen

Victoria had asked kindly after her, from which she judged that she was not included in the Royal disapproval. She was also reassured by one general's wife, Katherine Lyttelton: 'It simply said in the best words what most sensible people have been saying for weeks, but don't imagine that anyone lumps you with them. We all know that you have been really working and doing real good, and doing it well.' Mabell Airlie agreed that the Queen 'hit the nail on the head as usual; the whole situation here is undesirable in many ways, but I do think it would be hard if people like Violet and Lady Charles and I had to come back, because a lot of women choose to come out and behave badly – Birdie and Dosia behaved like fools.'

Mabell's husband David commanded the 12th Lancers and the Airlies stayed with Lord and Lady Roberts at Bloemfontein for 'a perfect fortnight with David . . . sitting in an arbour covered with vine leaves, where everyone forgot there was such a thing as war, or sadness.' Lady Roberts's grief for her son, Mabell said, was 'almost more than she can bear sometimes . . . She keeps it from Lord Roberts for fear of worrying him.'

The Airlies' brief idyll was to be their last together. A few short weeks later, he was shot through the heart by a Boer bullet at the Battle of Diamond Hill, the white pony he had had to exchange for his roan mount, which had been shot under him, making a clear target against the *veldt*. 'Thus the Empire lost one of its finest soldiers, one of its most honourable, well-beloved of men.'

Once again, it was Violet, capable and protective, who played a central part, helping the inconsolable Mabell back on her lonely voyage to England. During the rest of her long life, Mabell remained a sorrowing widow, notwithstanding her pleasure in her six children. She deified her husband – her moving book about him, *The Happy Warrior*, is even more hyperbolic than characteristic memoirs of that time.

Violet was by now preoccupied with her father's health, which had deteriorated on his voyage back home from South Africa. In May he died of typhoid, possibly contracted at Bloemfontein. At least, Violet wrote, his end was 'drowsy and painless'. His death left a terrible blank and meant, too, the dispersal of her girlhood home, Dunley Hill, with its happy memories of hunting and rollicking amateur theatricals with her brothers and sister, contrasting sharply with the reality of the drama in South Africa in which she was now playing a part.

In her grief at the telegrams from home about her father, Violet turned to the dependable and reassuring Alfred Milner. What hap-

Milner and his staff at Government House late in 1899. Back row: *Bend'or, Violet, Captain Chester-Master;* middle row: *Cecily Bentinck, Alfred, Colonel Hanbury-Williams, 'Ozzy' Walrond;* front row: *Captain Davenport, Annie Hanbury-Williams. Violet's stance, with her hand on the back of Alfred's chair, reveals a supportive possessiveness startlingly in contrast to the conventionally posed group*

pened between them, on the night of 18 June 1900, to make it so momentous a date for Violet that she remembered it ever after in her diary? Not unusually, she came to stay at Government House and they spent a large part of the evening together. This time, though, his ADC and Ozzy Walrond had gone out and they dined alone. As always, Alfred worked after dinner, on this occasion until midnight. Something made this evening a watershed in their relationship, certainly for her and apparently for him. Was it a declaration of love? A more than usually tender expression of affection? We shall never know precisely, but from this day on Alfred had the supreme place in Violet's heart.

To have the devotion of this pretty, high-spirited woman in the lonely eminence of Government House at this time of crisis meant a great deal to Alfred: 'A letter this a.m. from Alfred Milner. His letter shows his life vividly,' Violet wrote disingenuously in July 1900, 'the masses of work, the anxiety, the disappointments and the lack of everything entertaining "I always say Sir Alfred Milner lives like a monk, poor man", as the French Consul's wife said.' However, Violet's effect on His Excellency's usually formal, buttoned-up self did not pass unnoticed at Government House: 'Sir Alfred is very happy and full of jokes, and chaffs everyone. One sometimes can hardly believe he is the same man as last July,' wrote Annie Hanbury-Williams to Violet, a year after Violet had come to Cape Town. In fact, His Excellency's life at this time included fun as well as government and good works: in late June, he followed a solemn address to a crowded meeting of the Society of the Propagation of the Gospel by joining, next day, a large hunting party from Groote Schuur and the Mount Nelson Hotel: 'A good run and a kill at the end: Winston Churchill is dining . . . Sir Alfred is really wonderful I only hope he won't have tired himself today,' Annie Hanbury-Williams wrote to Violet. 'Don't you think he is the most attractive man you ever met?' she added artlessly.

Many women at the Cape did. His friend Clinton Dawkins wrote to Violet, 'London is a curious place. Politicians seem to be as much interested in the reported feminine intrigues around our Milner as in the struggle on the veldt. One told me gravely that Mrs. Walrond! [Ozzy's mother] and Mrs. Dick were tearing their eyes out pour ses beaux yeux.'

They were all out-manoeuvred by Violet: 'I do think she wants watching from "the intrigante" point of view,' Mabell Airlie had commented to Alice. 'I am a beast to say this, but you will not betray me. She is extraordinarily clever, and there is no doubt that *she alone* has prevented Sir Alfred from marrying Mrs C., I said so to her one day and she admitted it practically. She is far too clever to have any vulgar flirtations with small fry, but I believe there have been stories about her and Lady Charles though I never heard them except through Violet herself and then as the maids say "no names mentioned."'

Certainly Violet and Lady Charles had many admirers, from whom letters poured in from the front: from Lord Stanley, with Roberts at Bloemfontein, asking if Violet could procure him ostrich feathers to make into fans, halved black and white, his racing colours; from Colonel Ridley, describing the ludicrous manoeuvring needed to organise the Mounted Infantry up country. However, Violet was no Society butterfly, despite the vapid impression given in his book by the historian Thomas Pakenham: 'Still more beautiful was the young, flirtatious Lady Edward Cecil, invited by Roberts to visit the front at the end of March, when she inspected the guards. "What great big men" she commented.' In fact, Violet made this remark several months previously in a letter to Lady Salisbury from Cape Town and it is taken out of context.

Violet was, if anything, *too* earnest in conversation, as her brother-in-law Robert had concluded in exasperation. She was well up to an intellectual relationship with Alfred, to discussions of political events and theories, and was involved in future plans for the country in which they had both come to believe. Milner appreciated her sympathy with the Imperial Cause. He thrived especially in the company of young, free-spirited people; and they rewarded his friendship with their devotion. His so-called 'Kindergarten' of political disciples after the war was a celebrated manifestation of this. In a sense Violet was a female member of that Kindergarten, a devotee of what some derisively called the 'Religion Milneriana'. Few men had Alfred's intensity of vision and steadiness of focus – least of all Violet's husband. Adventurous officer though he was, Edward had no such drive to shape the world. Nor did she feel she could rely upon him, as she could upon Alfred.

But Edward was her husband and there is no clear evidence to show, *pace* Thomas Pakenham and other historians, that Violet and Alfred had a full affair at this time. It would not have suited him to compromise either of them; and such recklessness in that context would have been a major distraction from his duties. Their *amitié amoureuse* was characteristic of that period: 'The men of the nineteenth century,' as the historian A.J.P. Taylor put it, 'had the art, now lost, of displaying violent emotion without carrying it to its logical conclusion.' From the Duke of Wellington and Lord Salisbury's mother to Arthur Balfour and Mary Elcho in the opening years of the new century, the shades and variations within acceptable bounds of relationships between men and women, married or otherwise, were infinite. They could flourish without scandal, giving the comfort and solace of female companionship to men burdened with public duties and responsibilities in a predominantly male world, and to women who were married and had families, like Violet, they offered an emotional expression, and romantic diversion.

Violet was young enough to enjoy the social freedom of Groote Schuur while being the centre of attention of an almost exclusively male group. She was also socially confident enough to act, when necessary, as the unofficial hostess of Government House, showing a finely-tuned degree of playfulness which never overstepped the mark. Thus she leavened the formality which sometimes threatened to overwhelm social occasions there, making a face at Alfred if proceedings dragged on.⋆ Her affection for Milner and her flirtations with officers at Groote Schuur were within the context of her life as a married woman: she was clever enough, female enough, to combine them without drawing unwelcome attention to herself.

All this was to come to an end with the relief of Mafeking. As Lord Stanley observed to Violet:

> What a changed world it is too for you and Lady Charlie – no more Groote Schuur – no more freedom – no more upsetting of mustard pots in people's plates – no more champagne in people's eyes – no more bearfighting – it is too terrible to think that you two will deteriorate into two – comparatively – respectable married women . . . what will Groote Schuur be without you? Rhodes – our spare luggage – and nothing else . . . best love to you and the other Groote Schuur darling.

⋆ Thomas Pakenham has interpreted her doing this during a particularly stuffy evening as meaning that Violet disliked diplomatic life, and that this was a drawback in her as far as Milner was concerned; but Violet was an extremely skilful hostess, with enough experience of Hatfield and Arlington Street, and as Lord Edward's wife, to know how to manage formal occasions to an acceptable degree.

CHAPTER THIRTEEN

The Relief

WITH THE COMING of the New Year in Mafeking and no sign of relief after eight months, the inhabitants of the 'little veldt-forgotten hamlet' began to wonder if they could hold out for much longer. Alarming though the sniping and shelling were, more demoralising was the hunger. 'I used to watch Lord Edward Cecil in the office,' James Shimwell wrote: 'he got so thin – I was often afraid he would eat me.' Everybody had become so emaciated, Bell observed, that 'If you haven't see a man for a month, he is barely recognisable.'

Baden-Powell and Edward made every effort to devise a fair ration plan. On 8 January Edward issued the order reducing the bread ration further. It was not long, however, before starvation became a reality, and Lord Roberts having warned that Mafeking could not be relieved until May, Baden-Powell took the momentous decision to reduce the town's population by sending Africans out through the enemy lines under cover of night. Bell witnessed the departure of a group on 27 February: 'The long line of women and children in the starlight had a weird and impressive appearance. One might almost have ridden over them before they could be seen.'

Baden-Powell would not have achieved the remarkable feat of keeping the town alive and in good spirits without considerable toughness. His reputation has suffered from accusations of cruelty, particularly to the black population, but for the most part he was punctilious in insisting that they be treated humanely, including them in the issue of free food and reminding patrols who went out to reconnoitre or recover cattle that on no account were they to burn African farms or injure women and children. 'Women and children, whether White or Native, are to be treated with every kindness and care.'

In the face of shortages and siege fatigue, rows about health, as about food, multiplied. The diplomatic Lord Edward was frequently

Edward at Mafeking

called on to solve disputes between doctors and between the civil and military authorities. By February typhoid was claiming lives. The wards of the Victoria Hospital were thronged with rowdy young soldiers and many desperately ill patients could get no rest – it was 'more like a music hall than a hospital'. There was a dearth of medicines and trained nurses, and the civilian doctor was shirking his duties. By April, as fever spread in the town, Edward was at least able to use his influence with Ben Weil to find ways of supplying the hospital with vital necessities; but the squabbles persisted, and as CSO he had to bear the townspeople's resentment.

In general nobody was really strong or fit for hard work on the miserable diet to which they were now reduced. 'Sowen', a thin porridge of oat husks and water, was a staple diet. By 23 April stocks of this unappetising gruel were running low. Weil's two tons of starch were soon used up in porridge or to thicken soup. A kind of brawn was made out of horse hides: 'Curio hunters – of whom there were many in Mafeking at this time – longed to preserve a slab of it for presentation to the British Museum, but the feat of self-abnegation was too hard to be endured.' Ancient Dutch medicines with even a drop of spirit in them had long since been used up. Face powder, too, entered the diet, as did locusts, reportedly as tender as chickens and tasty as prawns.

A frightful rumour of cannibalism arose – a case, the ever-sceptical Edward felt, for the Court of Summary Jurisdiction, as he told Bell: 'Herewith a wonderful yarn. I fancy they are trying to pull our august legs but if we can "down" the liar we will pull his by placing him in temporary retirement or letting him pay a tanner for his joke.'

The news, on 11 May, that 1,000 men were on their way from Bulawayo to join Colonel Plumer's relief force, was dismissed, in the absence of confirmation, as a regular Mafeking yarn, even though it squared with a telegram from Lord Roberts, published in the town more than a month earlier, that relief would be taking place within a few weeks. The next morning, 12 May, the long-feared attack by the Boers under a youthful commander, Sarel Eloff, was finally launched on the citizens and garrison.

At 4 a.m., covered by a hail of fire from General Snyman's main besieging force, a party of 300 Boers charged through the British lines, invaded the Stadt and set fire to huts as a signal for a general attack. Then a section of this advance force, led by Eloff, seized the British South Africa Police Barracks, where a sizeable part of the garrison was beginning, bleary-eyed, to face another day of privation. Thanks however to swift action by Baden-Powell, Edward and other staff, the remainder of the garrison force moved rapidly. Charles Bentinck was among the foremost and before long his own and other units had stopped the Boers within and without the town from reinforcing Eloff's group, which was now trapped.

Every man was rushed to the defence; prisoners were released from gaol and armed. Many men were killed, including the gaoler, Heale, whose face had become so familiar to Edward over the months at the Court of Summary Jurisdiction. Under the resolute direction of Major Godley, and assisted by men of the Bechuanaland Rifles, Barolong chieftains led their people in a vigorous struggle to cut off the enemy in the Stadt. The Boers held out obstinately, expecting aid from Snyman's force outside. Finally Eloff, cursing Snyman for his cowardice, hoisted the white flag on the barrack and gave himself up, dirty and ragged after fourteen hours' continuous fighting. 'May Satan and all his angels torment you and all yours so that you'll have nightmares for the rest of your lives and may some of you die,' he scribbled bitterly on a letter he received from the Boer camp, feeling himself betrayed by Snyman.

The defenders of Mafeking had proved themselves: nurses risked death to rescue wounded on both sides, and Barolongs saved many lives by capturing a strongpoint before Boers could reach it. Many officers and men of the garrison exposed themselves continuously to murderous fire. Above all, Baden-Powell's command and his supporting staff had proved equal to the occasion.

Meanwhile Colonel Mahon's relieving force travelled north in a gruelling march of 240 miles in twelve days and on 15 May joined up with Plumer's smaller column coming south. During the afternoon of the 16th, staff clerk James Shimwell, at work in Baden-Powell's Office, heard Edward Cecil come in and announce that a battle was going on outside the town. Runners had reported that the two columns had arrived – intoxicating evidence that they were about to be liberated. The garrison artillery was sent up to give support; the pathetic spectacle of their broken-down horses, hardly able to walk as they pulled the guns, symbolised the town's exhaustion.

At 7 p.m., the few individuals wandering about the Market Square lifted their tired gaze to an incredible sight: Major 'Karri' Davies and eight scouts of the Imperial Light Horse, the first of the relief force to enter Mafeking, riding into the centre of town. Davies, one of the toughest of all the Johannesburg Uitlander leaders – a gritty bunch – had also been the first man to enter Ladysmith. It was his way of avenging himself on the Boers who had imprisoned him after the Jameson Raid, four years before. A crowd rapidly gathered, opening bottles secreted against the great day, and cheering and singing until they had no voice left.

Outside the town, the attack of the main British force on the enemy cleared them away within two days. The British soldiers looked in admiration at the abandoned modern-looking breech-loading Boer guns, so much superior to the 'little, miserable, muzzle-loading, out-of-date-antedeluvian seven pounders' with which, to the last, the town had been successfully defended; and they flung themselves on the food supplies left behind. There followed a sight no defender of the town would ever forget – the triumphal march past Dixon's Hotel. After 217 days, Mafeking was formally relieved.

It was some time before communications with the outside world resumed – the post, the road traffic and, erratically, the telegraph service. On 9 June at 5.30 p.m., the first train arrived from the south, bringing food: 'Everyone who could ran to the station and cheered lustily. The soldiers on the trucks returned the cheers shouting "Well done Mafeking".' And they had done well. The reports of Baden-Powell, and diaries of men like Bell, Shimwell and Plaatje, record the courage of men, women and children, black and white.

What the besieged did not realise, cut off on the veld, was that they had become heroes: Mafeking had come to symbolise imperial courage, and, dear to British hearts, ingenuity and defiance in the face of the enemy. Messages of congratulation began to arrive: from the Queen, from Lord Roberts and from towns throughout England and the Empire. Halfway around the world, wherever the map was pink, Union Jacks were raised and celebrations held. Nowhere was there more rejoicing than at Hatfield House. Four-year-old George Cecil was the star of the day: while his father was under siege, he had been given a toy cannon which fired peas at toy Boers surrounding a nursery floor Mafeking. Now he planted an oak in Hatfield Park with a ceremonial spade and christened it 'the Mafeking Oak' with a bucket of water; in the afternoon he and his cousin Moucher led a 'children's procession', and in the evening he lit with a red, white and blue taper an enormous bonfire, in memory of the glorious victory far away on the edge of the desert. On 1 June Alice Cranborne wrote to Edward, certain this time that her letter would reach him: 'I wish you had heard him [George] and Moucher rush in on Saturday the 19th, shouting "Mafeking is relieved, three cheers for Baden-Powell and God Save the Queen."'

When it came to doling out medals and promotions, however, there was, predictably, less generosity in recognising worth. Baden-Powell was raised to the rank of Major-General on 27 May; Captain FitzClarence, who had killed four men with his sword on one day, got the VC – well-deserved, for his award was for more than one engagement. As a General in the First World War he was later to fight and be killed alongside his men, a rare occurrence for 'top brass' in that war. There were some, however, who privately disputed his honour, on the grounds that other defenders of Mafeking, such as Charles Bentinck, himself later awarded a DSO for valour in the Great War, who had equally obeyed orders with great danger to their lives, were not similarly honoured. The black African defenders, some of whom also displayed exceptional courage, could not be officially rewarded because it had been decreed from on high that this was a white man's war, and the fiction had to be maintained outside Mafeking that officially they did not fight; it was ill-judged and ungenerous, like most actions in the war concerning the blacks.

And what of 'Lord Edward Cecil, whose splendid ability and services in Mafeking, have made him world-famous', as Louis Creswicke, contemporary historian of the war, described him; a man whose 'tact, patience and good sense smoothed over many a perilous situation'? Despite his foresight before the siege in doing a deal with Weil to buy up provisions; despite his many and varied acts of gallantry and fortitude, helping to exchange Lady Sarah Wilson, thus ensuring her safety within British lines, meting out summary justice with a fairness and patience which many lesser men would not have troubled themselves to exercise in the circumstances, Edward was passed over for promotion to the rank of Colonel.

He had not been involved in actual fighting, admittedly, but he had played a significant part in maintaining morale and running the military organisation alongside his more conspicuous superior; besides, nobody during the siege was out of the firing line. When James Shimwell, a shrewd observer, summed up his impressions of the siege he singled out Edward for praise: 'Who can help admiring . . . Major Lord Edward Cecil, who by his kindness and cheerfulness has shown everybody an example? Many a time I believe I should have done something desperate had it not been for the way in which he bore his troubles which were far more than mine.'

Edward had been ordered to the Western Transvaal as Acting Commissioner at Zeerust and in this difficult posting needed to bolster up his authority. His lack of promotion was a severe disappointment: 'Rather depressed as they have refused to make me Lieutenant-Colonel, so I revert to Major,' he told Violet. 'I think it is hard as it was part of the inducement to me to take it. If I am to be merely civil clerk to the Commandant I scarcely think they have done me well and I really cannot bother to agree with every ass of a colonel they send through. However we must take things as they come . . .'

The most likely reason for his being passed over was that he was an outsider, with no African campaigning experience – a disadvantage in the eyes of those who had it. Contributory, too, was the fact that the Cecils, as a family, were not self-promoters; they were brought up to believe in public service for its own sake and for the good of others, and not for personal ambition. Like 'Bobs' in Rudyard Kipling's poem, they did not 'advertise', as the common parlance was, and they criticised those, like George Curzon or Baden-Powell, whom they considered to do so.

The British triumphs continued. On 5 June, tanned and travel-stained officers celebrated the surrender of General Louis Botha and the Transvaal capital, Pretoria, with bottle after bottle of Heidsieck, in the city's Grand Hotel. The Belgian military attaché with the British forces, Count Vrede, well expressed the mood of the time as he rode through that pleasant garden city, 'the metropolis of Boerdom': 'Now de war is overre, ve go home. Oora! oora!'

But it was not over. Many of the enemy remained in arms and did not accept defeat. The Army was committed to further fighting by Alfred Milner's insistence on unconditional surrender. Lord Roberts was optimistic he could secure this: the British needed only to push the remnant of the Boer troops into a position where they could be outnumbered and outgunned in the field and the victory would be complete. He stuck rigidly to this strategy during the next few months until he left for England, even though the successful Boer guerrilla tactics were proving him wrong. For Edward, the Mafeking siege, harrowing as it was, had at least ended in a kind of triumph; to be able to leave that hated place had been in itself a deliverance. The campaign in which he was next to be plunged brought only humiliation, to him personally and to the name of Britain. During the months of fighting that followed he became deeply embittered.

His base was the small town of Zeerust, pretty and strategically important, sixty miles north-east of Mafeking. As Acting Commissioner in an area of fertile land the size of Scotland – the Rustenberg district, in what was, as yet, unconquered enemy territory, the Western Transvaal – he played a key part in pacification, accepting Boer surrenders, as required by Roberts, and collecting a huge quantity of rifles.

Violet set out from Cape Town for her reunion with Edward at Mafeking by rail on 26 June, the very day she received confirmation of the news she had dreaded – her father's death. What should have been a joyous reunion was overshadowed by her grief. On the monotonous rail journey to Mafeking she gazed out at the vast plains, her thoughts full of memories of her father.

Her meeting with Edward was poignant, she later wrote: 'We had each had an irreparable loss and he had been under continuous strain for the seven months of the Mafeking siege.'

They met across a gulf of separate and deeply felt experience. For Edward the siege had been a combination of the horrors of war and the petty miseries of a prison; for Violet the war, so far, had been a time of exciting responsibility and social success, a new emotional entanglement, and nagging anxiety about Edward and little George in England; both Violet and Edward had been far away from a beloved parent at the time of their death. After their reunion, they stayed at Weil's house, talking about the war and the future; Edward told her he enjoyed his new work, but complained of 'being fairly fed up with the military' in his district and particularly with the interference of Colonel Vyvyan, Baden-Powell's successor in command at Mafeking: 'I have to reverse his orders and it does me no good. He is a heaven-born meddler with a head like a bad potatoe [sic] and an awful fuss besides but I try to keep the peace.'

Jem Cranborne was also in Mafeking, commanding his battalion of Bedfordshire militiamen, who were based there. Reaching Zeerust, Violet and Edward stayed at the old-fashioned Central Hotel, kept by an Englishman and his wife. To Violet, it was very like an English coaching inn of a century before: 'I feel as if I were in the opening chapter of a Scott novel, the rather long-winded part,' she told her mother. After the arid and desolate scenery round Mafeking, the country appeared a land of plenty. 'At Botha's farm, a few miles over the border, there is an orchard of orange trees, twenty-five feet high and with more fruit than leaves. From Ottoshoop to Zeerust the country is alive with little streams.'

The war seemed far away; news of the fighting was hard to get – exasperating for Edward and those responsible for administering the area, but conducive to a relaxed, almost sleepy atmosphere. There was plenty of food, everyday life appeared to go on as normal, and superficially, at least, there was no feeling that this was a defeated country. A little English church with 'a very nice English parson' completed the picture.

Edward's new work kept him on the move, a relief after the claustrophobia of the siege; it called for diplomacy and political as well as military decisions. The Boers round Zeerust seemed overawed by British power and sick of war; they handed in their weapons, swore the required oath of neutrality and were allowed back to their farms, under British protection. Some even took service in the new administration.

Edward was patient with them but distrustful, unappreciative of their acclaimed independent spirit and unspoiled existence: 'They are a set of barbarians, scarcely educated, with holes where the bumps of honesty and morality should be.' He felt he could achieve more permanent results if Baden-Powell were not in charge in the region: 'That great soldier's view is to pacify the district by the old world method of shooting half and exiling the rest of the population. This to dull dutch minds is disagreeable and leads to soreness.' Also he was convinced B–P's determination to arm the Africans, as at Mafeking, would discourage the Boers from surrendering their own weapons. These open criticisms did Edward's career no good.

In this 'stronghold of Afrikanerdom', there was a continuous threat to bases like Zeerust from marauding Boer forces, though owing to poor intelligence and disinformation by the enemy, Boer numbers were wildly exaggerated. Edward and B-P were agreed in disliking Lord Roberts's 'climbing down policy', which they were supposed to follow, that garrisons should be withdrawn from towns if threatened by a superior force, to avoid British troops being locked up in long sieges. Edward felt it would undo what he had achieved and destroy Britain's image of invincibility.

In mid-July came news of an imminent attack on Zeerust. Armed with his experience of Mafeking, Edward reinforced the town's defences: 'Every position, every tree, every mark that could be used had been measured and the range marked off to make our artillery as efficient as possible. Nothing was lacking that care and military skill could accomplish, to make the position secure.' The plentiful water supply was safe; and there were provisions to last for six months. While trenches were dug, Edward walked among the townspeople and garrison, chatting serenely as if there were no crisis.

Because of earlier unsuccessful enemy activity, Violet had been sent back to Mafeking, but now, so confident were Edward and the garrison commander that he urged her to return – her very presence there would steady the district more than anything and 'I do so seem to lose all interest in things when you are away. I don't think you know what a support and inspirer you are to me. No one else seems to understand what I say. They merely guess at what I mean before I speak.'

She now thought definitely of settling in the Western Transvaal and sending for George – and Olive, grief-stricken by their father's death. Undeterred even by Alfred Milner, who wrote that he did not like her travelling to and fro in a war zone, she boldly set off alone, save a driver, from Mafeking to Zeerust, reckoning an escort would merely provoke Boer gunfire.

Her journey there was without incident, but she was disappointed to find the situation unpredictable and Edward without clear directions from British High Command, even about his authority to make on-the-spot decisions. Despite attacks on Zeerust and nearby Rustenberg, however, he stayed calm; he was so used to bullets that he no longer regarded them as a danger and he was confident of holding out against even a large force. He reassured Violet: 'It might be a bore for you but you would be quite safe in the house. Bullets very rarely go through a wall and they won't shell the town.' However, at church on 21 July she heard a sermon on the text: 'As the shadow of a great Rock in a thirsty land'. Reflecting on the present uncertainties, she thought of the great human rocks that had stood out during the last twelve months, 'of one, in particular, down at the Cape'. There she resolved to go, while she could.

On 23 July, she made her way out of the town and back to Cape Town. Part of her train journey she spent in company she could hardly have chosen – that of Mrs Chamberlain. En route, she heard that Rustenberg had been relieved even before she had left. Edward had been right. The threat was not so great, and they had only needed to keep their heads. Even so, arriving at Cape Town before breakfast, tired and dirty, Violet was grateful to be back at Government House, and to shelter beside the Great Rock.

Alfred Milner had looked forward eagerly to her return. They walked together in the garden that evening before dinner, which was a rather formal occasion, but the following evening her old friend Cecily Bentinck was a guest. Violet returned with Cissie to Groote Schuur. Before her arrival there had been furious gales, whipping up the sea round the Cape into great waves. Now, though it remained blustery, there was sunshine and superb long green rollers surged lazily shorewards to break on the granite rocks, throwing white masses of sparkling spray high into the air.

For just over a month it was like a return to Violet's old Cape Town days, with light-hearted moments when she and Cecily led their guests at Groote Schuur – who included Alfred – in many rounds of after-dinner guessing games. One guest was stumped by having to guess 'the needle with which Lady Roberts worked the flag which now waves over Pretoria'.

Alfred's friend, the journalist E.B. Iwan-Müller, who was staying at the Mount Nelson Hotel, came to recognise how indispensable Violet was to Government House and to 'H.E.'. It was to her that Iwan-Müller turned when he wanted someone to organise a dinner party for Sir Alfred, which would include several prominent Cape politicians; the table was decorated with red camellias, white 'badge flowers' and blue violets; also, it was thanks to her understanding of the nuances of Cape political life that the evening was a great success. When Iwan-Müller went to the Cape Parliament to watch the debates, he frequently found her there, in the Governor's box, and during over-long speeches they would gossip together.

Meanwhile up in the Western Transvaal, on 1 August, Lieutenant-General Sir Frederick Carrington, leading a force of 1,200 men and ten guns from Mafeking to protect a huge waggon-train loaded with supplies for Rustenberg, was attacked by a small Boer force. Despite being a South African veteran campaigner of many years' standing, Carrington proved unequal to the task and ordered a retreat. Later, his force found themselves on open ground outside Zeerust. Believing, erroneously, that Boer forces in the vicinity were numerically superior, Carrington concluded that Zeerust itself was untenable. He ordered the garrison to evacuate, destroying most of their supplies.

Edward was devastated. He protested without avail that there were enough troops close at hand in Mafeking to come to the Zeerust garrison's aid if they were needed. When the order came to leave, he is reported to have wept like a child; he called it the bitterest day of his life. It is not hard to believe. After the long months in Mafeking he had taken part in a successful campaign where the lessons of the accursed siege had been put to good use. Now all that was being undone, and the district remained unpacified until late in the war.

The general's predictions about a Boer presence were absolutely wrong. It took thirty-six hours for the Boers to get round to occupying Zeerust, with a force of only thirty men – a major moral victory for their side which encouraged the doubtful to join them. General Baden-Powell had lost a well-guarded and well-stocked supply base essential to his campaign; worst of all, the Boers who had surrendered and put their trust in the British were endangered. Many must have regretted their earlier submission, as they awaited reprisals from their own people.

Eventually, a force under Kitchener rescued British forces pinned down by the Boers; meanwhile on 13 August an order arrived from Roberts ordering Carrington to re-occupy Zeerust, reversing the earlier policy.

In ordering the evacuation of Zeerust, Carrington had only been following the Commander-in-Chief's general strategy. Lord Roberts was wholly opposed to using up his field forces on the defence of less important places, when they were needed to engage and overwhelm the main Boer armies. This argument would have been stronger had many of his forces in the field been led even half as competently as the garrisons in places like Zeerust. Roberts in any case did not see that the days of pitched battles in this war were over. As the dashing feats of the Boer General de Wet showed, it had become a guerrilla war; to hit back successfully, the British must have supply bases like Zeerust. General Baden-Powell felt thwarted when Roberts ignored his arguments. He and Edward became disillusioned with Roberts's leadership and denounced his strategy openly.

Now Edward joined Violet at Groote Schuur. Much of the time he spent sleeping or going to Government House for meals where he talked to Alfred about his predicament at Zeerust. E.B. Iwan-Müller, at dinner, found him highly entertaining, reminding him of Lord Salisbury in appearance and manner – 'only dresses better'. Edward was anxious to get back to the Western Transvaal and he left on 9 September, seen off on the night train by the two 'Groote Schuur ladies'. By the middle of the month Violet abandoned hope of rejoining him at Zeerust, now a battle zone. 'After 3 weeks of uncertainty, of *wobbling*, I decided that I had better go back to England, and leave Lord Edward to follow when he could. A letter from M. Clemenceau gave me the final push. He wrote: "Why are you not in England where Olive greatly needs you?"'

Necessary though her departure was, she was sad to leave Alfred, now dejected that when Britain had supposedly won the war, its forces seemed to suffer an unending string of defeats. On 19 September he wrote in his diary: 'I have been so frightfully overworked now for months, that I can't distinguish one day of exhaustion and boredom from another.' Every day during the week before Violet left they met for walks in the garden, rides in his carriage out to the Kloof, to talk in the Council Room before dinner, to go to church on a windswept Sunday. On Tuesday 2 October he held a farewell dinner in her honour: among the guests were D.D. Lyttelton, Doctor Jameson and

Cecily Bentinck. The next day they walked together for the last time in the garden and said goodbye, after more than a year.

Annie Hanbury-Williams, Cecily Bentinck and the Duchess of Westminster saw Violet off on the *Saxon*. 'It was a pang to leave South Africa,' she wrote later. 'Such a crowded 14 months of my life had been lived in that beautiful country.' On the journey back she kept mainly to her cabin, resting, for she was pregnant.

Alfred found the separation hard to bear. Despite the lovely weather and a bracing ride on the sands before breakfast he felt 'very low indeed', and was 'still feeling profoundly depressed' the next day. A week later he left Cape Town for Pretoria to discuss the state of the war with Roberts and Kitchener, which was 'a revelation indeed. *Chaos* is a mild term for the state of things here as regards civilian business . . . Pretoria is a lovely little spot – full of water, trees and gardens, ruined by the most horrible vulgarities of the 10th rate continental villadom – German architecture of the Bismarckian era at its worst.'

At breakfast, with members of Kitchener's staff, Edward was present, and the two men had an interview afterwards. Edward was desperate to get Alfred's support for his efforts in the Western Transvaal. His gloomy view of the situation left Alfred with the impression that he was overstressed.

When Jem Cranborne saw Alfred a month later in Cape Town he raised Edward's problems in the Transvaal. Although Alfred did not disagree, he intimated the difficulty of his intervening in a military matter. On his advice, Edward took three months off to recover his health. Alfred emphatically did not wish him to give up his post – for more reasons than simply a desire to help him.

Edward arrived in England on 19 December. In the early evening, accompanied by Violet, he reached Hatfield, where he was presented with an illuminated address by the townspeople. Waiting for them was Lord Salisbury's carriage, which people pulled along by hand; a large crowd cheered Edward. On the steps of the house he was reunited with his father and the rest of his family. With them, too, were the Lansdownes, Gerald and Betty Balfour, George Wyndham and Mr and Mrs Alfred Lyttelton.

Edward addressed the crowd from the steps. Modestly, he said that their cheers should not be for him alone, but for all Her Majesty's troops in South Africa. Lord Salisbury thanked the townspeople for their welcome to his son after his many tribulations in South Africa. There were refreshments for all, round a bonfire lit by George Cecil

*George Cecil at Hatfield with his aunt Gwendolen and cousins Mimer
and Bobbety (later 5th Marquess of Salisbury) in her electric car;
she had little control over it and on one occasion it ran her over*

in the park, while the reception committee was entertained to supper
in the Marble Hall.

Apart from his joyful reunion with George, that Christmas was not
a happy one for Edward, who was having to get used to Hatfield
without its guiding light, his mother. Like many a returning soldier,
he was surrounded by relations who can have had no notion of the
tensions and privations of the war and he was unable to convey its
reality to them.

Violet, at least, had an idea of the nature of his ordeal at Mafeking
and Zeerust but they differed deeply as to what he should do next.
She urged him to return to South Africa; once the war was over, they
could all settle there as a family. They would, in effect, be part of
Alfred Milner's plan for a South Africa settled by the British. Violet
hoped that her brother, Leo, would go and edit the *Cape Times*, and
Ivor would also make his future there. None of her hopes was real-

ised: Ivor rose to eminence in the British Army; Leo was content to continue editing the *National Review*. As for Edward, South Africa, where the war dragged on inconclusively, held no charms for him. As far as he was concerned, there was only one thing worse than being holed up in Mafeking and that was seeing British military gains undone by the misguided policies of the High Command. He cannot, either, have felt easy about his wife's feelings for Alfred, and getting her away from Cape Town would have removed one element of tension in his life.

The British Empire at the end of the century was large enough to offer destinations which interested Edward more. Finally, it was to Egypt and the Sudan, where he had been successful and happy as a soldier under Kitchener in 1898, that he turned again. Lord Salisbury encouraged him; he was coming to see Egypt as central to Britain's foreign policy.

Edward applied for secondment to the Egyptian Army. His old friend Sir Reginald Wingate, now Sirdar and Governor-General of the Sudan in succession to Kitchener, had recommended him as someone to be trusted. Edward received a two-year contract, and, in March 1901, sailed for Egypt. This would be, in effect, home for the rest of his life.

Violet did not accompany him. She remained quietly at the house they had lately bought in Park Street, Mayfair. Here a daughter, whom they named Helen, was born on 11 May – one cheering event in Violet's life during a dark time for Britain. For the Boer War still dragged on, without prospect of peace; and Queen Victoria, symbol of an era of imperial supremacy, had died earlier in that year.

CHAPTER FOURTEEN

Rifts

ALFRED HAD COME to mean more than her husband to Violet. Despite her copious editing and destruction of their correspondence in later years, eliminating all endearments, its sheer volume testifies to the importance of their relationship. Alfred continued to confide in Violet about his stormy political life. When he was on leave in England they met frequently. While he was in South Africa they wrote regularly and she became his political 'mole' in the high political circles in which she moved in England – for example, through her close friendship with Lord Midleton (then Secretary for War).

South Africa had made Alfred world famous. In Britain during the summer of 1900, he and Joseph Chamberlain and Lord Roberts had been national heroes to the country which had signalled its approval that autumn by voting in the Conservatives, led by Lord Salisbury, for a further term of office. In many localities, especially the recruiting grounds of the large boroughs, this had been a 'khaki' election.

In May 1901, when Alfred returned to England for a hard-earned rest, he was given a triumphal reception. In London he was met at Waterloo station by Lord Salisbury and leading members of his Government: Joseph Chamberlain, the Colonial Secretary, Arthur Balfour, the Conservative leader in the Commons, Lord Lansdowne, the Foreign Secretary, and Lord Halsbury, the Lord Chancellor. Together he and Salisbury drove in an open carriage to Marlborough House. There the King was awaiting him and conferred on him the title of Viscount Milner of St James (where he had his rooms) and Cape Town. That evening, at Arlington Street, Lord Salisbury gave a dinner in his honour.

After the ceremonies and the speeches of congratulation came the private visits: following lunch at Claridges given by Joseph Chamberlain on 25 May, Alfred went to see Violet in nearby Park

*Lord Salisbury, the Prime Minister,
greets Alfred Milner at Waterloo
station, on his return to England
from South Africa in May 1901*

Street, recovering from Helen's birth two weeks earlier. Two days afterwards, he called on his longstanding mistress, Cécile, in Brixton, for lunch and to spend the afternoon. The next day he saw Violet again, and met her frequently throughout June. A highlight of that month was dinner and the night at Hatfield, where his old friends Clinton and Loulie Dawkins were also guests. He took Lady Gwendolen in to dinner and had Violet on his left: the next day, Violet showed him round the house, where the portraits, particularly, fascinated him, and they strolled together through the park in beautiful summer weather. Alfred's 'very delightful' visit culminated in a short, pithy talk with Lord Salisbury on South African politics. During the course of the following week, Alfred visited Mrs Dick Chamberlain again, and immediately afterwards returned to Brixton for a night with Cécile.

During the Season of 1901 Alfred's diary was crowded with house parties, dinners and shopping trips with Violet. One of his most agreeable visits that summer was to Walmer Castle on the Kent coast. Violet had installed herself and her children in this handsome ancient fortress at the invitation of Lord Salisbury, who was Lord Warden of the Cinque Ports with Walmer as his official residence. Salisbury found the place inconvenient and insanitary: it was here that Lady Salisbury had first fallen ill, and it had gloomy associations for him; also, 'the moment he put his head outside the portcullis of the castle he was mobbed by enthusiastic political admirers. He hated this and it made him miserable', privacy being essential to the happiness of this most private of public men.

To Violet, the castle was romantic and mysterious. It was a perfect seaside home, on the very edge of the shore, with the beach and bathing huts below from which they could all swim in the sea; or they could sit on the ramparts, sheltered from the wind, where 'it felt like being on board an unusually steady ship'. One September night, at low tide, when the sea had retreated far out, Violet called George down on to the sand where 'he danced about in the moonlight, shouting with joy. I then found I had nothing to dry him with and he was soaked . . . So I took him on my back and carried him up to the Castle . . . That night was a full moon and the ramparts looked like *Hamlet* or *Tristan and Isolde*.'

The artist Wilfred von (later, de) Glehn stayed at Walmer and painted Violet in the rose-filled castle gardens, carrying Helen in her arms, with George in a blue suit at her side; the portrait was one of her most cherished possessions.

Guests enjoyed visits to Canterbury and bicycle rides, taking the train to some far-flung village and cycling many miles back through the beautiful Kent countryside. Violet and Alfred walked by the sea together, and Leo and he sat up discussing South African affairs well into the night after the ladies had retired. Clemenceau, also a visitor, met Alfred for the first time, the beginning of a long friendship. What would the British, this '*peuple planétaire*', do, he asked with a blend of irony and admiration, when the next Lord Milner wanted to take over another continent and found there were none left?

Her two summers at Walmer Castle were some of the happiest Violet spent. Here she was the *châtelaine*, with none of the constraints of her family-in-law at Hatfield. She was free to invite her own family: Leo and Kitty, who played the piano to them every evening, as well as Olive and her mother – and those friends she wanted, chief among

them Alfred Milner. The household was run as economically as possible with her new maid, Alice Campion, aged eighteen, who was to
stay with her for the next eighteen years; the children's nurse, Clear;
a 'summer cook', kitchen-maid and odd-job man. She had her two
children with her, and could go to London for events during the
Season. She did not need her husband in the life she had chosen and
achieved.

Other enjoyable summer visits included a large house party at
Mells, with the Horners, on a hot July weekend; Alfred and Violet sat
talking in the garden until midnight. Their fellow guests were
Millicent, Duchess of Sutherland, renowned for her beauty, the
Asquiths and Arthur Balfour with the woman who loved him, Mary
Elcho.

In London Alfred was given the Freedom of the City at a ceremony
at the Guildhall, and at Marlborough House was sworn in as a Privy
Councillor, along with Cecil Rhodes and Lord Cromer – a high
imperial moment, stage-managed by the ever-flamboyant Joseph
Chamberlain.

All too soon the summer sped past, and Alfred's return to South
Africa was imminent: Violet and he met for the last time for dinner
on 8 August. They would not see each other again for nearly two
years.

Edward had sailed alone to Egypt in March 1901. His marriage to
Violet was never to be the same again. From now on, over the next
seventeen years their relationship veered between rows and sulks,
coolness and courtesy, and even by some good fortune a reconcilia-
tion towards the end of Edward's life. But the divisions between them,
though papered over for appearances' and their children's sakes, were
irreconcilable. They had existed from the beginning. Alice Salisbury
went so far as to consider that their marriage had been

> a fatal mistake, as the years showed, for never were two people more hope-
> lessly unsuited. Their outlook was different, their ideas different, their
> whole scheme of life different. All the best things in him, all the fine qual-
> ities that lay beneath the surface in him made no appeal to her, she simply
> did not believe in them, while all her views of life, her ambitions, her
> friendships, were all to him equally impossible to understand.

Alice went on to remark that Edward was 'much too young and undis-
ciplined at the time of his marriage, and his conduct appeared and

indeed was selfish and inconsiderate.' For the first four years, having neither money nor a home of their own – which meant that they lived with his family – put an additional strain on the marriage. In the cold light of matrimony, the fun and wit, good humour and high spirits of the romantic young Guardsman which had first attracted Violet in Dublin days were not enough to live on.

Edward had matured by the time he had come through the Sudan campaign and the Boer War, but there were other misunderstandings, as Alice Salisbury recounted:

> She was very much interested in politics, and had intended and had thought he had agreed that he would leave the army and go into the House of Commons when he married and she felt she had been cheated when he remained a soldier. I never understood how the misunderstanding came about for there never had been a suggestion of it but it was unfortunate as it did produce a sense of grievance which was never dispelled and which coloured other things.

Alice's clear-eyed portrait, written after Edward's death as a valediction to the brother-in-law to whom she was devoted, nowhere alludes to Alfred as the reason for the unhappiness of the marriage; nor do any family letters. Violet herself destroyed nearly all evidence of unhappiness between Edward and herself, just as she played down the importance of her feelings for Alfred, who had crystallised her disaffection for Edward and replaced him in her affection.

Edward knew that his wife was greatly taken with Milner, but neither man was the type to discuss it, to bring it out into the open, nor was there any point in making it an issue. Violet was Edward's wife and he intended that they should stay married. Alfred was as private as he was discreet. His reputation was not that of a ladies' man – quite the opposite; he was no seducer. Some even thought of him as 'not the marrying sort', devoted to his clever coterie of young disciples, the 'Kindergarten'. Rumours of his homosexuality persist to this day, but so does one that he sired an illegitimate child in Egypt. Neither is substantiated in his diary.

From 1901, the more the Cecils lived apart, the more they drew apart. Violet was disappointed, as Alice said, by Edward's decision to stay in the Army when she watched the progress of his brothers, Jem and Hugh, now an outstanding parliamentary orator, as she thought right for sons of the Prime Minister. But Edward went his own way, to Egypt, where he was to achieve high office. Clemenceau's prediction at the time of their marriage, that never was a woman so capable of working upon her husband as Violet, was not destined to come true.

It was also a question of timing, Edward was a late developer, and as his sister, the ever-perceptive Gwendolen, remarked in a letter to Maud in 1906, 'I was again impressed with his great ability – his powers have really developed, widened and deepened in the last few years – and that without losing his old talent for delightful description which makes everything amusing in his hands.'

Alas, this late flowering of her husband's abilities had come too late to be appreciated by Violet. His family motto, *Sero sed Serio*, translated as 'late but in earnest', did not work. In the twelve years they had been married, their differences – his insouciance as to arrangements and time, his flippancy, so charming when they were young – had come to seem irresponsible and irritating to her. Violet, an extremely ambitious woman, was exasperated by what she saw as her husband's lack of initiative and by his family's habit of discussing their affairs in minute detail, instead of plunging in and getting on with life, as her family did.

This was not lost on the observant Gwendolen, who wrote,

As regards his domestic position – well I think that if the watershed is not already passed he will be over it soon. He probably thinks he wants Violet still but I am afraid I think that it is almost too late for her to change now; – I don't think he would be now quite as happy with her as he is without her. That wasn't so a year ago – perhaps it isn't quite as yet – but it's a near thing. If he doesn't live till he's too old and dies in harness I don't think his life as it is arranged at present will be below the average of happiness . . . all of which would contrast favourably with a rather grumpy wife who didn't 'keep a place' for you to come when you felt inclined but had a right to be annoyed if you didn't come whether you felt inclined or not . . . with such a socially attractive man as Nigs it was sure to be like that – oh isn't she a fool!

She concluded that Violet's going to Egypt to set up house with her husband would *not* necessarily be a success.

Alice's character sketch concludes:

Fundamentally they were completely unsuited and living apart so much, their difference of outlook became accentuated. She felt he had failed her in the beginning and no subsequent change was of any use, she felt no further responsibility for their life. Deep and great as his remorse was and hard as he fought against it, yet I think he resented this and her difference of outlook and absence of religious understanding made a perpetual bar and sorrow.

There was no question of an official separation, as there had been with Violet's parents, still less of a divorce. Quite apart from the Cecil family's profound religious convictions, that would have meant a public scandal. Edward and Violet remained man and wife, even if their marriage had little of the day-to-day companionship and mutual support normally provided by that institution. Whatever the Cecils may have thought of Violet, she was still a member of the family, and George and Helen were invited to stay with their cousins at Hatfield – although not as often as Violet would have liked.

The Egypt to which Edward sailed in March 1901 was technically neither a colony nor a protectorate of the British Empire. As an autonomous province of the Turkish Empire with an hereditary viceroy, or Khedive, it was subject to the Ottoman Sultan at Istanbul; but although theoretically nothing had been done to limit the Sultan's legitimate rights over Egypt, the British were the *de facto* rulers. They ran the Egyptian Army, and British 'advisers' sitting on a powerful council effectively controlled the departments of state and the Khedive's ministers. Lip-service was paid to Egyptian representation in government, but the bodies set up were deliberately ineffective. The Khedive's authority had been whittled away and the real power in the land lay with the British Agent and Consul-General of Egypt.

That 'the veiled protectorate', as Alfred Milner described it, worked effectively was largely on account of one man: Evelyn Baring, Lord Cromer, who with Curzon, Milner and Kitchener was one of the British Empire's grandees. He had become Agent – the modest title chosen to play down Britain's domination – in 1883, when he was forty-two.

The British army had occupied Egypt since 1882, when it entered the country to crush an Egyptian nationalist revolt, led by Colonel Arabi, against the Khedive and the Turkish Sultan, which, the French and British realised, would threaten their own influence in the country. For even before that France and Britain had tried to control the country indirectly, to ensure that the Egyptian government repaid to foreign creditors the colossal debts run up by the Khedive Ismail. After Arabi's defeat, the new British 'veiled protectorate' inaugurated seventy-four years of British domination. The French, who had failed to help Britain in the crisis, were excluded from this arrangement and remained a resentful element in Anglo-Egyptian affairs until the Entente Cordiale of 1904 and, to some extent, after it.

Cromer, 'the Lord', or 'El Lud', laid the foundations of British rule in Egypt along lines which Alfred Milner admired and had hoped to emulate in South Africa. Like Alfred, Cromer had been nominally a Liberal, with socially progressive views, but his imperialism meant that he had more in common with the Conservative Party. He was a master of finance, and in modernisation and economic improvement his achievements in Egypt were impressive. He successfully fought corruption, though to his disgust *baksheesh* continued to oil the wheels of trade. The use of forced labour by villagers for public works – an inefficient and oppressive system – was abolished. The *courbash*, or whip, used to enforce law and order and persuade labour gangs to work, was generally discouraged. Brutal punishments such as eighty lashes for smoking in the street during Ramadan, and excessive police powers, were suppressed. The result was a rise in crime, but such was the price of humanitarian reform.

Following the financial reforms set in train by Cromer and Edgar Vincent, the Financial Adviser, foreign investment in Egypt revived, and with it major irrigation projects such as the Nile dam at Aswan, 800 miles south of Cairo. The amount of cultivated land increased by a quarter during the next thirty years and the country – and the government – enjoyed an unprecedented prosperity from agriculture, mostly cotton. With stringent government economies and an honest administration, at last the huge debts incurred by past Khedives could be paid off.

While Salisbury did not envisage that this arrangement and the concomitant military occupation would last long, and feared their effect on relations with France, Cromer was convinced that Egypt, the flagship of Empire, though not formally part of it, must continue to lead the way in economic progress and enlightened administration. Salisbury finally accepted the strategic argument that Britain had to stay there to safeguard her Suez route to India. Cromer also persuaded British official opinion that England's mission was 'to save Egyptian Society', and it would be irresponsible to give Egyptians their independence before they had learnt how to rule themselves, which would take at least a hundred years.

He had no high opinion of his subjects. He despised 'the feeble organising powers of the Oriental', and called the 'contemptible flattery' which accompanied all the Egyptians' dealings 'a thorn in the side of the Englishman in Egypt'. To Cromer, 'The want of accuracy which easily degenerates into untruthfulness is, in fact, the main characteristic of the oriental mind.' He thought the Egyptians improvident, superstitious and mentally torpid: 'devoid of energy and initiative, stagnant in mind, wanting in curiosity about matters which are new to him, careless of waste of time and patient under suffering.' For this he largely blamed Islam for what he saw as its intolerance, its subjection of women, its acceptance of slavery, its fatalism, its approval of harsh, excessive punishment.

Consequently he dismissed Egyptian nationalism either as Pan-Islamic Muslim fanaticism – dangerous, but little to do with Egypt as a nation – or else as fashionable salon political talk. It had no reality, he argued even as late as 1907, because there was no Egyptian nation: the true Egyptians, the majority of the population, the peasants or *fellahin*, had always accepted foreign domination. There was no native ruling class above them. The other 'Egyptians', including those in government, were Coptic Christians, Greeks, Armenians, Syrians, Turco-Egyptians, Jews and other Levantines; or they were North Africans and nomadic or 'semi-sedentary' Bedouin. He saw little threat, therefore, from nationalism as such, but to be on the safe side he discouraged spending on advanced education for fear of creating an unneeded class of over-qualified professionals clamouring for political power. When nationalism revived in the mid-1890s under the influence of the lawyer Mustafa Kamel, Cromer continued to ignore it and Kamel's nationalist paper, *Al-Lewa*. He believed it would wither away as national prosperity and peasant land ownership increased, which was happening, albeit slowly. After a few years, support for Kamel did indeed decline; but many grievances over rural poverty and indebtedness remained and it only required an 'incident' to start up the nationalist cause again – as was to happen in 1906, five years after Edward arrived.

Edward had known Cromer since the Sudan campaign. Now he was destined to work with him directly and, gradually, he came to see Egypt through the Agent's eyes. For the next seventeen years he remained a supporter of Cromer's views on Britain's mission in Egypt: to clear the government's debts by promoting irrigation, agriculture and trade and curbing public expenditure; to promote law and order and justice; to raise the *fellahin* from their condition of abject poverty;

to inculcate principles of honest and responsible government in the Egyptians; and to uphold British power there until its job was done, however long it took. He found Cromer had much in common with Lord Salisbury as Foreign Secretary and also matched his industry, working daily from six in the morning till eight at night with few breaks. Cromer, like Salisbury, was cultivated and well-read. He had started life as a soldier and worked his way up in the Army, but it had been his diplomatic skill and grasp of international affairs – and finance – which had raised him to his high position. He had a gift for languages, and had taught himself ancient Greek, but was no solemn and pedantic scholar. Strangely – almost perversely – he had never troubled to learn Arabic, relying on staff to do so and to find out for him what he wanted to know. Among his friends as a younger man had been the painter and master of nonsense verse, Edward Lear. He was impressive to meet without being intimidating: 'Lord Cromer is a real man and it is a pleasure to know him,' the young diplomat, Cecil Spring-Rice, had found. 'He is a stalwart, high coloured man with white hair and clean-shaven face and a quick kindly way of talking which is unlike that of most diplomatists that I have ever met.' Those who worked for him did so willingly, for he inspired strong loyalty; but they were also well aware that behind his patrician assurance and considerate manner were a formidable intellect and will which came down hard on slackness and incompetence. He was an autocrat and he ruled Egypt autocratically, albeit benevolently. 'Everything centres round him and he looks as if he knew it and liked it,' Spring-Rice wrote. 'No sign of worry or anxiety, but confidence which inspires confidence.'

A few months after Edward's arrival, Violet and George, with Olive, came out to join him in Cairo. The baby, Helen, was left in England. For much of the time during their stay, Edward, on army duties, was far away in the Sudan, a dangerous region, forbidden to European women. When he was in Cairo, the young couple were sought after and sociable. Cecil Spring-Rice, who arrived in Cairo at the same time as Violet, found that 'The Cecils are certainly the most charming and fascinating company: each and both, especially both. I see as much of them as I can.' He thought Violet 'clever enough for ten: also extremely nice to look at, and eminently alive'.

Violet immediately came up against the strictures of the English colony which revolved around the Cromers, whose every move, and guest list, was watched and analysed. There was little intercourse with the, mostly Muslim, Egyptian women, who lived secluded lives. While Violet was in Egypt, one high-ranking officer in the Sudan service, who married a Muslim woman, was demoted by Sir Reginald Wingate ostensibly on other grounds, much to the annoyance of Cromer, who thought well of the man. The fact was that mixed marriages were frowned on, though Wingate was widely criticised for his handling of the affair by his colleagues, and Violet was clearly shocked. Such social contact as there was with Egyptian women remained formal and limited, not conducive to forming friendships.

Two days after her arrival, an afternoon which Violet spent with Lady Wingate encapsulated life there:

> I had to be 'presented' to the Khediva . . . Lady Wingate took me in a carriage preceded by running footmen to a dreary looking 'Palace' outside Cairo. The Khediva was a heavy looking woman. She spoke a little French and our conversation was formal and banal, but one of her daughters (she had no son) had recently had typhoid and I asked her how the Princess had been treated during her illness. She had, of course, no European Doctor or Nurse. 'Oh', said the Khediva, 'we moved her every day to a new room.' It really wasn't a bad plan to run away from the germs they couldn't control.
>
> One thing amused me on the way home. Our coachman overtook and passed Lady Cromer's carriage. Lady Wingate was dreadfully upset. I told her that Lady Cromer wouldn't even notice the incident, but she wrote and apologised, and Lady Cromer and I, comparing notes about this, felt that we both had a great deal to learn.

Violet was married to a man who cared little for protocol, beyond normal good manners; the niceties of dress and precedence meant nothing to him, as had been the way during his upbringing at Hatfield. But in Egypt Violet, as his wife, would have been expected to observe them rigorously – which she found constricting, especially after the freer atmosphere of the Cape.

Cromer's second wife, Katherine, a daughter of the Marquess of Bath, whom he married in 1901, three years after his first wife's death, was an exception: large-hearted, socially broad-minded and sympathetic, she was able to move without too much friction into the semi-regal position thrust upon her by marriage to 'El Lud'. She loved Egypt, ancient and modern, as much as she was indifferent to the expatriate social life.

The company to which Violet was for the most part restricted

*Lady Cromer, wife of the British Agent in Cairo,
with her son, the Hon. Evelyn Baring*

consisted of the English administrators and their wives, a coterie which she regarded as at best narrow and at worst self-congratulatory, who contented themselves with gossip and household affairs; at dinner their husbands tended to talk shop. There was a limit to Violet's interest in irrigation and the prospects for the cotton crop and what 'El Lud' had said to whom and why he had not said it to someone else. The excitement, the status which she had enjoyed in South Africa could not be replicated in Egypt. At Cape Town, the scene of a major imperial drama, thronged with some of the liveliest and most entertaining of the British aristocracy, her social gifts and talent for organisation had been continually employed. In Cairo society, among Egyptians themselves, women had a subordinate role, and too much self-assertion and enterprise among the British wives of officials were felt to harm the British image in Muslim eyes as well as arousing petty jealousies.

Cecil Rhodes and Dr Jameson visited Cairo at the beginning of 1902. Rhodes's progress through the old part of the city was characteristic, scattering largesse indiscriminately, talking to all-comers, from the priest in the temple to the pumpkin-seller whose cart he had inadvertently upset, with his usual unselfconsciousness. He was also generous to Violet, as he had been in South Africa; he presented her – insisting that she must accept it as a gift – with his fine black horse. The horse joined the menagerie of donkeys and other mounts at the house just outside Cairo which Violet took at the end of January when the rainy weather made the city unappealing: 'the smells are indescribable, the mud simply dreadful'. Here, in the pure air of the desert, Violet enjoyed riding, sometimes with Cecil Spring-Rice and Count Gleichen, who was also stationed in Cairo, and George who went out on his donkey.

Nevertheless, Violet was not sorry when the temperature rose and the 'Khamsin' wind started blowing in March, the signal for her departure for England and her reunion with Helen. She was not to return to Egypt for ten years. Increasingly disappointed with her marriage, she was also disappointed with Cairo itself. Although a fashionable destination at that time, it no longer lived up to its reputation for international elegance. 'It is now nothing but an entirely dull and ordinary place in which everyone is pretentious and idle and inclined to be smart,' wrote Spring-Rice, 'except the workers, whose salaries are low and don't count.' He meant the Anglo-Egyptian officials like Edward. He described the *nouveaux riches* who were drawn by the international financial world dominating Cairo; and the newly-built palatial hotels, thronged with rich Americans spending their husbands' money and surrounded by bowing uniformed attendants. Edward was to find this too: 'All the people who used to go to Monte Carlo come here and gamble in land and stocks. These people don't care what they spend and drive the prices up daily.' Cecil Spring-Rice, like Violet, was relieved to leave. In 1903 he went on to the Embassy in St Petersburg, and his successful diplomatic career took him eventually to Washington as Ambassador, and lasting fame as writer of the hymn 'I Vow to Thee My Country'.

Violet knew, too, that the children's health would be at risk in Cairo. Olive was bedridden with typhoid for many weeks of their stay, which had meant removing little George from the household out of the way of infection. Before Violet was the difficult dilemma faced by many wives throughout the British Empire: to stay with their husbands and part with their children, or bring the children up in England, seeing their husbands only rarely. Violet soon decided. She wanted no more long separations from her children, and she preferred to make her life in Europe. Also, she would have more fun there.

On her return to Hatfield, Violet noticed the decline in Lord Salisbury's health. He had slowed up, and Violet described him as

Lord Salisbury in old age, with two of his grandchildren,
Robert ('Bobbety') and Beatrice ('Mimer')

'torpid' as he shuffled slowly across the polished floor of the Long
Gallery or was wheeled in a chair to the chapel. 'I think he misses his
work, misses the grindstone on which to sharpen his mind.' But he
still enjoyed family life above all, as she wrote to Alfred: at dinner,
'Lord Salisbury was delightful. Linky was explaining that the reason
why the clergy are more popular with the poor than with the rich was
because the rich "never see the clergy except at a disadvantage". "You
mean in the pulpit," said Lord Salisbury at once.'

In July 1902, two months after the Boer War had finally ended,
Salisbury, who had stayed on to maintain continuity, felt that he could
retire as Prime Minister. He missed the old Queen and disliked Edward
VII, although the King honoured him at his last audience at
Buckingham Palace with the gift of a little jewel case which Lord
Salisbury thanked him for and took home without opening: when
asked what was in it, 'I don't know,' he replied indifferently. Gwendolen
opened it and found a jewelled Grand Cross of the Victorian Order.

For the King's Coronation he was content to stay at Hatfield while his family attended Westminster Abbey. Violet wore a gown of pink brocade with thick écru lace, a wrap of pink chiffon and black velvet detail; she wore 'all the jewellery I possess'. She enjoyed driving to the Abbey in the Salisburys' carriage with Bob, Nelly and Gwendolen. From her seat in the north choir she had a good view of the throne and altar. Below were the massed ranks of the peers: 'I could have dropped a biscuit on Bend'or's head'. She greatly admired Queen Alexandra, 'a dream of beauty', as much as she despised the portly, vulgar King and the company he kept. Afterwards, Lord Salisbury was 'a very good audience . . . ready to listen by the hour to our accounts of all the doings he was thankful to have missed.'

His health was not helped by his regime: 'he lives on stimulants, claret, brandy and soup', and he hardly took exercise. His 'speech is less to the point. Only when some of his old subjects are talked of, Turkey, Persia and the like, does he show his old powers.' Attended by the devoted Gwendolen, he continued quietly at Hatfield during the next few months. In the summer of 1903 Edward was telegraphed with news of his father's rapid deterioration; he left Egypt immediately, but arrived too late to see his father, who had died peacefully, surrounded by his family. Salisbury was seventy-three. The simple funeral was delayed until Edward's arrival; on the last day of August his father was buried beside the wife he had so loved, with his extensive family thronging the Cecil burial ground in the little parish church.

The death of such a dominant and much-loved father left a gap which was hard to fill. Jem Cranborne, aged forty-two, became 4th Marquess. The emotional void was particularly hard for the unmarried Gwendolen. Her father had been all in all to her; she had been his constant companion and amanuensis. During her mother's last illness she had shouldered many of her responsibilities, and after her death Gwendolen accompanied her father on public visits, to the Queen at Windsor, for example, and organised the household at Hatfield.

Edward showed a sympathetic understanding of her particular loss, writing to her shortly after Salisbury's death:

> Please remember what the Bishop [Talbot] told you and that you are suffering from a real illness and not at present fitted either to judge or decide anything about your future yet . . . remember that not one hair of

your head falls to the ground except by the will of the most capable and best judge of your affairs. There are still many to whom your happiness is of the deepest concern and for their sake you have much yet to do and much happiness to bring to them.

Gwendolen's visit, with her brother Hugh, to Edward in Cairo that winter was the tonic the three needed, not least because in Lord Cromer they found many of the same characteristics as in their father, and someone who could talk to them about him with the affection and familiarity of an old friend, as well as commanding their respect as a statesman: 'Cromer has the same breadth and grasp of a question, the same almost contempt for all the petty sides of a question and the same gift for witty jeers at the topics of Egypt and the day' as Salisbury. In him was the same combination of irreverence and capability, of courage to take responsibility, decisiveness and statesmanlike breadth of vision.

Gwendolen concluded less reverently, 'He would be attractive anywhere, but here on his own dunghill he is quite delightful. He talks continuously, indiscreetly, and largely about his own business; with a keen sense of humour and an absolutely original and unconventional way of treating every subject . . .'

Katie Cromer deftly managed to mitigate the formality of Agency life. 'She is amusing in the character of an uncrowned queen (which position she accepts with much wry grimacing).' To Gwendolen's relief, she accepted the idiosyncrasy of her own wardrobe with equilibrium: 'There's a good deal of society for which my wardrobe is singularly unfitted. With one morning and high evening gown, both old and rusty, I have attended royal and official banquets, and Khedival functions in the height of the Cairo season. Luckily Katie has a soul above dresses.' This was the highest compliment Gwendolen could pay to one of her own sex.

Under Cromer, Edward's promotion was rapid: based at Cairo from 1903 to 1905, he was Agent General of the Sudan Government, with responsibility for liaison between it and the external world; primarily, he was the sole channel of communication between the Sudan government departments and Cromer. In addition he was head of Military Intelligence. No British soldier or civil servant was well-paid, but his income did improve. 'He is sending or about to send £300 home out of his pay, which is really a sign of grace . . . he is in high favour here, and his work is certainly important and responsible. The office is really an entirely new one – one for which he is specially fitted and, if you can say so to anyone, necessary, owing to his peculiar personal relations with both Cromer and Wingate.'

Edward by now had an Egyptian Army rank, *Lewa*, equivalent to that of Major General in the British Army. His highly responsible position was not reflected by his rank in Britain, which remained that of Brevet-Major; and the War Office in London, sticking to the book of rules, suddenly warned him, in 1903, that he would revert to a mere Captain unless he sat an exam including, among other things, military history, a subject he had long since pushed to the back of his mind. He agreed to do this, with eventual success, after appeals from Wingate and Cromer to the bureaucrats of the War Office, to his regiment in London and to Lord Roberts had failed to get more than a postponement of this pointless imposition. It was, as Gwendolen said, 'farcically exasperating' and humiliating, considering that he was involved in crucial civilian work.

His responsibilities increased as Cromer's and Wingate's confidence in him grew. In 1904 he was entrusted with the supreme command of all troops in Egypt whenever the Sirdar was absent. In the same year Cromer appointed him Under-secretary for War in the Egyptian government, and in 1905 Under-secretary for Finance. His Sudan work had already involved him closely in economic affairs; as Gwendolen reported, he was 'practically minister of commerce and plunges boldly into questions of tenders, concessions . . . markets etc. – I have no doubt with admirable effect.'

The country was entering a new and more tense phase. In the summer of 1906 the British authorities overreacted to an incident at the village of Dinshwai in the Nile Delta, when peasants killed a British officer and attacked others following a misunderstanding largely of British making. Amid fears of fanatical Muslim sedition, a tribunal was set up to try the case. In a tragic miscarriage of justice, several *fellahin* were hanged and others lashed or imprisoned for life. Overnight, the Egyptian nationalist movement gained a million supporters, and Cromer's reputation as a just ruler plummeted; for though he was in England on leave and was upset by the sentences when he heard of them, he shared the Foreign Office view that it would undermine British authority to set them aside.

The Dinshwai incident, like many important episodes in the history of the British Empire, started insignificantly, but it was destined to have profound repercussions on Britain's role in Egypt.

In Cairo, Edward lived in what amounted to a bachelor establishment. Not domestically adept, he allowed servants of varying degrees of competence to run the household. He missed family life. Loneliness ran like a thread through his letters, sometimes manifest as homesickness, sometimes as a nostalgia for 'pre-war' days – pre Boer War, that is; sometimes he could detach himself and throw himself into his work; sometimes melancholy threatened to overwhelm him. The tenets of Christianity, which included, of course, the holy and irrevocable sanctity of marriage, increasingly sustained him. 'As time goes on I seem to see the dawn brighter and clearer in the sky' – the dawn of the celestial kingdom. His father's death, 'whom of all mankind I loved the best and for whose sympathy and counsel I would pay any price' was made more bearable by the conviction that they would be reunited in the next world. Sometimes his father and his mother both seemed very close to him, so close that he could hardly believe that he could not communicate with them in the material sense.

CHAPTER FIFTEEN

Alfred Milner, Success and Failure

ALFRED MILNER had been sucked back into popular politics. Soon after his return to South Africa in 1901, he was to fall victim to the waywardness of the British electorate that he had always mistrusted. The leading opposition party in the British Parliament, the Liberals, were divided by the war – one reason for their failure at the 1900 general election. A small but influential section, the Liberal Imperialists, strongly supported the war effort. They included admirers of Alfred such as H.H. Asquith, R.B. Haldane and Sir Edward Grey. On the opposite wing was an equally small faction of 'pro-Boers' whose leading members included the young and radical David Lloyd George. In the middle, the majority of the party, led by Sir Henry Campbell-Bannerman, accepted the fact of the war, while being very critical of Chamberlain and Alfred Milner's policies.

The Liberals' opportunity to savage the Conservatives came in the summer of 1901. A scandal blew up about the policy, inaugurated by Lord Roberts, of gathering Boer non-combatants (and many blacks) together into 'Concentration Camps'. This was in order to prevent them from providing supplies and refuges during the prolonged guerrilla war, which was the form Boer resistance now took throughout the territories the British had conquered and much of Cape Colony. Boer farms were frequently burned. Neglect of sanitation and supply by the British Army – already a scandal in its own hospitals – rather than from any motives of 'ethnic cleansing', led to the deaths of thousands of women and children from malnutrition and disease as a result of their incarceration. Miss Emily Hobhouse, a leading opponent of the war in the indomitable Victorian upper-bourgeois mould, exposed the frightful state of these camps. It was a foul blot on Britain's humanitarian reputation, and is still remembered today, when the war has almost faded from popular memory.

In this, Sir Henry Campbell-Bannerman at last found a cause under which to draw together his party by blackening the Government. Alfred bore the brunt of the Liberals' attacks. The shrewd Campbell-Bannerman detested the Milner cult, as staunch House of Commons men always detest non-parliamentary *éminences grises*. In fact Alfred, as soon as he heard about the state of the camps, was appalled. He inspected them and enforced immediate reforms, which the military accepted. This was not enough to redeem him in the eyes of most Liberals, who held him responsible for all the failures of Britain's policy in South Africa. Now they attacked him whenever they could, and the 'calm' Alfred of the first year of the war, who seemed to be keeping his head when all about him, in the words of Kipling's 'If', were losing theirs, became embittered and felt persecuted.

The war ended at last in May 1902. Over the next three years in South Africa Alfred flung himself into the enormous task of reconstruction, which demanded all his best qualities of patience and careful thought. At his side was the dedicated team of clever young men from the Colonial Office and Oxford – the 'Kindergarten' – who were to perpetuate his ideals into the next generation. They would work for a strong, united South Africa and a Federated British Empire across the globe whose members would be close partners of Britain. These devoted supporters included Philip Kerr, subsequently British Ambassador to the USA; Lionel Curtis, afterwards founder of the Institute for International Affairs at Chatham House; John Buchan, the future novelist and Canadian Governor-General; Fabian Ware, subsequently creator of the Imperial War Graves Commission; and Geoffrey Robinson (Dawson), later Editor of *The Times*. For these the Empire represented the future and modernisation – not domination and exploitation. Their vision, and Milner's, was the product of many years of hard thinking and practical responsibility and it rested on an unquestioned assumption that it was Britain's right to impose this world order on the territories she had conquered.

In August 1903, when Alfred returned to Europe on leave, he visited the German health resort of Karlsbad. Here one of his flirtations was with the famous romantic novelist, Mrs Elinor Glyn, who was infatuated with another imperial statesman, George Curzon, though she boasted – as was her wont in talking of illustrious men friends – that Alfred loved her. This was an exaggeration; he saw her occasionally, in London and Paris, over many years, but too briefly for her to rival Violet in his affections.

At Karlsbad, Arthur Balfour, Salisbury's successor as Prime Minister, telegraphed him, pressing him to take the post of Colonial Secretary – to no avail. Alfred refused, believing he could serve his country better in Africa and he was confident of eventually gaining a British Cabinet position.

He had not bargained for one of the most contentious issues of his South African career, indeed of his whole life – the Chinese labour question. The war had disrupted the Johannesburg minefields. To revive the country's economy and thus encourage immigration from Britain, gold production must resume in addition to lesser industrial and agricultural activities. It was proving hard, however, to attract African labour back to the mines after the war, so, to meet immediate needs, a large contingent of low-paid indentured labourers arrived early in 1904 from China. These unfortunates, separated from their families, were mostly confined in compounds when not working long hours down the mines for six days a week. They were subject to various summary penalties without legal redress. Alfred, as the man responsible for the ordinance establishing this unhappy arrangement, was furiously attacked in Parliament by the Liberals.

The worst part of his ordeal was to come – in England. In spring 1905, increasingly frustrated by political wrangles in South Africa, he decided to resign as High Commissioner. It emerged that before he had finally left Africa, he had authorised the use of 'light corporate punishment' to deal with outbreaks of violence among the Chinese coolies. Apart from humanitarian considerations, it seems almost incredible that, after the earlier angry response in Britain to Chinese labour, he did not judge how disastrously this introduction of summary caning would play into the hands of the Liberals baying for his blood. But there was an oddly ruthless streak in the upright and honourable Alfred where important imperial issues were at stake. As far as he was concerned, punishment by caning was hardly more, after all, than Englishmen had long been accustomed to at their public schools. What mattered to him was that this temporary Chinese workforce should behave itself and get on with the job of speeding up the country's economic recovery.

The political furore over the 'light corporal punishment' moved beyond Parliament. After a series of defeats on other matters, the Conservative Government decided to resign at the end of 1905. The election of January 1906 that followed was a disaster for their party. They had been in office too long; and their opponents, briefly united, brought every weapon to bear against them. The spearhead was an attack on them – and Alfred – for the iniquitous treatment of the Chinese labourers. Liberal politicians dwelt on the all-male labour camps where unnamed 'vice' was said to flourish, and on the threat which cheap imported labour from the Far East signified for labouring men everywhere. During the election, the slogan 'Chinese Slavery' was enough to raise an anti-Conservative roar; and one Liberal candidate employed a party worker, dressed as a 'Chinaman' in shackles, to stand dumbly on the platform during denunciations of the Conservatives and Alfred Milner. Meanwhile, Alfred's old Liberal allies, Grey, Haldane and Asquith, already embarrassed by the Chinese revelations, were persuaded to work with Campbell-Bannerman and accepted leading positions in his Cabinet.

As a result they did not defend Alfred publicly in March 1906, when he was censured in the House of Commons for authorising the practice of summary flogging. Owing to an amendment by Winston Churchill, the censure refrained from naming Alfred, but Churchill's speech was, according to Asquith, 'ungenerous, patronising and tactless' and the slur on Alfred's reputation remained, extending, by implication, to his whole conduct in South Africa. Thus the once widely admired Proconsul – 'a Roman of the Augustan age', in Philip Kerr's not wholly original description – became the whipping-boy for the Liberals, his reputation tarnished. Was it for this, Alfred asked himself, that the long-drawn-out war had been fought?

Conservatives in the House of Lords and in the Commons prepared for battle, inaugurating a party struggle which would rage until the First World War. A resolution passed in the Lords applauded Alfred's African administration. Among these supporters, the former High Commissioner had come to represent the disinterested man of integrity in dark times – a champion of his country against socialism, class war and the destruction of Empire which the trivial Liberal hacks and radicals were aiding and abetting. This had long been Violet and Leo Maxse's view.

As well as the Colonial Secretaryship, Alfred had been offered the post of Viceroy of India, but he had refused this too, reluctant at present to accept any further burden of responsibility.

In July 1906, he bought the country house where he was to live for the rest of his life, Sturry Court in Kent. In *Country Life*, a writer, typically of that period, linked it with the achievement of its owner: 'an old quiet Kentish house on the edge of a Kentish village, in view, up

Sturry Court, Kent, from the church tower. Violet, along with other artistic female
friends of Alfred, helped to restore and embellish the house and gardens

the Kentish river scene, of the lofty towers of the Kentish cathedral.
The scene is England of the English, still and peaceful, yet alive and
prosperous. It is exactly right as the choice and cultured retreat of a
great public servant.' However, during the years after his return, the
'great public servant' appeared a defensive and disappointed figure to
his less intimate acquaintances. Beatrice Webb, the pioneer Fabian
socialist, went with her husband Sidney and the manager-playwright
Harley Granville-Barker to visit Alfred in his new home. The Webbs,
as patrician and theoretical in their way as Alfred, had earlier supported his South African war policy as representing the forces of mod-
ernity and improvement against backward bigotry. Beatrice, a tireless
inquisitor, impatient with social niceties, described their meeting:

> An old Tudor house, giving almost the impression of an inhabited ruin, a
> garden surrounded by a deserted backwater . . . seemed a fit setting for
> that stern rigid man, brooding over the South African victory – or disas-
> ter? At first he was constrained; but after lunch he unbent and, from
> democracy to the present government, from the present government to

their policy in South Africa, from this to the war and its results, we drifted on until we reached intimate conversation. We tried to cheer him by suggesting that after all the friction and abuse after the war and its devastation, there remained the two republics merged in the Empire. That was (if you believed in its rightness) a sufficient accomplishment for one man. This government would not last more than four years and they could undo little of the past. But he would not be comforted. 'It is well for you to be optimistic,' he retorted. 'You say you are always in a minority, but events are moving your way; whilst my house of cards is tumbling down.'

Alfred defended his actions over Chinese labour to them, his only regrets being that he had given his opponents their chance. Both the Webbs and Granville-Barker – whose controversial plays tore the mask away from Victorian public attitudes – felt the loneliness of the man and his moral detachment, as they saw it, coupled with his high integrity. As she listened to 'his feeble, forceful voice, watched his rigid face and wrinkled narrow brow, noted the emphasis on plentiful capital, cheap labour and mechanical ingenuity', Beatrice felt him impoverished by his arid nationalism and his lack of any loving relationship:

> Milner, though a public-spirited, upright and disinterested man, does not believe in the supremacy or even in the relevance of the spiritual side of things – goodness is a luxury to be arrived at after a course of money-getting by whatever means, and of any blood-letting that may be necessary to the undertaking . . . A god and a wife would have made Milner, with his faithfulness, persistency, courage, capacity and charm, into a great man: without either he has been a tragic combination of success and failure. 'He would have been made by being loved,' summed up G[ranville] B[arker] as we rode away.

Beatrice Webb was always quick to condemn; but she was not alone in her views which have contributed to the myth of Alfred as the unfeeling, theoretical solitary. There was a core of loneliness in him, and he nursed a deep political grievance. His mind did indeed turn largely on figures and theories. His reading was often of the driest, such as Shadwell's *Industrial Efficiency*; like General von der Goltz's *Das Volk in Waffen* (A Nation in Arms), the books impressed him greatly, being on a subject dear to him: the efficient mobilisation of a nation's resources. Yet he had an aesthetic side, responsive to poetry and natural beauty. Clearly, too, the Webbs knew nothing of Violet's devotion, and made no allusion to any attachment on Milner's part – only to the lack of it. In fact, however, alongside his dedication to his work as South African Proconsul, he had maintained his many close friendships with women, some of whom were strikingly attractive, and nearly all of whom, as ever, sought him out as a confidant. They included a childhood friend, Bertha Synge, the author of books for children about the Empire, the Marchioness of Londonderry, Mrs May Gaskell, who had been in love with Burne-Jones, Lady Helen Vincent and Lady Desborough. In South Africa, Mrs Poppy Annesley, the younger sister of Loulie Dawkins, was frequently in his company at his official residence in Johannesburg during 1901, almost as though she had replaced Violet as his companion there. His relationship with Cécile was discreetly compartmentalised, revealed only in the briefest of entries in the diary he kept all his life.

The loyal Alfred never, it seemed, dropped anyone to whom he had given his friendship. Cécile eventually married and went to America (but she and Alfred had a reunion in England several years later); 'Mrs Dick', 'seen off' as a matrimonial prospect by Violet, remained in his life; and he and Margot Asquith corresponded at length for years.

A glance at his diary, even in 1906 when his attention was taken up with the Chinese labour affair, is enough to show how much pleasure he took in women's company. Before moving into Sturry he rented a house at Sutton Courtenay on the banks of the Thames, an idyllic spot in where he enjoyed many romantic evenings on the river, one at least with the alluring Norah Lindsay, with her Grecian profile, famous as a garden designer: 'We drifted slowly down to Clifton Hampden and returned by moonlight', he wrote.

Alfred also had a wide circle of male intimates to whom he had strong emotional ties. Of these, Clinton Dawkins, like Alfred, had been Private Secretary to George Joachim Goschen as Chancellor of the Exchequer, and later Under-secretary for Finance in Egypt. In the summer of 1905 the urbane Clinton fell ill with the heart trouble that would kill him at only fifty-one. Alfred spent some time with the Dawkinses on Lake Como; at the Villa d'Este hotel they played cards, went for rainy walks and read Dante aloud. Alfred was at pains to consult the doctors, reassure the distraught Loulie and make their daughter Dolly's sixteenth birthday a happy one.

Ever since he too, had worked at the Exchequer for Goschen in the 1880s, Alfred had been welcomed at his home at Seacox, near Hawkhurst. When Lord Goschen died in 1907, Alfred grieved. The old man, a robustly-built avuncular figure, with his Victorian gravitas, his great bushy-browed head and mutton-chop whiskers, had been his mentor, teaching him the highest standards of financial administration, and sharing with him a brand of Liberal Conservatism which cut across sharp party divisions. His exuberant Irish granddaughter Moira, orphaned in her teens, later became a close friend of both Alfred and Violet.

Goschen and Alfred had another important element in common – their German antecedents, although both were disturbed by the growth of Germany as a world power. Alfred still kept up his German friendships. In 1903, for example, he made an elaborate detour on his return journey from South Africa to visit his parents' grave at Tübingen, to organise its restoration, and to call on old schoolfriends, cousins, and, in a nursing home at Winningen, his father's second wife Elise, old and broken in health but overjoyed to be reunited with her renowned stepson.

This was characteristic of Alfred, the benefactor of many, not just illustrious, friends. His promising private secretary in South Africa, Ozzy Walrond, lately awarded a CMG, suffered a paralytic stroke on their voyage back to England in 1905. Alfred took endless trouble to get him the right medical help and enabled him to resume some kind of a career. Eleven years on and throughout his highest wartime responsibilities, Alfred repeatedly visited in an asylum another friend, Charles Boyd CMG, Cecil Rhodes's former political secretary, who became insane in 1916 – visits which were very distressing to Alfred. To the end of her days, Alfred also gratefully paid a pension to Lizzie, an old servant who had looked after him and his alcoholic cousin, Marianne Malcolm. He never forgot Marianne either and devotedly tended her grave.

In the summer of 1905, Violet took Wanborough Manor, later famous as a training base for secret agents in the Second World War and a short train ride away from where Alfred was lodging with Clinton and Loulie at Polesden Lacey, a graceful Georgian manor near Dorking. Violet and he met frequently for lunch or walks. When he came to stay, she and George met him in a pony cart and trotted back to the house while Alfred's confidential servant, Axten, followed with the luggage. Afterwards at nearby Compton they visited the Watts Memorial Chapel, shrine of pre-Raphaelite admirers such as Violet. In town, now that Alfred was beginning to take on directorships in the City and other responsibilities, they met at Violet's club, the Ladies' Empire Club at 69 Grosvenor Street, to lunch at the Savoy and walk in Battersea Park, or to see the progress of the portraits by the painters Maxwell Balfour and Theodore Roussel for whom he was sitting.

Late in the year, Alfred was constantly at the Dawkinses' London house, keeping vigil at Clinton's bedside. When his friend died he helped the grief-stricken family, arranging the funeral and obituaries. For the rest of his life he continued to be the family's protector, and while Violet was destined to be his greatest love, Loulie Dawkins seems to have been, for years, his most frequent female companion.

The following year, he moved into Sturry Court. Its name was derived from the stream that meandered past, the Stour, meaning 'river'. The house, reflected in its waters, had once belonged to the Abbey of St Augustine until its dissolution in 1538, and had been the home of the last abbot. Parts dated from monastic days; an upper bedroom was still known as the chapel. Among the ancient buildings on the estate were a fine fourteenth-century tithe barn, a gazebo and a brick Tudor gateway with an avenue of pleached limes beyond it. Alfred first slept there during September, in 'the Monk's Room'. Violet helped him to choose curtains and carpets, and encouraged his restoration of the neglected house and gardens. He enjoyed making these improvements which included a graceful Chinese wooden bridge and a pavilion designed by the otherwise mundane architect Sir Reginald Blomfield. Inside, Alfred kept the furnishings simple, more like a traditional farmhouse than the palace that his illustrious neighbour, Lord Kitchener, was making of Broome Park, with its works of art and fine porcelain. Sturry Court and its estate soothed and inspired Alfred in times of stress over the next twenty years.

He was now a director of the London Joint Stock Bank and the Bank of Egypt, and later of a marine insurance company, of the British Bank of West Africa, of the Egyptian Mortgage Company, and, eventually, of the Rio Tinto mining company. He was also a trustee of the Rhodes Trust – alongside Kipling, Jameson and other close friends – which met regularly throughout the year; its financial affairs and scholarships and its promotion of imperial projects in Rhodes's memory occupied much time, as did his enormous, empire-wide correspondence. He found it difficult to shake off his worries about the future of the empire, particularly that his political enemies at the Cape might dismantle his efforts – as he often wrote to Violet over the years – and he brooded on Britain's incapacity to defend herself in a war against a continental enemy. He was not alone: this was fast becoming a national obsession, and the constant theme of articles in papers such as the *Daily Mail* and the *National Review* as well as in 'invasion-scare' and spy novels, a very popular genre.

Over the next ten years the pursuit of his imperial aims was to involve Alfred in most of the major political conflicts of the period. In 1906 Joseph Chamberlain, the most powerful voice of the New Imperialism in politics, suffered an incapacitating stroke following a carriage accident. Alfred was full of foreboding, though he cheerfully drank 'Great Joe's' health at a huge banquet where he was guest of honour on Empire Day, that now long-forgotten date of celebration on 24 May. Many began to think of Alfred as Chamberlain's successor. Chamberlain had largely converted the Conservative Party to tariff reform, a policy to protect all the industries and agriculture of the British Empire with a tariff system, but chiefly intended to bind the Empire closer together. It fitted Alfred's ideas of a 'permanent organic union' and led him now to support actively the party which believed in it. He travelled to Canada to preach the message. The opposition to federation in the Dominions, which cherished their own sovereignty, proved a major obstacle to achieving his dream.

At first the British public was unreceptive to tariff reform, aware that it would put up the price of bread. However, during the high unemployment of 1908, the idea of a protected British industry began to appeal, particularly as the Conservatives promised to use the customs duties to pay for social reform. The Liberals began to lose by-elections, so in 1909 they countered with Chancellor David Lloyd George's famous budget which, without sacrificing the sacred principle of Free Trade, offered a package of social reform to be paid for by increased income and inheritance taxes and a new tax on land. Because it attacked landed wealth, but above all because it eclipsed the social appeal of tariff reform, Alfred and his Conservative associates were incensed. Their leaders resolved to veto it in the mainly Tory House of Lords. Traditionally the Lords could not contest money bills, but they argued that this budget was radical social change masquerading as a fiscal measure. In retaliation, the Liberals decided to abolish the veto powers of the House of Lords, which the Tories, powerless in the Commons, had been using repeatedly to throw out Liberal legislation and embarrass the Government.

In 1910 Alfred was to emerge as an uncompromising champion of the House of Lords alongside the aristocratic old guard, such as Hugh Cecil, Willy Selborne and Jem Salisbury. They rallied Tory backwoods peers to defend the veto; but the Liberal Government, narrowly surviving two general elections that year, threatened to overwhelm the Tory Lords with hundreds of newly created Liberal peers. The majority of the Lords, opposed by a 'die-hard' rump which included Alfred and members of the Cecil clan, accepted defeat and the loss of their permanent veto, keeping only a two-year delaying power.

The Parliament Act of 1911 signalled the end of the peerage as a central political force, though it remained important for several decades through wealth, experience and social influence. The struggle was to bring Alfred new friends and allies; and the bitter debates primed him for his aggressive campaign against Home Rule in the following years. They were to alienate him from his former friend and political admirer H.H. Asquith.

With imperial defence much on his mind, Alfred joined the National Service League, led by Lord Roberts, which campaigned for compulsory military service to match the huge conscript armies on the continent. Violet helped him and Kipling too was a major crusader. Alfred was also to attract a circle known as 'The Round Table' which shared his hopes of closer Empire ties. This included members of his South African Kindergarten, old allies such as the author and politician Leo Amery, and new friends such as the writer–entrepreneur F.S. Oliver and the multi-millionaire Waldorf Astor. They published a heavyweight journal, the *Round Table*, on political and social topics. Members of the group gathered for periodic 'moots' to discuss the issues of the day and imperial federation. Oliver was often their host, at his town and country houses; Leo Amery too, Waldorf Astor at Cliveden and Jem Salisbury, eager to discuss imperial defence but not sharing Alfred's views generally, at Hatfield. Here two of the Kindergarten, the high-minded Philip Kerr and the loquacious Lionel Curtis, met Jem's astringently humorous daughter Beatrice (Mimer) and both proposed to her; she refused, thus escaping, it has been said, 'two of the greatest bores in the British Empire'.

For much of this period, Alfred operated almost conspiratorially, as suited his subtle nature. Real political power was to elude him until the end of 1916.

CHAPTER SIXTEEN

Great Wigsell

Now violet too found the house of her dreams, although to
many the derelict manor of Great Wigsell, near Hawkhurst on the
Sussex-Kent border, would have been a nightmare. But she saw past the
rat-gnawed floorboards, the rot-infested walls, the uncut grass growing
up to the front door, to a romantic vision of the Jacobean age, waiting
for her sure touch to bring it back to life, and to surround it with
smooth lawns, mellow brick walls, topiary and sweetly-scented roses.

From its date – 1635 – incised over the deep stone porch, to its
setting in a wide hollow near a river, and the potential twenty-five
acres of good farmland, everything about Wigsell enchanted her. Not
the least of its attractions was its convenient distance from Alfred at
Sturry, fifty miles away, which meant a journey of about two hours
by motor or train to Canterbury. Other connections with Alfred in
this area were their mutual friends the Kiplings, eight miles away at
Burwash, and at Hawkhurst both the Goschens and the Readys,
Alfred's mother's relations. Alfred himself knew and loved the area
since as a young man he had toured it on his bicycle. On 29 August
1905 Violet took him to see the house for the first time, travelling
from Charing Cross with a picnic hamper. They looked over it all
thoroughly inside and out, and picnicked in the overgrown garden.

Wigsell had been an ironmaster's house for centuries, the property
belonging to one family, the Culpepers, for 300 years. In its heyday it
would have been a grand establishment, since this heavily wooded area
had been the centre of British iron production before the Industrial
Revolution and the age of coal. Iron was mined in the Sussex Weald,
where charcoal from the forests had originally been used to smelt it; near
the house were seven ponds used in the smelting process, and the iron,
mainly destined for guns for the fleet, was transported to the nearby
Robertsbridge foundry or down the little river Rother that flowed

through the estate, past Bodiam, the ancient moated castle (restored after the Great War by George Curzon) and on to the picturesque port of Rye and thence to the sea. The same route came to be used, in reverse, by smugglers, and, by the time Violet came to Wigsell, it had a disreputable reputation as a hideout for the notorious eighteenth-century Hawkhurst gang who brought their contraband there: the ghost of one of these piratical villains is said to haunt the attics to this day.

This was a region of rural England much celebrated by such leading writers as Belloc, Wells and above all the Cecils' neighbour, Rudyard Kipling, whose house, Bateman's, had also been an ironmaster's house, of the same date and scale and built of the same warm pale stone. The counties of Kent and Sussex were lauded as much for their historical resonances as for their beauty, all the greater for the wildness into which hedgerows and fields were falling in that time of agricultural decline. Now, thanks to the railways, Londoners could escape the urban sprawl, take their bicycles on the train and alight at the rural stations of Etchingham, Robertsbridge, Withernden and Battle, all about fifty miles from the metropolis. In the *The Wheels of Chance*, H.G. Wells described the Sussex countryside with positively Keatsian lyricism, through the eyes of a suburban shop assistant thirsty for its pure rural delights:

> There were purple vetches in the hedges, meadowsweet, honeysuckle, belated brambles – but the dog-roses had already gone; there were green and red blackberries, stellarias and dandelions, and in another place white dead nettles, traveller's joy, clinging bedstraw, grasses flowering, white campions, and ragged robins. One cornfield was glorious with poppies, bright scarlet and purple white, and the blue cornflowers were beginning. In the lanes the trees met overhead, and the wisps of hay still clung to the straggling hedges. In one of the main roads he steered a perilous passage through a dozen surly dun oxen. Here and there were little cottages, and picturesque beer-houses with the vivid brewers' boards of blue and scarlet . . .

The history of that enchanting corner of England also struck a chord with contemporary writers, architects and artists: that great age of literature and commercial enterprise, which had acquired an empire overseas under a renowned queen, saluted another, that of the Tudors, Good Queen Bess, Shakespeare and naval adventurers. When Kipling switched his creative focus from the Empire to the love of England, here was its beating heart, the land for which to strive, and for which both the Kiplings and the Cecils were ultimately asked to

pay with the sacrifice of their only sons. Indeed, among that generation of young men a number were later to be acclaimed, after their
deaths in the Great War, as the 'New Elizabethans', combining a
manly adventurous spirit with literary creativity.

It was also a great time of enthusiasm for 'Tudorbethan furniture',
for half-timbered suburban houses, and for rediscovering, through
popular historical literature, the life of the sixteenth- and seventeenth-
century countryside:

> See you the dimpled track that runs
> All hollow through the wheat?
> O that was where they hauled the guns
> That smote king Philip's fleet

wrote Kipling, in 'Puck's Song', of the Sussex and Kent that he loved,
where every field and ancient building told a story:

> See you our little mill that clacks,
> So busy by the brook?
> She has ground her corn and paid her tax
> Ever since Domesday Book . . .

Kipling's celebrated children's stories, *Puck of Pook's Hill* and *Rewards
and Fairies*, describe Una and Dan, based on John and Elsie Kipling,
being taken back to earlier periods – to the far-off neolithic men of
the Sussex Downs, to the Normans on the Kent coast and to Queen
Elizabeth giving lessons in statecraft. In one, the children meet the
seventeenth-century herbalist Nicholas Culpeper, who has a 'cousin
at Great Wigsell'. From the richness of British history in which they
rejoiced they drew lessons which were propaganda for the Empire.
These books appeared in George Cecil's schoolroom as they were
published; and he and his contemporaries would have absorbed messages about dying for England from one haunting tale in which King
Harold survives the battle of Hastings, and about how to be a good
imperial soldier from another about a Roman legionary.

When she discovered Wigsell, Violet had been house-hunting for
a long time for somewhere accessible to London and Hatfield, and
reasonably cheap – cash was forever a problem with the Cecils – where
George, then eleven, and Helen, just five, could grow up in healthy
country air and Violet could entertain in some style, and lastly, which
would be a welcoming home for Edward on his leave from Egypt. All
those requirements, except the last, were to be fulfilled.

The surveyor who inspected the house minimised neither its dereliction, nor the need to spend money on improving the more modern
'service wing' at the back – an addition which did not obtrude upon
the older original, and enabled the family to live in a degree of comfort
that earlier inhabitants of Wigsell would not have enjoyed. He concluded that 'the picturesque old house will justify such an outlay being
made.' And so, on 21 November 1906, with the help of a loan from
Cox's bank, Violet and Edward paid £3,259 for the manor of Great
Wigsell, the farm buildings, a pair of cottages, and twenty-five acres.

Violet wrote to Edward that she had told the architect, 'We do not
mean to spend more than £2,500 on doing it up,' though 'as a matter
of fact we can make it £3,000 but I thought I had better have a
margin'; by scrupulously overseeing the workmen and buying what
furniture and rugs she could at auction, Violet contrived to keep
within that budget.

In 1902, the Kiplings had paid £9,300 for Bateman's with thirty-
three acres; so Violet had got a bargain – but one for which she had
to work hard. Her choice of architect was significant: she turned to
Ernest George, whom the Admiral had used for the building of
Dunley. Father and daughter had the same aim – a self-sufficient small-
holding. This was possible at that time of agricultural depression with
plenty of cheap labour; in 1910, Violet's accounts show for outside
workers an annual wages bill of only £327 12s: for the handy-
man/bricklayer, and the carpenter, 25s a week; the two farmhands,
17s a week apiece; the gardener, Wood, who was to stay with her until
well after the 2nd War, 24s a week, and the under-gardener 18s a
week; most, if not all, of these would have had tied cottages.

In her recreation of Wigsell, Violet replaced the eighteenth-
century sash windows with stone mullions, which gave a lesser, but
authentic, light within and transfigured the facade outside. The car-
penters and joiners she employed to repair the magnificent elaborately
carved central staircase were masters of the vernacular tradition of fine
rural craftsmanship, which had been allowed to languish as a result of
mid-nineteenth century mass production and urbanisation; aesthetic
perfectionists such as Violet and Kipling and the great gardener
Gertrude Jekyll were enthusiastic in reviving it.

Two years to the day after his first visit to Wigsell, on 29 August,
1907, Alfred noted with pleasure in his diary that Violet had settled in
to her house, where he visited her before motoring back to Sturry.

The Blue Room on the ground floor, so-called from the colour of

The chatelaine of Wigsell, photographed in 1911 by Edward

the damask curtains at its tall windows, became Violet's sanctuary. There she wrote her household instructions, her daily letters to George when he went away to school, her weekly news to Edward in Cairo, and her copious correspondence with friends such as Alfred; from here she could slip out through a little door into the walled flower garden she created.

On the floors above, up those handsome, ancient stairs, where the smell of beeswax and wood smoke drifting up from the fires was reminiscent of Hatfield House, Violet made a set of bedrooms and a sitting room from an open gallery previously used for exercise during bad weather. In the main guest bedroom, named the Clemenceau Room after the statesman who was a regular visitor, was French furniture – a wicker-backed day bed and *bergères*, a four-poster painted pale grey and hung with pink-flowered silk, and an armoire lined with pale apricot silk, contrasting with the severity of the stone-mullioned windows and wide stone fireplace. On a round mahogany

The handsome staircase at Wigsell, restored by Violet, was a hazard: both Alfred Milner and Ivor Maxse fell down its highly polished steps

table, flowers and a pile of books welcomed guests. Regency prints and paintings on glass hung on the pale painted walls. A door connected it with Edward's bedroom, where the *lit en bateau* was dressed in red damask to match the curtains. On the top floor, with its sinister ghost, were the attics for the servants and extra guest rooms.

Everywhere were memories of Violet's girlhood, from the Clemenceau Room, with many of his books, to the works of Meredith, bound in red Morocco and gold-tooled, in the library with Violet's book-plate, designed by Burne-Jones. Kipling's books were added as they were published.

The house was comfortable but not luxurious; there was no telephone or electricity. At Bateman's the Kiplings had an old mill and they harnessed their stream to turn the mill wheel and generate their electricity. At Wigsell the flickering light of oil lamps and candles added to the mystery of the shadows on the stairs, where the carvings threw grotesque patterns as the family climbed up to bed at night. It was not an easy house to heat, the draughts whistling up through the gaps between the old floorboards despite numerous rugs. But the delicate tracery of the frost on the windows on winter mornings was thought to be all of a piece with the old house; and there were fires in the main rooms and bedrooms – six at least, in winter time – fed by the estate's plentiful wood.

Throughout the summer of 1907 Violet camped in the nursery rooms upstairs. Finally, she wrote to Edward, George was able to join her, 'tremendously excited at coming here and got up at 5.30 on Monday morning to go prowling round. Yesterday we went over and lunched with the Kiplings and George was very happy playing with Kipling and his children . . . Imagination is wanted to see [Wigsell's] great beauty in its present carpetless and curtainless condition.'

George reported to his sister: 'Wigsell (at this moment) is surrounded by little heaps of brick, over which you invariably fall and you land in a ditch equally stony. We have got lots and lots of rats. In the brook there are many eels Willie and I have caught.'

By the following year Violet could declare, 'The house is a joy to live in and in this new flush of Spring seems to gain new life from the beauty around it.' As she created the gardens and designed the yew hedges into topiary shapes her pleasure intensified in Wigsell, the first home that was properly hers, where she felt her children could be brought up happily.

There was one piece of the equation missing, however: Edward Cecil did not share his wife's delight in Wigsell. The fruit of Violet's most sensitive and imaginative side gave him little pleasure, so the family life created there was as lop-sided as Violet's own childhood with her parents living apart. In fact Helen, at five years old when they moved there, was the same age as Violet in 1877 when her parents separated; so the family pattern was repeated.

Edward never felt at home at Wigsell. Anxious about his chest, which had been weakened by tropical illness, he had asked Violet to find a house on a hill, built on well-drained land and within easy reach of London by rail. Wigsell was none of these: its low-lying situation was neither dry nor bracing and it required two train changes to reach from London. Edward felt his wishes had been discounted and he constantly reminded Violet what a strain the restoration was on their limited finances. For her part, she resented having expended so much time finding and creating a family home only for Edward to criticise it. His lung trouble was a reality and it eventually killed him – but the root of his discontent probably lay in his uneasy relationship with Violet. Wigsell was her achievement and preoccupation and when there he seems to have felt supernumerary, not part of the established routine and social life, even a stranger in his own household.

On his annual leave in the spring or summer Edward visited and saw his children there, as well as staying with them at Hatfield and in London. It was a way of life typical of families divided by the Empire and united only once a year. But the tension between Violet and Edward made the separation worse.

From his room, at the front, Edward looked up the drive towards the two fine young South African tulip trees that Violet had planted; near the babbling river, from a stout branch, hung a child's swing. He landscaped some of the woodland beyond the orchard and paddock, planting a bluebell wood, and damming the river with George's help. But, poignantly, at Wigsell he seemed to care most about the wallflowers that he planted in profusion . . . flowers traditionally a metaphor for being on the margins, not at the centre of things.

As the presence of her husband receded from the house, that of Violet's son George seems to have taken its place. He was 'crammed' for the testing entrance exam to Winchester College which, thanks in large part to Violet's supervision of his work, he passed. In 1909, his departure for boarding school at fourteen was followed by a flurry of letters from his mother, often two a day, to 'darling George'. To his father George reported that life at school was 'like Tommy Atkins and a disgusting French play mixed.' Of corporal punishment, which was doled out frequently, he concluded, 'it just teaches boys to lie their way out a situation.'

Several times Violet took George, whose French was good, on her annual trip to Paris, and these were to be among her happiest memories of him at that age, proud of him – 'not a bit forward and yet quite taking his share' – at dinner with Clemenceau. When Clemenceau was staying at Wigsell, he went with Violet to visit George at Winchester. The appearance of the Prime Minister of France caused a sensation. Clemenceau for his part was enchanted by the beauty of the late medieval buildings.

George had his fair share of adolescent indolence – 'He would

Georges Clemenceau shooting at Wigsell, where he was a frequent guest

make a quite admirable king in a limited monarchy, but unfortunately it is not open to us to enter him for this profession,' complained Violet. When they went to stay at Breamore in Hampshire, he was happy 'missing birds or not catching fish – I am bound to say that he works as little at pleasure as he does with his head – unlike most Englishmen'. Breamore House, a seventeenth-century brick manor, and its surrounding estate of woods and open downland, belonged to the Hulse family. Nearby was a strange turf-cut 'mizmaze' of great antiquity, encircled by yew and hawthorn. Teddy Hulse was a few years older than George and had inherited this romantic seat, and the family baronetcy, in 1901 when his dissolute father, a professional soldier, had killed himself in South Africa. Teddy was at once called home from Eton and so escaped a fire at the school, which destroyed the wing of the boarding house where he normally slept, claiming the lives of several boys. His own life was preserved only until the greater conflagration that awaited the young men of his generation. His mother, Edith, was an intimate friend of Violet and Olive and Breamore was one of their favourite retreats.

Violet wrote to George every day while he was at Winchester, her neat handwriting in blue-black ink filling sheet after sheet of azure paper, with anecdotes of home and of their neighbours the Kiplings: 'A.J.B. said, with a rather superior air to him "I can't help being rather broad minded" – to which Kipling answered very earnestly "If you work hard, Sir, that is a fault you can overcome, perhaps; I was broad minded when I started but I never let it interfere with necessary work."'

She commissioned John Singer Sargent to draw George and sent a copy of the picture – 'the living image of the boy on his jolliest side, with that look of real goodness which is his characteristic' – to Edward. The drawing shows an amiable, stalwart face, with curly hair: 'Sargent thought it not handsome enough for George, whom . . . he thought very handsome indeed – so he is – as I realised when I saw him among his fellows,' continued the doting mother.

The children became accustomed, although not reconciled, to their father's absence. Alfred Milner was a constant presence in the family circle; an avuncular figure, he visited Wigsell at weekends and the children frequently stayed at Sturry. Although he was always busy, 'Uncle Alfred' had time to talk to the children about their interests and what they were reading; from him as from Rudyard Kipling and Edward, George and Helen learnt about all manner of things from botany to battles. When Alfred stayed, as the only guest, at Wigsell in September 1908, the talk was of Canada and the great imperial scheme of tariff reform, which Alfred intended to preach to the Canadians when he visited them. In the New Year he took the family to a matinée in London, *Pinkie and the Fairies*, which he enjoyed as much as they did.

Violet and Alfred also met frequently in London. Yet she was still only one among his circle of attractive women friends. Norah Lindsay spent days on end with him at Sturry, and Mrs May Gaskell stayed at the same hotel and shared a sitting room with him on holiday in Italy. There may have been no shade of scandal in either case, but they indicate his firmly maintained status as a bachelor, free to travel where he wanted with whom he wished. Society did not single out Violet's relationship with Alfred from this upright statesman's many respectable – it was assumed – *amitiés gallantes*. It was just as well. Picnics and strolls through Regent's Park may have been innocent enough; but the note in his diary that he and Violet travelled to Tunbridge Wells to spend the day there together and a night in the same hotel, points to the other, likely conclusion that they had become lovers in the full sense; perhaps had been, at long intervals, for years. Somehow, however, they evaded gossip, as prominent people could then and could not today.

Like other wives whose husbands were on imperial service, Violet had the hard work of the children's upbringing, had most influence on them, and had to discipline them. With George she was careful to mitigate any criticism with affection. Her letters to him reveal a side not

Helen and George Cecil at Wigsell, c. 1907

always shown to those around her, expressively affectionate, concerned with his happiness and wellbeing, appreciative and encouraging.

On 15 December 1910 her letter to him was headed 'Colenso 1899', after Britain's humiliating defeat by the Boers a decade earlier; and on 27 February 1911 her letter is headed 'Majuba, Paardeburg': 'I cannot resist writing down the great defeat Majuba – the great victory – Paardeburg (1900 in the "great" Boer War) on their anniversaries.' In 1906 George's uncle Ivor Maxse published a book, a tribute to a brother officer killed during the Boer War: *Seymour Vandeleur, Lieutenant-Colonel, Scots Guards and Irish Guards: A Plain Narrative of the part played by British officers in the acquisition of colonies and dependencies in Africa representing a dominion of greater extent than India added to the British Empire in less than twenty years.* The title was eloquent of the goal for which Violet, Edward, Kipling, Alfred and the Maxse brothers were striving and for which George was expected to strive too: 'It is meet that the story of his life should be recorded – as an instance of the toll exacted by Empire and a reminder to us that sit at home that there still are men whose pride it is to render service to the State,' Ivor wrote. Such a child of Empire, too, was George.

By the time he was sixteen George had grown to a height to match his father's. He was strong, rather clumsy, with huge feet. Once in 1912, shortly after the sinking of the *Titanic*, when everyone's spirits were cast down by that terrible tragedy, George and his father were

present at an awkward social occasion when everybody was trying not
to refer to the painful subject. As he and George rose to leave Edward
looked down and commented, 'My God, George, your feet! They're
titanic!' These same feet drew teasing remarks from his younger
cousin, David Cecil.

David was of an age with Helen; their aunt, Gwendolen Cecil,
described the two cousins talking precociously of the metaphysical
nature of Time and Space – the beauties of Botticelli, religion and
ethics, Shakespeare and music. 'George, I need hardly say doesn't
indulge in those flights,' she continued. 'He's quite delightfully
British, coming down with a sledgehammer of "all rot" upon metaphysics and philosophy generally.' In many ways George was the unso-
phisticated model schoolboy, cheerful and sociable, a keen cricketer,
fresh and simple, but also serious and anxious to do well. His aesthetic
responses, however, were more mature than those of an average
schoolboy: life at Hatfield and Wigsell had sharpened his eye for beautiful buildings. He enjoyed wild nature, too, and avidly read Richard
Jefferies, the doyen of country writers, and absorbed himself in
botany, spending a day looking for the orchid *Gymplatanthera Jacksonii*,
named after one of the Winchester schoolmasters, which he explained
was 'a cross between *Gymnadenia Cornopia* and *Habenaria Viridis*'.

The Cecils, anxious about George's and Helen's religious education, wanted them to have a firm spiritual foundation. But Violet only
impressed religious study on her children as a duty, not a necessity for
their spiritual wellbeing. George was evasive when Edward tried to
probe him about his religious knowledge and whether he was reading
his Bible, as he had been enjoined to do. He felt too embarrassed to
admit to his father that, bored with keeping up his Bible reading, he
had dropped the habit.

When he was confirmed his godfather, the pious Lord Brownlow,
sent him a handsome leather-bound King James Bible, urging him
to 'Cling to God and fight the Devil with all your might . . . and
thus show yourself worthy of the great and honoured name you
bear.' The Cecils did not express themselves in these terms, but they
profoundly believed that any claim to importance that they – or any
other illustrious family – might have, would be the poorer for a lack
of religion.

Helen inclined naturally towards religion, like her father. She cross-
questioned Rudyard Kipling, whose opinion they all revered, on what
he really believed, receiving the answer that the closest contact

mankind could have with a higher presence came when people worked together for a great constructive purpose.

From an early age George's greatest enthusiasm was for martial matters. He knew the names of the leading generals in the different armies of the day, notably among the Germans, who led the way in modern strategic ideas. 'He was always quoting General von der Goltz,' wrote his aunt Nelly, 'and trying to explain military mysteries to me – assuming that I knew exactly what happened at Badajoz etc.'

He pressed his opinions with an intensity not unlike his mother's. As a little boy, if he wanted agreement, he would say, 'I insist.' Sometimes, however, he met his match: 'I was rash enough to argue with Kipling about the Greeks as a nation,' he told Edward. 'Of course he turned me inside out and and roared with laughter.'

George was in the Junior Officer Training Corps (OTC) at school – an organisation more or less obligatory for all boys over fifteen. The OTCs were an innovation, part of the Haldane army reforms of 1907–8. These reforms provided a highly efficient, though small, British Expeditionary Force of regular soldiers; they also furnished an elementary military education through a new volunteer part-time 'Territorial Army' with battalions in local regiments, and through the OTCs at schools and universities. It was the beginning of a British society prepared for military life – a phase of the country's history that was to last until the end of National Service in the early 1960s.

On Corps field days the Winchester School Corps joined forces with other Junior OTCs and fought mock battles. George asked his father to take him out on a practical demonstration of Infantry Attack and Assault at Wigsell. His father's support and approval mattered to him. He wrote regularly to 'Eggs', as the children called him following a telegraphic mis-spelling of 'Nigs', but during these formative years his children had all too little of his company and missed him: 'Though I have been with the very nicest uncles and aunts yet it is not the same as one's very own people, is it?' said George.

In 1912 he won a prize cadetship to Sandhurst. Many of his older friends were also beginning their military careers. Edward Hulse 'has got into what is known in the Scots Guards as the "Peerage" clique,' George told his father, adopting the breezy military style: 'John Manners whom you thought was such a young blighter is now being reformed by the Grenadier Guards. They gave one look at him and then ordered him to cut his hair in a different way and not to speak till he was spoken to.'

The Kiplings entertained him to dinner at Brown's Hotel in London and Carrie reported on his good start at Sandhurst:

> We did not have any one else to dine so we might hear his talk, and about 10 Rudyard took him to the *Morning Post* office and they showed him everything there to his great interest.
>
> Rudyard said 'better than a theatre, gives him fresh notions.' Also he 'looks well, a bit thinner, but more in possession of his body. He looked so nice as he came in to the dining room . . . Of course one must always trouble about them but as far as one can see he is happy and all is well.'

Rudyard added, in what was like a parody of his own writing:

> He has come on splendidly – sage, as ever and altogether delightful in his account of the new life, and keen as mustard. The engineer in charge of the linotype machine (George went through 'im very thoroughly) said to us behind his hand:
>
> 'Oo is the young gentleman? most of 'em only say:- "'ow wonderful" an' go on. E's asked me every dam question he ought to ask about a new machine.' Not bad . . .

When George passed out of Sandhurst he joined his battalion, the 2nd Grenadier Guards, at Chelsea Barracks in January 1914, along with John Manners. After the Trooping of the Colour ceremony in June Violet wrote proudly that he was 'absorbed in his regiment and new work.' At Wigsell in mid-July he got up a cricket team, the Sussex Rabbits, for which he recruited the Kiplings. 'Do they still scoff at the club?' he asked his father, who was seeing some of George's young friends who were visiting Cairo. 'Tell them that they won't when we play the MCC at Lords in 1920 and their names are omitted from the list of our 11.'

Life was full of fun and promise and George lived every minute of it to the full.

CHAPTER SEVENTEEN

Edward in Egypt

E DWARD, BEING so much in step with Cromer, had seemed assured of his high position in the government of Egypt. But suddenly, in 1907, Cromer resigned, his constitution worn out after twenty-six years as supreme ruler, and retired to England. His successor, Sir Eldon Gorst, disliked Edward and resented his influence.

'Lord Edward Cecil had frequently said to me: "If Gorst succeeds Lord Cromer, I leave Egypt by the first boat," but as a matter of fact he did not,' recounted the stalwart Harry Boyle, Cromer's Oriental Secretary and right-hand man, who left a vivid account of the years after 'the Lord's' departure. They were the nadir of Edward's life.

Cromer had chosen a successor with an exceptional grasp of finance and long experience in Egypt: nobody had proved his worth better than the ambitious 'Jack' Gorst, especially in presenting Britain's Egyptian case to the French when the 1904 Entente Cordiale was forged. Now in his late forties, he spent every day in a whirlwind rush of strenuous work, competitive sport and purposeful entertaining; but his pace was too fast for Egypt, and Cromer was a hard act for anyone to follow. Small in stature, plain and bespectacled, although determined and astute, Gorst lacked either authority or dignity. When Violet had met him out in Egypt she had thought him the cleverest man in the Egyptian service, but cynical and a bad influence: 'He said to me the other day that patriotism is only a passing phase . . . he does not believe in honour and honesty.' She thought him 'a cad with women and shows this at once . . . Having started on the wrong leg with me the other day, he now drapes himself in patriotism and the Union Jack.' She had voiced her fears to Katie Cromer; the Cromers were disturbed to find her remarks confirmed by others. But Gorst had continued to impress with his work and in due course had made a suitable marriage, so Cromer for a while suppressed his uneasiness.

Sir John Eldon Gorst, Agent and Consul-General in Egypt from 1907 to 1911

When he retired from Egypt, however, he began again to regret his choice of successor, in view of the increasingly delicate situation; the shadow of Dinshwai hung over the country. As he drove to the station in his carriage, Cromer passed through streets lined with armed troops: no farewell cheers, only silence, greeted his departure.

Cromer had always held that eventually the Egyptians must take over the running of their country, but he had never tried to hasten the process. Edward himself doubted whether they would be ready for independence for decades. 'I am not anti-Native but I believe in speaking the truth and saying that this country must be in leading strings for many years to come,' he declared.

Gorst, on the other hand, believed that the process could be accelerated; the Liberal Government at home encouraged him. He was impatient to move on to greater glory as a career diplomat and eventually to a position in British government, as he confided to Harry Boyle. Treating Egypt as a stepping-stone did not go down well with the non-self-advertising, dedicated Anglo-Egyptian officials, to whom it was 'bad form'.

Gorst decided to involve the Khedive much more in government: he held regular, confidential consultations with him. He tried to strengthen respect for the authority of central government by recruiting more Egyptian ministers and increasing the number of Egyptians in responsible administrative posts; and he allowed a greater voice to representative institutions.

This seemingly generous policy of liberalism was full of contradictions and drew criticism even from the Egyptians. The Khedive was counting on regaining his former despotic powers and the furious Egyptian government ministers suspected him and Gorst of conspiring to control the country between them. Likewise, the Egyptian representative bodies, such as the legislative council, were angry that the Egyptian executive had been made stronger at their expense. Worst, for Gorst, the nationalists, who could have been placated by these changes, were simply encouraged to campaign for greater independence.

As their agitation grew louder, Gorst clamped down on the nationalist press with an ineffective and unpopular press law, easily evaded. This was followed by a disastrous political defeat when Gorst and his Prime Minister, the able Boutros Ghali, gave way to nationalist pressure over the position of the powerful Suez Canal Company, always a cause of discontent. A nationalist assassinated Boutros for having sided with the British against Egyptian interests. Hanging the killer merely created a martyr.

With more imagination Gorst could well have had a limited success: the future lay with his policy, rather than with Cromer's. But he was overconfident while at the same time failing to win over his own British officials, many of whom carried out his policies reluctantly, resenting having to cover up the mistakes of newly-appointed Egyptian colleagues to maintain the prestige of government, disliking his secretive dealings with the Khedive and resenting giving up their jobs to men less capable than themselves. Edward considered the relaxing of British authority entirely counter-productive:

> If we really want to teach these people to govern themselves some day (and unless we do I don't see what we the Anglo-Egyptian officials are here for) we must teach them by example. Our administration must be the pattern which will gradually work into their minds and which will be their guide hereafter. If we cover up abuses, deceive them, fool them, how shall they believe that we are anything but hypocrites when we preach good government and practise 18th century opportunism?

There was no question now of Edward's hoped-for promotion to the key post of Financial Adviser. He remained an Under-secretary in the Ministry of Finance and was taken off the Council of Advisers, on which he had occupied an unofficial place under Cromer, when much of the financial business had been delegated to him. Gwendolen wrote to Maud: 'In that atmosphere of semi-oriental despotism, Nigs came to be treated as the favourite at court and treated by everyone accordingly. Now that is all changed.' He was no longer apprised of government policy: 'He knows nothing and of course he is pitied by the surrounding society as a fallen favourite.'

Edward began to feel that the old values he represented were about to be swept away. This matched his brothers' mood in England, where they were endlessly defending the cause of the established Church and the landed aristocracy in Parliament against the Liberal Government of the day. The fact that his disillusion was so widely shared in Cairo did not make him feel less alone. He had found, in common with other colleagues, that since the Dinshwai incident many Egyptians who had appeared relatively friendly to British rule had become colder. He felt beleaguered and his letters became full of extravagant religious sentiment, so much so that Gwendolen and Jem feared that he was heading for a nervous breakdown.

Despite his subsequent success, Edward never got over the disenchantment of these years and he increasingly felt it risky, in that narrow governing circle, to unburden himself to anyone: 'My heart does ache for him,' wrote Gwendolen. 'It is just a time when a wife would have been everything!'

'Things are about as bad as I thought they would be. Or a trifle worse, whichever way I look the outlook is as bad as it can be,' Edward agonised to Violet, at the same time resenting her indifference towards him. 'If I were not so poor I should not mind as I could quietly go on till the smash came but when I think of you and the children and Wigsell my heart goes into my boots. To be married to a man you don't care for is bad enough but to an unsuccessful man to boot is poor luck.' He also had a practical purpose, asking her to copy his letter, leaving out the bitter reflections on their relationship, for his brother, Jem Salisbury, and his cousin Arthur Balfour, as head of the Conservative Party, hoping that they would find some way of using their influence to remedy the situation. 'My sentence', he told Violet, 'is Penal Servitude for life . . . stranded in my old age with nothing to do and as poor as a church mouse.' The talk was that all 'Cromer's men' were to go and be replaced by men trained by Gorst. 'Shall I stay on and risk it?' he wondered. 'Or try to get moved. If so where?'

Whatever her personal differences from Edward, Violet was outraged by his treatment. She denounced Gorst to the wife of the Permanent Secretary to the Foreign Office, Arthur Hardinge, a rash act, for her criticism was sure to get back to Gorst himself and would make matters worse for Edward. According to Gwendolen, Lady Cromer had heard of 'that perfect ass' Violet's indiscretion and had been very shocked. In November 1907 Edward's brothers and Gwendolen held a council of war at Hatfield – without Violet: 'It is a rather gloomy commentary on the whole thing that at no time did any of the family think of consulting Violet or even of speaking to her,' Gwendolen wrote. They decided to approach Cromer through his wife to ask his advice and to emphasise that Violet's outburst had been at her own initiative, not Edward's. Pained though he was by what had happened, Cromer was in honour bound to utter no word of criticism against Gorst. The message that came back to the Cecils was that Edward should hang on, however disagreeable it might be.

Edward tried to submerge himself in his work. He took up photography and astronomy and travelled – some remarks of Gorst's about his ignorance of Egypt may have hit home. At Aswan he enjoyed the 'simple rugged country where problems don't exist or if they do, they are simple and easy of solution'. He showed the usual British tendency to romanticise the 'noble' desert people at the expense of the 'corrupt' urban Egyptians: 'At Korosko I had the pleasure of speaking to real Arabs again,' he told Kitty Maxse. 'What a relief it is to meet gentlemen again. Their dignity and educated way of speaking reminds one of the Highlanders and they look you straight in the face as one man should look at another . . . Of course they are barbarians and treacherous, but their treachery is the artifice of the sportsman not the low cunning of the pickpocket.'

Visitors to Cairo included Jem and Alice Salisbury, travelling out with their daughters, Mimer and Moucher, who charmed and amused Edward. Alfred Milner's trip to Egypt in February 1908 gave Edward a little moment of triumphant gloom. Alfred looked tired and old and had 'lost his sense of humour a little. He said a few despairing sentences about South Africa but I naturally dropped the subject.' Professional etiquette dictated that Edward could not unburden himself to Alfred about the Gorst regime, and he could only hope that Alfred might see below the orderly surface of things and report home accordingly.

Because of the break in Cromer's policy, fissures had opened up

Eggs is looking so pleased because they have brought him his letters and he thinks one is from BABY *he is opening it.*

Edward Cecil photographed by himself in Cairo for an album he made for Helen
('Baby'), showing his daily life. The children called him 'Eggs'

which international financiers saw opportunities of exploiting. The opulent figure of Sir Ernest Cassell, 'money incarnate', the favourite of Edward VII, 'is here having his boots licked by every soul . . . at the Savoy yesterday after dinner during the dance. All the people came up and claimed friendship or acquaintanceship in the most loathsome manner. It is far worse than any form of snobbery.' Cassell spent his time, according to Edward, with German entrepreneurs and politicians, whose influence was growing. Cassell's pre-eminent position was not undeserved: in 1895 he had financed the biggest engineering project in Egypt, the Aswan Dam, and between 1907 and 1910 pressed for its height to be raised to increase its irrigation capacity. The returns in agricultural productivity were large, but Edward, like other officials, was alarmed at Cassell's power over the country's economy.

He much preferred another visitor, Winston Churchill, 'who always makes me laugh.' He hastened to assure Kitty Maxse who, being married to Leo, regarded Churchill as a nuisance: '. . . I don't agree with one view in fifty of his. He is very clever and amusing and knows I am not taken in by his various poses.'

But his natural melancholy intensified:

> I don't think you women with all your many troubles and suffering, great though they are, realize what it is to live by one's self in a semi-hostile environment with no friend in whom one can really confide. There is a loneliness about it which makes physical suffering almost a relief [he wrote to Violet].
>
> I suppose I know it is all my own fault and certainly you would never have married me if I had not asked you to. I am not blaming you only as Baby [Helen] says I'm awfully sad. But it's no use repining though the strain I am sure will do for me somehow. I don't believe one can go on feeling as I do for ever . . . I am afraid you will have an awful struggle to keep down expenses. Poor darling if I had known I would have drowned myself before I led you into such bothers.

Although Violet was prepared to stick up for him, however misguidedly, in England, she did not consider this crisis in his life in Egypt required her to be by his side, when she was occupied with the children's education and the restoration of Wigsell. The Cecils disagreed and their attitude towards her hardened.

'I'm afraid,' Gwendolen wrote to Maud, 'she has lost the last chance of making the marriage a success now – if she had been sympathetic and gone to him now that he is in low water it might have retrieved much. He made one bitter allusion to her want of sympathy in his letter – though he didn't mention her name. From what one learns she is now entirely absorbed in furnishing this new house – none of her old friends see her. I don't think she is quite sane, really.'

However Edward had many good friends among his colleagues, such as Edward Goschen, whose sons were friends of George, and, later, Ronald Lindsay; he was popular with their families, their wives pitied his bachelor existence and their children enjoyed his company. We glimpse him through the eyes of one little girl, Priscilla Hayter, who welcomed his visits 'even if he arrived in the middle of the sacred parental hour in the drawing-room'. Coming across her elder brother 'building a bridge of bricks across a river of polished floor between two Persian rugs he would immediately and silently involve himself in this operation, getting the scheme without having to be told.' He even completed it by building 'a lighthouse with a lighted candle at the top surrounded with stained glass windows, and turned off all the lights and caused us to be ships in the darkness keeping away from the rocks.'

William Hayter, the children's father, who was in the legal department, had also like Edward spent several years in the Sudan, which he left in order to marry; he forsook 'the rigours and simplicities of life in the Sudan with regret, to involve himself in the tortuous labyrinths and the complicated tensions of multi-racial Cairo'. Hayter was a man of intelligence and humour and, in common with Edward, had a vision of Egypt's future, which he imparted to his daughter as they strolled together by the Nile on the eve of her ninth birthday:

> We walked now hand in hand, discussing the independence of Egypt. It was to be a country solvent, secure and free; with the fellahin earning a living wage for their unending labour, with no more bullying of the poor . . . no more selfish exploitation in the midst of misery. It was a dream to which he had cheerfully dedicated his life; more, in a characteristically English way, by accident than design . . . Without self-righteousness, and without even much self-consciousness, he was a missionary for good government, regarding it as the beginning of the relief of misery. He and many like him were in some ways as selfless in their task as a missionary could be.

The same could be said of Edward Cecil: he, too, was working wholeheartedly in Egypt, as Priscilla in her memoirs put it, 'not in self-enrichment, not in safety, not in comfort; but enduring long separations from home and family, a summer climate often lethal, strange diseases, strange foods, and the certainty of straightened means at the end of it all, retirement on a small pension and probable ill-health. They had also the virtual certainty that everything they had done would be roundly abused at the receiving end.'

The delicate balance between such men and the Egyptians was upset by Dinshwai and now by Gorst's policy. British prestige had collapsed by 1911; Cromer was saying privately that all his efforts in Egypt had been thrown away in four years. Then suddenly Gorst's energies seemed to flag. Fatally ill with cancer, he left Egypt in April and died shortly afterwards.

Cromer lost no time in recommending to the Foreign Office that Kitchener should replace Gorst. And so it was that in September 1911 an Agent built on the same large imperial lines as Cromer came out to Cairo – but how different the two men were! Compared with Cromer's consistency, Kitchener's talent was, as David Lloyd George once observed, like the rotating beam from a lighthouse, brilliantly illuminating all before it, then swinging away leaving the scene in impenetrable night. 'I am glad Kitchener has been chosen,' Cromer wrote to Edward: 'My last Cairo speech was somewhat prophetic. – I said if my jog-trot became a gallop, the horse would fall down and break his neck – and this . . . is what has happened.'

A new rider was on his way and Edward, who knew Kitchener so well, expected the route ahead, though probably in a direction he approved, to be a rough one. On 29 September, returning now as Agent, Field Marshal Earl Kitchener of Khartoum and the Vaal stepped out of the train at Cairo station, immaculate in grey top hat and frock coat; the civilian nature of his new job had been firmly impressed on the imperial warrior by the Foreign Secretary, Sir Edward Grey. The crowd of cheering Egyptians welcomed the strong man who would bring tranquillity to their country (or perhaps they simply thought it sensible to show enthusiasm). His unexpectedly jovial expression, like everything else about that formidable hero, was faintly disturbing – the smile of a tiger, but a tiger come as saviour.

Kitchener's instructions from the Government at home were to restore order and British prestige. With a mixture of toughness and evasiveness which would have been the envy of Queen Elizabeth I, he set about dampening nationalist activity, and contesting the influence of the Khedive, Abbas Hilmi, and the legislative council of Egyptian notables. He was expected to continue Gorst's liberalisation programme, but could see no sense in trying to democratise Egypt too swiftly, and made only the most conservative alterations to the constitution. More important for him, and for the mass of Egyptians in that vast territory, were his ambitious land drainage scheme, and a plan to wipe out the debts of most of the *fellahin*, in defiance of their European creditors; this made him a hero to the peasantry, the majority of Egypt's population. He got his way through a benevolent despotism, using his virtually unlimited powers as Agent and Consul-General.

Edward thoroughly agreed with Kitchener, that the *fellahin* deserved better treatment. The peasants, the backbone of the Egyptian economy, were still as financially vulnerable as they had been in the days of the Pharaohs; they needed the protection of the British against unscrupulous financiers and politicians. Edward backed Kitchener fervently in his battle with the Khedive: 'We can never do much real good as long as the fat little man is at the top out here. He is working like a beaver to bring trouble on and will probably partially succeed.'

Edward was astounded by Kitchener's disregard for the rules. 'Kitchener is very comic,' he reported to Violet in February 1912.

> He presided over the Church Committee yesterday. It was done in his best robber baron style. I nearly died of suppressed laughter . . . when he explained how he proposed to raise money. It ran along the edge of the criminal law almost the whole time. He is governing the country well but eccentrically. He complained to me that the ministers were rather in the way also the laws and judges but he hoped to 'get on better now,' as I suppose he will do away with them. He treats us all as Personal Staff and one does all sorts of work one was never meant to do.

Edward was promoted at last to Financial Adviser, '*Sisely Malia*' (Finance), as he was known among the Egyptians. The post of Financial Adviser was pivotal, ranking next to that of Agent; he effectively controlled the funding allowed to each department. Although not always agreeing with Kitchener's methods, Edward admitted their effectiveness and accepted that, for most purposes, he and his fellow officials were simply tools of the Agent: 'What we shall all be like when he goes I dare not think.' Kitchener kept everyone working at full nervous stretch; it was a relief when his state tours took him to visit his precious *fellahin*, leaving his 'tools' to enjoy a spell of peace.

Kitchener, in his turn, recognised to the full Edward's popularity among colleagues, and his ability to glide gracefully out of difficult positions and always to deal tactfully with the Egyptians. Edward was not a particular expert on finance; as in South Africa, it was his diplomatic sensitivity and common sense which counted. 'K. flattered me hugely,' he told Violet proudly, 'by saying an article in the Graphic saying that I am to be his successor, was "not a bad idea".'

As during the Boer War, after a while in the saddle Kitchener became impatient to finish and get away, driving himself and his officers ever harder and becoming more unmanageable with exhaustion. He was increasingly moving towards Egypt's outright annexation by the British Empire, and the political work for his underlings became more difficult during 1913. The Khedive was almost openly at war with him, paying French journalists to attack him in their press. Kitchener began to take steps towards deposing him, but was deflected by Cromer, who warned that this might lead to rebellion in Egypt and fury in France. Edward shared these fears; he did not want to see Kitchener run into trouble – 'Hustling the East is a difficult, dangerous and fatiguing game,' he said, paraphrasing Kipling.

Kitchener, often lonely in his pre-eminence, came to rely increasingly on Edward as confidant, sitting up late over tumblers of whisky and water. He suggested that Edward should visit the Agency several evenings a week before dinner. 'He says he is dull. Nothing to what I am. You know much as I love him how I hate shop and soup combined. High talking and low feeding are inseparable.' Kitchener dragged Edward off with him to Alexandria: 'K wants me to act as cross between a clerk and a referee for 12 hours a day . . . and I am wrongly supposed to be the only one he will listen to.' On tour Kitchener was treated like a king, with obeisance and fulsome compliments. The journeys, speeding in a car over miles of earth roads, could be exhilarating: 'One bounds about just missing falling into the canal or a drain I drove with a very fat Egyptian and he flew up in to the air at each bump. I thought every minute he would come down and crush me flat. It was fun,' he told Helen.

As a reward for prolonged attendance on his chief Edward was made Knight of the Cross of St Michael and St George – 'after only six months as F.A. rather a record . . .' Kitchener 'was awfully nice about it and very nervous in telling me. He is a funny shy old thing and he looked as if he was having his teeth pulled out when I thanked him but liked it all the same in an odd sort of way.'

However, Edward could not dispel the feeling that the whole exercise of British paternal rule in Egypt was thankless and futile. From time to time he wished himself on a coral atoll somewhere away from it all. 'I wade in filth, dishonesty, treachery and viciousness such as in the West is unknown and if one is well one laughs at it but if one is not one feels sick.' He said that he should give up dining out because he had become such depressing company that 'old ladies break out into uncontrollable sobs with the fish.' Kitchener too, he later recollected, saw the absurd side to the endless round of intrigue which was the stuff of Egyptian political life. Edward concluded that it was best not to take either oneself or Egypt too seriously, for

> It is in reality a huge joke or series of jokes, not all perhaps in the best taste but very humorous nevertheless. It is not, as some falsely hold, a corner of the empire inhabited by future proconsuls and the grateful people they govern (as if any one did like being governed!), but an enormous and unending *opéra bouffe*.

The pattern of his day in Cairo was breakfast at his club, work at the Ministry of Finance, followed by a light meal and an hour's sleep, and conscious of an expanding waistline, a walk or tennis or golf at the Sports Club, in the former palace grounds of the Khedive Ismail on the island of Gezireh. Going round the course was a sociable business and a chance to flirt with dashing lady golfers. On his walks he explored the old parts of the town, with their narrow, dark streets, some roofed over and full of small shops selling wares from all over the Middle East, North Africa and India. He returned to work until dinner which he also frequently took at his club, the Turf, a gathering place for other British officials whose families were in England. Dining outside on the terrace was cool but noisy, reeking of ancient drains discharged from the Coptic school nearby, and with a view over the new synagogue, an *art nouveau* building which Edward thought hideous. If he had to share a table, he sometimes had a 'purgatorial dinner' with someone determined to talk shop. Afterwards he might play billiards or cards before going to bed with some 'stodge' on financial administration to read. 'I am still torn between the dullness of my life if I go to bed early and the vile effects of staying up late.'

Some evenings after a formal dinner party, Edward, in white tie and tails, would go on to a ball thronged with 'the *jeunesse dorée* of pashadom' at one of the smart hotels. Socially, he had little contact with Egyptian high society, though he seems to have liked one member, at least, the Oxford-educated Governor of Port Said. Dinners with the Khedive were a hazard: 'H.H. (rightly) tried to poison me. The poison was apparently of an inferior quality for though painful it did not do more than give me a sleepless night.' One of the worst culinary ordeals was at an Agency ball mismanaged badly by Kitchener.

> Only selected members of each family were asked, sometimes the wife, sometimes the husband, often the deceased. I never saw a ball room full of such irritated people, but the crown was the supper which consisted exclusively of some rare and curious old prawns and a particular brand of champagne at 1/3d the bottle. My, how ill everyone was . . .

After many hilarious evenings with his friends exchanging anecdotes about the horrors of their Cairo life, Edward wrote down his impressions in sketches which he sent to Violet. She enjoyed them, and at his request showed them to Kipling.

Relations between them had improved somewhat: Edward's promotion brought a rise in salary to £1,800 a year. He began to build a house on the fashionable river island of Gezireh, and with his brother Jem Salisbury's unexpected help, bought two neighbouring plots of land – 'I am so delighted I can only just stop singing in the office.' 'Villa Cecil' was painted on the gateposts, a garden was planned and he asked Violet to send out furniture and light fittings, as the lamps on sale in Egypt were 'terrible, Art Nouveau as seen by a hashish seller.'

He could now write more objectively to Violet and apologised for his irritability, a feeling familiar to fellow Anglo-Egyptian officials, indeed to officials throughout the British Empire.

> It must be some excuse for my gloom and crossness at times that they come from my other life out here. It must seem very unreasonable to you, like watching people dancing when one cannot hear the music. If things go ill out here and I quarrel with my friends, the effect appears in my letters but not the causes. I say all this in explanation of my letters to you of a blue tinge. It is so odd to think that none of you at home know really anything of my hopes and fears, loves and hates, failures and successes.

This was true: Violet was interested, as many wives would not have been, in the general political picture, but his accounts of byzantine intrigues among his colleagues and friends naturally meant little. But he would allude to such people as though he expected them to be familiar to her, without explaining why associates fell into or out of favour – why, for example, he should suddenly speak of Ronald Storrs, the Oriental Secretary, as 'the greatest ass (for a clever man) I have met for some time'. Storrs reciprocated this dislike.

With Edward's eminent position, and precisely because he needed her less, Violet felt better able to cope with life in Cairo. In January 1913, for the first time in eleven years, she came out to Egypt. Alfred Milner was making his annual visit to Cairo on Bank of Egypt business, staying at the Heliopolis Hotel. The Cecils gave a grand dinner for financial officials which he attended and he met Violet several times *à deux* for lunch and tea. Her visit, sweetened by this ingredient, went well and she repeated it in December that year, this time bringing Helen. Aged twelve, Helen loved this, her only visit to her father in Egypt, staying at his pretty white-painted house in Gezireh. They drove out to the Pyramids in his carriage and scrabbled about in the sand for bits of pottery and faïence beads; at the zoo Said, a tame hippo, would rise out of the water on command. In the bazaar 'Each shop was like a tiny and most luxuriant room'. On their visit to Lord Kitchener she and Violet admired his icons and antiquities (he was an avid collector) while Edward and his chief walked up and down the immaculate Agency lawn deep in conversation.

When mother and daughter returned to England, in March, Edward's mood fluctuated between tolerance of his exile and pessimism: 'I do like pleasant things so much and pretty people and laughing and I get so sick of the grind and black looks . . . No nerves left, my home broken and nothing to look forward to but a dreary old age.'

Kitchener's regime was deteriorating. Far from being a rock of strength in a storm, he was becoming a major cause of the storm himself. His rudeness to the Egyptian ministers and British officials at their meetings was a nightmare, and Edward looked forward to Kitchener's annual leave. 'He is very troublesome . . . He is I think displeased with my inability to make money out of sand.'

The biggest crisis of Kitchener's Egyptian career came in May 1914. His health and nerves were worse than ever at a moment when the Khedive decided to get rid of the Prime Minister, Mohammed Said, whom he regarded as too pro-British. It was crucial for British prestige that Khedive should not be allowed to do this, but Kitchener seemed to have lost the ability to negotiate with him. Edward and other colleagues pressed Kitchener to stand firm: any change should be on *his* terms: 'We had a most fearful row and I told him this was ruin and destruction . . . that he had several times assured the Ministers that as long as they stuck to us they had nothing to fear and that if he now threw them over we should never be trusted again.' Kitchener, nearly weeping, ignored Edward's point of view as impractical. Yet his own feeble efforts over the next few days allowed the Khedive to outmanoeuvre him and appoint ministers of his own choice in place of Mohammed Said and others.

'It is the most awful defeat I have ever been in,' Edward wrote, 'and the result is exactly what I thought. Our prestige is gone for the moment, the Khedive is omnipotent . . . the Ministers completely out of hand and pay no attention to what one says.'

Afterwards Kitchener was in an abject state, talking of letting things slide until after everyone had taken their leave and still furious with Edward for criticising him. Edward, bewildered, wrote to Violet: 'I should just as much have expected the Nile to run south as for him to behave like this . . . Shan't I be glad to get away in July. You must be extra nice to me when I do come because I shall need it.' When he came home at last, at the end of that month, he was delighted with the progress of his son in his old regiment and to be reunited with twelve-year-old Helen, musical and growing fast, with long slender hands. Her health then and for the rest of her days was uncertain, but she responded to life that spring and summer with a particular intensity: 'The days I am now spending are so happy that when I grow older I should like to remember them,' she confided to her diary for 1914. The only cloud on the horizon was the possibility of civil war in Ireland; and though that did not disturb the young people's summer plans, Edward found his contemporaries almost obsessive on the subject.

Asquith had half-heartedly introduced a Home Rule bill in 1912, principally to please the Irish Nationalist Party, now propping up the Liberal Government which had lost its parliamentary majority. The Northern Irish Protestants of Ulster signed a mass 'Covenant' to resist being overwhelmed by a semi-independent Catholic-dominated Ireland. In thousands they joined an Ulster Volunteer Force which equipped itself in April 1914 with a huge armoury from Germany.

Alfred Milner had emerged as the English leader who was most extreme in their support: 'For the last three or four months I have really worked hard – at public things – for the first time since South Africa,' he told Violet. By mid-1914 he had mustered around two million signatures to a 'British Covenant' against the bill. He was recklessly adamant that Home Rule must be defied even if it passed into law, going further in plotting resistance to the elected British government than the British public, though strongly anti-Home Rule, could ever have accepted. It was as if the ancient Ulster conflict had dragged this progressive rationalist back to the sixteenth century, when politicians planned treason and faced the axe for their beliefs.

Despite the 'demoniacal rush' of these months he and Violet still met often, as on 7 June, at Taplow, where she brought George, the house party being largely for young people. On 18–20 July at Sturry, Helen and Violet enjoyed, as Alfred's guests, one of the legendary golden sunlit weekends of that last summer before the war, punting on the Stour and listening to him reading aloud. Helen went on to stay with the Kiplings at Rider Haggard's house, Kessingland, near Lowestoft, so close to the edge of the cliffs that they said it was like living on a boat. She always treasured this memory of her talks with Kipling in the study, the wide-open views of the North Sea, the picnics and walks along the sands. In London, Alfred showed Violet the house in Great College Street, Westminster, that was to be his new London base. Over dinner together, they discussed its decoration.

Then suddenly the news from the Continent dominated everything else. What began as trouble in the Balkans ran out of control. Europe's statesmen snatched blindly at new opportunities or lost their grip altogether; the fragile peace, which Lord Salisbury, above all, had so painstakingly preserved in earlier years, broke down. Most people in Britain were bewildered. Could this crisis really be more important than the Irish question? Even experienced statesmen like Arthur Balfour remained sceptical: as late as 29 July, when Leo Maxse had observed, 'Well the Germans mean business this time,' Balfour's only comment was: 'Did you hear what that lunatic Leo said?'

Within days, Europe was plunged into the greatest conflict it had ever known. For a while the Liberal Government had wavered over Britain's involvement: European war was not part of their political vision. Like Bob Cecil and other Conservatives, Alfred felt that Britain must at least show the Germans that they would oppose an invasion of Belgium – of which he had heard news on 3 August – and should send the British Expeditionary Force to the Continent at once. On the morning of 4 August, he and Austen Chamberlain urged Lord Lansdowne, as the former Conservative Foreign Secretary, to press this on the Government. That same morning, news of the German invasion of Belgium had been confirmed to the Cabinet, which finally authorised the Foreign Secretary, Sir Edward Grey, to ask the German Government whether they were prepared to respect Belgian neutrality. This ultimatum went unanswered. By midnight, Berlin time, Britain was at war in Western Europe for the first time in a hundred years. 'It is better,' Alfred commented, 'to have an end of the uncertainty.' This was an echo of his old Boer War impatience with shilly-shallying. Yet war itself does not eliminate uncertainties and it was soon to create an agonising one for Violet and Edward.

Edward was immediately recalled to Cairo, as was his chief. But hardly had Kitchener boarded the ferry at Dover than a message came summoning him to the War Office. He left at once. Two days later he became Minister of War. Edward continued the long journey upon which he had started, back to Cairo and his duties in Egypt.

Before Armageddon came: Edward and George together at Wigsell in 1907; they were not destined to meet again after August 1914

CHAPTER EIGHTEEN

George at War

WHEN WAR BROKE out George was impatient to see action with the British Expeditionary Force. 'If ever anyone suggested he wouldn't go his face fell,' Helen wrote, 'but he knew what he was in for, as when Mlle, saying goodbye to him, "Au revoir, Monsieur," he answered "Au revoir Mlle ou à jamais."'

George's battalion, the 2nd Grenadiers, was a crack fighting unit, part of the most intensively trained force ever before to leave British shores and the first to reach French soil since the Napoleonic Wars. According to the battalion's historian, its officers, from highest to lowest, were dedicated men:

> It was a very close, tight-knit community that took the Guards battalions to war in 1914. They all knew each other well and many, like George Cecil, had succeeded their fathers in the Regiment. To them, as much as to their soldiers, the Regiment was a way of life, a family . . . which commanded their ultimate loyalty. They went to war with high spirits, confident in their ability to defeat anything that the enemy could send against them. They entirely justified that self-confidence, although at a terrible cost to themselves; perhaps their most striking characteristic was their self-discipline.

Edward, Prince of Wales, later recalled the Guards as 'a great club, and if tinged with snobbishness, it was the snobbishness of tradition, discipline, perfection and sacrifice.' George had other clubs. His last letter before he left England was from the Garrick, to which he had just been elected. He also had his own private group of intimates, consisting of his mother, Kipling and Angela Manners, sister of his fellow-soldier John, and a favourite dancing partner. 'I shall always remember that sweet compliment,' Angela told Violet later of being invited to join George's chosen circle,

George Cecil at the Royal Military Academy, Sandhurst, before he joined his regiment early in 1914

'because I know he felt it was more honour than being given the [Order of the] Bath; <u>and</u> it <u>was</u>.'

On 12 August, George and his battalion set off for France to join the 4th Guards Brigade. Helen recorded their last hours together: 'The morning of the day he went he would not say goodbye to anybody but being too restless to stay quiet went about with Mumey and me in a taxy . . . I rubbed noses with George instead of a kiss; it was our usual salutation . . . I saw Mumey cry for the first time in my memory after George had gone out of Barrack square.'

They said their last goodbyes at Nine Elms station, from which soldiers departed for the front, in a hectic rush along the railway platform.

> We come up with 1 basket of pears 1 basket of plums just as the train is preparing to start. As we pass running the band strikes up 'God save the King' we give the things to George and John Manners the train starts the band plays remembrances of old langsine, the noise is tremendous, soldiers cheering happy jolly faces out of all the windows . . .
> Blank after.
> The thing I could hardly bear was a porter who burst into tears when the train went.

Violet's last vision of her son was 'his flushed excited face thrust out of the window behind John Manners, and I waved until the train was out of sight'. Their thoughts remained with him, wherever he might be across the Channel: 'Somehow my pen falls from my hands when

I think of the heat, the fatigue, the plain of Belgium, where I under-stand our troops are going – my only news is in the *Homme Libre* which has twice as much news as any English paper . . . I only hope the postal arrangements will be good.'

Alfred went to stay at Wigsell, spending quiet evenings alone with her and Helen. These beautiful days they spent mostly outdoors; Violet was to remember that still, sunny weather for the rest of her life. For Alfred it was a momentary respite from exhausting work, but not from their chief preoccupation: 'impossible', he wrote, 'to talk and think of anything but Armageddon.'

The War Office took over his Sturry estate as billets for the West Kent Yeomanry. Officers slept in the house, there were horses in the barn and a forest of tents pitched in a field. For the time being Alfred was excluded from his country haven, and lodged nearby on his occa-sional visits. The much-loved house soon showed signs of rough treat-ment by the military. Territorial and Yeomanry units were stationed all round as the south-east coast was deemed especially vulnerable to invasion. The German armies in France and Belgium were pushing hard towards the coast and the tension in Kent mounted, reaching a climax in October when the enemy advanced as far as Ostend.

Much has been said about Britain's unreadiness for war in 1914. This was so in terms of manpower and guns, but many in the highly-trained BEF were tough Boer War veterans. The German Army, though its officer corps and NCOs were well versed in modern methods and formidably equipped, lacked experience under fire.

George went in the First Army Corps of the British Expeditionary Force, alongside battalions of the Coldstream and the Irish Guards. The General Staff organised their transport with great efficiency and exceptional speed. They crossed the Channel in the *Cawdor Castle*, on a dead calm sea, which was just as well because the ship was packed with soldiers, and seasickness would have been disastrous. Until they got under way, even the ship's Captain did not know their destination – Le Havre. Here they were greeted by cheering fishermen, the *Marseillaise*, cider and women bringing flowers. Their first, blisteringly hot march in the early morning, through the docks and the town to the rest camp five miles off, saw men falling out in tens, as a result of the heat and the unfamiliar local brew; many reservist troops were unfit for marching with new boots and ninety-pound packs across the unforgiving *pavés*, which were almost as uneven as cobblestones. George, trained in route marches, would have had a better time of it, despite the heat. On 15 August at 2 a.m. they entrained for Belgium. En route they camped for four nights, training and receiving inoculations against typhoid, and comparing themselves favourably with the Coldstream Guards whose saluting drills they considered sloppy. George's fluent French impressed the soldiers whom he helped to buy food; he also had to explain to the wine dealers that they were not to sell drink to the men.

Violet's only news of him was the newspaper announcement that the whole Expeditionary Force had landed and been given a wonderful reception in France and Belgium. She was pleased that Brigadier-General Robert Scott-Kerr, with an excellent military reputation, was commanding them. She had written to him about George; she was more afraid for her son's health 'than I am of the bullets', and she wished there was an older and more experienced soldier to look out for him: 'at 18 to undergo such a strain as this campaign seems to me excessive – to say nothing of his never having ever done a brigade training.' She had a poor opinion of Colonel Corry, his battalion commander, for 'not changing both George and John into a battalion which will come out in three months time, though of course John is twenty-three, harder and though more ignorant militarily than George, less likely to succumb.'

How little Violet, and everybody at home, knew about the tactics, the conditions and above all, the whereabouts of the BEF! The soldiers themselves were bewildered in a war of such rapid movement. This was the last period of mobile war on the Western Front before the trench warfare which was to endure from the end of 1914 until the final summer of the war itself, four years later: there was no proper liaison, in the armies of either side, as the Germans moved swiftly across country.

After midday on 20 August George's brigade marched towards the Belgian border where, ominously, they could hear the gunfire, and realised that the Germans were much nearer than they had thought.

On 23 August, at 3.30 a.m., the Guards were ordered to advance towards Mons, in Belgium, through an unlovely region of mining villages, slag heaps and pit heads. Here their drums were silenced, so as not to give away their whereabouts, although the German planes could see them all too plainly in the summer light and the drums were a help in keeping up the men's marching rhythm and their sense of being a unit.

At 1.30 p.m., near the outskirts of Mons, they had to abandon their first proper food that day when the Germans drew very close, forcing the French and the much small British forces into retreat. George's Brigade struggled for twenty miles along roads crowded with refugees and artillery to the little town of Landrecies, where the 1st Army Corps, under Sir Douglas Haig, had established headquarters. Scarcely recovered from their march, they began their first engagement with the enemy, during what the Grenadier Major Lord Charles Gordon Lennox described as 'one of the longest nights I have ever spent'. George's company was defending the river bridge to the rear of the front line, and pulled up paving stones to make shelters against enemy missiles. During the battle George himself was orderly officer to Brigadier-General Scott-Kerr.

The Guards were trained, like the rest of the British force, to fire so rapidly that the enemy believed them to be using machine-guns. With the aid of two real machine-guns and a field howitzer, the German attack was held back; but behind the Guards, in the town, Haig and his headquarters had evacuated in near panic after a shell had hit the house they were occupying. At 4 a.m. the Guards themselves pulled out, abandoning much of their kit, including entrenching tools. Some of their companions, too, they left behind, dead. The injured were evacuated, those who could walk staying with the marching columns.

The retreat from the town was achieved before daylight: the British defenders were all but asleep on their feet as they made their way along the hot dusty road to Oisy, eight miles away. Next day they continued down the road through Etreux, destined later that day to be the scene of one of the war's epic engagements, when the 800-strong 2nd Munster Fusiliers, following behind them, fought a twelve-hour battle with a force six times their size. Only 200 survived and were led, after firing their last shot, into captivity – a whole battalion destroyed. It was a taste of things to come. By the end of 1914 there would be little of the original BEF left, and soldiers spoke of the 'dead little, red little army'. Now, George and his 4th Guards Brigade remained doggedly determined, as the BEF hastened south along roads and across country, bewildered by repeated rumours of impending attacks from three sides: the 'fog of war' was as impenetrable as ever – signs of a German assault from St Quentin turned out to be the dust from a column of British lorries.

Violet, who lived in suspense since saying goodbye to her son, wrote to Edward on 27 August: 'It feels to me 100 years since I wrote, but it was only a week ago.' All she had to report was a brief note from George, dated 21 August, while they had been still advancing. 'He said that up to date it had all been the most glorious fun.'

The fun had long since ceased. After another exhausting march of nineteen miles, the Brigade crossed the Oise, having evaded the enemy all the way. Not one Grenadier fell out along the route. They rested one day, then at 3 a.m. began a long trek, relentlessly hot when the sun rose, although much of it was through forest. After a mid-day stop followed a six-hour march of twenty-three miles, when again, miraculously, no one fell out.

In London the papers were publishing the mostly optimistic reports of correspondents then roaming northern France and Flanders in pursuit of elusive facts: they heralded as a great victory a resolute holding action by the British 2nd Army under General Smith-Dorrien at Le Câteau. Sometimes, though, to inject a note of urgency and drama into their reports they put matters more plainly; one telegram, published by *The Times*, on 30 August, referred to 'the broken bits of many regiments' which was extremely distressing to the public, particularly those such as Violet whose sons and husbands were in the BEF. As Lord Northcliffe, the owner of *The Times*, had calculated, it also caused a surge of young men to join up to serve their country. At Violet's request Alfred busied himself with arranging for several English volunteer nurses to be sent to France to aid the French wounded, following an urgent message from Clemenceau. Alfred, Violet, her mother and Helen were joined at Wigsell by the Kiplings, 'even in these bad days, very delightful company'. Alfred, although no better informed than anyone else about the state of the war, was clearsighted enough to know that it was going against Britain and France, especially after hearing from one of the nurses whom he had sent over. Yet he did his best to cheer up Violet.

On Monday 31 August, just after crossing the Aisne river, the Grenadiers lost their first man to fall out by the way. He fainted in the presence of a singularly pretty French *ambulancière* and, the brigade needing to move on, he was left in her care, while the troops marched on in the heat eleven miles to their next bivouac in thickly wooded country. In the stillness of the night the soldiers could hear the rumbling wheels of transport vehicles somewhere to their north. At 3 a.m. they were woken to prepare for action. George's company was posted forward to look out for the enemy. Unable to see anything through the mist and dense trees, but realising that a German attack was beginning, they fell back, as instructed, to join the other companies, and took up a position on a woodland ride leading westward from a small clearing, Rond de la Reine, two miles north of the town of Villers-Cotterêts. As the mist lifted and sunbeams broke through the dark green late summer foliage, the woods were for a while delightful, despite the hidden danger; British Lancers and Scots Greys on their horses, from the 5th Cavalry Brigade, stopped to chat with friends in the Grenadiers. As one diarist wrote,

> It was very pleasant coffee housing in the shady ride, for all the world like a big field hunting in the New Forest on a spring day . . . Very shortly after the Cavalry had moved off, we heard a good deal of firing from the direction of the northern edge of the forest, and after a bit a herd of deer appeared opposite my two companies. They looked extraordinarily pretty and at first didn't spot us as we lay quite still, but when they did spot us, they galloped off to our right. It was hard to believe it was War!

Not for long. Near 11 a.m. a clamour of rifle fire was heard approaching Rond de la Reine. George and his companions waited at a position to the west of this, but so thick were the woods that they could not see their enemies who were also coming round them from the east. In a couple of hours, on the west, other companies of Coldstream and Irish Guards, falling back, found the German troops, tall Brandenburgers from the 35th Regiment, getting round their flank and suddenly in among them, firing at point blank range. This desperate and confused mêlée was akin to a scene in the Battle of Waterloo. The Brigadier, in agony from wounds, having been carried off the field by the brigade Major, left the brigade for a while leaderless and without orders. George's platoon seems to have attempted a counter-attack to cover the retreat, but neither this nor other efforts by the Guards turned the tide. The Germans could have been repelled had the British made a stand *en masse*, for there were not many more of them and they were equally tired. But as the bulk of the British were continually retreating, actual fighting at any given moment was left to just a few men; and the woodland concealed from them the Germans' relatively small numbers. Eventually, leaving the enemy masters of the field, the Guards Brigade managed to re-form and retreat in good order at nightfall through Villers-Cotterêts; its men had been marching, fighting and digging since 3 a.m. Their retreat continued for another four days until they were twenty-five miles from Paris. Then the French and British began to push the Germans back the way they had come, to the river Aisne, where the British had been on 30 August.

Those missing after the woodland battle included Lieutenant-Colonel the Hon. George Morris commanding the 1st Irish Guards; Lieutenant Geoffrey Lambton of the Coldstream Guards; and among the Grenadiers, 160 'other ranks' and three officers. Lieutenant the Hon. Francis 'Buddy' Needham had been wounded and taken prisoner; his platoon and that of Lieutenant the Hon. John Manners, also missing, had never received orders to withdraw and had been cut off. The third officer was George, reported wounded: had he died, or taken shelter, or been captured by the Germans?

'Wounded and missing' was all Violet heard from a letter from a fellow-officer, which she received on Tuesday 8 September – a whole week later. She immediately travelled to London, 'terribly distressed and looking very ill,' Alfred wrote. Neither the War Office nor Walter Page, the American Ambassador to London, to whom she turned for help as representative of a neutral power, and whom she found considerably upset himself, could enlighten her as to George's fate. From the enemy no co-operation was to be expected. 'So far the Germans have refused to open a war Bureau to give names and conditions of wounded,' she wrote to Edward, trying to soften the news for him. 'I know it will be a knife stroke,' she went on, 'but we have both expected it in these tremendous days, though the blow is dreadful.'

Violet summoned all her ingenuity to establish George's fate: Alfred, also in a state of shock, went down to Wigsell where the family had been joined by their young cousin David Cecil, as a companion for Helen. Uncertainty about George hung like a pall over everything. Although news had come of an Allied victory on the river Marne, Alfred was too realistic to rejoice: 'while it was undoubtedly a success and seems to indicate a turn in the tide, I am afraid the extent and decisiveness of the victory may be rather over-estimated.'

Violet had wired her cousin Ernest Maxse, then working in Rotterdam; perhaps he could find out whether the Germans were holding George prisoner. She grasped at straws – that George could have crawled, wounded, to shelter in a French house and be there still, sick but alive. 'I have every reliance on George's resourcefulness and brain. But he may be too ill to think.'

CHAPTER NINETEEN

Bereavement

ON 5 OCTOBER, Rudyard Kipling, in a letter to a friend, encapsulated Violet's travails:

An old friend and neighbour of ours had her son reported wounded and missing more than a month ago. She went over to Paris the other day and covered all the country near where he fell in a vain search for news. A sympathetic French peasantry assuring her he was all right; the guns growling far off, and she wandering from one piled mound of graves to the next. She hears nothing save a report that he was seen dying in a ditch (the boy is 18). She comes back to England . . . On that very day comes word from the boy's battalion that a returned prisoner saw the lad blown to pieces by a shell. And so the horrible see-saw goes on; she dying daily and letters of condolence *and* congratulation crossing each other and harrowing her soul. Meanwhile the boy's father thousands of miles away and cut off from all save letters and wires.

Alfred Milner tried to dissuade Violet from going to France in September. He had gathered from his friend Fabian Ware, who had undertaken a 'Red Cross hunt' for George, that the situation was too hazardous: 'the massed opposing sides were ranged against each other along the line of the Aisne, neither had the mastery and the losses on both sides were horrifyingly high,' Alfred wrote in his diary. But Violet was determined to go, and she had the opportunity to travel with her brother-in-law, Bob Cecil, a volunteer in the Red Cross Missing and Wounded Department, which was carrying out investigations on behalf of hundreds of distracted parents and wives.

In a sad travesty of the jaunts across the Channel that she had last enjoyed with George himself, brother and sister-in-law, united in apprehension, crossed to Dieppe on 19 September; Clemenceau, to whom she had appealed, had followed up the possibility that George might be taking refuge in a French household and had also made enquiries in the hospitals and ambulance depots around Compiègne, but, he reported to Leo Maxse, '*George n'est dans aucun village, hôpital, ambulance, famille privée. Je le crois prisonnier des Allemands.*' This was another false trail.

'I at once wired to Clemenceau for a pass to get me to Villers-Cotterêts and beyond to Vivières,' Violet wrote to Edward. 'The difficulty was that the Battle of the Aisne, which has now been raging for 3 weeks is very near that part of the world. Villers-Cotterêts was last week, I daresay it is still – the headquarters of the French western army – Vivières, to the north about 5 miles, was even more difficult to attain.'

In the event, Violet could not accompany Robert Cecil on his visit to the scene of the action as she had given up her seat in a Red Cross motor ambulance to a nurse. Balked of that opportunity, Violet now pulled all the strings she could and somehow – with the help of Myron Herrick, the American Ambassador in Paris, who lent her his car and one of his military attachés – she managed it. Her journey was as disheartening as it was dangerous. The French soldiers whom she questioned 'were nicer than you can imagine but they had all only been there a few days. We had a miserable hour turning round and round in a circle.' She admitted that 'although I have not with my instinct been able to believe in his death, my reason told me that hope was practically dead.'

In addition, Bob Cecil saw, in hospital, Needham, the only one of the missing Grenadier officers to turn up. Needham had seen nothing of George, but Needham's servant, when he was a prisoner, had seen George lying badly wounded in the head in a ditch and believed him to be dead.

At the end of a fruitless week in France, Violet telegraphed that she was returning to Wigsell. Alfred met her at Folkestone and they drove back to Wigsell together, too drained to talk. 'There is no good news of George Cecil,' Alfred wrote, 'and I think she had altogether despaired of seeing him again alive.' Late the next afternoon, however, a telegram came from her cousin Ernest Maxse reporting a rumour that George was a wounded prisoner at Aachen. 'This started again,' Alfred continued, 'the fitful hope and racking uncertainty, in which she has lived for three weeks.'

But then came a letter from Colonel Wilfrid Abel-Smith, dated 26

September. Smith had taken over as the officer commanding George's battalion and had written to 'My dear Ned' in pencil on two leaves torn from his military pocket note book:

> You will, I am sure, know by now about your poor boy, and I have only delayed writing to you till I could get good evidence of how he died. A prisoner who returned to us yesterday tells me that he saw him killed by a shell. I am afraid, therefore, there can no longer be any doubt. He was an excellent boy, and everybody speaks highly of him . . . it may be a comfort to you to know that he can have suffered no pain, and that he was buried by our prisoners near where he died. You will know now that I am not allowed to mention names of places.

Violet sent this letter on to Edward with Ernest Maxse's letter, the two being completely at odds, and with an account of another story she had been told about a drummer boy who said he had buried George and John Manners.

> You see it is 5 weeks since it happened, 4 weeks since I heard. I have kept sane, but this is all I can say . . . I have practically no reasonable hope. I don't feel as if George could be dead, but that is simply because I saw him last so well and full of life. My instincts tell me he is alive – my reason that he is dead, the evidence is too good. I cannot write about what I feel, the loss and the loss to Helen of this warm heart and capable head. George's power of love is among the great things I have seen in my life . . .
>
> I write calmly – I eat, I walk, I talk, I sleep, I feel hot and cold, I write my letters. I have all the appearance of a live person and one not in ill health. I am so dreadfully sorry for you stuck in Cairo and only dependent on these letters in which – alas – there is never any good news.

Alfred and the Kiplings, 'a very sad party,' consulted together at Wigsell. They felt they must still investigate the rumour, however unlikely, that George was a prisoner.

> Kipling has been kindness itself . . . [Violet wrote to Edward] and makes the wildest suggestions and some very good – for breaking down the German wall of official silence. One can truly say that nothing has been left undone . . . and before you get this letter I shall I think be able to cable definitely and either tell you the worst or something which will make you almost happy again.
>
> Your loving Violet.

In London, Alfred enlisted a friend with German contacts, Philip Ashworth, the traveller and German scholar, to sail to neutral Holland. But after exhaustive enquiries, he telegrammed that George Cecil was not and never had been at Aachen. The last vestiges of hope were demolished when Wilfrid Smith confirmed his earlier news.

Smith had supposed the Cecils would have heard officially long before, but so unreliable were communications at that stage of the war, that his handwritten letters posted from the front reached England comparatively speedily, whereas his official report was not relayed to George's family.

Throughout this ordeal Alfred was a constant support to Violet and to Helen, whom he helped to buy a little terrier pup for company. He found Violet's grief 'deplorable in the extreme' and was himself too distraught to eat or work properly. His depression deepened when he learnt on 15 November that Lord Roberts had died while visiting the Indian troops at the front. Over the British nation as a whole, reeling from their tragic losses at the front, came, with the death of their beloved soldier hero, a melancholy mood. There were many dire moments to come in that war, but few more sombre: 'It was extraordinarily dark, damp, and chilly,' wrote Alfred, who attended Roberts's funeral at St Paul's Cathedral, on 19 November.

On the same day a telegram told Violet that George's body had been identified in one of the graves at Villers Cotterêts.

Bob Cecil and others of the Paris Branch of the British Red Cross had gone with a team of labourers to investigate what had happened to the missing soldiers at the Villers-Cotterêts battlefield. There was a grave, deep in the forest, that they wished to examine. Lord Killanin accompanied them; it was his brother, Lieutenant-Colonel George Morris, the commanding officer of the 1st Irish Guards, who had been missing since the action. Killanin's account told of the grisly process of disinterring the dead, which went on for three days, and revealed ninety-eight bodies crammed, entangled, into a pit twenty-five feet long and twelve feet wide. The state of the corpses after two and half months' burial, with faces smashed and features masked with clay and blood, made identification an ordeal, but many still had name discs round their necks. The four officers' bodies were dug up at a late stage of the search, after Robert Cecil had to return to Paris. Colonel Morris was identified by his wrist watch.

Very soon afterwards, the remains of another officer were found. The buttons showed that it was the body of a Grenadier, but no disc could be found on the body, but we were of opinion, from the description of George Cecil's figure supplied to us, and especially from the size of the boots, that it was his body and this was confirmed by finding on the front of the vest the initials 'G.E.C.' which we cut off. As a memento for his mother we took three buttons off his uniform. His remains were placed beside those of the other officers.

It was possible to see that George had been wounded in the head and chest.

The grave was enlarged so that the bodies could be properly laid out and the ninety-four 'other ranks' were immediately re-buried with prayers. The following day, the four officers were put into coffins. The Mayor of Villers-Cotterêts, M. Mouflier, and his family brought a pall and flowers to place over these, and they were buried in the town cemetery, the sound of gunfire ever-present in the background. Some twenty French officers snatched time from the nearby fighting on the Aisne to attend the funeral.

On both the grave in the forest and in the cemetery, wooden crosses were erected giving brief details. George's read: '*Le Lieutenant George E. Cecil, des Grenadiers de la Garde – Tombé au champs d'honneur le 1er Septembre 1914.*'

Bob Cecil accepted, from Lord Killanin, George's pathetic relics – a painful moment for them both. 'I think the future of Bob's life went away with him,' confided Nelly to Edward later. Childless and affectionate, Bob had been devoted to his promising, generous-hearted nephew. The desperate sadness of that search for him in France brought home to Bob the reality of war. After the world conflict was over, he devoted the rest of his active life to trying to achieve a world without war through the League of Nations.

Killanin intended his consoling thoughts to help Bob to come to terms with the loss of his nephew and the ghastly work of exhumation: 'Their remains were rescued from an utterly unknown grave and a most indecorous burial, and have been laid to rest . . . when everything possible was done to show respect and reverence and affection and honour to their glorious and loved memories.'

Bob sent Edward an abbreviated, less painful, version of Killanin's report and his own deeply felt words of comfort:

Sad, terribly sad as it was I can honestly say that it was in a way deeply consoling – somehow the great beauty of the place – a beech forest in hilly country combining the charm of woodlands with occasional glimpses of green distance together with the real sympathy of the French people and their genuine gratitude and even enthusiasm for what our troops had done for them – made one see a little that even war with all its horrors was consistent with the Divine government of the world. And then the very loss of all aspect of humanity in the dead, gruesome as at first it was, made one understand how little a part of the true personality depends on the body. I never had so vivid an impression of the immortality of the soul as in standing by that open grave . . . My dearest Nigs, when I think of your grief and Violet's it is dreadful. But it is impossible to grieve for him – a wonderfully perfect life – so affectionate, so upright so true so innocent – followed by a painless and glorious death. We have lost much but he has gained immeasurably more.

Edward had already received the final terrible telegram – 'grave opened George believed identified broken hearted Violet Cecil'.

Without their Christian beliefs in this earthly life as only symbolic of the realities of the eternal life to come, Violet could not agree with Bob and Edward that even war with all its horrors was consistent with the divine government of the world, nor take comfort in George's soul being for evermore with God; least of all that the very loss of all aspects of humanity in the bodies in the mass grave by which Bob had stood in sorrowful contemplation was in fact evidence of the unimportance of the body, of the triumph of the spirit and the soul's immortality. To her, George's mangled remains were just that: his remains. Reality was her darling boy's handsome features and upright body being destroyed, as he lay – for how long? she agonised – wounded, perhaps crying for her, until dying, alone in the same anonymous French ditch, he was

> thrown like carrion into a pit; when I think of the inhuman waste of a beautiful life I can hardly endure myself or to be part of a world where such things were possible.
>
> George had grown (was hourly growing too) to be so exactly what any fond and ambitious mother would wish – with character, looks and remarkable brain and heart that to think of him is to think of his death only as the most cruel waste of material for his country and desolation for me. He was my future.

In their grief husband and wife were isolated from one another, by his religion and her lack of it. Recognising this, Violet threw at least one letter she had written on to the fire: 'You see you and I can't talk about any of the great vital things without my saying something which might touch upon your religious views so I won't write about the Great Dissolver, Death – we have no common ground at all about it. Your beliefs are incredible to me and my consolation different to yours. I had written and . . . then came your letter with a reference to "future life" and I felt mine had better go into the fire and the whole subject remain untouched,' she wrote to Edward on Christmas Eve.

Violet's letters make painful reading: one can only imagine their effect on Edward, as alone in Cairo as she was in England. In her next letter, on Boxing Day, she alluded to her tactlessness and made a determined effort to discuss more general topics, international affairs and the progress of the war. The regular letters that she dutifully penned on the elegant Wigsell writing paper, now bordered in black, were courteous but hardly sympathetic. Edward had to take his comfort, as best he could, elsewhere: in his religion, his friends and his work.

To Alice he wrote that Violet's want of religious faith made him grieve the more for her. 'I'm very unhappy about Violet. It's awful for her to believe that she will never see him again and that he is only dust. I pray and hope that she may be helped to see.' In letters to his beloved Helen he tried to give her the comfort of his Christian beliefs in the afterlife. The tragedy of her brother's death intensified her spiritual yearnings. In her thirteen years she had never seen such grief as Violet's, and the intensity of her mother's feeling frightened her. She did what she could to console her, sleeping in her room, and putting fresh violets in their usual place behind George's photograph at her bedside. On her walks outside in the wintry garden she struggled to understand what had happened. The swing on which she and George had played became a symbol of her past, childhood, happiness. 'I love the swing, it has many dear recollections of George and exhilarates one to praise God,' she wrote in her diary.

There was a sense of time stopping for Violet with George's death: the past obliterated, the future empty, the present days and sleepless nights to be endured. All was still that Christmas at Wigsell; the cold penetrated the thick stone walls, and up the old staircase to the attics

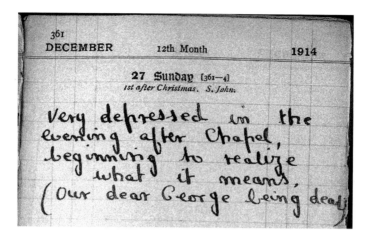

361
DECEMBER   12th Month   1914

27 Sunday [361—4]
1st after Christmas. S. John.

Very depressed in the evening after Chapel, beginning to realize what it means, (Our dear George being dead)

*Extract from Helen Cecil's diary while she
spent Christmas 1914 at Hatfield*

where George had played as a child. Outside, too, was the same still-ness, when Violet roused herself to walk through the orchard, where the fall of a solitary withered apple was the only movement; through the fields, where the sheep paused in their munching to gaze at her as she passed. Pheasants rose, squawking, bringing memories of George's enjoyment of days out with his gun.

Helen spent Christmas at Hatfield, but she felt isolated in that cheer-ful throng of relations. Many of the young were in khaki, ready to go to France. Randle, aged twenty-five, and Victor, aged twenty-three, the elder sons of William and Florence Cecil, had already gone to the front. Violet had given Victor George's spare kit, which had been sent back home. Jem Salisbury was responsible for the organisation of the Hertfordshire Territorials, with general's rank. His son, Bobbety Cranborne, was in the 2nd Grenadiers and would be in France by the spring, if the war continued. Jem wrote to Edward, telling him that he had given George's unopened letters, passed to him from the military authorities, to Violet. He added: 'I have only as yet sent five officers to the front and three of them killed and one wounded. But I suppose that is nothing out of the common. God grant it may be soon over. But for you the worst has happened. In a few weeks time we may be in a like case.'

Kipling felt the same; he was aware when he hunted for clues of George how soon he might be facing Violet's ordeal. For John Kipling was eager to get to the front. On 31 October he had said,

'We have a pretty stiff training in the Brigade, but it is great fun. With luck I ought to be out at the front in eight weeks, but it is mostly a question of luck.' Kipling was still doing all he could to help Violet piece together George's last hours and the exact circumstances of his death, interviewing four Grenadier survivors of the battle of Villers-Cotterêts.

According to one, Private Snowden, whose account he trusted, the platoons of George's company were eventually cut off and nearly all killed in and around the 'sunken lane', a grassy wide ditch from which the men were firing at the Germans closing in on them to their left. Snowden said he then saw George running through the forest behind the line of men, firing from his revolver, apparently the last officer of the company still on his feet. He was hit in the hand, stumbled, jumped up again, drew his sword and said: 'Charge lads, and we'll do 'em in yet!' – a form of words which Snowden repeated and insisted on. By that time, with fire coming from all sides, he was shot in the head and killed immediately.

This, as Kipling said, was 'as far as you will ever get it from the soldiers present at the fight'. Violet was grateful to him: 'One can't help wanting to know it all even though it is nothing but agony. One always wants to know the truth.'

At Wigsell, 'it was bitterly cold outside and inside great sadness,' Alfred wrote. 'I am so thankful to think you are going down to be with Violet,' her mother told him. 'I am sure she must not be left alone. It is all heart breaking and one can do nothing to help her except give her all our tenderness – and love.'

Violet spent New Year's Eve at Alfred's new house at Great College Street, Westminster. Then she and Helen went to stay at Sturry Court where he had hired a piano, and Helen played Chopin to them. Violet encouraged her to seek solace in music, as the Cecils did in religion, and Helen enjoyed her walks with Alfred, feeling safe and comforted in his care.

As far as his public life was concerned, Alfred, like Bob Cecil and many others in the Conservative party, was restless and frustrated. Longing to use their experience to help the war effort, they felt that the Liberal Government should build on the party political truce that had prevailed since the start of the war and give them greater responsibility. Both Alfred and Bob Cecil flung themselves into voluntary, humanitarian work. For Alfred, the case for National Service seemed ever more pressing, as the carnage grew daily more terrible.

In February he was able to visit a prisoner-of-war camp at Holyport near Maidenhead for an investigation similar to Kipling's, this time among German prisoners, Brandenburgers of the 35th Regiment of Foot. In strangely civilised circumstances during a war in which both sides were beginning to bombard their populations with hate propaganda, Alfred spoke in German to two officers, one of whom had been in the thick of the fight in the woods near Villers-Cotterêts. Both were willing to help, as were the British authorities who arranged the meeting. However, they could add little to the existing evidence; in that wooded country the Germans had been as confused as their enemy and unable to gain any general idea of the action. Their picture of unremitting exhaustion among their ranks as they advanced and then retreated was very similar to that of the British forces matched against them.

On the Western Front the troops of both sides were now entrenched. The surviving ranks of the Grenadiers, the gaps left by their fallen comrades filled with drafts from England, gazed over a bleak, rain-sodden landscape towards the seemingly immovable enemy lines.

Violet spent long solitary hours compiling a little volume of letters and diaries chronicling George's last weeks. She interwove them with the letters home of his companion-in-arms, John Manners, and testimonies from the wounded Brigadier Scott-Kerr, whom she had been to see, saying that he had no son of his own, but he would have been proud to have called such a boy as George his son.

She sent the leather-bound notebook with gold and floral end-papers to Edward, keeping a copy at Wigsell, now bereft of its heir. Many bereaved women carefully compiled these pathetically slim, commemorative books, an agonising process, but one they needed to go through to try to cope with their grief. Mary Elcho, who lost two sons, wrote to Arthur Balfour, 'I know I ought to feel grateful for the many happy years, but when I sit on the floor alone among heaps of "dead leaves", fluttering papers of the past – I see the glorious crowns of life nipped off and life's hopes and aspirations – and incidentally one's own heart! – lie bleeding in the dust – the long years of preparation leading up to the holocaust. Religious people say this life is but a preparation . . . well . . .'

Sometimes Violet gave in to bitterness: why had her son been singled out while others seemed immune? Bobbety Cranborne had severe colitis, which kept him at home. In fact his condition seems to have been part of an overall debility after exposure to the ferocity of trench warfare, in particular going over the top at the battle of Festubert in May. Alice and Jem thus, ironically, 'reap a reward for having neglected their children's digestion. If I had done the same,' wrote Violet to Edward, 'perhaps George would have come home with appendicitis (as George Nugent's boy did on the retreat). Everything I ever did for him told against him and sent him to the place of peril and kept him there.'

By the time Edward received this letter, in July, he would also have had the news of William Cecil's son Rupert's death, 'killed instantaneously, shot in the head whilst running to see to his men in their trench,' Violet told him. 'Next week,' she went on, 'it will be a year's agony one has lived through and human nature being so strangely tough and resisting, not died of. It is certain that grief does not kill the body – England is full up of people who prove that fact.'

The year brought an unremitting sequence of casualties. Among friends and family, Teddy Hulse, aged twenty-five, was killed in action at the battle of Neuve Chapelle in March. Violet went to Breamore to be with Edith, 'whose heart is as surely broken as mine.' In May, George's good comrade, Lieutenant-Colonel Wilfrid Abel-Smith, died of wounds, aged forty-five. In June, Julian Grenfell also died of a head wound, and, on the last day of the following month, his brother, Billy:

> 2 golden curly heads, Julian and Billy [wrote Violet]. They have one boy left, just going to Sandhurst. Billy seems to have lost his life in a vast muddle in which the Greenjackets suffered dreadfully, 800 men killed and wounded, they have not recovered his body, nor has the Public ever been told there was an engagement. We are told nothing. All we know is that we are bereaved.
>
> Today last year was George's last day in England.
>
> Tomorrow I shall not even be able to say 'last year'.

Breamore, Hatfield, Taplow and the other households Violet knew so well from peacetime visits somehow came to terms with the deaths of their boys, with the knowledge that there would be no heirs, and with living in the shadow of deaths to come. 'Willy [Selborne] tells me Bobby Palmer [his son] is on his way to Mesopotamia with a draft. So that they are about to enter the period of anguish. [He was to die at the battle of Um–El–Hanna in January 1916.] Gradually I see all my friends approach that zone and how it changes them!'

The young, too, grieved for their friends. John Manners's sister, Angela, wrote to Violet, artless, ill-spelt letters like the fluting of a beautiful, wounded bird in a world altogether changed by war. She described how at Taplow she walked along the cedar walk, where she had so often strolled with Billy Grenfell, whom she had loved, looking down on the great house:

> That hideous house looked gaunt and sad, I'd never seen it anything but <u>crammed</u> full of youth and brains and the joy of life; and as we walked up Ettie, Lord Desborough, Monica and Imogen were sitting in the garden trying to look and be the same.
>
> I cannot tell you what her [Ettie's] courage is. She has put on the <u>whole</u> armour of faith, and lives in the thoughts of what they were and what they did and how they died. She will not, anyhow to an outsider like me, allow one to see that there is any tragedy or resentment. We walked and talked

Lord and Lady Desborough and their family. Billy (standing) and Julian (with dog) were killed in 1915

of them for an hour and I never heard her say a bitter word, and it was me who said them all and alas felt them. It hurts to see such courage in so frail and sad a face. Bill's body has been found and he was buried just as he fell, they are relieved about it, for of course they never knew for <u>certain</u> till now that he might not have been wounded and tried to crawl to a trench, but there is <u>no</u> doubt now, he was 20 yards in front of all the rest and lead the whole attack, such if it had to be I suppose he would have it. Poor Lord Desborough he is simple in his grief and grudges his beautiful boys and seldom stops crying, Oh the sorrow of it all why were we born to this.

But I've loved coming and seen such lovely letters.

Angela Manners threw herself into looking after children bereaved by the war – 'How interested John and George and Bill would have been,' she finished her letter.

Ettie Desborough was admired for not 'breaking down', an admiration mixed with incredulity at such resilience. Violet also did her best in front of others. 'I try to keep up an appearance of courage but it is a mere show – all the stuffing is out of me. I have wished each breath I drew was the last, ever since I was sure of George's death. I try to hide what I feel from Helen, try to lift a corner of her load.'

Walter Page, the American Ambassador to London, wrote of the staunchness and restraint of the women who came seeking his help: 'At intervals they come all day. Not a tear have I seen yet. They take it as part of the price of greatness and of empire. You guess at their grief only by their reticence. They use as few words as possible and then courteously take themselves away. It isn't an accident that these people own a fifth of the world. Utterly unwarlike, they outlast anybody else when war comes.'

In September 1915, a year after George's death, Rudyard and Carrie Kipling's only son John went missing during the Battle of Loos. The Kiplings had the same anxious, fruitless search as Violet, who now did everything she could to help. But John's body was never found, and Carrie and Rudyard were forever broken-hearted. Rudyard, always doing his utmost to suppress his grief, began physically to decline from then onwards.

In George's memory Violet had commissioned a rifle range at his old school, Winchester, and Kipling opened it, made a patriotic speech to the assembled school and scored a bull's eye with the first shot.

The 'Great Push' at Loos, which had cost John Kipling and countless others their lives, had failed to break through the German line

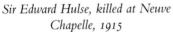

Sir Edward Hulse, killed at Neuve Chapelle, 1915

John Kipling, killed at Loos, 1915

on the Western Front. In Asia Minor, the Gallipoli campaign against Turkey, originally masterminded by Winston Churchill early in 1915, was now being wound up after a string of defeats. America still refused to join in. At home volunteers for the Army were dwindling, but the Prime Minister, Asquith, remained wary of introducing military conscription because it contradicted fundamental Liberal beliefs.

Asquith was still very much in control, although since May, his was now a coalition government with the Conservatives. As a concession to them, he had dropped Winston Churchill – condemned over his management of the Gallipoli campaign – from his post as First Lord of the Admiralty, and R.B. Haldane – pilloried since the start of the war for having once spoken of Germany as his 'spiritual home' – from the Lord Chancellorship. These changes pleased Violet who, like most patriotic Conservatives, regarded Haldane, despite having been an old friend of the Admiral's, as a danger to the country, and Churchill as an untrustworthy egomaniac. But Asquith had given no key jobs, save the Admiralty to Arthur Balfour, to any Conservative politician.

Alfred Milner was palmed off with a committee on wartime agriculture. He, as usual, took immense trouble to interview farmers and agricultural experts, yet his sensible conclusions about land management and food production were disregarded by the Cabinet.

Violet cursed the Government, especially Asquith, for his laziness, for his indecision about conscription and for hiding awkward truths from the public. 'Asquith who reduced the army and talked peace when he knew it was war, is still Prime Minister. Grey whose blunders and mistakes, whose blindness and whiggery took us up to the guns blindfolded is still foreign minister, Haldane who helped the Germans organise their victorious march into France is drawing £5,000 a year.'

Such talk of conspiracy and incompetence was the language of Leo Maxse's *National Review* and, increasingly, of Lord Northcliffe's patriotic press, reinforced by the gossip about Asquith's frivolity, drinking and philandering. Alfred told Violet that his friend Norah Lindsay spent a Sunday with the Asquiths. 'The war was not mentioned. Asquith flowed on with pleasant gossip. He is in excellent spirits, played golf all day, and bridge all the evening and cuddled Mrs Montague in betweenwhiles.' He was no longer nicknamed 'Squiff', she told Edward, 'but "*Soif*", in compliment to our allies.'

Military conscription, long desired by Alfred, Kipling and the Maxses, came at last in January 1916. Destined to provide another two and half million men for the armed forces, it also, momentarily, checked the Conservative critics anxious to pull down Asquith's Government. Like many, Violet and Edward considered those who did not join up until compelled were little better than shirkers – unfairly, for thousands of conscripts had conflicting obligations to work and families, and were often relieved to have the decision made for them.

Nonetheless the volunteers of 1914 and 1915 commanded a particular respect which Violet shared: she offered to take in the five-year-old son of a 'Kitchener Volunteer' officer whose wife was living on ten shillings a week. Victor Chapman, wild and 'black and blue with home beatings', was for all that 'a jolly little chap'. However, the poor child proved a handful. Hugh Cecil, by then an elderly and erratic pilot in the Royal Flying Corps, mercifully kept from flying duties, told Alice of his unease at seeing his sister-in-law 'going through the antics of maternity with a child who was not her own'. Neither the efficient Violet, the patient governess nor the affectionate Helen could cure Victor's screaming fits. After several months, Violet, who had never been fond of him, Gwendolen thought, gave up the struggle and he was passed to another guardian.

Violet and Helen decided to spend Christmas 1915 quietly at Breamore with Edith Hulse, rather than trying to keep up cheerful appearances at Hatfield.

The Mizmaze on Breamore Down XXXII.

View, drawn just before the Great War, by the antiquarian Heywood Sumner, of Breamore Down, from the turf-cut medieval 'mizmaze', a spot from which Violet drew solace when she stayed with the Hulses

CHAPTER TWENTY

Last Years in Egypt

THE YEAR 1916 brought a death in some ways as devastating for Edward as George's. Kitchener was drowned in June en route to Russia, his ship torpedoed off Scotland by a German submarine. Edward had become devoted to that lonely, powerful figure, whose support had been central to his career. He had last seen his chief in England in August 1914. As Minister of War, Kitchener had raised two and a half million volunteers for his new armies, and equipped them with the shells that rained down on the enemy, up until the second month of the battle of the Somme in July 1916.

Meanwhile, in Egypt, during the last crucial months of 1914 Edward had played a guiding role until the arrival of Kitchener's successor, Sir Henry MacMahon. The situation was extremely delicate: Turkey, Egypt's nominal overlord, declared war on Britain and her allies. Would the Egyptians take Turkey's side? Should Britain annex the country to forestall this possibility? Edward agreed with Sir Milne Cheetham, the acting Agent, and Sir John Maxwell, the commander of the British force in Egypt, that outright annexation would provoke a nationalist uproar. As far as possible they must not disturb the existing arrangement: so, instead of being a 'veiled protectorate', the Foreign Office decided Egypt should become a formal protectorate under Britain, with a High Commissioner rather than an Agent. A British, non-Islamic, suzerainty replaced that of Turkey. The anti-British Khedive, Abbas Hilmi, conveniently in Constantinople at the time, was deposed, and a compliant member of his family, Hussein Kamel, stepped into his place. Edward's diplomacy had been stretched to the full in steering Britain's course through this tricky passage, without violent objections from the Egyptian government or a nationalist revolt, and in instituting realistic economic changes, such as limiting cotton production in favour

'Sisely Malia':
Edward as Financial Adviser
to the Egyptian Government

of wheat, to ensure Egypt's self-sufficiency when grain supplies were cut off by the war.

Kitchener's death had a significance not only for Edward but for other Egyptian officials who had Cromer's aims of improvement at heart: although absent during the war, Kitchener had been there in spirit, upholding Cromer's ways. It was always assumed that the Egyptians would be given their independence eventually, but the Foreign Office, which had ultimate control, was increasingly intent on speeding the process, to avoid an Egyptian revolt or friction with other powers, such as France, whose ambitions in the Middle East were reviving. With Kitchener dead and Cromer mortally ill, until Alfred Milner entered the British Government at the end of 1916 there was no strong champion of the old policy left. With hindsight, that policy seems to have been impossible to implement in an age of national self-determination; at the time, to Edward and other Cromerites, however, the Cromer approach was immeasurably preferable to the economic exploitation of the *fellahin* and the widespread financial corruption they believed would follow if their efforts were relaxed. Kitchener's death was a blow to England at war, and 'Here in this small corner it is a disaster,' he told Violet. 'We are now handed over bound to the bureaucrats of London . . . I fear, though it is a small point, that it ends many dreams of mine as to the future – not personal dreams but just dreams of what *might* be done.'

For him the Foreign Office 'bureaucrat' was personified by Sir Ronald Graham, the Adviser to the Ministry of the Interior and a follower of Gorst, trained in the Diplomatic Service. Graham's readiness to compromise with Egyptian politicians and entrepreneurs, no matter how bad the schemes they were floating, simply for a quiet life, undermined British obligations to guide them responsibly. Edward's lifelong principle was that a public servant's position must be earned by achievement; Graham seemed to him a second-rate man promoted by self-advertisement: 'Great are the uses of Advt.,' he wrote scathingly:

> Ask Dukes and M.P.s to dinner, stuff them with your own importance and good deeds and fear nothing even if every man in your department says you're weak, hopeless unreliable or anything. For that is the truth of R.G. . . . carried by other men, his advice despised, and his administration laughed at but through Advt. and a nice talent for letter writing he has been shoved on and promoted to do his appointed amount of harm to the Empire.

Edward was angered by Graham's refusal properly to organise Kitchener's funerary service in Cairo. 'I wish I could have kicked him just once after the ceremony it would have consoled me. But . . . "why spoil your boots?"'

Organising the service fell to Edward and he made every last effort for his chief:

> I got my boys together, and one or two men from the Interior and all our part i.e. asking people, putting them in their places, arranging etc went very well. I had long interviews with the generals who were running the thing and very soon it was decided to have [it] in the open air and after a struggle we got the inside court of Kasr el Nil Barracks . . . We asked all we were allowed to but heaps of Egyptians were left out for want of space. At least the soldiers would give no more tickets.

Edward's concern for Egyptian feelings gave the lie to the charge of arrogance levelled at him by Graham; fortunately the Moslem holy men, Anglican clergymen, Copts, Armenians, Greeks and Jews did sit all together on the dais during the service. Edward managed to control his feelings until 'The Last Post . . . took my entrails out of me. I ran about for him as I used to do and for the last time and I was awfully glad to do it,' he wrote to Violet.

Although in Government circles Kitchener was reckoned to be old and obstructive and to have outlived his usefulness as Minister of War, in which he had lately, anyway, had a much more limited role, for the masses he had always been the symbol of the national will to resist, as embodied in the famous recruiting poster of his face and pointing finger: 'YOUR COUNTRY NEEDS YOU'. His death deepened the depression of the British public about the unending war.

Alice Salisbury had long been devoted to Kitchener and she revered his memory for the rest of her life. Thirty years later, she handed on his photograph to a grandson, so that he too might learn to admire him. Now she wrote to Edward: 'There are few heavier blows that could have fallen on you than this and . . . to you one of the great loves . . . of your life has gone. There were few people who really knew and loved him and you were one of them and he you.' She added, 'You are about the only exponent left, of K's great policy in Egypt and so absolutely necessary there to carry it on.' She told Edward that Lloyd George, Kitchener's chief critic over his management of munitions, had taken his place as Minister of War. 'Sometimes I feel like David "The wicked flourishing like a green bay tree and the evil man is exalted."'

Wartime Egypt seemed one enormous army base, first for the Gallipoli Expeditionary Force and later for the Egyptian Expeditionary Force sent to ward off the Turks from the Suez Canal and to launch an attack into Ottoman-held Palestine. 'The place is stiff with generals,' Edward told Violet, 'none of whom seem to know what they are doing.' As was the way with the military, they enjoyed telling the civil authorities how to run the country. 'We take it all smiling and wait till they will cry to be helped out of the various scrapes into which they are getting. Meanwhile we continue to prepare for the Turks who so far don't seem to want to come at all.'

He described the Australian troops in Cairo and Port Said, omitting their notorious attack on a brothel after numbers of them had become infected with venereal disease: 'The Australians are wonderful fighters though unattractive in other ways. They must be very like Nelson's sailors. They are hopelessly insubordinate they drink like fishes they have every sort of row and a strong criminal tendency – but they are men.' The Australians' heroism at Gallipoli had greatly moved him, and the eventual failure of the Allied campaign there depressed all the British community in Egypt.

So, too, did the fate of General Townshend's Mesopotamia Expeditionary Army, which was forced to surrender to the Turks in April 1916 after four months' siege at Kut-el-Amara on the Tigris river. The relief force under General Nixon cabled the Egyptian government urgently for help with transport; but the Nile at that time was too low for the old steamers, which were offered, to make their way down to the Mediterranean, and no crews seemed to be available for the long sea voyage to the Persian Gulf. Something of Kitchener's determination entered into Edward: 'his restless impatience seemed to appreciate no limitations to the object he had in view,' wrote a military colleague, 'and rising from his seat with the urgent cable from General Nixon in his hand, and striking the top of his desk, he said: "If Kut falls without assistance from Egypt, the responsibility will be on Egypt."' As a result of Edward's urgings the steamers reached Basra, on the Gulf, a good two months before Kut fell and before the relief forces were ready to use them – though cruelly, this did not save Townshend's army from surrender and terrible hardship in captivity.

Edward had managed to get home on leave to England in February 1916. For fifteen-year-old Helen his kindly presence lifted the gloom of mourning at Wigsell, and of her teenage solitude. Making up for their long time apart, he took her for carriage rides round London, told her romantic tales of the Arabs, and talked late into the night with her, about politics or religion or Violet's distressed state of mind – but also frivolities: 'Papa drivels beautifully. Talk, talk, talk, talk, talk . . .' At Wigsell they gardened together. Violet and he got on so much better that Helen even admitted to being a little jealous: 'he has helped [Mama] a lot already. I am so selfish that though happy in their unity and absorbtion in one another I feel very lonely . . .'

While in England, Edward, warned of a severe shortage of coal in Egypt and anticipating a great rise in prices because of demands on shipping and German submarine attacks, seized the chance to purchase for the Egyptian government, on his own responsibility, 250,000 tons, at a price of £1,570,000. This courageous action, little recognised, recalls his bold deal with the Weil brothers before the siege of Mafeking.

His return to Cairo, 'dry unwholesome and unpleasant . . . reminds me of dirty sawdust,' he told Violet. 'Perhaps you spoilt me a little this time at home. It was so awfully nice seeing you and being near you and I do miss you dreadfully.'

One escape he had from the 'village squabbles' of Egypt was teaching himself astronomy. 'I am only really happy with my stars who are very nice friends, almost as nice as a garden very restful and beautiful.'

He also spent some days with the Egyptian Expeditionary Force. Inspecting Cairo's defences, he was surprised to find how much they resembled those at Mafeking: 'They are a little deeper and narrower but the pattern is the same and the ideas of concealment very similar.' Edward had long wanted to return to the army full-time and had pressed to be allowed to do so. He felt his experience might be of help; at any rate, he could not be as much of an ass at the job as some of the men he saw around him.

The fifteen-year-old Prince of Wales, later Edward VIII, was in Egypt with the Guards. Like many others before and since, in royal company Edward felt embarrassed: 'I cannot tell you how even a Serene Highness absolutely paralyses my sense of humour, befogs my intellect and leaves me without a hope or wish in the world except to get away.' The boy seemed nice enough, though immature. Edward noticed various traits in him which were destined to endure – his vanity ('his main terror is getting fat') and his obstinacy, which Edward optimistically, but mistakenly, saw as a sign of strength. 'I think one day he will fall in love and then he will suddenly grow up but what he will be like when he does so I have no idea at all.' The answer would be his abdication twenty years later.

A colourful presence for a while was the ever-dashing Bend'or Westminster whose passion for Rolls Royces had led him to inaugurate and finance a Division of twelve Silver Ghosts, their bodywork replaced with three tons of armour-plating apiece and machine-guns mounted in revolving turrets. Under his command, these pioneering armoured cars had a success in France, then moved to Egypt where Bend'or led them to the rescue of British survivors of the SS *Tara* – sunk by a submarine – who had been taken prisoner by ferocious Senussi tribesmen. The Duke and his cars went on to help T.E. Lawrence, 'Lawrence of Arabia', in the Arab revolt against Turkey.

In Anglo-Egyptian circles, the pettiness and intrigue continued. 'I

believe that Egypt makes people fight,' Edward wrote, 'it is the light
or the air or something.' His good relationship with Sir Henry
MacMahon, Kitchener's successor, aroused jealousy, particularly as
MacMahon did not interfere with his very considerable power. It was
repeatedly alleged that there was a 'Hatfield plot', reaching back to
Kitchener's friendship with Alice Salisbury and the family's close relations with the Cromers, to advance Edward's career in Egypt. Ronald
Graham suggested that Edward was poisoning MacMahon against the
Egyptians, MacMahon naturally denied it. In the narrow British
administrative community Edward's criticisms of Egyptian colleagues
and admiration for Kitchener and Cromer were common knowledge,
but so too, as testified by the Legal Adviser, William Hayter, were his
good manners and patience with Egyptians, repaid with their
confidence and respect, if not liking. Edward could be very firm in
refusing favours or the myriad dubious financial schemes proposed to
him. Ronald Storrs insisted he was very unpopular with the
Egyptians, but Storrs overestimated his own knowledge of the Arab
world and language and his evidence is unreliable.

Soon afterwards Graham was transferred to the Foreign Office in
London, where, Edward believed, 'they know absolutely nothing
about Egypt', to take charge of Egyptian affairs. An example was their
over-estimate of the dignified but sickly Khedive, or Sultan, as he was
now known, Hussein Kamel: 'I never dared to say when they praised
this wonderful Sultan in London that the man was far advanced in
drug taking. Poor man he has used drugs and now has to reduce them
enormously which I believe is a real torture.'

Owing to Graham's influence in the Foreign Office, MacMahon
was dismissed, on the grounds of his ignorance of Egyptian affairs,
with a brusque lack of tact which shocked many, even within its ranks.
Thanking Edward for his support, from the boat which carried him
and his wife back to England, Lady MacMahon wrote: 'Henry and
I felt leaving you more than anyone or anything else in Egypt . . .
even the Foreign Office cannot strip us of friendship such as you have
given us.'

Edward tried to enlist Bob Cecil's influence with Sir Edward Grey,
the Foreign Secretary, to re-examine MacMahon's case, but then Grey
himself lost his job. A palace coup expelled him and the other ministers closest to Asquith, who was himself unseated as Prime Minister in
favour of Lloyd George. The country, weary of the unending deaths,
the disappointing campaigns on the Western Front and the mass sink-

ings at sea by German submarines, welcomed the change, for Lloyd George was not only popular but a far more dynamic war leader than Asquith. The Cecils, including Violet, had mixed feelings. Bob was upset to lose Grey, a man of integrity, but he and the other Tories had lost confidence in Asquith; on the other hand they did not like Lloyd George, the scourge of their class. For them, Lloyd George as Prime Minister was simply an expedient, perhaps a temporary one. They were consoled by the appointment of Arthur Balfour as the new Foreign Secretary and of those supreme administrators, George Curzon and Alfred Milner, to an executive cabinet established to run the war instead of the large, cumbersome, peacetime-style cabinets where quick decisions determining the fate of thousands were impossible.

For many months Alfred had been intensely critical of Asquith's Coalition Government – over its neglect of his agriculture committee findings, over its hesitation in introducing National Service, over not having anticipated rebellion in Ireland during Easter 1916, above all over its failure to provide a coherent, resolute war policy with decisions made and implemented quickly. He had headed a group of politicians, commentators and newspaper men known as 'the Monday Night Cabal', which discussed with increasing urgency the possibility of overthrowing Asquith – principally through press agitation. By December, David Lloyd George, the Minister of War, had emerged as the most likely alternative to supplant him. Alfred, his excitement mounting, kept Violet posted on the drama:

> The rumpus here is simply awful . . . About 2:15 yesterday [2 December] my telephone suddenly went mad and it has not completely recovered sanity yet . . . L.G. is really making a Gigantic Effort to get rid of H.H.A[squith] . . . and form a small real War Govt. All the perfectly useless members of the Govt. – some 16 or 18 out of the 23 – are clinging round H.H.A.'s knees and beseeching him not to give in. No thought of what is happening to the country – you may observe. It is just *their* positions . . . H.H.A. . . . wants to see L.G. this evening. Thereon much depends . . . My fear is – that there will be another compromise and a patch up. Two to one on the patch up, but there is a chance of smash . . . [5 December] No fresh news of the crisis . . . I cannot see what L.G. is waiting for.

On 8 December, as Alfred was changing to go out for dinner, a note had arrived from Lloyd George summoning him to the War Office – to a 'War Committee'. Alfred penned a quick note to Violet:

Back in power: Alfred Milner in Downing Street

'Whether I am to be in or not, I have as yet not the least idea . . . my own disposition is strongly against being in the Govt. at all, most strongly against being in it unless I am part of the Supreme Direction'. That evening he was offered the first high-ranking job which he was prepared to accept since leaving South Africa in 1905. Like George Curzon, he was not put in charge of a government department; he was a 'Minister without Portfolio' whose function it was to run the war, to provide a central drive and coordination. The Cabinet consisted at first only of Lloyd George as the new Prime Minister, Curzon, Milner himself, Andrew Bonar Law, the Conservative Leader, as Chancellor of the Exchequer, and the Labour Party leader, Arthur Henderson.

At sixty-four, Alfred once more had a compelling purpose in his life and was as energetic and incisive as ever. It was ironic that after entering the Cabinet he became very close to Lloyd George, who had been one of his most aggressive critics over the Boer War and 'Chinese

Slavery'. Willy Selborne was one of those amazed by this turn of events. Succinctly he told Edward: 'Milner could not bear gippies or Boers because they economised truth, and yet he gets on with a man who hasn't got any to economise.'

In Cairo, Edward's new boss, Reginald Wingate, formerly Sirdar of the Egyptian Army and recommended by Ronald Graham, was an old friend since Dongola and Ethiopia days. Despite Edward's hope that he would 'do excellently', Wingate was neither up to the job nor a support, toeing the Foreign Office line by pushing him into a subservient role – a bitter blow to Edward, whose real ambition was to be at the head of Egyptian affairs – 'as I would have been if Lord K had lived'.

When Edward took leave in the spring of 1917, he searched for work more closely involved with the war, even active service. He found a post in London as assistant military adviser to the Ministry of Munitions, but soon resigned from it, feeling his duty lay in Egypt, for better or for worse.

He discussed with Arthur Balfour, and Bob Cecil, whose Blockade Ministry was part of the Foreign Office, how control of Egypt could be transferred from the Foreign Office, which was not trained to administer Egypt's internal affairs, to a separate government department specifically created for the purpose. Only thus could Cromer's aims be achieved and the policy of indiscriminately appeasing the Egyptians, as he saw it, be ended. The Chief Secretary of the Foreign Office, Lord Hardinge, was incensed. However, a top-level committee consisting of Balfour, Alfred Milner and George Curzon considered Edward's proposal. Balfour and Curzon settled for a cautious compromise, but Alfred warmed so strongly to the idea of root-and-branch reform that he was able, though in the minority, to get a final decision postponed so that Edward's ideas were not altogether rejected, and might be implemented after the war.

Edward's health improved during his leave in England. His weak chest strengthened: 'Native air is a wonderful thing,' he told Violet. 'Last night I had no rattle and did not wake up in the night.' He and Helen became closer. The more she saw of him, the more she loved him. She had always accepted her mother's view that Edward was neglectful and selfish; gradually, her feelings of adolescent rebellion against her dominating mother came to make her believe that Violet had deceived her and cheated her of the father she came to love so much: she never forgave Violet for this. All these years too, Helen felt

Sir Reginald Wingate as Sirdar

the weight of her mother's sorrow for George's death which eclipsed her feelings for her living child.

When Edward returned to Egypt, Wingate, having been told of Edward's scheme to sideline the Foreign Office in the running of the country, was enraged, more because he felt Edward was usurping his authority than because he agreed with the Foreign Office. Edward was unrepentant, especially when he saw how strongly Egyptian nationalism had grown, largely, he believed, because of Graham's hints that the Egyptians could expect great advances in self-rule after the war – which would inevitably lead to disappointment. In Edward's view, Hussein Rushdi Pasha, the Prime Minister (actually no fire-eating nationalist but quick and capable), was now walking round and round 'poor little W' the whole time 'and we shall come off very second best'.

Edward's contempt for 'poor little W' grew. Because of Wingate's fear that unwelcome news might upset native loyalties, all news was subject to rigorous censorship and Egypt was now extraordinarily isolated from the outside world. Rumours – often damaging – replaced accurate reporting: 'This secrecy after the event is quite the acme of military-cum-civil stupidity,' Edward wrote. Egyptian cotton producers and traders, backed by the Sultan, protested that they were being cheated of profits by the British Government's efforts to control cotton prices in wartime; Wingate was terrified when the Sultan threatened to resign, for fear, Edward thought, that he would lose his own job. 'Everyone is very nice to me,' Edward told Violet, 'and says thank heaven I'm back etc. but as I thought, I can do nothing. What can you do with a weak frightened man of inferior intellect?'

Over the management of Egyptian affairs, Edward was finally to achieve a modified victory; he did not get what he had wanted, a separate government office for Egypt in London, but at least a new Middle Eastern Department of the Foreign Office was created, ensuring that the Foreign Office took advice more widely. This decision came too late, however, for Edward to benefit by it. Despite a brief rest in the drier conditions of Helwan, his health declined alarmingly. His cough grew worse. During an attack of fever he lost a pound in weight a day. He clung to the hope that it was only 'septic bronchitis', a common enough ailment in the Army, but finally came the diagnosis he dreaded – tuberculosis. At once he was dispatched to a sanatorium at Leysin in the mountains of Switzerland. 'It was quite wise to stop at once when your health gave way again,' Alfred Milner wrote to him. 'But it has been very, very bad luck indeed for you and Egypt.'

CHAPTER TWENTY-ONE

The Death of Edward

EDWARD TRAVELLED TO Switzerland via France, eluding submarines. 'During my voyage,' he wrote to Nelly, 'everyone has treated me with the lachrymose respect one pays to the dying. The commander of the antiquated ark they called a ship that brought me to Marseilles said it did not matter how one died for one's country, either in the battle, or slowly in bed.' On his reaching Switzerland early in January 1918, the Vice-Consul in Geneva 'said it must be a great comfort to me to look back over a useful life.'

Violet was relieved that he seemed happy in his new surroundings and so more optimistic: 'Your Leysin sounds very like the atoll you have always been asking for.' He slept well, and relaxed with the latest 'shilling shockers'. The purity of the cold fresh air brought a well-being he had not experienced for years. From his pen and typewriter poured the wild letters typical of a tubercular patient, uninhibited and all-encompassing. In his solitary days on his 'atoll' he brooded on the war and its aftermath. He foresaw a reaction against its management and against democracy; he imagined Field Marshal Haig being stoned on the streets as Wellington had been in the era after 1815.

Violet's letters from Wigsell were necessarily more down-to-earth; country life in England was changing with the need to bolster food production – this owed much to a bold scheme from Alfred Milner's agricultural committee of 1915. So that Britain should be self-sufficient in grain, landowners were ordered to put all available acres under the plough. At Wigsell the kitchen garden expanded across two acres and ewes and their lambs grazed the lawns. In Violet's well-tended borders, flowers made way for fruit and vegetables. With able-bodied men away at the front, much of the ploughing was done by German prisoners, 'the only Germans who will ever have been at Wigsell, or, with my consent, who ever will be here.' As the harvest approached, Violet's mistrust intensified: 'The German prisoners . . . need very careful watching as their object is to destroy the cultivation as far as they are able.' Her hostility to their increasingly familiar presence never abated: 'This place is polluted by German prisoners who are ploughing . . . I hate to see them in the field Helen and George used to ride in. They are brutes to the unfortunate horses too.'

Edward agreed: 'The Germans have retrograded and become a savage barbarian race which is a positive danger to civilisation.' Such anti-German feeling, like Leo Maxse's, was more extreme than in the rest of the Cecil family. Willy Selborne, for example, praised the courage of Bishop Henson of Durham for saying he found it incredible that of the eighty million Germans, every man, woman and child must be absolutely terrible and wicked. Selborne called this much-criticised statement 'about the best thing Henson ever did'. But from Leo Maxse's *National Review* came a predictable diatribe against the bishop. Bob Cecil was hardly a Germanophile; he wanted to see Prussian militarism overthrown and the Kaiser put on trial after the war. Nonetheless he, and even more, Nelly, drew back from extreme anti-German views. As British Blockade Minister he was the Germans' most hated enemy, now that they were suffering severely from the Allied blockade; he learnt this through the wife of a Blockade Ministry official, Mrs Leverton Harris, who had recently visited a German cousin, a prisoner-of-war in England. When it became known that the wife of a government servant was making these visits, there were widespread calls for Harris's resignation in the press and from Noel Pemberton-Billing, the fanatically patriotic MP and editor of *Vigilante*. Bob Cecil took his subordinate's side and threatened himself to resign when Harris was forced to leave the Blockade Ministry, declaring that he would rather sweep a crossing than do the bidding of a cad like Pemberton-Billing. So there was a certain defiance of public opinion in Nelly Cecil's spending time with Harris's wife.

Nelly refused to condemn all Germans as monsters. 'They are human beings . . . I don't see why we shouldn't expect some pacifist Germans in Prussia . . . Jem says prisoners here work industriously and peacefully, look very harmless and are on the friendliest terms with the inhabitants. I have had similar accounts of our men on German farms. It's all so d–d silly, isn't it?' she wrote to Edward.

But Violet was outraged by such tolerance. 'London is full of well-intentioned donkeys,' she told Edward, 'and Nelly – who is a very clever woman – has always been miles away from reality.' People ought to support their own side wholeheartedly instead of 'speaking on one side and shooting on the other to show impartiality' as she remembered Lord Salisbury saying of the Duke of Devonshire.

She described an acrimonious exchange about Mrs Leverton Harris with a young Balfour cousin, 'an Aggravating Young Fool':

> V.: Would you give your hand to a man whom you *knew* had put out the eyes of a Belgian baby?
> A.Y.F.: We are told that it is our duty to forgive.
> V: It is very good of *you* to forgive a man for putting out a Belgian Baby's eyes!
> A.Y.F.!!!! (collapse, real and unaffected).

The vindictive anti-German feelings shown by Violet and a great number of her fellow countrymen in those months may seem shocking today, particularly when Germany has arisen from the ashes of a far worse system than the Kaiser's to become a modern democracy. Yet they were all too understandable in a Britain exhausted by three years of war and bereavement and suddenly in the spring and early summer of 1918 faced with the possibility of total defeat.

In January the Germans had imposed a shattering peace treaty on Bolshevist Russia by which the Baltic regions and the Ukraine, with its vast corn supplies, passed into their hands. On the Western Front, in a series of highly effective offensives, they pushed the Allied armies far back along a forty-mile front, reversing for the first time the small gains achieved at colossal cost since September 1914. The Allied front was on the point of disintegrating. There were fears that the Allies' nerve had collapsed after the fearsome campaigns of recent years and it was true that, in their alarm, the French and British armies ceased to trust one another.

Alfred Milner, who was now Minister of War, hurried over to confer with the French President Poincaré, Clemenceau, Prime Minister since November 1917, and the British and French military commanders. On 26 March, at Doullens, close to the fighting, the fate of the Allies was in the hands of eight men under intense pressure, with Marshal Pétain close to breaking. The differences and misunderstandings were calmly straightened out, largely on Alfred's initiative helped by his friendship with Clemenceau. On that fateful day, the conference decided that all the Allied forces on the Western Front should be co-ordinated under one *generalissimo* – Marshal Ferdinand

Foch. This turning point was principally to the credit of the man who had been called 'a less than perfect diplomatist' in dealing with President Kruger before the Boer War.

Although their line was not broken, the Allies' retreat continued through March and April 1918; to such families as Violet and Edward's it began to seem that all the sacrifices their nation and the French had made since 1914 had been in vain. Politicians rushed to blame generals, and generals to blame politicians. Most foresaw a struggle going on for years. Writing to Edward, Nelly Cecil did not hide her gloom about the German successes.

Bob Cecil, however, was determinedly confident that the Allied front would hold. He was right: there were nearly a hundred times more British troops in the line than in the days of Mons when George Cecil had gone to war. They were far better equipped and, compared with the early trench warfare, tactically far more sophisticated. Prepared intensively by Ivor Maxse as Inspector-General of Training – his greatest achievement – the British forces, with the tough and resolute French and, eventually in force, the Americans, turned the tide and by 10 August cracked German resistance. As Blockade Minister Bob had a clear view of the world economic situation: Germany's financial position could only get worse in the long term, even if its food supplies were replenished by its new Russian conquests.

Bobbety Cranborne, who had been out of the fighting since 1915, returned to the front with a staff job in July when Jack, the third of William's four sons, also reached France, from the Middle East.

Violet found no social life to speak of when she visited London with Helen. 'I have not had on an evening dress since we came up,' she reported. They were reduced to taking cookery classes alongside Olive and Alice Salisbury. Violet was relieved to return to the country, but seventeen-year-old Helen was lonely at Wigsell. Elsie Kipling had become sallow and withdrawn – 'the girl who took the wrong turning', as Violet privately described her. At Bateman's Carrie and Rudyard mourned John: 'Poor people, they all make each other worse. He is now as gloomy as she is. I came away feeling very low. Because it is their very affection for each other which has produced this.'

Violet and Helen spent a Sunday at Hatfield, most of which had become a convalescent home for wounded soldiers. The Salisburys now occupied only a corner of the great house, but there were still masses of babies and perambulators belonging to relations; for a

Hatfield House was a wartime convalescent home and welcomed disabled servicemen, seen here with Alice Salisbury

moment Violet was transported back twenty years, to a memory of George in his pram, part of a procession of infants being pushed by nursemaids through the park.

Helen found a new interest, training as a nurse. As for many women, the war offered her a first chance of independence. Their old friend Helen Vincent began training as an anaesthetist at the same time. Violet seized at every encouraging bit of news: in June, 'The Americans are at last coming in'; in July, 'The guns have been very loud for a few days' (this was the start of the 'Hundred Days' when the Allies finally pushed the Germans back). Nelly thought Violet's spirits improved and commented with a touch of irony, 'she always looks so particularly nice in mourning I think, quite a treat after the floppety women one sees all about.' At Wigsell Violet, deprived of her maid, Campion, found herself up against the 'servant problem', the bugbear of her class now that most young women were working in munitions factories, in transport and on the land. She made or made over her clothes herself, and even put her cooking lessons into practice; this was not a part of the English social revolution she embraced eagerly.

At the beginning of 1918 Cissie Maxse died after a short illness, aged seventy-eight: 'The loss of my mother is one of those elemental huge great things gone from a life already made empty by much loss. I do not want her back. She is at rest, I know. But the loss is great . . . all the past [is gone].'

Violet was thrilled to see Clemenceau on three occasions in London during 1918. Their first meeting was an emotional moment. No one had told her he was coming, and she heard the news only by accident. She found out when he was going to see Lloyd George, and waited on the pavement opposite No. 10 Downing Street: 'Clemenceau, whom I had not seen for three years, fell upon my neck . . . Almost gibbering with excitement,' she accompanied him inside the building, where she had not been for eight years. Afterwards they dined together with Olive: 'I have never known him in better form in my life,' she told Edward. Clemenceau was the very spirit of his country's endurance. Dark times had called out a man equal to the occasion; Bob Cecil, talking with him in Paris, was impressed by the old man's lion-hearted indifference to his popular standing. 'Clemenceau really is a big man and he has an immense advantage in having no future' – leaving him free to act as he thought right, without worrying about his popularity.

He was of great help to Violet in arranging the journey she and Helen took through France to visit Edward, whom they found in good spirits, his health improving and amused by the gossip of Leysin. He had befriended some of the sick British and French prisoners-of-war whom the Red Cross had arranged to be transferred to neutral Switzerland from German camps, awaiting repatriation. He had also been writing his recollections of Lord Kitchener, in what was to be his most enduring literary effort.

Early in September Helen and Violet returned via Paris. From Alice Salisbury's younger daughter Moucher, who was there with her husband Eddie Hartington, then engaged in secret liaison work, they heard that Jack Cecil had been killed late in August, the third of William and Fluffy's sons to lose his life: 'Poor Fluffy,' Violet told Edward. 'He was her only joy and chief pride. The news came yesterday and extinguished us entirely.'

Violet also met Alfred Milner in Paris: he had good news for Edward – Egyptian affairs were coming under a man who could be trusted at the Foreign Office, Sir Eyre Crowe. 'Egypt will now really be understood in London. I know you will be glad,' she wrote to Edward. Alfred and Bob also thought Edward might again be given major responsibilities in Egypt.

Clemenceau arranged for her to be driven out to Villers-Cotterêts: 'The forests where George fell are untouched, the cemetery has been shelled, though his grave was not touched. I stayed awhile both in the wood and at his grave side.'

In Paris, she found, most people considered that the war would continue through the winter, and in the spring the Germans would attack again, but the Allies, after eight or ten months, would gain the final victory on their terms. In England, despite the prospect of the dreadful slog to come, the atmosphere in the autumn of 1918 seemed more buoyant than it had been for years.

Jem Salisbury set off to Switzerland to see his brother in September, despite Edward's anxiety that the 'Spanish 'flu' pandemic, then sweeping the world, had descended on Leysin; to the enfeebled TB patients, it was particularly dangerous. Edward described a talented young Belgian pianist, almost cured of TB, who caught the 'flu in Geneva. On her return on Leysin, 'she gave a tea party to all her friends, warmly embracing all the females whom she had not seen for ten days. She then came down to dinner and shook hands with those of her acquaintances who had not come to the tea party and retired to bed with a temperature of 104°.' It was decided to isolate her and her infected friends in a chalet at the end of the hotel garden under conditions of secrecy, to avoid alarming the other inmates. 'I was just going to bed,' Edward told Violet,

> when I heard stage whispers in the garden and numerous people tiptoe-ing backwards and forwards so I went out on to the balcony . . . the staff at the hotel appeared carrying a procession of stretchers. By the moon-light, which was very bright it looked like the burial of Sir John Moore in triplicate. Just the kind of thing the War Office would love. The effect was however destroyed by the patients who apparently thinking they were to be buried or put in the destructor, commenced wailing and screaming that they were dying. It was like a scene out of Defoe [*Journal of the Plague Year*] and made me feel quite uncomfortable. Meanwhile every one in the hotel was on their balconies and those who were strong enough had hyst-erics and the rest coughed sympathetically. Every bell started ringing and one lady arrayed in a not very voluminous white garment commenced packing and demanding a carriage to go down to the valley. She forgot to

dress . . . A solemnity was attached to the incident however by what I thought were minute guns but it turns out that the Russian lady overhead fainted five times in succession and her faithful maid missed her each time but revived her when on the floor.

Now at last came the days of triumph for the Allies. More quickly than they could have imagined, the German resistance was collapsing. The British War Cabinet, including Alfred Milner, was caught up in a whirl of negotiations at Paris and Versailles for an Armistice. On 11 November what Edward called the Great Horror finally ended. 'A wonderful day,' reported Alfred, who had been woken by a War Office despatch telling him the Germans had signed the peace terms at Compiègne at 5 a.m. The Armistice would be effective at 11 a.m., signalled by the firing of maroons, the ringing of church bells, the sounding of bugles, and Big Ben was to start striking again after a silence of four years.

'The face of everything is transformed by the Armistice,' wrote Violet who came to London directly after Alfred had told her the good news was imminent; when he rang and told her all had signed she went to Whitehall, where, she described to Edward

such scenes of spontaneous and *heartfelt* rejoicing as I never thought to have seen . . . The traffic was quickly transformed into a perpetual procession of Victory – drays, buses, taxis were all boarded and driven full speed – I counted 22 people in and on one taxi, and 6 people on a motorbicycle. The Scots Guards band that came along walked in a heavy surge of people . . . Lloyd George came out in Downing Street and had a great ovation, but the person who really had the fun was the King. The Army Council and Milner had gone to Buckingham Palace to write their names down and had to stay there! Milner said there were 50,000 people and that whenever the Grenadier band stopped playing they chanted 'We *want* King *George*' over and over again . . . he was very, very pleased.

She and Alfred had had dinner together and he afterwards walked her back through the crowded streets. 'The striking thing was that there were no police and no disorder . . . the crowds of girls and young men danced in the street, but I saw no drunken people and no prostitutes. Just the English without their mask!'

London remained *en fête*, and for weeks foreign heads of state were welcomed: 'Wherever Foch and Clemenceau are recognised they are greeted with cheers,' Alfred observed. The Army commanders returning from France in December were given a triumphant reception at an elaborately decorated Charing Cross station. In the election held that month, Lloyd George's coalition was returned with an overwhelming vote of confidence, after a jingoistic campaign. On 26 December, the American President, Woodrow Wilson, dapper in top hat and tails, was met by the King and Queen when he arrived on this, his first visit to Europe. For many he was the saviour who would bring perpetual peace.

Violet left London on 12 November to stay with Edith Hulse at Breamore to rest in that quiet country spot: two bereaved mothers together, hardly able to take in the 'silence heard around the world' with the cessation of the holocaust that had deprived them of their sons.

On his 'quiet mountain shelf', Edward received the Armistice news. He had been writing a report on the interned prisoners, who were all off home, as he observed wistfully. He felt better than ever. The weather was fine, cold and brisk. Then the influenza caught him and a year's progress was undone in a few days. At once Violet went out to him, escorted by Jem Salisbury. She stayed at his bedside for much of each day and night.

Edward was sometimes delirious, though when his fever dropped, he spoke to her quite normally; his features grew gaunter and he could hardly move his legs. He died on 15 December. He was fifty-one years old, the only one of his brothers and sisters, apart from William, not to live into their late eighties or nineties. 'I think he had been feeling the burden of life for some time,' Gwendolen wrote.

Close at hand to help was Violet's old friend from the South African War, General Hanbury-Williams, who had been responsible for the welfare of British prisoners-of-war. He arranged the cremation. Violet travelled back via Paris, to see Clemenceau, her strongest living link with her father. On Christmas Eve she returned to England and on Christmas Day she spent the morning with Alfred at Great College Street before going on with Helen to Hatfield.

Edward's memorial, a handsome stone slab, lies next to his parents' grave beneath the venerable trees in the family burial ground by Hatfield church. The house and family who meant so much to him, whose vivid life shaped his character, had received him back after his long exile abroad on imperial duty, in wilder lands, under bluer skies.

Edward's Cairo property on fashionable Gezireh realised £10,000. A £2,100 war loan and the proceeds of various sales proved in the end

Edward's memorial in the family burial ground in the churchyard at Hatfield.
In the background is the old royal palace, dating from the fifteenth century

more than enough to meet the death duties, a mortgage and other debts; while from his shares Violet now received the income of several hundred pounds a year for life.

Violet relied on Cairo friends like Teddy Goschen to wind up Edward's affairs. His personal papers were returned to her together with twenty bottles of old brandy from Edward's cellar.

This unassuming man was mourned more than he could ever have expected among his contemporaries in Egypt. Teddy Goschen was typical in telling Violet how much he missed Edward – so much so that he himself was going to take the first opportunity to leave the Egyptian service: 'I positively hate going into his house where I had so many happy talks with Ned . . . There is no one like him here, and never will be . . . Egyptians have realised, and are hence tired of saying so, the loss of Ned to this country. He had the knack of dealing with these people in peculiar crises . . . he could make people work for him wholeheartedly . . . he was . . . irresistible.'

Goschen comforted Edward's servants: 'Poor Nasr wept very bitterly. He would, I know, have done anything for Ned, and his grief was really sincere. He asked me to thank you, but I can't, in English, reproduce his fervent expression of deep-felt gratitude.' Others also had reason to mourn at the time, such as a needy younger colleague, Percy Stout, to whom Edward had always been generous.

Edward's sketches and memoirs of Egyptian life which he had been keen to see published in some form, appeared, more or less as written, in 1921, as *The Leisure of an Egyptian Official*. This was Edward letting himself go, talking, as it were, to his diary or to close relations at home. It is a pity that there was no editorial guidance. As Lord Salisbury, thirty years before, had pointed out to the young George Curzon when he proposed writing of the Shah of Persia's wife 'as a woman who looked like a melon and wandered about her home in a ballet dress with naked legs . . . it would not be "safe to handle the Shah with the truth and freedom which is permissible and salutary in the case of Mr Gladstone."' Curzon reluctantly removed personal references to the lady and his franker opinions of the Shah. Edward's book did not have the benefit of such practical advice. So although his pieces are often hilarious and enjoyed considerable success and good reviews, the impression they leave today is patronising, narrowminded – and facetious. The jokes of yesteryear are as fleeting as its snows. The butts of Edward's humour included tiresome colleagues, female visitors to Cairo, club bores, crafty Egyptian officials and antediluvian servants. 'Ninety per cent at least of the men out here are good fellows and capable men, but they sometimes conceal these facts with wonderful care. Under the nerve-irritating Egyptian conditions all our natural eccentricities assume abnormal proportions.' Edward describes them all, from 'A Member of the Prisons Department . . .

entering the room in his usual state of suppressed fury. He is far advanced in the national disease of irritability,' to the Scottish doctor whose 'flow of talk has made so many of us feel more sympathy with suicide than is right,' to his servant, four foot odd in height, who 'makes more row than a giant . . . he has discovered how to drop a woollen garment on a thick carpet, and make it sound like a plank falling on a pavement.'

These pieces have a hideous authenticity, but they altogether leave out his concern for the Egyptian *fellahin*, the majority of its population, on whose behalf he worked tirelessly. Nor would the reader have any idea of his courtesy, and his genuine liking for many people, Egyptian and British, with whom he worked and and his hopes for Egypt itself.

Some of his fellow Anglo-Egyptian officials, at the time when he wrote the pieces, before the war, were amused, and one, an anonymous reviewer for *The Spectator*, asserted too, that it gave its readers 'a closer insight into the psychological conditions which affect the Government of Egypt than they will get from many weighty volumes by more serious and less perspicuous authors.' But this very authenticity to historians of a post-colonial generation 'unconsciously explains much of the lack of harmony in Anglo-Egyptian relations'. Another has described it as 'an exercise in unclouded self-esteem and superciliousness (sometimes witty) towards the people he served'. Some Egyptians accepted the book in the light spirit that was intended. The distinguished scholar Magdi Wahba saw Edward's parody of his cultivated and clever father as humorously grotesque and not to be taken too heavily.

The second edition, in 1929, had an anonymous preface which remarked that the lightness of sketches and the fun they describe, concealed the hardworking life of the author, because

> being English, he wrote only of what he cared least about, and the subjects chosen were those that entertained a mind often wearied with the fret of difficult work, a mind, however, that no fatigue could deflect from reality . . . There were no phantoms in his outlook and no illusions; but there was a great deal of toleration and understanding of Egypt and its inhabitants. He had, too, a sense of political direction and a knowledge of Home and Foreign politics which enabled him to keep his sense of proportion in a life of exile. There is no talk of state craft in this volume, but under the sparkle of Lord Edward's wit, his serious concern for things that matter may be seen, even in the Egyptian Sketches.

Edward does include a brief tribute to Cromer and, best of all, an illuminating memoir of Kitchener, whom he had known so well. On the right subject he was an excellent stylist, and these passages, if no others, deserve to survive.

Jem and Alice Salisbury, always protective of the family's reputation, took the line that Edward himself would not have published the sketches in such a form. This is probable. They blamed Violet's insensitivity – which was also a fact – but, out of respect for his words, she was tentative about tampering too much with them. Besides, she herself thought the articles entertaining and shared his views to a fault on the awfulness of colonial dinner parties and the absurdity of Egyptian politicians.

Considering his position, it is not surprising that Edward found relief in satirising the Anglo-Egyptian way of life. There would have been hardly a moment when he did not have to consider the ramifications of any decision he took, or any overture he received, among endless different but interlocked nationalities – Egyptian, British (military or civil), Maltese, Coptic, Armenian, Syrian, Berber, Sudanese, Italian, Greek – any one of which might take offence. All the time Britain's status was being challenged by nationalists, or undermined by Turkey's supporters and, even in wartime, by the French. Bribes were thrust at Edward daily; he was endlessly watched, endlessly conspicuous. There must also have been powerful amorous temptations for an unattached man of his romantic and affectionate nature, given the exceptionally seductive charms of the Greek and oriental ladies he encountered in the voluptuous atmosphere of Cairene society. Many of his contemporaries fell – as well as to other allurements such as hashish. Soldiers of some British army battalions departed from Egypt for the Western Front giddy with the fumes of Indian hemp.

The book, which became something of a classic among colonial memoirs, must be seen in context. Edward's attitude was that of a whole generation of administrators. The tragedy of the Empire and colonialism was that it was inseparable from some element of racial contempt felt by even the most humane rulers for their subjects. There were of course a few exceptions among the British community in Egypt, as revealed in the letters of Bimbashi MacPherson, a talented teacher and public servant whose time in Egypt overlapped that of Edward's; while Ronald Storrs' somewhat precious and self-conscious memoir, *Orientations*, shows more appreciation of Arab culture and life.

Not that Edward was immune to Egypt's beauty. In one of the few passages where he allows himself to be serious, he describes the evanescent early morning view from his window, symbolic of the ever elusive promise of that land: at first he sees only 'masses of white mist lazily moving in the light morning air', then, as the sun rises,

> the mist turns a delicate pink, in the far distance the bright blue hills of the western desert begin to show, and the horizon line is cut by the pyramids, starting out of the sea of blushing cloud. Incredibly quickly change follows change. The cloud now turns to liquid translucent gold, and through it dimly appear the feathery palms and the graceful sails of the passing boats. In a moment more the rising breeze has swept away the cloud, and the houses round show again their familiar but not beautiful forms. The morning pageant is over, and though I have seen it more times than I care to be reminded of, it never finishes without causing me a slight pang of regret that anything so beautiful should cease to be.

As for the Empire, for which he worked all his life, first as a soldier, then as an administrator, he regarded it as a responsibility Britain must not shirk. Like Lord Salisbury, he believed it was justified by the better standards it brought to its people, but not by any arguments of national destiny or mission. In this Salisbury and Edward differed from such men as Joseph Chamberlain, Leo Maxse, Rudyard Kipling and, most signally, Alfred Milner. Violet shared Milner's ideal of an imperial mission, which itself amounted to a veritable religion, whereas to Salisbury and Edward the Empire was far less important than the Christian religion. This belief was another fundamental difference between Violet and her husband. But by publishing his book and so enshrining Edward among the selfless servants of Empire, Violet came to terms with the unhappiness of her marriage.

Alfred Milner respected the achievement of Edward and his colleagues in the difficult circumstances of Egypt in the past decades. He and Violet contributed their thoughts about him to a brief entry by William Ormsby-Gore in the *Dictionary of National Biography*. Thus was Edward transformed in Violet's mind into an admirable, increasingly remote figure, like a well-polished imperial medal, its tarnish kept at bay in a drawer marked 'Egypt', and only occasionally taken out and dusted when the grander contents of the 'Hatfield' drawer were put on display. In later years Violet used to say, 'When I married Hatfield,' never, 'When I married Lord Edward'.

CHAPTER TWENTY-TWO

The Return of Peace

THE WORLD IN 1919 was an altered place for Violet and her family, for the other Cecils and for all their friends. Superficially Britain looked much the same, with almost none of the bomb damage that scarred the landscape after the Second World War. But the inner landscape of the survivors had changed for ever. Of the Cecils, William had lost three sons, Randle, Rupert and Jack; Maud her eldest, Bobby; and Violet, George. Ettie Desborough had lost her sons, Julian and Billy Grenfell; Moucher her close friend Charlie Mills. John Manners had died with George, Teddy Hulse at Neuve Chapelle, John Kipling at Loos. Of the younger relations of the Souls circle, Raymond, Margot Asquith's stepson and Edward, Frances Horner's son, were gone. Among the young survivors, Alice's cousin, Wilfrid Ewart, was shell-shocked and Helen Cecil, Imogen and Monica Grenfell, Elsie Kipling and Angela Manners never got over their brothers' deaths.

It was a new epoch for the aristocracy. Although the inter-war political world is associated with many of their names – Halifax, Derby, Churchill, Linlithgow, Cranborne, Londonderry, Curzon, D'Abernon – far fewer young men from landed families went into Parliament. Many were impoverished by double inheritance taxes when the eldest son's death in battle was followed shortly by that of the family head. There were massive land sales, partly because farming was in a depression. Big town houses were demolished to make way for hotels and apartment blocks; and the armies of servants dwindled, for fewer people chose to go into service. Great displays of wealth had been thought tasteless in the grim atmosphere of war and the old style of grandeur had gone for good. Jem Salisbury's coach and four with liveried coachmen and postilions would have attracted no particular notice before the war, but when it drew up outside Arlington Street early in 1919 a crowd gathered; thereafter he abandoned the practice of driving in it to Parliament.

Violet was now on her own. Helen and she were never to be close, for Helen felt she had had more in common with Edward, the father of whom she had been cheated, in girlhood by her mother and as a young woman by his early death. She shared his religious temperament. Now she found escape from her unhappy home life in her love for twenty-five-year-old Major Alec Hardinge MC, the son of Lord Hardinge of Penshurst, the former Viceroy of India. Like so many of their generation, Alec and Helen had come together under the war's shadow. Alec had been in George's regiment and, like her, had lost a courageous elder brother, close in age, in 1914. Violet told them to wait, as Helen was too young, at eighteen, for marriage. But they were engaged in October 1919.

Violet was not well off. In place of Edward's salary were only tiny pensions for her and Helen – £140 apiece per year, terminated if either married – witness to the selfless dedication of members of the colonial service. Luckily the only large bill was for his months in Switzerland. Although Wigsell was Violet's absolutely, she feared that she and Helen might no longer be able to afford to live there. Soon, however, a gift – anonymous, but almost certainly from Alfred Milner – rescued them with loan stock worth £200 a year: 'All my dearest memories of my dear boy,' Violet wrote to the solicitor who arranged the transfer, 'are centred round the home he loved so dearly. The reference to Lord Edward's work in Egypt enhances the gift and my debt to this donor.'

By the spring of 1919, Violet was back where she most enjoyed being – at the centre of things. Paris, since January, had been the focus of the world's attention, as the Allies argued about the peace terms for vanquished Germany. Alfred Milner, recently appointed Colonial Secretary, was one of the plenipotentiaries representing Britain and the Empire at the Paris Peace Conference, who would sign the Peace Treaty; Arthur Balfour was another; Bob Cecil was a key negotiator. Clemenceau led the French delegation.

In May Violet rented a little house in the Bois de Boulogne where, accompanied by Olive and Helen, she tasted once more the pleasure of a Parisian springtime in a city emerging from four grim years, when it had been virtually under siege, menaced by long-range shellfire, impoverished by shortages, filled with soldiers on leave hungrily seeking distraction, its atmosphere frenetic and strained. Mementoes of the war were ubiquitous, from the many bereaved women in mourning, among them Violet herself, to the captured German guns lining the length of the Champs Elysées on both sides from the Arc de Triomphe to the Place de la Concorde, to be melted down eventually, it was said, to make into church bells. The city lights were dimmer than in pre-war days, though brighter than London. But Paris soon recovered the gaiety and elegance which all visitors craved.

Violet plunged into the activities of Paris, whither hundreds from the British upper classes were flocking to take part in or to savour the diplomatic drama. There were private balls, embassy and official parties, as well as sumptuous dinners given by celebrated hosts such as Mme Fitzjames, Mme de Porges, Princesse Marie Murat, Mme d'Aunay and Boni de Castellane. Their guests admired the art treasures now brought back from the country where they had been stored away from the bombs. At such gatherings there was a great mixture: politicians, society beauties, foreign royalties, journalists, diplomats, financiers, political adventurers, food experts full of the horrors of starving Europe. Great men regaled their fellow-diners with reminiscences of the war and the conversation sparkled or faltered in good, bad and execrable French.

Military bands played at the balls and receptions. There were visits to the theatre, musical comedy and opera, some of it poignantly makeshift after the years of scarcity and human loss; and to restaurants like the Ambassadeurs, and the legendary Tour d'Argent. Women looked longingly at the latest fashions and were soon wearing them: short skirts, longer at the back, quite straight, without waists, and short hair decorated with ropes of pearls or tall ostrich plumes.

In Paris Violet also met members of the younger generation of the Cecil family: Mimer accompanied her husband, William Ormsby-Gore, later Lord Harlech, who had lived in Edward's Gezireh home while he was in Switzerland and had been an executor of his will; now he was in Paris advising on Middle Eastern affairs. Moucher was with her husband, Lord Hartington, who was also on conference duty. One of Bob Cecil's assistants was Bobbety Cranborne, who, with his wife, Betty, had taken a flat; she regarded their whole visit as an enthralling holiday and was sorry to leave the capital when the conference was over. Seventeen-year-old Lord David Cecil enjoyed jaunts to the vivid squalor and gaiety of the Left Bank with Eddy, the son of General

Sackville-West who was a key figure in the Inter-Allied Military Organisation at Versailles. Violet's old friend Edgar Vincent, now Lord D'Abernon, was there and the newly appointed British Ambassador was Eddy Stanley, now Lord Derby, whose brother Arty was staying as well.

Above all, Violet would often meet Alfred, to buy presents – 12 May was Helen's eighteenth birthday – to walk in the Bois, to motor out to the woods around Versailles, or to dine. Socially, it was almost like turn-of-the-century Cape Town all over again.

Violet and Helen lunched with Arthur Balfour, ill and sleepy and by then thoroughly dissatisfied with the mismanagement of the negotiations. His apartment in the Rue Nitot was near that of the British delegation's leader, the Prime Minister David Lloyd George. The apartment was luxuriously warm, especially to British visitors accustomed to the cold, and decorated in modish green silk and leather, with white and gold walls. Balfour had imported his butler Coleman, and was accompanied by his suave and resourceful secretary Sir Ian Malcolm, who had fitted out the flat, and was on hand to rescue his chief from trying social situations, or to bully him into keeping appointments. At lunch also were Alfred and the Cranbornes.

Alfred, like most of the British delegation, stayed at the Majestic, 'a vast caravanserai, not uncomfortable, but much too full of all and sundry, too much of a "circus" for my taste.' As the months passed, the hotel became squalid with cigarette fumes and overcrowding. An army of British official staff lived there, working twelve to fourteen hours a day, and in the evening dances and amateur theatricals were put on for them by enterprising Foreign Office clerks such as the future Lord Vansittart.

Violet also saw Clemenceau, his face the colour of old ivory, black-coated like the other delegates, and wearing lavender cotton gloves. He had been slightly wounded in a recent assassination attempt and was sick of politics, longing for the peace of his Normandy farm with his beloved dogs.

Violet lunched several times with Bob Cecil; weighed down by large responsibilities over Europe's crippled economy, he had taken to smoking heavily. He told Violet that the Peace Treaty would heap up disaster for the future: events proved him right.

Alfred was exasperated by the disagreements among Allies and colleagues who had worked together stalwartly in wartime. 'Now there is peace,' he brooded, comparing this spring with the previous one, 'but I am not sure that the outlook for this country and the world is not even blacker today than it was then.' Alfred's old impatience as a negotiator – so manifest in South Africa though not at Doullens – with politicians and electorates alike, and his aversion to horse-trading and compromise, were exacerbated by exhaustion from the strain of running the War Office during 1918, and the exceptional tension felt by everyone at the conference. Nonetheless he impressed people by his reasoning and command of detail.

Both Alfred and Bob Cecil had disagreed with Lloyd George about the harshness of the terms that Britain should impose on Germany – as much from a practical as from a moral point of view. Both felt that fierce financial and territorial terms would turn Germany Bolshevist and wreck Europe's economic system. Lloyd George had been committed, against his own better judgement, by his election pledges of December 1918 to squeezing the last penny from Germany in reparations to pay for the cost of the war. By the time he was converted to a milder settlement, the changes he achieved were too few and too late to prevent a punitive peace.

Bob and Alfred were also opposed to Clemenceau and the French delegates, who were determined that never again should Germany be in a position to invade and wreck France: her economy must be broken by reparations and she should be stripped of land and military power. To Bob, the French were 'the worst diplomatists in Europe. They were quite incapable of giving up some tuppeny-ha'penny bit of international swagger, and would much rather sacrifice a really important interest in its place . . . Even Clemenceau, who is in many ways the best of them, is not free from these defects.' He concluded that 'the only explanation of their conduct is that the war strain has literally knocked them a little off their balance.'

Clemenceau, for his part, did not find Bob easy: '*un Chrétien qui croit et veut vivre sa croyance, avec un sourire de dragon, barré aux arguments.*' As for Alfred, Clemenceau complained, 'if he does not agree with you, he closes his eyes like a lizard, and you can do nothing with him.' But recollecting him later, when the tension of 1919 had subsided, Clemenceau was kinder: 'a brilliant intellect crowned with high culture, extreme gentleness and extreme firmness . . . A man who, during an official report on a night journey from London to Versailles at one of our most trying moments, paused to speak of the loveliness of the moonlight and the young spring grass.'

For Alfred personally, the economic ruin of Germany bore heavily on his private as well as his public conscience. He worried about those who had been friends of his family during his happy childhood days in Germany, and later he sent money to an elderly woman friend in Tübingen, a small gesture of kindness following on so much cruelty between the nations.

He was growing disenchanted with Lloyd George, though he continued in office under him as he considered this to be his duty during the post-war reconstruction. While Alfred was still Minister of War at the end of 1918, Lloyd George had humiliated him in front of his Cabinet colleagues, furiously accusing him of being dilatory over military demobilisation. It was then that he had moved Alfred to the Colonial Office, replacing him with Winston Churchill. The Prime Minister had a cruel streak and was fond of exploiting the weaknesses of vain men like George Curzon, whom on one occasion he reduced to tears. Alfred was less vulnerable but he felt the slight: 'Wrote a long and stiff letter to the P.M. about the rather indecent proceedings of the Cabinet in the morning.'

Bob Cecil had been appointed as official representative of Britain to draw up a scheme for a League of Nations to prevent future wars. He did this with conviction, to compensate for the merciless economic blockade imposed on Germany. He yearned, as his father had done, for a strong international organisation and legal framework to replace for ever 'the cold cruel arbitrament of war'. Back in England, Ivor Maxse, knighted and a general, holding the British Northern Command, but a shade bitter than he had not been promoted higher, was sceptical about the new peace organisation. 'I prefer a League of Tanks to a League of Nations,' he proclaimed gruffly in an after-dinner speech. This caused an outcry; summoned by Winston Churchill, the Secretary of State for War, to explain his conduct, Ivor was unrepentant. Most military men – and Violet – agreed with him; so did Clemenceau and the other French leaders who favoured collective defence against their mortal enemy.

Violet's amiable American diplomat friend, Henry White, who had been one of the Souls in those far-off days at the end of the last century, was plenipotentiary for the United States; he did little more than follow the line of the autocratic President Woodrow Wilson. The USA, through its supreme economic position, had become the arbiter of Europe and the champion of liberty, a fact much resented by some big powers but welcomed by small nations, especially in Eastern

Europe, which hoped to gain backing for their nationalist schemes. Paris was full of Americans.

The many Allied countries represented at the conference scrabbled for whatever recognition, territory and security they could gain. Other nationalities and movements excluded from the negotiations lobbied for their causes: T.E. Lawrence canvassed the claims of the Emir Feisal in the Middle East; arguments about Zionism, only too familiar in later years, were vigorously delivered. Sinn Fein campaigned for an independent Ireland; Indo-Chinese (Vietnamese) for independence from France; proponents of schemes ranging from Esperanto to World Labour organisations streamed to the hotel offices of great power delegates.

It was a strange world in which old enemies from former days were brought together – like the Boer General Louis Botha and Alfred Milner: 'Seventeen years ago today,' Botha declared in May 1919, his hand on Alfred's shoulder, reminiscing about the Treaty of Vereeniging which had ended the Boer War, 'the terms were hard, but they were generous. You know the result.' Alfred was all too aware of how much South Africa had gone the Boers' way since then, but Botha was one of their leaders who had done more than many to embrace partnership with Britain in the Empire.

Many visitors had come to France to mourn their dead and to see for themselves the terrible devastation of the Western Front where a generation of sons, husbands, brothers, nephews and fathers had perished. 'It was a grey windy day of scudding clouds,' young Eddy Sackville wrote after going up to the front with David Cecil, 'the trees were the grimmest things of all – great avenues of gaunt black fingers . . . Great stretches of barren country pierced by shell holes and here and there a half-ruined house.'

Bereaved families searched for the last resting place of their dead, often amid the homely relics of trench life. Alice Salisbury's cousin, Wilfrid Ewart, had survived the war as a Guards officer and now made the pilgrimage to Delville Wood on the Somme with his sister, Angela Farmer, to find her husband's grave. He wrote:

> Everywhere lies the ordinary debris of occupied trenches – bully beef tins, biscuit tins, traces of half-executed meals . . . A dented white basin with traces of soapy water stands on a box; shaving tackle all spattered with soil and mud spreads itself upon an improvised table. Something of a meal remains – a marmalade jar with tin plates and rusted knife and fork. A pair

Devastation on the Western Front: British soldiers gaze into a German trench at the end of the war

of muddy, hardened boots is set down near the entrance . . . Will we find our friend, or do the dead lie too thick – are the crosses too many? We pause in our search, a profound disappointment upon our faces. Already sundown is here, and it is the hour of the frost. Already great shadows begin to lengthen across the battlefield, blotting out the hollow places, adding infinitely to the vast tragedy of this land . . . What bitterness lies there!

Violet took Helen to Villers Cotterêts to see where her brother had fallen.

Violet was to join Kipling, Fabian Ware and Alfred in helping with the Imperial War Graves Commission which had been founded by Royal Charter in May 1917 to commemorate the Empire's million war dead, to dig graves and build cemeteries on the battlefields. Alfred was its first chairman, Kipling its adviser on suitable memorial lines: it was he who chose the words 'Their name liveth for evermore' from Ecclesiastes, as the Commission's sacred pledge.

In time, the Imperial War Graves Commission created a memorial for George and the other ninety Guardsmen killed at Rond de la Reine. This spot was to be a point of pilgrimage for Violet which she visited every year save 1941–44, until she was very old. It stands in the heart of the woodland, close to the site of the mass grave where their bodies had been found. George's body was moved back there. The beauty and remoteness of this little graveyard, the extreme youth of George and other boy soldiers killed in the same forgotten and desperate engagement, make it one of the most moving sites on the Western Front. On George's stone is carved the grenade symbol of his regiment and the simple words:

SECOND LIEUTENANT
GEORGE EDWARD CECIL
GRENADIER GUARDS
1ST SEPTEMBER 1914 AGE 18

ONLY SON OF
LORD AND LADY EDWARD CECIL
KILLED IN ACTION
NEAR THIS SPOT

The Peace Treaty with Germany was at last signed at Versailles on 28 June. Alfred was still heavily involved, however, in the negotiations over settlement with Turkey, which dragged on for months afterwards. In London there was a great Victory Parade on 19 July which Alfred watched from Buckingham Palace – an immense and wonderfully managed spectacle, he said, led by the American General Pershing, which took two and a half hours to march past the royal party.

Alfred's final achievement as Colonial Secretary was to head a commission on Egypt's future, following predictable nationalist riots. He reported in 1920; realistic enough, in the post-war turmoil, to recognise the force of Egyptian nationalism, he urged abolition of the old ambiguous structure of British and foreign influence over the country's government. Egypt henceforward should be treated as an independent constitutional monarchy and an ally, where Britain should maintain, under treaty, only a minimal civilian presence and a larger military one, to promote imperial interests. Alfred's conversion was a great victory for the Egyptians, though it did not satisfy their wishes for full independence. In British governing circles he was heavily criticised and his recommendations initially blocked. Violet, too, disagreed with his report, though this never came between them.

A few months later the Government came round to his views, but by then sheer weariness had led him to resign from office for good, leaving in February 1921 with the highest honour, the Order of the Garter.

This had an absurd sequel: shortly afterwards, when about to attend a court levée, always a social minefield, Alfred realised he did not know how to wear his new honour. He decided, incorrectly, to wear the riband over the right shoulder instead of the left. George Curzon, shocked to the depths of his ceremonious soul, wrote to him afterwards, that it was 'almost inconceivable' that anyone who had been given this ancient order should not even take the trouble to find out how it was worn. A few months later Curzon, confused in his turn by the elaborate medieval rules about 'Collar Days', turned up wearing both his Garter collar *and* his riband – extremely bad form to those who cared. Alfred was delighted to overhear the King point out this mistake, and wrote to his pompous friend – repeating Curzon's words precisely – on his 'inconceivable' breach of the dress code.

George's grave

CHAPTER TWENTY-THREE

Lady Milner

HELEN CECIL AND Alec Hardinge were married on 8 February 1921, at St Paul's, Knightsbridge, in the fashionable heart of London. Had Edward been alive he might have had a moment's regret that his beloved daughter was marrying the son of his old enemy, Lord Hardinge, who as head of the Foreign Office had backed Ronald Graham and other thorns in his flesh in Egypt; but he could not have disapproved of Alec Hardinge himself, a brave and entirely suitable young man.

Alec had recently been appointed Assistant Private Secretary to King George V. Following the King's death in 1936, he was to become Private Secretary to Edward VIII, and after the abdication, to George VI. So Helen and Violet were to be drawn into royal circles. For Helen's family, Alec was to prove a valuable support, affectionate and devoted to his young bride, whose nervous vicissitudes did not always bring domestic serenity. Many a time in years to come, it was Alec who kept the peace between her and Violet.

Because Alec was a courtier, King George V and Queen Mary were present at the wedding. The Queen's splendour – gold and mauve toque and purple velvet gown – contrasted with the plain black of her lady-in-waiting, Mabell Airlie, still in mourning for her husband's death in the Boer War, and also that of her youngest son Captain Patrick Ogilvy, MC, of the Irish Guards, in 1917.

Violet wore a dress of dark brown soft silk known as 'charmeuse' under a gold-embroidered coat trimmed with the sable collar, cuffs and bow which were then so fashionable. Her touch was evident in the flowers, early spring bouquets and miniature orange trees, and also in Helen's wedding dress of old *point d'Angleterre* lace, which had belonged to Cissie Maxse, with a train and halter collar of rich white satin; traditional orange blossom held her veil in position and encircled her waist. She carried a simple bouquet of lilies of the valley.

Helen Cecil, aged 20, and her bridegroom, Alec Hardinge MC

The guests seated on the bride's side of the church encapsulated Violet's past life and the tragedy of the war: the Cecil family and her Maxse brothers and sister; from Dublin days, Sir Herbert and Lady (Aggie) Jekyll; from her London life of the 1880s and 1890s, Lord Midleton (St John Brodrick), Lady Horner, Ettie Desborough, and Cynthia Mosley, wife of Oswald Mosley, the future fascist leader, representing her father George Curzon; from South African times, Cissie Bentinck and Major-General Sir John and Lady Hanbury-Williams; from Egypt, Katie Cromer and Sir Henry and Lady MacMahon; and friends Violet shared with Alfred – the Kiplings, Loulie Dawkins, Lord and Lady Goschen, her neighbours near Hawkhurst, whose eldest son had been killed in Mesopotamia, and whose niece Moira Somerville, a nurse during the war, had become almost a member of Violet's family.

Jem Salisbury gave Helen away and Lord William Cecil officiated. Helen's bridesmaids and pages in the Cecil colours of blue and silver, included Eve Cecil, Lord William's second daughter, and Lady Elizabeth Bowes-Lyon, the future Queen: both of them had lost brothers in the war. The bride and groom emerged to a great peal of bells and a guard of honour from the Grenadiers.

At the reception afterwards, in the library of the Salisburys' house in Arlington Street, the guests admired the array of presents including a blue enamelled clock from the Queen, and the King's gift, a silver bowl bearing the royal arms.

That evening Violet and Alfred dined *tête-à-tête*. No doubt they discussed an even more momentous wedding which was to take place in three weeks' time: their own.

There had been no public announcement. Ever-secretive, Alfred chose to keep quiet about this astonishing turn of events which ended his life as one of London's most sought-after bachelors. He had simply announced that he was going abroad for six weeks. Nobody but his closest friends, such as Leo Amery, his successor at the Colonial Office, knew anything; the only guests were Olive Maxse, Loulie Dawkins (who had been considerably upset by the news) and Alfred's solicitor, who had arranged the ceremony, at St James's Church, Paddington, and whose brother, an army padre, officiated alongside the vicar.

It was strange that two such convinced atheists should go through a Christian service in a lofty Gothic Revival church encapsulating Victorian piety. Yet the event, a fulfilment of their deepest feelings, was of such solemn importance to them, that perhaps only such a dignified building, its sombre splendour largely the work of the famous architect G.E. Street, could have been an adequate setting.

Close friends and relations were pleased by the news. For Helen, still on her honeymoon, Alfred had been a steady, affectionate presence in her life since girlhood. Jem and Alice liked him, too, and it was no little relief that, with Helen also wed, Violet was off their hands. Alfred was nearly sixty-seven, and looked older, though friends found him more buoyant than he had been for years. Violet at forty-nine was still elegant: her satin wedding dress was her favourite colour, brown. After the service Lord and Lady Milner went to Olive's home for lunch with the few wedding guests, and they signed new wills. Then Alfred returned to Great College Street to say goodbye to his household who were still in ignorance, eluding a journalist hanging about outside. Before he left from Charing Cross station, where an official from the Colonial Office had brought his luggage, Alfred sent an official notice of the marriage to the Press Association.

Alfred and Violet spent the first night of their honeymoon at the Lord Warden Hotel, Dover. They walked before dinner in the brilliant starlight, and retired to bed after listening to a violin recital in the hotel foyer.

Then came some of the happiest weeks of Violet's life, in her beloved France, with the hero whom she had at last, after twenty-one years, been able to marry. They reached Provence without attracting attention, although the Sunday papers were full of their 'secret wedding'. At the Hotel de l'Europe at Avignon their reception was frigidly formal, until the management realised that they were the leading figures of the secret romance emblazoned on news posters everywhere. Despite an unwelcome migraine afflicting Violet briefly, the fortnight they spent at that comfortable, unpretentious establishment was so delightful that they could hardly bear to leave. They strolled along the medieval ramparts and drove in a hired car to nearby *villages perchés* and the spectacular monuments of France's medieval and Roman past, returning with armfuls of wild jonquils to decorate their rooms.

Alfred did not relax even on his honeymoon; as ever, for several hours of each day he dealt with correspondence, chiefly on the business affairs he was resuming. His sightseeing was equally thorough. After a day that would have exhausted most men of his age, in and out of amphitheatres and churches, he was disappointed at Arles, that they were 'too late for the Musée Lapidaire'.

As for Violet, she was enchanted by the beauty of that early spring with its spectacular starry nights and sunny days; by their leisurely picnics and by meals at the restaurant Hiély, that tranquil temple of *haute cuisine*, with its white-aproned waiters trained in the most arcane rituals of the table.

An unexpected arrival at their hotel was Arthur Balfour, bound for Cannes to recuperate from an exhausting meeting of the League of Nations Council. The two gossipy evenings Alfred and Violet spent in the charming, flippant company of this perennial bachelor suited their honeymoon mood. After Avignon, they went to the walled city of Carcassonne, north to Cahors, and returned home via Paris where they called on Clemenceau, full of fresh and interesting impressions of his recent trip to India.

On the evening of 12 April, Violet arrived at Sturry Court for the first time as Alfred's wife. They strolled together in the garden by moonlight. In the days that followed they enjoyed for a second time the onrush of spring which had exhilarated them in the South of France. In the woods, full of the sound of nightingales and cuckoos, the bluebells were out in great drifts. Alfred had 'never known this place more beautiful and more attractive than during this first week'.

Not even the national coal strike, which threatened to spread to other industries, could undermine his contentment.

As mistress of Sturry, Violet brought out the beauty of the hand-some red brick Tudor manor as she had at Wigsell, sympathetic to its essential simplicity, while introducing improvements such as electric lighting. Nothing could have checked her initiative, but for the first time she had as her companion someone who made decisions for her and on whom she could completely rely: 'Alfred is truly a rock and has the best judgement of anyone I have ever known,' she told Olive. Mutual interests, romantic feeling, devotion, admiration and gratitude all played a part in their deep contentment. The independence to which both had been accustomed for so long was at an end. For Alfred the *tête-à-têtes* with Mrs Glyn, Mrs Lindsay, Mrs Dick Chamberlain and nearly all the sirens *d'un certain âge* ceased; the exceptions were Loulie Dawkins, Bertha Synge, Mrs Arnold Toynbee and Mrs Gaskell, none of whom were seen as a threat. Even so, he retained a greater degree of autonomy than the average husband and Violet was clever enough to accept this.

Alfred sold his London house to one of his wartime private secre-taries, John Arkwright, author of the yearning memorial hymn to the war dead, 'O valiant hearts'. The Milners moved into a larger, double-fronted house, 14 Manchester Square, across from one of Violet's favourite haunts, that most civilised of galleries, the Wallace Collection.

Until they eventually let Wigsell to Sir Ralph Verney and his family in 1923, they occupied it each summer and early autumn. Alfred helped Violet to tend the groves of oak and chestnut she had planted, to light great bonfires and gather windfalls of apples after storms. One evening in July they counted forty-eight glow worms as they wan-dered along a lane nearby. At Sturry they passed many hours arrang-ing the books in the shelves and in the evenings reading aloud to each other: Dickens, George Meredith, Walter Raleigh, Byron, David Garnett – or drier fare, such as Penty's *Post-Industrialism*. 'Read aloud some of Dr Roberts' book on a National Health Service to Violet' is a typical entry in Alfred's diary.

He could not be kept away long from public affairs such as agricul-ture, planning, industrial relations and imperial politics. Now an exec-utive director, once more, of the Rio Tinto mining company, international economic problems preoccupied him.

As a couple, they dined in town with friends such as Waldorf and

Nancy Astor, to meet the King and Queen; went to the wedding of the future King George VI, then Duke of York; stayed with the Rothschilds at Mentmore; and attended the Rhodes Trust ceremonies at Oxford. George Curzon, when Foreign Secretary, invited them to lunch at Carlton House Terrace in 1923 to meet Edvard Beneš, the Czech Prime Minister and future President. They were closely involved too, in the 1820 Memorial Settlers League (named after the big English colonisation of the Eastern Cape Colony in that decade) which promoted British immigration to South Africa – Alfred's key solution for preventing Boer domination after the Boer War. Old South African friends, to whom he was still a hero, came to see him, including Sir Percy Fitzpatrick, the ebullient Irish former 'gold-bug' and Jameson Raider, who had done so much before and after the Boer War to persuade Alfred that he was on the right course. 'Fitz', an enterprising promoter of British settlement in Cape Colony, stayed at Wigsell, joining in mushroom-picking after weeks of hot weather followed by rain produced a bumper crop. Rudyard Kipling came over from Bateman's and the three men talked of starting a new tariff reform campaign and of the iniquities of Boer nationalism.

Lloyd George was forced to resign as coalition Prime Minister in October 1922 by a strong revolt among the Conservative leadership, including Jem Salisbury. Bonar Law, at the head of a new administration, tried to entice Alfred back into politics, offering him any job he chose. 'Oh no Bonar, no no, under no circumstances,' Violet heard him say on the telephone. George Curzon also tried to persuade him to return – as Ambassador in Paris. 'He was very eloquent about the importance of the post, my fitness for it, also Violet's gifts,' wrote Alfred, who nevertheless refused, anxious to use the time remaining to him as he pleased.

The decline of British influence in South Africa, the rise of Indian nationalism, and the independence of Ireland appalled both of them and they were deeply distressed by the assassination by Sinn Feiners of their friend Sir Henry Wilson, in June 1922, outside his home in Eaton Square. They had believed him a great force for reinvigorating imperial policy and national self-esteem. Alfred went directly to comfort Lady Wilson, who was keeping a vigil in her husband's room, his body laid out in his Field Marshal's uniform which he had been wearing when he was shot. Violet had to attend Court that evening to present a friend to the King and Queen; it was all she could do not to break down in tears.

The already rapid urban expansion before the war was now increasing. The 'beast', as the architect Clough Williams-Ellis described it, had begun to descend on the British countryside, with ribbon development, automobiles and commuters – of whom Alfred, ironically, was one. He was depressed to count more than 262 cars in less than a mile's walk along a usually quiet Kent lane on an August bank holiday. Worse still was a squalid intimation of Sturry's future as the dismal urban overflow from Canterbury it has become today. One March day in 1923 he 'surprised a man and woman behaving in an indecent manner with another male and female presumably having done or about to do the same. I turned the four out but I am afraid with a growing population all round the preservation of duty and order in the world is going to be difficult.'

Despite Violet's new contentment – her first grandchild, George, was born in 1921 and her second, Winifred, in 1924 – continued migraines filled her with depression. Their cause, though mysterious, was partly, Alfred suspected, psychological: 'It is a bad time of the year for her,' he wrote on 25 August 1922, the eighth anniversary of George's last week of life, 'and I think she dreads the visit to France next week.' His understanding of her continuing grief for George's death meant much to Violet. That year the pilgrimage included a ceremony to inaugurate a monument she had commissioned from the sculptor Pierre Sicard to mark the spot at Rond de la Reine where George was killed. This stele or pillar of classical Greek design bore the figure of a woman, with a French inscription inviting the passer-by to pause a while.

When Alfred accompanied her there in 1923 he was impressed by the dignified patriotism of the Mouflier family, who continued to look after the grave, and their sorrow for their ravaged country: their home town had been a battleground in 1914 and 1918, so it was not surprising, Mouflier told them without bitterness, '*si je trouve les allemands un peu encombrant*'.

On a trip to Paris by herself in January 1923, Violet saw Clemenceau every day and went to his party in the green room of the Opéra Comique, wearing the smart new Parisian clothes which she was now delighted to be able to afford. When he came to dine with her 'the whole staff of the hotel was crazy with excitement'. She and Alfred twice stayed with him at his home, Bel-Ebat, on the Atlantic coast. Like her, Alfred was captivated by the simple life he led there, crab fishing, visiting the ancient druidic monuments and going to the markets where Clemenceau exchanged cheerful banter with stall-

*Return to South Africa: Lord and Lady Milner on
their last journey together, Cape Town, 1925*

holders, particularly 'one enormous lady at a fruit stall, Mathilde by name, who must have been a great beauty in her time'.

To Violet, Alfred was the ideal travelling companion, considerate and knowledgeable, and their voyaging was more luxurious than she had known before. In spring 1922 they went to the Middle East, stopping first in Egypt: 'The whole of Cairo appears to be flocking to meet Alfred at Port Said,' Violet wrote proudly.

In November 1924 Alfred and Violet returned to South Africa. Nearly twenty years had passed since he had left, and for her twenty-four. At Cape Town they stayed at the Mount Nelson hotel and visited the white granite Rhodes Monument on the mountainside above Groote Schuur – featuring a figure mounted on a galloping horse, representing Rhodes's 'colossal' energy. They visited Alfred's old opponent, later ally in the Great War, Jan Christiaan Smuts, at his farm

Irene, near Pretoria. The dwelling, once an officers' mess hut, 'he has certainly not troubled to beautify in any way,' while the farm had 'the usual air of Boer disorder, and the cattle we caught sight of were poor,' wrote Violet.

Smuts greeted them with his celebrated charm, but Mrs Smuts, a 'stout, active-looking woman, with black curly hair cut short all over her head,' seemed flustered, having been, until recently, very anti-British. Violet professed to like her 'naturalness' and thought 'the whole household was a lesson in simple life and abundant warm-hearted hospitality', though irritated by the endless 'Oupa's and 'Momma's that punctuated the General's interchanges with his wife. She remembered Rhodes saying the same about Boer domestic talk: 'I hate their paas and their maas.' Their lunch, an unpretentious Malay *Babootje* – meat and vegetables – was accompanied, to Violet's surprise, by an excellent champagne. Of Smuts she later remarked that he 'was much too certain of himself to think of making a difference between one set of people and another'.

During the meal and in Smuts's large study, hung with moth-eaten, captured German standards and the old Boer 'Vieur Kleur' flag, Alfred and Smuts talked avidly of European affairs, which they had not discussed together since the war and the Paris peace conference, when Smuts, like Alfred a member of Lloyd George's Cabinet, had stepped on to the stage of world politics.

'Knowing the mentality of the Cape Dutch,' Violet wrote subsequently, 'I was not surprised, when my husband died . . . General Smuts should have given to the press a very inaccurate account of the talk he had had and the views he held on the South African situation – views dramatically opposite to those he actually held and expressed.' It was an episode characteristic of Smuts's reputation for not being completely on the level, while Violet's belated revenge – a sardonic account of the visit in the *National Review* years afterwards – was equally characteristic.

Further south, in the Eastern Orange Free State, Alfred was delighted to find a part of his vision for the whole of South Africa realised – Englishmen, known as 'Milner settlers' of the post-Boer War period, who were farming with apparent contentment in that fertile country of green hills and newly planted woodland. They visited Bend'or's estate, Westminster, with its fine plantations and stylish house by Herbert Baker. Alfred commented optimistically on the 'splendidly healthy looking' children on the farms, and the 'prosperous, cheery and grateful' stamp of men he found there. Although he knew that his plans for a massive British settlement in South Africa had so far failed, he still clung to such hopes for the future. In the semi-autonomous native state of the Transkei, at a famous beauty spot, the Tsitsa Falls, his celebrated vigour failed him climbing down the slippery path: 'I presently found myself too exhausted to go on, and it was all I could do to clamber to the top again without assistance.' He had been unaccountably ill for several days, and the last leg of his journey, through the Eastern Cape Province, was a struggle, although the large English population there received him like a hero.

At Cape Town, he and Violet attended the opening of the Union Parliament. Under the newly-elected General J.B.M. Hertzog, the South African government was now uncompromisingly anti-British, but Alfred wisely ventured no criticism, for though a private visitor, he was bound to be taken as the voice of the English Government. Cape Town seemed different: white people had cars, and many Africans, all of whom formerly went on foot, were mounted, often on good horses, which cost little. Few of the old type of Boer farmers, with wide-brimmed hats and long beards, were around; more prosaic figures, lawyers and ministers of the Dutch Reformed Church, in dark suits, walked the streets.

The Milners paid a nostalgic trip to nearby Muizenberg, by the sea. There Alfred's friend, the millionaire politician Abe Bailey, had a house next door to the cottage where Cecil Rhodes had died – and where Violet and Cissie Bentinck had stayed as a respite during the Boer War. To Alfred's chagrin, the suburban railway line now ran between the houses and the sea, and the village 'had become a crowded and rather vulgar seaside place and lost all its old charm of solitude and unspoiled natural beauty'.

But their last fortnight in South Africa was particularly happy. Alfred was fêted by Bailey, and while he spent his time at masculine gatherings, Violet tactfully stayed with his devoted friend, the writer Dorothea Fairbridge. Once they made their way together up Table Mountain, overlooking Kirstenbosch: 'The silver-trees, and flowers innumerable, and the unsurpassable views on to two seas – Table Bay and False Bay – and again across the Cape Flats to the great army of mountains from Hottentot's Holland on the right to Tiger Bay on the left, are sights impossible to describe or forget. These were perhaps the most enjoyable hours we spent during the whole of our journey,' Alfred wrote.

As they sailed out of Table Bay bound for England, seen off by a crowd of Alfred's admirers, he and Violet wondered whether they would ever see South Africa again. On 'the most lovely afternoon conceivable', they watched, until it disappeared from sight, the noble outline of that mountain which had been the backdrop for the central drama of both their lives a quarter of a century earlier.

On his return, in March, Alfred seemed to friends like Rudyard Kipling much aged. His health was failing. Briefly, he led a normal life, working late as usual, but soon the doctors advised complete rest.

Their remedies were useless: by the end of April he was losing the power of speech and was partially paralysed. Only then was he diagnosed as having 'sleeping sickness' (*encephalitis lethargica*), contracted, apparently, from a tsetse fly bite in Africa. Still friends had faith in his resilience, though not for long. Violet had to ask for the church bells to be silent on Sunday so as not to disturb him. She had him brought downstairs to the sitting room so that he could look out at the garden and was with him all the time. 'He was often conscious during the day and night – always patient and his lovely smile.'

In default of other candidates he was elected Chancellor of Oxford University on 12 May 1925. It was too late. The following day he died, under Violet's distraught gaze. He was seventy-one. A service for him was held in Canterbury Cathedral, conducted by the Archbishop. Then, in a coffin wrapped in a Union Jack and decorated with Sturry flowers, he was buried at Salehurst Church, a few miles from Wigsell, on the very edge of the graveyard, looking out over the quintessentially Kentish landscape that he cherished: fields of barley, fringed with bright flowers, and dotted with oast houses with their pointed, quaintly angled turrets and tall stacks of silver-grey hop-poles.

CHAPTER TWENTY-FOUR

The Widow of Wigsell

ON HER FIFTY-FOURTH birthday, 1 February 1926, Violet wrote
in her diary: 'Never was a more complete change. Last year, all
affection, solicitude and adorable companionship. This year – Oh, my
dear, dear love, where are you?'

She decided to leave Sturry for Wigsell and to commemorate
Alfred at the church where he was buried. Here she proposed to make
a chapel, with a tomb supporting two recumbent figures, Alfred's and
hers. This she felt would be in keeping with an ancient church full of
interesting memorials. But the authorities disagreed. On 23 March
1926, Alfred's birthday, Violet went to the church with flowers and a
wreath, and to discuss the possible 'Wigsell Chancel' with the church
wardens. But 'though I can see the beauty of my plan,' she wrote 'they
cannot.' The dispute was eventually settled by a consistory court in
Violet's favour; tenacious though she was, however, the remaining
complications forced her to drop the idea – a pity, as the planned
chapel, to Lutyens's design, would have been a spectacular addition for
Salehurst's old church.

Outside, Lutyens's tomb to Alfred, finished in April 1927, was in
the style of his war memorials, of white stone, dignified and unob-
trusive. At first it struck Violet as 'rather fortress-like', but when she
had decorated it with flowers, it looked 'less desolate'. The first
garland Violet laid there was of all the flowers they had loved best,
especially those they had seen on the honeymoon: 'periwinkle for
South Africa, grape hyacinths for Carcassonne, fritillaries for Cahors,
polyanthus for Sturry and magnolias for my deep love, rosemary,
forget-me-not, iris.' She would sit on the stone bench she had placed
near the grave and think about Alfred; and when she was out of reach
of the churchyard where her dead love lay her thoughts returned
there. She had cypresses planted, a row of dark green between the
stone graves and the golden corn.

Violet offered Sturry Court to King's School, Canterbury, as a junior school, and endowed a Milner Scholarship. In January 1927 she left the house for good. The Kiplings – 'I bless them for their kindness' – came over to keep her company at the last. On her final afternoon there, she walked alone in the twilight, 'the river gleaming . . . I paused for a moment to say good-bye to it all and to bless the grassland, the wooded hill, the bare brown earth and his river . . . Now I am sitting by the fire. The house is still. The wind can be heard in the chimney. The room is already strange. I turn the page. Goodbye, my darling Love, once more goodbye.'

Something of Alfred's house was incorporated into Violet's when she created the 'Sturry Parlour' at Wigsell, on one side of the hall, by installing a partition of fourteenth-century panelling from Sturry Court. She had stained glass windows designed with the various family coats of arms in vivid colours – Cecil, Maxse, Milner. She even designed a tapestry in the manner of *La Dame à la Licorne* in the Museé Cluny, Paris, which she embarked on sewing herself.

On the other side of the big hall Violet also made a library–dining-room, the bookshelves designed by Lutyens when he came to work on the Milner tomb. Hand-blocked William Morris willow leaf wallpaper was complemented by specially mixed subtle green paint. In the centre was a seventeenth-century oak dining table. New bathrooms, a telephone and electricity, driven by her own generator, were also installed.

Her links with the Kiplings and Clemenceau were stronger than ever. In New Year 1926 Violet visited Clemenceau, now in his eighties and retired from politics, for the first time since Alfred's death. Sitting in his familiar room in the Rue Franklin she was too choked with emotion to converse much: 'that room has too many memories and I was too miserable.' Yet she gained comfort from his indomitable spirit: 'Once more, out of the darkness, light, even though it is held by an old hand and is only a flickering torch. He will hold it until he dies. He longs to go, but until he goes he will bear witness and stand for truth and a sane understanding of what is around us.'

On a later visit, in March 1929, Violet was very moved to see with Clemenceau Monet's *Nymphéas* in their new, permanent home at the Orangerie. 'About the great pictures he was inspired. He had seen them grow under his friend's hand and had watched every phase.' To her, 'the 4 vast canvasses of water lilies in different lights are one of the noblest creations of man. The State would have refused them, but for Clemenceau; he got them accepted and got them worthily housed.' On that Sunday afternoon, there was 'the usual stir and excitement when he appeared, and one or two very adhesive people followed him everywhere, a man noting down all he said.' Because of Clemenceau's deafness, Violet had to talk loudly to him, and he enjoyed himself by answering equally loudly with his usual lack of inhibition. 'He talked most enchantingly and indiscreetly.'

She took the train down to his seaside home at Bel–Ebat where life by the rugged Atlantic shore refreshed her spirits. Her bedroom led on to the garden with the sea beyond, swept by the wide arc of the lighthouse; she left her door open at night and saw the dawn break, pearly pink across the ocean. Also staying was Monet's daughter-in-law Blanche Hoschedé, herself an artist, who sketched the seascape, pictures Violet later bought from her, memories of that paradaisical spot, where the humming of the bees round the flowers mingled with the still vibrant voice of her friend. Every morning she would walk straight out of her little bedroom and swim in the clear, cold waters; then back for a hot tub and breakfast with Clemenceau in his ornate dressing-gown and cap. His conversation was as lucid, fresh and uncompromising as ever. Needless to say, Violet found much in common between him and Alfred: 'Clemenceau has, in fact, though so totally different in temperament, exactly Alfred's outlook. When you have done your *utmost*, then you can do no good by being miserable over your failure. He is certain there will be another war.'

Her last visit to Clemenceau was in September 1929, a few days before his eighty-seventh birthday. 'He has been far away – I felt him slipping through my fingers, I could not catch and hold him.' A few weeks later he died.

Afterwards, Albert, his loyal manservant, told her that M. Wormser and others of his ex-staff had never left him at the end, but 'his family were unspeakable. They had a perpetual tea party in the dining-room. I saw that George's photograph was not in its usual place, so Albert hunted it out of a cupboard and it is to hang near Papa's.'

Clemenceau's flat in Rue Franklin was subsequently preserved, thanks to a rich American benefactor, as a museum, and remains today exactly as it was when he died there.

For Violet, Clemenceau was an integral part of her life: a major link with her father and girlhood, when she had first come under the spell of his exuberant personality, and of Paris itself; with her memories of George, regarded by Clemenceau as a grandson; with Alfred too, who owed to her his close acquaintanceship with Clemenceau, so crucial during the war; and even with Wigsell, where the 'Clemenceau Room' was filled with his gifts and furniture she had bought in Paris.

She was glad that her last visit to her dear friend was on the Britanny coast, by the ocean as indefatigable, clear and powerful as the man himself.

Violet could not go to Paris for his funeral, for her brother Leo was dying of cancer. She offered to take charge of the *National Review*, which he had been editing for nearly four decades. What began as emergency work was to last for the next eighteen years: 'Bringing out the Nat.' became the pattern of Violet's life: the monthly scramble to get to the printers on time; chivvying contributors; sifting through books sent for review. She also wrote the commentaries on public affairs, the 'Episodes'. Composition took her a long time, yet she achieved an easy idiomatic style. She and her devoted secretary, Diana Mayne, worked round the clock to prepare the copy for the printers; the completion of every issue she recorded with pride in her diary.

Leo died early in 1932, after repeated remissions and long periods when Violet moved into his house to look after him. She was now sixty. 'It seems incredible that I should have lived so very long and out-lived so much that was infinitely precious.' Not that she had aged greatly; her figure had broadened, but she still played tennis vigorously and, despite her debilitating headaches, depression and feeling of exhaustion, her constant activity was proof of her enduring energy and her powerful will. Even Violet's closest assistants, such as the good-natured Diana Mayne, had to hold their own or become doormats.

As always, solace came for her in restoring and beautifying the buildings and garden at Wigsell, designing a little pigeon house into which she introduced a couple of 'whiffle ptarmigans'. In the summer of 1930 the magnificent tulip trees brought from Africa when she first came to the house twenty-four years before flowered for the first time. Her grandchildren continued to delight her: a third, Elizabeth, had been born in 1927.

Leo had not been interested in the business side of the *National Review* and despite its many loyal readers it had been losing money for years. Violet proved an effective manager, using a good team well; by March 1930 they had turned a net loss of £120 a month to a tiny profit. They put the *National* on a firmer basis by making it into a company, Violet raising the £5,000 they needed from supporters in a few weeks. After Leo's death she achieved a notable coup when the legendary Lady Houston, whose generosity the year before had

*Leo Maxse. Passionate about tennis,
the younger of Violet's brothers played
even during his last long illness*

enabled Britain to win, for the third time, the Schneider Trophy for high speed flight, offered the magazine £15,000 in Leo's memory so that the price could be reduced to two shillings and sixpence and thus attract many new subscribers. Violet, overwhelmed by the paper's renewed success, wished 'darling Leo could have known. He often thought his work was wasted, like good wine poured down a sink.'

The *National Review* retained good contributors from its heyday before the Great War, as well as its lively, radical right-wing stance. Violet saw herself as the guardian of her brother's views, committed like him to causes such as tariff reform, and imperial defence, particularly against a revived Germany. Hitler's rise made her family's outspoken views seem more perceptive and less paranoid. Violet never used the 'Nat' to campaign for women's rights. Always confident of the *private* power of women like herself, she considered their outward political status irrelevant.

In the 'Nat' Violet attacked anti-British legislation in South Africa, and the moves to deprive the Cape's black Africans of the vote. 'The "Colour Bar" is the infliction of a legislative or administrative bar

Lord Robert (Bob) Cecil, British co-founder of the League of Nations at Geneva, by the caricaturist Aloys Derso

upon British people of colour, solely because of the colour of their skin,' the *National Review* declared. 'No barrier of race, colour or creed should be applied to British citizens of the Commonwealth.' Privately, she sent money and encouragement to the Cape Natives Vote Convention, to defend their political rights – a losing battle.

The 'Nat' applauded, in February 1932, when the Government introduced a 10 per cent tariff on all foreign goods save meat and grain, but granted free entry to all produce from the British Empire. Thus the battle which Alfred, Leo, Kipling and the Chamberlains had fought was at last won, though it came too late to bind the Empire more strongly together, as the Tariff Reformers hoped.

One of the chief targets for the 'Nat's' attacks was 'Internationalism', as represented by the League of Nations, of which Bob Cecil was Britain's elder statesman. Violet, equating it with cloud-cuckoo-land, political weakness and national betrayal, was dismissive of the 'misapplied energy of a group of Englishmen in this huge unwieldy affair'. Firm patriotism and tough action, not some wishy-washy brotherhood of nations, were the only ways to deal with aggression – she drew a homely parallel with the spirited ducks on the pond at Wigsell that she had watched driving off an invasion by much larger and more numerous geese. Bob Cecil enjoyed an argument but he came to dread meeting Violet. 'My patience!' he would exclaim, escaping from her tirades across the Long Gallery at Hatfield, 'that's the most tiresome woman I know!'

Although less influential than in earlier years, the *National Review* was still respected and Violet made some powerful friends, glad to feed her information and valuing her advice. Even Stanley Baldwin occasionally took notice: once, when he was visiting Wigsell, she tried to bring home the realities of Europe to him: 'Never forget, Prime Minister, our frontier is on the Rhine.' 'What?' he asked, and she repeated what she had said. Not long afterwards he used the same phrase in a radio broadcast, strongly impressing listeners. In general, however, his policy, and that of his successor Neville Chamberlain, of 'appeasing Germany' remained the same. Both men were terrified of provoking another war and of committing Britain to military action without adequate arms or funds or the backing of the Dominions.

Among Violet's old friends, the Kiplings had remained robustly pessimistic about a world demoralised by the Great Depression, where Britain and her inadequate leaders seemed to have gone soft, unnerved by the ordeal of the Great War. As Rudyard put it – and Violet agreed – 'most children and all nations when they have hurt themselves, instinctively run indoors and ask to be told a pretty tale. So it is with us.'

The intestinal pain Kipling had felt ever since John's death meant that he always had to be within reach of a doctor and no longer travelled far. Violet made a point of visiting him when he shut himself away at Bateman's. He would read his work aloud to her and sometimes: 'He laughed so much he could barely read.' Some of this verse he contributed to the 'Nat'. When he died in January 1936, Wigsell itself seemed strange and empty: 'I have always felt as if it partly belonged to him. Sussex is bereft. There is no light shining there.' After Carrie, too, died late in 1939, Bateman's was left, under Rudyard's will, to the National Trust, among the earliest houses to come into its possession; Violet was invited to be on its committee of administrators.

Rudyard's funeral address was to be delivered by his cousin, Stanley Baldwin, who came to consult Violet. He confided to her that King George V was dying. This was the beginning of a nightmare for her son-in-law Alec Hardinge, as Secretary to the new King, Edward VIII.

In November 1936, Alec told his mother-in-law that King Edward was set on marrying the American Wallis Simpson whose second husband was divorcing her. Violet's dislike of Edward for his bad manners and bad judgement intensified during the abdication crisis which followed: '*On dit qu'il est fou. Je le crois.*' When it became publicly known that Alec had confronted Edward with the scandal that was certain to follow, and advised Mrs Simpson to go abroad, Violet was full of praise for her son-in-law's courage.

On 9 December Violet took a Turkish bath 'to wash off the dirt of this horrible crisis'. She heard Lord Halifax read the King's message of abdication in the House of Lords the next day. The Peeresses' Gallery was packed, with many sitting on the floor. The following night, HRH Prince Edward, as he had now become, addressed the nation on the wireless, 'a good speech,' Violet observed, 'but how lacking in control must a man be who does what he has done! And talks about it!' Geoffrey Dawson told her that Edward had kept up Prime Minister Baldwin till late at night shouting orders at him – orders which were wholly unconstitutional. 'He thought he could be Hitler!' Violet scoffed.

She was greatly upset by the whole affair, not simply on Alec's account, but because she wholeheartedly supported the monarchy, the focus of loyalty for the Empire. She could see only a scheming woman and a spoilt man inflicting, through their self-indulgence, an unpardonable humiliation on the country. British prestige undoubtedly suffered out of proportion to the triviality of Edward's passion. The monarchy had gone to Hollywood, so to speak; nor was Edward's irresponsibility lost on Hitler, who welcomed the couple as guests the following year, exploiting for propaganda purposes their obsequious salutes to his sinister regime.

As a peeress and widow of an eminent statesman, Violet had a seat in Westminster Abbey for the Coronation. Showing a style unusual in English ladies of a certain age, however grand, she had her gown made by her Parisian dressmaker.

As the menace of Hitler grew on the continent, Violet's stance was anti-German first, anti-Nazi second. She hardly distinguished between the modern ideology and totalitarianism of Nazism and the nationalism of the Kaiser's regime. However, the anti-semitic atrocities of Hitlerism incensed her; she helped a Jewish acquaintance to escape from Austria, and went with Jem Salisbury to join the great protest rally at the Albert Hall against the *Krystallnacht* pogrom of November 1938, when Jews were brutally attacked and their property vandalised or stolen all over Hitler's Germany.

Throughout the Thirties, and especially as the world crisis gathered momentum, she surrounded herself with like-minded friends, to whom she gave lunches at her club, where she expected everyone to be well informed and eloquent – a stimulating if alarming experience. A frequent guest was the elegant Lord Lloyd, defiantly expressing imperial ideals of the pre-First World War period. He soon rose to be Colonial Secretary, but died of leukemia in 1941, yet another of Violet's heroes whom she outlived. Other intimates included the diplomatic correspondent of *The Times*, Iverach McDonald, whose views on appeasement were very different from the peace-at-any-price line taken by Geoffrey Dawson, his paper's editor; the journalist F.A. Voigt, German-born but naturalised, a British Army veteran of the Great War ('an embittered ex-idealist, a brittle intellectual who has cracked beneath the strain', declared Violet, who liked him and admired his attack on Hitler and on British government policy, in his book *Unto Caesar*); the rising right-wing Conservative politician Alan Lennox-Boyd; the forceful Ned Grigg, an old disciple of Alfred's, liberal in outlook and resolutely anti-Nazi; and 'Polly' Poliakoff, a Russian journalist who looked like Mussolini and enjoyed striding up to the Italian Embassy and frightening the doorman. These were often joined by British and French diplomats and Czech exiles, including Jan Masaryk, son of the former President of Czechoslovakia.

Violet's nephew, Bobbety Cranborne, the future 5th Marquess of Salisbury, had emerged, in his early forties, as one of the most forthright parliamentary opponents of the Conservative Government's appeasement policy. Even so, Violet was dubious about his stand on the rule of law in international relations, as upheld by the League of Nations; this had convinced him that Britain must show equal toughness towards Mussolini for breaking the international law as to Hitler. Violet, who considered it wiser to court Mussolini than drive him into the arms of Hitler, thought Bobbety wrong, but as the crisis mounted, she forgave most anti-appeasers for such aberrations – even Winston Churchill: 'For three or four years Mr Churchill has done national work which is beyond praise. He has steadily and eloquently warned of the dangers ahead.' Nonetheless, Violet was so constituted that an enemy usually remained an enemy and a hero always a hero.

Violet, here seen lunching with Neville Chamberlain, was to fall out with him over the appeasement of Hitler

Churchill, with his 'mountebank stuff', had always been suspect in her eyes, the more so since his parliamentary attack on Alfred as long ago as 1906.

For Neville Chamberlain and the other appeasers, Violet was unsparing in her abuse, despite the fact that they included some of Alfred's disciples: Geoffrey Dawson, Editor of *The Times*, Philip Kerr (now Lord Lothian) and Lionel Curtis, whose Institute of International Affairs she described in 1938 as 'worse than I thought possible . . . we all talked round and round, nothing good. I walked nearly the whole way home, feeling the need of <u>decontamination</u> after the really dreadful atmosphere of Chatham House.'

In March 1938 Germany was on the march. Hitler took over a willing Austria and in May began to agitate about Czechoslovakia, protected by the peace treaties. As Britain waited in suspense to be plunged into a new Armageddon, Violet wondered whether to burn all her papers, 'for who, that comes after me, will take the faintest interest in them?' Like most Londoners she feared an instant attack from the air, so she removed her jewellery and silver to a bank near Wigsell.

After the unsatisfactory Munich agreement between Britain, France and Germany, war in the West at least seemed to be averted. Violet did not share the general relief: 'Neville has yielded everything he went to defend. He was received as though he were a conqueror, by shouting crowds. They won't shout long!' In December she went to Paris to present the Musée Clemenceau with her old friend's letters – 165 of them; the President of the Senate, flanked by his family, various politicians and Clemenceau's son Michel, greeted her.

On 15 March 1939, Hitler marched into Czechoslovakia, ignoring the limits agreed at Munich. Despairing of Britain's leadership, the rationalist but romantic Violet began, as people do in times of stress, to seek non-rational comfort. Staying with friends at Stepleton in Dorset, a place which, like Breamore, had always exercised a healing power over her, she climbed the lofty Iron Age earthwork at Hod Hill, long a sacred ritual for her. From this ancient fortress she gazed across the sheep-cropped downland and the tapestry of fields spread below; she 'found a wonderful fairy ring, round patches of dark green grass. I stood in the middle of it and asked what Gods there be for three things. Power to see, to understand and for strength to endure.' Music, as ever, gave her comfort and fortitude. She was a friend of John Christie, the founder of the opera theatre at Glyndebourne in Sussex, where she was almost overwhelmed by the singing and the productions that year. The intimate theatre, the fine house and garden, were antidotes to the forces of evil she felt closing around her beleaguered island.

At this time, Violet's lease of Manchester Square ended and the house was sold by her landlords. It marked another separation from Alfred: 'It was our real married home, not his, nor mine, but ours.' From now on, she stayed in London at her club or Olive's flat. As Editor of the 'Nat', a prominent francophile, socially well-connected and with friends at Court, her life in 1939 was as full as ever with political and social engagements. In one week there was a party at 10 Downing Street, where a photograph of Mussolini still glared at the guests – the time had not quite come for Mr Chamberlain to remove such dubious tokens of friendship – followed by another at Buckingham Palace, graced by a bevy of beautiful duchesses, Devonshire, Buccleuch, Northumberland, stately in their diamond tiaras; and Violet was invited to dine at the French Embassy to meet the King and Queen and President Albert Lebrun. 'The whole governing class were there!' Violet wrote. Such grandeur seemed a swan song, almost a replay of the months before the First World War.

By 25 August German troops were massing on the frontier of Poland, Hitler's next target. Violet invited Gwenda, Iverach McDonald's wife, with their baby son, to come down to stay out of harm's way at Wigsell. She also gave shelter to her aunt Kate, her mother's invalid sister, now aged ninety-two. 'I couldn't bear to think of that darling old girl with the bombs raining on her.' The weather was lovely, Violet observed, at 'the last moments before the crash'.

1 September came, the twenty-fifth anniversary of George's death. 'War has begun. Germany attacked Poland at 5 a.m. this morning.' One thousand evacuee children arrived in the Wigsell neighbourhood for distribution round the houses of nearby villages. The next day general mobilisation was announced and the country went on a war footing. On Saturday, 3 September, Violet listened in to Chamberlain's tired and disappointed broadcast declaring war on Germany.

The first months of the war confirmed her conviction that the Cabinet – 'nearly all the incompetents and cowards' – of ten, not four or five, as when Alfred was in the Government during the last war, was too cumbersome to conduct urgent business, and its members mostly too complacent. What was the Government doing? she wondered. By the end of Poland's epic struggle Britain had done little more than drop pamphlets on Germany. Gradually, however, the country prepared to fight. In October searchlight batteries moved into the neighbourhood of Wigsell and Violet was soon entertaining the officers to meals.

The 'phoney war' ended next year with the German invasion of Norway and Britain's retaliation. Violet, realising that it would not be long before Germany turned its attention to France, decided on a last trip to Paris, risking fog and mines to make a crossing on 28 April. 'Paris, elegantly and not too much darkened, is lovely. The Place de la Concorde seemed illimitable.' She was invited to visit the French Prime Minister, Paul Reynaud, at the Quai d'Orsay. He was dog-tired; his only memorable remark was about the seventy-seven-year-old Lloyd George, who was making pronouncements about war policy from his retirement: 'Why on earth does Lloyd George go on when he is past everything. He is like Sarah Bernhardt, *qui jouait même avec une jambe de bois!*'

Brandishing a military permit, Violet even managed to make her annual pilgrimage to Villers Cotterêts, now in an army zone; she was relieved to see the two monuments were still beautifully tended. On 10 May, she was woken at dawn by shrieking sirens, not because of enemy planes but to alert the nation, for German troops had entered Luxembourg, Holland and Belgium: 'The war on the Western Front,' she recorded, 'has begun.'

Back in England, she watched France struggling over the same territory as in the First World War, with Villers Cotterêts once more a battleground. She shared the agony of a country on its knees, feeling the humiliation of the terms dictated to the French in the railway carriage at Rethondes on 22 June, 'Hitler,' Violet recounted bitterly, 'sitting on Foch's chair.' Under these conditions, France was half occupied, half a puppet ally of Germany – and the enemy of Britain.

Great Wigsell, from the front

CHAPTER TWENTY-FIVE

Wartime at Wigsell

TWENTY-FIVE YEARS earlier, in the First World War, Alfred and Violet, down in Kent and Sussex, had heard the guns throbbing in Northern France. During the late summer of 1940 the Battle of Britain was fought directly above Wigsell. The house itself was hit on the night of Saturday 24 August. Violet was saying goodnight to her guests, Iverach and Gwenda McDonald, when they heard a sound of thunder and a terrific rattling on the roof. Looking out of her bedroom window, she found the whole scene lit up by incendiary bombs which the Germans dropped in clusters of fifty, nicknamed 'Molotoff's breadbaskets'. One of the roof gables was blazing. McDonald swiftly got all the fire buckets in the house and, scooping up the sand in his hands, threw it down on to the blaze from an upper-floor window; the two maids reinforced his efforts with jugs of water, and thus the fire was extinguished. When the Hawkhurst Fire Brigade arrived, followed by the Battle Brigade, the police force of Hurst Green and a contingent of military police, there was little left for them to do except have 'a beer-drinking party' until 2 a.m.

Four days later – the air once again 'full of bullets and zooming planes' – a Spitfire crashed in flames near the house. 'The pilot was dead. The flames burnt for nearly an hour,' Violet wrote. She picked some flowers to lay on the young man's remains. 'As I waited with my flowers for the van carrying the body to come down the lane, I saw in my mind's eye the figures of the boys, my own George, who so often walked that way, and who lived here, and of Helen's George, who I saw come along there carrying the first rabbit he had shot – I thought of them and of this boy – the unknown boy – who was now coming along the same path.'

August and September were always a bad time of year for Violet, when her lost boy was uppermost in her thoughts. 'This day I think even more of him, of the bitter loss.' She went to the funeral of the dead pilot and talked to his parents and fiancée.

Her grandson George, now eighteen, left for the Navy, and Violet enjoined on him the same sentiments of love of country and the Empire on which her George had been brought up. The boy was bemused by her talk of Empire – the diminished power of which she disregarded – and her view that Britain should declare war on Russia and Turkey (for their hostile neutrality) as well. He went through agonies of fear before going off to sea, as he poured out to Diana, Violet's secretary, at night-time when he could not sleep – which made all the more courageous his performance of his duties over the next five harrowing years.

Meanwhile the battle to bomb Britain into submission continued, day after day, night after night, throughout that autumn and winter; and even after the Battle of Britain and the Blitz, Violet watched enemy bombers fly over throughout the years that followed.

> Sometimes we see as many as four flights in a day. They always present the same picture. The German bombers come in at a great height flying in formation . . . they disappear in the direction of London. A few minutes later they come hurtling back with Hurricanes and Spitfires on their tracks. For a flash the actual fighting can then be seen – the swooping, whirling battles that are over in less than a minute of time, a minute that is frozen into an age by the emotion of the watchers.

By moonlight, starlight, searchlight, the blacked-out house a silent silhouette behind her, Violet scanned the sky. In the daytime, she found a new outlet to relieve her anxiety: trimming the yew hedges, 'very steadying'. As the planes droned over with their deadly cargo, clip-clip-clip, her shears cut round the topiary peacocks and the smooth walls of dark green. In the evenings, too anxious to read, unable to sleep for the racket overhead, she would spin the sheep's wool she gathered in the fields; a neighbour supplied her with a hand spindle and taught her how to spin, and eventually there was enough wool to knit a shawl.

As the next year passed, and Britain's plight remained perilous, huge flocks of seabirds, driven inland by the fighting three miles over-head, became a familiar sight over Wigsell. On 12 February 1942 Violet recorded that 'thousands of seagulls, flying very high, streamed overhead from Dover towards Lewes, and Tunbridge Wells. We heard the news of the battle on the midnight news. Very disappointing. Singapore is near surrender.'

Three days later came the definite news that 'Singapore has fallen. The day has been fine but I have been utterly depressed to think of anything but the mismanaged war.' For Violet had little confidence in Churchill: in March, when he announced the intention to grant Dominion status to India after the war, she saw it as 'severing our connections with India. Churchill has once again turned his coat, once again returned to his vomit. He has now laid the trail for the general imperial break up.

'This is our sunset. Whatever military successes we may have later on – if we do have them – nothing will retrieve the disaster of such policy. I feel more discouraged tonight than I have ever been before.' For Violet, Britain's frontier was not simply on the Rhine but wherever the map was painted pink. Gloom about Singapore was warranted, and universal: the surrender of the city's 64,000 British troops to an inferior-sized Japanese force was the greatest blow ever suffered by the Empire. To accuse Churchill of putting his own power and reputation before British rule over India was, however, grossly unfair. The promise of self-government for India within the Empire, as for South Africa, Australia, New Zealand and Canada, was simply the recognition that unless the loyalty of so many millions of His Majesty's subjects was rewarded by such a gesture, they would be certain to press for total severance from Britain.

Now, too, early in 1942, the Americans as a condition of their assistance were pressing for an end to Imperial Preference after the war and for free trade everywhere. From Leo Amery and others Violet heard hints that Churchill might betray the imperial tariff policy, the economic keystone of the Empire for Alfred, Leo Maxse, Kipling and Joe Chamberlain. But the ideals and policies of these imperial colossi were growing outdated; the world had moved on, and leaders like Churchill might possibly also have to move with it. Violet could not. When Lord Lloyd's erstwhile private secretary, the young James Lees-Milne, now Historic Buildings Adviser to the National Trust, visited her on his way to Bateman's, she told him George Lloyd's death ranked as a disaster with Munich and the fall of France. 'She said too that there was absolutely *no* able man in England today. This convinced me that, clever as she is, she lives in the past and is out of date.'

Other unexpected visitors to Wigsell were a couple of hapless American Kipling fans who had appeared, unannounced, during the Battle of France, having travelled to England to solicit support for a 'church and mortuary' in Los Angeles as a memorial to the writer. 'My lips were touched. I felt I was saying what dear Rudyard Kipling would have said,' wrote Violet in her diary. Iverach McDonald, who was staying at the time, remembered her reply:

> 'Now I want you to listen' she told them: 'Do you hear anything in the distance?' One American answered that he could hear a noise like thunder.
> 'It is the sound of guns – our own and the enemy's. We are in a war – we are far too busy getting on with the war – too busy to bother with Kipling's mausoleum, so will you go back to America and stay there?'

The Wigsell household was better off than most for food, by dint of ploughing up extra land, keeping ducks in the walled garden, poultry in the plum orchard and extra cows and sheep. Foxes sometimes decimated the poultry and poachers were a menace, shooting whatever they could for the black market: blocking the gates to prevent them bringing trucks in to collect their trophies did not deter them.

Violet took produce as presents whenever she visited London. To publish the 'Nat' every month, she travelled there regularly. For all the toll its production took on her energies, she was glad of this respite from war anxiety. The paper's unfailing appearance, in reduced form because of paper rationing, was an expression of Britain's will to fight – and of her own will to stay in public life. It also brought her some social life: she saw much of the Columbia Broadcasting Service's Director of Talks, Ed Murrow, and his wife Janet. Lean and dark, with a rakishly tilted trilby and perpetual cigarette, Murrow had come to embattled England from the USA as an unexpected angel of comfort. He perceived in the crisis the chance to raise American awareness of the world-wide threat to freedom. For British people, the knowledge that his broadcasts were going out, and for those like Violet who met him, his words of encouragement, delivered in a relaxed, musical voice, boosted morale. Despite his ironical manner he was an idealist, and his celebrated talks presented vivid images of a nation holding its own bravely at war, and of the capital during the nightly Blitz, 'the beautiful and lonesome city where men and women and children are trying to snatch a few hours' sleep underground'. Years later Murrow told Ned Grigg's son, John, that for him the indomitable spirit of wartime England was represented not by Churchill, but by Violet Milner.

In the wearisome blackout Violet visited the theatre occasionally with her granddaughters. In May 1943 Elizabeth and she saw *Love for Love* with John Gielgud, with brilliant set designs by the artist Rex Whistler, who was killed a year later on active service in France. In May, too, Win Hardinge became engaged to Anthony Murray, a Guards officer, and Violet used her last dress coupons to help her granddaughter with her trousseau. After Win's wedding, in the Guards' Chapel on 10 July, when the register was signed by Princesses Elizabeth and Margaret, Violet, in a characteristically romantic gesture, handed the groom a diamond ring to slip on to his bride's finger. When her other grandchild, George, became engaged to Janet Balfour the following February, Violet gave her a necklace of turquoises interspersed with black pearls, of Italian design. Jan was a member of the Goschen family, so many of whom had been friends of both Alfred Milner and Edward Cecil. George had known her from childhood and she became a favourite of Violet's.

And always air battles raged above Wigsell. On 21 January 1944 Violet described looking out and seeing 'search lights from all sides, and a German plane and then another caught in the beams'. They were attacking London, Chatham, Hastings and Eastbourne. The woods nearby were afire. The whole sky blazed with flashes and signal flares. Alone in the house, Violet could not sleep, and spent most of the night out of doors scanning the sky: next day she heard of terrible damage done. Once in a field nearby a labourer picked up an 'anti-person bomb' which exploded, blowing off his hand and half his face.

Violet never admitted to being afraid during the raids: she was excited, and after the excitement she described having a raging thirst and then feeling very cold. 'My hair is white from no other cause.' The most she ever owned to was being jumpy, during the summer of 1944, in the run-up to what would be the Normandy landings. 'The aerial armadas which fly over us are tremendous. This evening I counted one party of 72 planes going to France. I should judge Rouen – and other lots of 18 going further West. The noise is almost continuous of these machines going and returning.' It continued, and on 6 June Violet wrote: 'Last night the prodigious great air movement increased so much that I had no doubt that the great attack had begun.'

For the civilians the skies soon held a deadly new threat – Hitler's 'secret weapon', the V1 pilotless plane, nicknamed 'the doodlebug' on account of the throb of its pulse jet engine. From 15 June, and for the next five weeks, more than 3,000 of these 'Robot planes', as Violet called them, came over by day and by night. Near Wigsell some 'Robots', small, sleek and very fast, were chased and exploded noisily in the air by British fighters and some brought down by anti-aircraft fire. One that got through to London on Sunday 18 June destroyed the Guards' Chapel at Wellington Barracks where Win had recently been married. Two hundred Guardsmen and their relatives lay dead or wounded in the rubble.

Wigsell shook to its foundations every few minutes; sleep was impossible. Violet sat up and read Macaulay's *History of England*, with its message of unconquerable optimism. She spent the nights in a chair in the hall, out of reach of flying glass, or on a camp bed under the stairs. On 27 June, one V1, shot down, skimmed over the house, missing it by a few feet, and landed near Merriments Lane. Three days later Bateman's was hit by another, which luckily did not damage the main house but destroyed the mill, damaged cottages and broke windows.

On 4 July Violet and Olive became evacuees, going to Hatfield, where they slept well for the first time for weeks. The Salisbury family was living with a minimal staff in the east wing; the rest of the house was a military hospital with 300 beds. It was not all peaceful even there, however: while Violet was staying, an Italian prisoner-of-war committed suicide by throwing himself out of a window. Still, regardless of Hitler's weapons and shell-shocked prisoners, the roses bloomed. Violet admired one new to her – the single, scented, pale yellow *Mermaid*.

A short week later, Violet and Olive returned to Wigsell, where the situation had not improved: 'We arrived in the middle of a battle with Robots. From Robertsbridge Station we saw one apparently brought down on Wigsell. However, it was beyond it.' The V1s continued to come over in a constant stream and Violet and Olive retreated again to Hatfield 'to an accompaniment of bursting bombs'. On the wireless they listened to news of the attempt to blow up Hitler a few days earlier. Later in the month they travelled to Oxford for the wedding of George Hardinge to Jan. Violet took in her luggage a bottle of champage, a diamond brooch of her mother's for Jan, and for George the pearl studs that had belonged to his namesake, her George.

Although outside the RAF the carnage was less great for the British than in the First World War, the toll, now that the Allies were landing on the Continent, was very heavy, and parents of servicemen felt the same terrible strain. Nineteen-year-old Dickie Cecil, Bobbety

Robert Cecil, now the 6th Marquess of Salisbury, as an officer in the Guards Armoured Division; and Marjorie (Mollie) Wyndham-Quinn, whom he married just after the war, in which she served as a nurse

Cranborne's son, serving with the RAF, had a fatal accident. His elder surviving brother, Robert, was back in the fighting after a fearful wound. Their first cousin Billy Hartington, son of Moucher and Eddie Devonshire, and Helen's page at her wedding, was killed in action on the Belgian–Dutch border. Andrew, Billy's younger brother, won the Military Cross in circumstances of great danger. Two sons of Alfred Milner's ADC in Cape Town forty years before, Lord Kerry, later Lord Lansdowne, were killed in August 1944.

Violet rejoiced when Paris was liberated that month. To Francophiles as ardent as her, the fall of France had been one of the worst tragedies of the entire war. In August, too, thanks to RAF raids on the launching sites and storage depots in France, the V1s began to diminish in number.

In September the skies above Wigsell were full of planes from English airfields, flying low and towing gliders. In these aircraft were British, American and Polish paratroopers bound for Holland. At Arnhem the 1st Airborne Division, fighting heroically, suffered a terrible defeat. Elsewhere the Allied troops established a precarious hold

over the lower Rhine at Nijmegen and Eindhoven, reinforced from
the south by the spearhead of the 30 Corps, the Guards' Armoured
Division, among whose officers was Robert Cecil.

Gradually, in 1945, Europe was being freed from Nazi oppression:
this revealed the hitherto undisclosed horrors of the death and concentration camps. Violet listened to Ed Murrow on the wireless giving
'a fearful account of Buchenwald. He was there on the day it was
liberated.'

On VE Day, 8 May 1945, Violet was at Wigsell, celebrating as the
news bulletins came in over the wireless. She gave the staff a bottle of
port and wished that her beloved Alfred, Rudyard Kipling and Leo
could have witnessed the final defeat of Germany. 'The weather is
warm and bright. We are just beginning to realise that Peace is here.'

In June 1945, Violet paid her first post-war visit to Paris. 'As the
boat steamed into the harbour I found I was saying aloud "France,
France, France".' As after the First War, in Paris the Champs-Elysées
was full of khaki-clad soldiers, mostly American; there were no buses
or taxis to be had, just a few old horse-drawn *fiacres*, so she walked
everywhere, taking refuge in Mme Lanvin's shop in the Faubourg St
Honoré during a cloudburst and trudging along to the Musée
Clemenceau where Marie, Albert's wife, fell on her with cries of
delight. Despite sore feet and blisters it was thrilling to be able to walk
freely in those familiar streets once more and to talk the language she
loved. At the Louvre Violet gazed once more upon the unchanging
beauty of the Venus de Milo: 'there she was, serene and lovely, as I
have seen her for 60 years.' George Hardinge, working in Paris with
the Navy, attached to the British Embassy, was her companion on her
pilgrimage to Villers-Cotterêts, where they were relieved to find the
grave and the monument to George in good order, unravaged by this
second war. The ingenious Mme Mouflier rustled up a delicious meal
for them, and Violet gave her basic supplies of scarce tea, coffee, sugar
and soap.

Back home, what did the longed-for peace bring? In many ways
conditions resembled those in wartime: the same shortages and rationing of food, clothes and fuel. Violet was shocked by the huge Labour
majority at the general election in 1945; her world – the old order,
the aristocracy, and the Empire – was under threat. Some, including
close friends of hers, even departed for Kenya and Rhodesia, 'to
escape the welfare state'.

News came of 'another fearful new weapon of war, designed from

some sort of disintegration of the Atom. Very difficult, this, to understand . . . The accounts of the damage done by the atom bomb are
quite fearful. Revolting.' The bombs at Hiroshima and Nagasaki
meant the capitulation of Japan, but Violet felt, as Jem Salisbury did,
that the world had plumbed a new depth of barbarism.

Violet in her mid-seventies was still vigorous. When she had a
medical check-up, the doctor pronounced that she had the heart and
blood pressure of a young woman. Not until September 1948 did she
finally give up editing the 'Nat', which had belonged to the Maxses
for sixty years. The Griggs purchased most of the shares and John
Grigg, Ned's son, took over as Editor. Violet, delighted by a piece he
had written, concluded, 'I really can now say, "*nunc dimittis*".'

After the war few men or women returned to full-time domestic
service, and those who did expected higher wages. This created a
social revolution. Save in very rich households, the living-in servants
– if there were any – were now either old retainers or very young,
unskilled and temporary. Some of Violet's neighbours had no help at
all, and this became generally the established pattern for the middle
classes who had to do their own cooking and cleaning. Within twenty
years, women from this background, fed up with domestic servitude
and ambitious for a fuller life, responded to calls for greater liberation,
as many had clamoured for the vote before the Great War.

At Wigsell, in place of six outdoor staff previously employed, there
remained one, the faithful gardener Wood, now a great age. Inside,
the formidable cook, Mrs Edwards, remained while the housework
fell on inexperienced maids ('*deux jeunes filles sans aucune idée de leur
travail*'). The kitchens had no labour-saving devices of any sort. To
return the garden to its former idyllic state would take years; some of
it, designed by Alfred, had to be abandoned completely. Violet
enjoyed working outside – there was no stigma in women like herself
gardening, as opposed to housework, which was too demeaning. In
contrast with her hostility to them during the First World War, she
now admitted relief that German prisoners in their patched grey
fatigues were trimming the neglected hedges, clearing overgrown
ditches and unblocking streams and ponds – especially that autumn,
when her family had 'quite a pre-war party' for the christening of
George and Jan's first baby, Julian; Princess Elizabeth was godmother.
Violet rose to the occasion with a delicious lunch at Wigsell. Her
present to her first great-grandson was her George's silver christening
mug, now fifty years old.

Julian Hardinge's christening, autumn 1945. Back row, left to right: *Violet, Phyllis Balfour (Jan's mother), Frank Balfour (Jan's father), Alec Hardinge, Lord Goschen (Jan's grandfather);* front row, left to right: *HRH Princess Elizabeth, Jan (with Julian), Helen and George Hardinge*

During the winter of 1946–7, the coldest since 1881, the coal stocks ran low and with a restricted supply and a transport strike, an unprepared Britain froze. At Wigsell ancient oaks were felled to keep the house and estate cottages warm, and when the thaw came, the roof leaked and the surrounding countryside was flooded. Wigsell was luckier than many large old houses at this time, whose owners, in despair, sold properties which were often wantonly pulled down. When Hatfield ceased to be a hospital, Jem and Alice still continued to live in only a corner of their huge mansion. With the tax on his income now at nineteen shillings and sixpence in the pound (97.5p out of £1), even a great landowner like Jem could not afford to live lavishly.

As the years went by Violet entertained in style only on Sunday at lunchtime. Otherwise she would usually have a cup of soup and a chop for dinner, with a few tots of brandy afterwards. She remained socially enterprising, however, inviting new younger people whom she had got to know as well as her existing circle. To Violet's younger guests, for whom such luxury had become rare, it seemed as if nothing in the household at Wigsell had changed from an Edwardian expansiveness. Fruit was bottled or made into jam; hams were rubbed with herbs regularly for six months under Mrs Edwards's direction, milk and butter came from the home farm; chickens scratched about outside; rose petals and lavender flowers were made into pot-pourri.

Violet hoped that Wigsell would stay in the family for generations. She had settled it on her grandson George in her will, and in 1947 he decided to move there and make a career as a fruit-grower. For several years he worked hard at the farm before giving it up in 1953 to become a publisher. The house was divided, with Violet retaining her favourite rooms at the front, and they shared the entertaining of guests. She was glad to have the young Hardinges' company and support, particularly because Helen and she seemed further apart than ever.

For Helen and Alec, who had lived for so long in the correct atmosphere of the Court, Violet's sometimes extreme political pronouncements, delivered in an unbridled style recalling her Berkeley grandmother, were embarrassing. Violet was equally outspoken to Helen over the way she brought up her children. The differences between them were exacerbated by Helen's embracing of Moral Rearmament, the religious movement led by the American, Frank Buchman – 'or "Frankie", as his devotees call this plump bespectacled alien,' Violet had written during the war. She regarded MRA as a combination of political brainwashing and repulsive hypocrisy; to David Cecil she reported that 'Helen has joined the grim growdies.' MRA went against all her canons of individual independence of thought and choice. She was appalled when, in the bitter cold of February, 1948, Helen should have been so moved by her spiritual conversion as to fly to New York to 'Buchman's mischief centre'. 'It is lunacy. New York in February! and Buchman!'

In March 1956, The Queen Mother, elegant in a fitted feathered hat and a coat trimmed with silver fox-fur, visited Wigsell. Violet, flanked by Alec, welcomed her. Helen, no longer a 'moral re-armer', George and Jan were all present at the amazing lunch Mrs Edwards had prepared: *Oeufs Belges, Poulet Soubise, Oranges Zestes* and *Fromages*. The Queen Mother, who sat between Violet and Alec, was 'delicious, as she always is,' Violet remarked. It was the high point of Violet's social life in her beloved home and a civilised reunion of a not always united family.

CHAPTER TWENTY-SIX

Memories

T HROUGHOUT HER LONG widowhood Violet fulfilled her self-appointed task of commemorating George and Alfred, the two men – one no more than a boy – who had meant most to her. Not believing in any afterlife, she was determined that their memory should be perpetuated on earth. In Westminster Abbey and Canterbury Cathedral, in northern France and New College, Oxford, in Hatfield House and Winchester College, thousands of miles away in southern Africa and close to home in Kent, there appeared memorials and inscriptions, a tomb and a bronze bust, a school and a painting, stained glass windows, a grove of trees – all planned and erected, dedicated and planted by the energetic and increasingly formidable Violet.

Every year she recorded the days of their births and deaths in her diary. The anniversary of her marriage to Edward, 18 June, was rarely mentioned, and usually only because it coincided with the more significant date of the precious moment of closeness to Alfred, in Cape Town in 1900. This she alluded to often. Apart from his gravestone, her one memorial to Edward was also dedicated to George: a religious picture, chosen with care, which now hangs in Hatfield chapel.

To the world she always strove to present Alfred as the hero of the hour – in South Africa, far-sighted, humane; and at the Doullens Conference calmly saving the Alliance from falling apart under pressure of battle. On Armistice Day 1933 she had been invited to a ceremony in the Military Cemetery at Doullens itself, in the presence of the Mayor, who remembered Alfred in 1918. There she had unveiled yet another bust – by Pierre Sicard – of her late husband, expressed her adoration for France and Alfred in well-polished French and received the Légion d'Honneur.

Alfred had specifically asked for the publication of his letters rather than for a biography. The great labour of gathering and organising his papers was a way of staying in touch with him, keeping faith with him and enshrining him as an unblemished imperial idol. She had regularly sat up late, going through the records of his career and the biographies of his contemporaries, until too weary to read. In 1931 and 1932 the historian Cecil Headlam had brought out two volumes on Alfred as High Commissioner in South Africa, and in 1952, with Violet's help, her friend Edward Crankshaw produced a study of Alfred's imperial principles, *The Forsaken Idea: A Study of Viscount Milner.* The American historian Alfred Gollin wrote a penetrating study, on which he consulted her.

Each year of Alfred's diaries took her five hours at a stretch to read carefully. They began when he was a very young man and ceased a few days before he died. With these diaries she did not tamper; they were terse and unrevealing, save to a very careful investigator, about his private life, but she was anxious in general to conceal the full facts of her relationship with him, particularly from Hatfield, whose good opinion she wished to keep. She therefore suppressed any indication of their feelings for one another before they were married, typing out for posterity only the political passages from their letters. She destroyed the originals with a pang: 'Nowadays the passion for publicity is so great that I would rather not risk such personal papers ever being made public . . .' 'Adieu – Adieu, fair and happy hours.' Letters to him from Cécile, Norah Lindsay, Mrs Dick Chamberlain, and any other ladies who engaged his affections, have also been eradicated, probably by Alfred himself, though Margot Asquith's correspondence with him has been preserved.

Violet spared no effort to protect Alfred's reputation. Furious when *The Sunday Times* published two letters of his without leave 'in a scurrilous article by Margot Asquith', she rushed round to her solicitors who extracted an apology from the paper. She consistently played down the German part of Alfred's life, and, despite its importance to him, avoided any contact with his old friends and relations in that country. Her anti-German prejudices were confirmed when one Frau Press wrote to her, as Violet claimed, 'threatening to publish Alfred's letters if I did not send her £100. One cannot expect anything from a pig but a grunt!' Headlam's introduction to the *Milner Papers* depicted Alfred's parents as a purely English couple who just happened to be living in Germany. Violet preferred to stress her husband's agency in bringing England and France together at Doullens. One wonders how she would have reacted to Clemenceau's description of him in 1918 to an English general as '*un demi-Boche*' – referring to Alfred's insight into the German mind.

On the centenary of Alfred's birthday in March 1954, she arranged a ceremony in St Martin's Chapel, Canterbury Cathedral. The choir of the King's School sang, a trophy of flowers was laid before the great proconsul's bust, and Alan Lennox-Boyd delivered a reverent address.

In writing her memoirs, Violet also presented her story as she wished it to be known, basing much of it on the remarkable letters she wrote to her mother. She then followed her misguided practice of burning them. It is paradoxical, given the value she placed on continuity of family, culture, and tradition, that she destroyed so much of her own past. The New Year of 1950 had started with the usual paper holocaust, this time of the letters Olive wrote to her about the baby George when she was in South Africa, innocuous enough, surely. But, 'I can see that my dear young people will take care of nothing, neither "furniture" nor "effects" and that I must dispose of these myself or they will disappear and be lost.'

Ironically, it did not prove possible for those very 'effects' that she carefully disposed of to preserve Alfred's memory for ever – his Garter star and gold boxes and Menpes' painting of Rhodes and a Burne-Jones drawing – to be kept together in the 'Milner Room' which was created with his furniture at New College, Oxford. They are however well cared for by his old college, as are his papers, now transferred to the Bodleian Library; but otherwise, in the college where Alfred was a Fellow, the memory of the imperial statesman has faded away.

When Violet's memoir, *My Picture Gallery*, was published in 1951, it was quite a curiosity, so far in time did life already seem from the Victorian age. The book, covering the period 1872–1901, is lively and not trite. It is vivid on South Africa – for instance on Violet's adventures in the Western Transvaal, a neglected area in Boer War history. Despite personal omissions, it gives a fresh and occasionally critical angle on Hatfield, which greeted the book with mixed feelings. Nelly Cecil thought there was too much of Violet in it – she told Alice it should simply have been called 'My Picture'.

In the period of Violet's memoir, nothing could have been more intoxicating than the vision of Empire shared by her and all the protagonists in this book: a vast, newly opened world replete with promise of wealth, power and adventure – and all 'British' – being the very apogee of the country's destiny. As promoters of this vision

Alfred, Leo and Violet, alongside Joseph Chamberlain and Rudyard Kipling, represented the modern, progressive face of British imperialism, part of an eloquent radical right wing with wide public influence in the pre-war era. They looked forward to a federated empire bound together by an imperial parliament, an imperial defence force and imperial trade protected by a tariff system. They pressed for National Service, for 'National Efficiency' – a society organised in matters of health, education and defence on the model extolled in Kipling's short story 'The Army of a Dream'. To Alfred Milner the achievements of 'the British Race' were the products of a long tradition of fair dealing; methodical industry; and self-sacrifice towards a common cause – improvement. Kipling expressed a kindred view with his notion of a 'Law', an understood morality by which the best people in the trades and professions worked co-operatively in a brotherhood of Empire embracing all who accepted its ideals and principles, whatever their race and background. Those outside Kipling's 'Law' – 'the lesser breeds' – included cunning Boers, bandits and cutthroats, evil traders and selfish slackers.

These views of the radical right contrasted with the traditional Toryism of Edward Cecil's family. His father, the 3rd Marquess of Salisbury, as Prime Minister and Foreign Secretary, had not shared the imperial mood of the late nineteenth century. He did not look romantically on the Empire and its growth as a triumphant progress. To him it was an accidental, though almost inevitable, result of trade between modern advanced countries and technically backward ones; he acknowledged the prestige and commercial profits it brought, but apart from it sometimes helping to spread Christianity, and to check slavery and savagery, he did not otherwise consider that it had a clear moral basis. Of his children, Robert and Hugh were of much the same mind; but Jem, a part-time soldier, and Edward, a full-time one, were fired by Britain's colonial adventures and their beneficial results, a view shared by Alice, Maud and Willy Selborne, and Gwendolen.

All, however, opposed any idea of a society mobilised for imperial rule, as favoured by Alfred and the radical right, which would involve conscription and other interference by the state. Because of their innate conservatism they doubted the feasibility of moulding British minds, let alone those of subject peoples, to think imperially. Edward's family attributed tariff reform to selfish motives, both national and commercial; Jem specifically labelled these policies 'Milnerism' – 'a complete change in our method of Government from the English system to the German system'. The Cecils' High Tory priorities in that generation of their family, were the protection of Christian worship, the Anglican Church with the monarch as its head, and the maintenance of the law and the constitution, including the House of Lords. For them the Empire was a matter of obligation and service, but was not paramount among institutions which must be promoted and defended at all costs, however important for Britain's economy and influence.

From 1895 to 1914 such High Tory attitudes to Empire seemed old-fashioned and unprogressive, but by the end of the 1950s they were no more obsolete than those of Rudyard Kipling and Alfred Milner. If anything, they had stood the test of time better than those of the radical right; for while devoted administrators were still needed in the rapidly dissolving Empire until they were replaced, vanished was the glorious dream of imperial federalism, with British society organised for imperial service and driven by 'British Race Patriotism'.

Alfred's best-known imperial achievement – the subjugation of the formerly independent Boer republics and the recovery of South Africa after the war he had been instrumental in provoking – soon gave way to Boer dominance over the Union of South Africa. Nor were Empire tariffs, introduced in 1932, destined to have the unifying effect for which Joseph Chamberlain and Alfred had hoped. Conscription was introduced solely as a result of the 1914–18 war; it was promptly dropped afterwards until needed again in 1939, and after the Second World War was retained for only another fifteen years.

To Britain in the twenty-first century, therefore, Alfred, as a vision-ary leader, has nothing to say. As a toiler for the Empire making his name as a young man in Egypt, he, like Edward later, was one of the many who kept the show on the road. Those who did, perhaps achieved more good than those who decreed what the show should be; and before they left the stage they passed on an administrative structure and exemplary standards of probity to their successors around the world.

Gradually, as the elder generation of Cecils at Hatfield reached the end of their long lives, Violet came to identify herself with them as never before – despite having been out of step with them during her mar-riage to Edward. On the death of Gwendolen, at the end of September 1945, Violet added to David Cecil's obituary of her, observing that Gwendolen 'was as brilliant as any of her brothers' with a really original mind, as well as being the centre of Hatfield life half a century before. At the funeral Violet noted, characteristically, the beautiful flower arrangements, the short service 'and not too much about resurrection', an aspect of the Cecils' Christianity which still grated.

When she met Mollie Wyndham-Quinn, the fiancée of Robert Cecil, later the 6th Marquess of Salisbury, for the first time, Violet found the evening at Hatfield 'an immense contrast to when I first came here as a fiancée. Then there were always four married couples beside Lord and Lady Salisbury, Gwenny, the private secretaries and a great crowd of eager talking young people.' On that December evening in 1945 Alice and Violet talked by the fireside and the young couple played cards.

The romantically beautiful Mollie, in a simple white satin dress, married Robert at Westminster Abbey. The party afterwards at Arlington Street, given with the Salisburys' impeccable style, though constrained by post-war shortages, also contrasted with the weddings of Violet's youth. It was the last party to be given at that house, which was shortly to be sold to an insurance company. Everywhere in it Violet saw her past, her young self meeting her formidable parents-in-law for the first time: 'The contrast between weddings now and fifty years ago is that in our day there were no great aunts and uncles. They had all been decently buried! Today there were dozens and I was one!' She felt that she, and all of them, had outlived their time.

When Jem Salisbury died in April 1947, 'I can hardly take in what this means . . . how changed the circumstances from Jem's own succession fifty years ago.' Changed too, though she seemed to have forgotten it, was her reckoning of her brother-in-law, whom up to the 1920s she had considered neurotic and over-conscientious, an ineffective successor to his famous father, the Prime Minister. Now she viewed him, as most people did, as a dignified elder statesman, the wisest of his brothers, though not the most brilliant, transformed into a symbol of a departed age of idealism and honourable traditions. It was a fair estimate; for though late in life still a victim to intense depression, he had lived for years for duty and for his religion with impressive fortitude and integrity.

Alice, his widow, died in 1955, the same year as Olive Maxse. Olive's death, aged eighty-nine, was preceded by several years of decrepitude. Many was the time when after a long session at her flat Violet soothed her own agitation with a newly discovered solace, a

Alice and Jem Salisbury in old age

double Martini. Ivor, too, was slowing down; told of Olive's death, he said, 'This is rather sudden.' Violet wished Olive and Leo alive just to hear him say it. Ivor died, aged ninety-five, in 1958: 'the last relic of my youth going'. Violet was not well enough to go to his funeral. Three days later, she celebrated her eighty-sixth birthday: walking was painful, now, and she was deaf and breathless, but she knew 'there is nothing the matter with me but being too old . . . I own that I had no desire to live until now, a world which I can no longer understand (atom-bombing and automated) is difficult to live in and old age is without charm, though my state is no worse than that of others.' She enjoyed seeing George and Jan, but she realised that Jan was unhappy; the marriage, undertaken when they were too young, was on the verge of collapse.

Although she could not get out much into the garden, she enjoyed looking at the cherry blossom, listening to Schumann's concerto in A minor on the wireless (which Olive had played, in Violet's view, with greater taste) and going to London on 9 May to have lunch at the Connaught with Ed Murrow.

In July she was too tired to cut the roses, as ever the glory of Wigsell; she had lately planted a beautiful dark red Guinée and a crimson, richly scented Mme Isaac Perreire against the front of the house. September brought the anniversary of George's death and a letter from Mme Mouflier, 'who never forgets me at this season,' from Villers-Cotterêts. The cherished tomb, still beautiful, was covered with '*un ensemble de verdure et de violets qui est superbe, joli et frais . . . 44 ans!*' Mme Mouflier concluded passionately. '*Comme c'est déjà si loin! Mais encore si près dans les coeurs! Bien chère Madame, je pense si souvent à vous! À votre peine éternelle!*'

On hearing of the death of the composer Ralph Vaughan-Williams, on 26 August 1958, Violet noted: 'He was working as usual that day. What a lucky man! He was my age.' In the late summer, however, she was content to have her two great-grandchildren running in and out of the house and to hear about their lessons on the lawn tennis court and the gallons of homemade ginger beer they drank, 'just as George had done years before.' Then, on 8 October, came the penultimate entry in the diary she had kept every day since Alfred's death: 'Fred and Helen came to lunch. Fred is spherical,' she wrote crisply of her nephew, Frederick Maxse; an eccentric man, he, curiously, was among the few members of her family who continued to keep the faith by visiting the Moufliers and George's grave in the forest.

On 10 October Violet died peacefully at Wigsell. On her desk were piled papers for her next book of memoirs; of Egypt, of losing George, of Edward's death, and her marriage to Alfred. Outside, the empty swing Helen and George had played on as children with Elsie and John Kipling swayed in the autumn wind, which bent the tops of the tall tulip trees she had brought back from South Africa more than half a century ago; their yellow and russet leaves fluttered down into the stream and were lost from view.

Sources

MANUSCRIPT SOURCES

The Bodleian Library, Oxford University, Department of Western Manuscripts (BOD)
Violet Milner Papers (VM); Viscount Milner Papers (AM); South African Journal of
Ernest Bruce Iwan-Müller (with Milner Papers).

Hatfield House Muniments (HH)
Papers of 3rd Marquess of Salisbury (3M), and 3rd Marchioness of Salisbury
(3MCH); Viscount and Viscountess Cecil of Chelwood (CHE); Lord Edward Cecil
(EC); Lady Gwendolen Cecil (GW); 4th Marquess of Salisbury (4M); various
Balfour Papers.

Pembroke College Library, Cambridge (PEM)
Sir Ronald Storrs Papers.

The University of Durham Library (UDL)
Papers of Sir Reginald Wingate in Sudan Archive (SAD).

The West Sussex Records Office, Chichester (WSRO)
Maxse Papers – General Sir Ivor Maxse (Ivor); Leopold Maxse (Leo); Admiral
Frederick Maxse (Admiral); Cissie Maxse; Lady Caroline Maxse; Olive Maxse (Olive).

The National Archive of Scotland, Edinburgh (NAS)
Papers of Blackwood, publishers; Lady Frances Balfour; Elizabeth Balfour; Field-
Marshal the Earl Haig.

The Public Record Office Kew (PRO)
Records created or inherited by the Dominions Office (DO); Records of Colonial
Office (CO); Foreign Office (FO); War Office (WO); Papers of 1st Earl of Cromer
and 1st Earl Kitchener of Khartoum.

The British Library (BL)
Papers of Weil brothers (Weil); 1st Earl Kitchener (Kitchener); 5th Marquess of
Lansdowne (Lansdowne).

The National Army Museum (NAM)
Sir Evelyn Wood Papers.

The Brenthurst Library, Johannesburg (BLJ)
Papers of Sir Courtenay Bourchier Vyvyan; Lady Sarah Wilson; Samuel David Cawood; Lord Baden-Powell; Sir Leander Starr Jameson; Earl Kitchener of Khartoum; Viscount Milner; Joseph Chamberlain.

The Cory Library for Historical Research, Rhodes University, Grahamstown (COR)
Papers of Albert James Shimwell; Robert Bradshaw Clarke Urry; Charles Bell; Charles James Weir.

The Mafikeng Museum, Mafikeng (MAF)
Papers of Ina Cowan; John R. Algie; Sister Mary Stanislaus.

Cape Town Public Library (CTPL)
Cape Times.

Privately held
Hugh & Mirabel Cecil, Papers of the 4th Marchioness of Salisbury (AS); Milner family album.
The Hon. Lady Murray: Helen Hardinge private papers.

PRINCIPAL SOURCES

Book titles below appear in full in the Bibliography.

Chapters 1 & 2
Lady Frances Balfour, *Ne Obliviscaris*; David Cecil, *The Cecils of Hatfield*; Lady Gwendolen Cecil, *The Life of Robert 3rd Marquess of Salisbury*; Viscount Cecil of Chelwood, *All the Way* (hereinafter ref. to as 'Cecil, ATW'); Blanche Dugdale, *Family Homespun*; Lord Edward Gleichen, *A Guardsman's Memories*; Roger Lancelyn Green, ed., *Lewis Carroll Diaries*; Violet Milner, *My Picture Gallery* (hereinafter ref. to as 'MPG'); Andrew Roberts, *Salisbury*; Kenneth Rose, *The Later Cecils*.
AS, private collection, unpub. sketch of EC; HH/3MCH,/3M, notably John Strike's Memorandum Book 1877–84; EC's letters to his family at HH. WSRO, Ivor. Conversations with 6th Marquess of Salisbury.

Chapter 3
John Baynes, *Far From a Donkey*; P. Blanchart, *Henry Becque*; Alfred Cobban, *A History of Modern France, Vol 2: From the First Empire to the Fourth Republic 1799–1945*; Gregor Dallas, *At the Heart of a Tiger, Clemenceau and his World, 1841–1929*; Oxford *Dictionary of National Biography (DNB)*; George Meredith, *Beauchamp's Career*; MPG; *Pall Mall Gazette*.
BOD, VM8, unpublished memoir by VM of her mother's family; VM15, Admiral

to Lady Caroline Maxse, Clemenceau to Admiral; VM17, VM to Olive; VM18, Cissie Maxse to VM. WSRO, Maxse Papers (Admiral, Ivor, Leo, Lady Caroline). Conversations with M. Marcel Wormser.

Chapter 4
The Cable (farming journal), 18 Jan. 1896; Winston S. Churchill, *The River War*; Alfred M. Gollin, *Proconsul in Politics*; MPG; John A. Hutcheson, *Leopold Maxse and the National Review, 1893–1914*; Jane Ridley & Clayre Percy, eds., *The Letters of Arthur Balfour and Lady Elcho*; John Evelyn Wrench, *Alfred Lord Milner*.
BOD, AM Diaries; VM42, Pembroke to VM. NAS, Betty Balfour Papers. WSRO, Ivor, Leo.

Chapter 5
Sir George Arthur, *The Letters of Lord & Lady Wolseley*; Max Egremont, *Balfour*; Elizabeth Countess of Fingall, *Seventy Years Young*; Lord Edward Gleichen, *A Guardsman's Memories*; MPG; *The Times*.
BOD, VM23, 60, 37, letters of VM, Edward, and Clemenceau. HH/CHE;/3M, 3M to EC;/3MCH, EC to 3MCH;/GW, 5th, unpublished volume of Gwendolen Cecil's Life of 3M, 1892–1898. NAS, Frances Balfour, Betty Balfour Papers. WSRO, Admiral, Ivor, Leo.

Chapter 6
See refs. for Chapters 1 & 2; J.A.S. Grenville, *Salisbury and Foreign Policy*.
BOD, VM4, VM Diaries; VM8, VM, unpublished memoir; VM26, GW to VM; VM37, Clemenceau to VM. HH/GW, GW Diary, 1888.
Conversations with Iverach McDonald and the late Lord David Cecil.

Chapter 7
George H. Cassar, *Kitchener, Architect of Victory*; Lord Edward Cecil, *The Leisure of an Egyptian Official*; Winston S. Churchill, *The River War*; Lord Edward Gleichen, *A Guardsman's Memories*; A.B. de Guerville, *La Nouvelle Égypte*; Henry Keown-Boyd, *Soldiers of the Nile*; MPG; Trevor Royle, *The Kitchener Enigma*; Edward M. Spiers, ed., *Sudan, The Reconquest Reappraised*; Major F.R. Wingate, *Ten Years Captivity in the Mahdi's Camp 1882–1892* (Father Ohrwalder's story).
HH/EC, EC's Diary of the Sudan Campaign 1896. NAM, Sir Evelyn Wood Papers. PRO, WO32/6142, Kitchener's despatch.

Chapter 8
Winston S. Churchill, *The River War*; Count Gleichen, *With the Mission to Menelik, 1897*; J.A.S. Grenville, *Salisbury and Foreign Policy*; A.B. de Guerville, *La Nouvelle Égypte*, ch. 20; Cecil Headlam, ed., *Milner Papers, South Africa*; J.M.N. Jeffries, *Front Everywhere* (ch.18, Gibraltar); MPG; Sir Horace Smith-Dorrien, *Memories of Forty-Eight Years' Service* (ch. 7, Fashoda).
BOD, AM Diary; VM12, Lord Edward Cecil's Diary of Mission to Ethiopia, 1897; VM35, Brodrick to VM; VM73, Ivor Maxse to Edward Cecil. HH/CHE, letters of Lord Robert Cecil to Lady Robert Cecil; HH/GW; HH/3M, 5th Marquess of

Lansdowne to 3M. NAS, Blackwood Papers; Haig Papers. PRO, WO files, Atbara, Omdurman.

The late Lord David Cecil, information.

Chapter 9

James Bryce, *Impressions of South Africa*; *Cape Times Weekly*, 2 Aug.1899; Winston S. Churchill, *My Early Life*; Cecil Headlam, ed., *The Milner Papers: South Africa*, Vol. I; Mortimer Menpes, *War Impressions*; MPG; Lord Newton, *Lansdowne*.

BL, Weil 46848. BOD, AM Diary 1898–1900; AM, South African Journal of Ernest Bruce Iwan-Müller, 1900; VM16, VM to Leo; VM30, AM to VM. HH/3M, EC to 3M; 3M to J. Chamberlain: 'It looks as if he [Milner] has been spoiling for a fight with some glee, and does not like putting his clothes on again.'; HH/3MCH, EC to 3MCH; HH/GW, VM to GW. PRO, DO 119/358, EC to AM, AM to J. Chamberlain.

Chapter 10

Phillida Brooke Simons, Alain Proust, *Groote Schuur*; MPG; Mortimer Menpes, *War Impressions*; Graham Viney, Alain Proust: *Colonial Houses of South Africa*.

BOD, AM Diary 1899–1900; Iwan-Müller, Journal, Aug. 1900; VM18, Admiral & Cissie Maxse to VM; VM55 (correspondence with VM during Boer War). HH/GW, VM to GW.

Chapter 11

Major F.D. Baillie, *Mafeking, Diary of a Siege*; John L. Comaroff, *The Boer War Diary of Sol T. Plaatje*; Louis Creswicke, *South Africa and the Transvaal War, II, III, IV*; T.W.P. Hayes, 'Underground Soldiers and All'; Tim Jeal, *Baden-Powell*; *Pall Mall Gazette*, 2 May 1900 (J.E. Neilly); Iain R. Smith, ed., *The Siege of Mafeking*; Paddy Cartwright, ed., *The Forthright Man: Vere Stent, Reuters Correspondent*; Charles James Weir, *The Boer War: a Diary of the Siege of Mafeking*; Brian P. Willan, ed., *Diary of the Siege of Mafeking, by Edward Ross*: Ross Diary (on 26 March 1900, Ross lists some of Edward Cecil's stories: 'Cut off from the North'; 'Where would you like it My Lord?'[about Heale, the town jailer]; 'Come to tea tomorrow afternoon'; and Edward's account of finding an original letter by General Gordon in 'Khatoum' [*sic*]); Lady Sarah Wilson, *South African Memories*.

BL, Weil, 46848, 46849, 46850, 46852, 46853. BOD, VM23, EC to VM (wished he had died: 7 July 1907); VM55, letter ascribed to Sarah Isabel Delsey to VM, 8 October 1899. BLJ, Cawood Diary; Vyvyan Diary; Sarah Wilson Papers. COR, Shimwell, Bell and Urry Papers. HH/GW. MAF, Algie Diary; Ina Cowan Diary; Sister Mary Stanislaus Diary.

Re EC at Mafeking, Thomas Pakenham, *The Boer War*, p.118, writes: 'His marriage was, to tell the truth, a most unhappy one. Lord Edward had volunteered to go on this dangerous mission [to Mafeking] – had sent himself, almost as the biblical Uriah was sent to the front of the host. Death and glory. The Last Stand. It would make a fine ending for poor Lord Edward, who had long wished, as he later told Violet, that he were dead.' Pakenham also states: 'By contrast BP found . . . Major Lord Edward Cecil, his Chief of Staff – a considerable strain . . . [Cecil's] natural diffidence had been intensified by the unfortunate marriage with Violet and – since the siege had begun – by the news of the death of his mother, the woman who had dominated his life. Now his mood amounted to a kind of moral surrender. Fortunately, B-P was able to give him a task in which he could do no great harm – looking after an improvised cadet corps.'

Pakenham's view has never been corrected, even in his article 'The Besieged', in Iain R. Smith, ed., *The Siege of Mafeking* (published 2001), despite access to fresh material; rather, his misinterpretation has been perpetuated: for example, in the catalogue for a major Boer War sale in London on 20 October 1999, when EC's medals were auctioned (see bibliography), where the above quotation by Pakenham is given. Andrew Lycett, in his *Rudyard Kipling*, cites Pakenham and distorts the record in Chinese-whispers fashion: 'Cecil had volunteered as Baden-Powell's second-in-command so as to get away from his attractive, bossy wife Violet, who had found a role for herself stiffening the resolve of the High Commissioner in Cape Town' – a curious conclusion since EC was delighted for her to accompany him to South Africa and missed her in Mafeking, as his few letters smuggled out to her reveal.

As for EC being palmed off with organising 'an improvised cadet corps', Brian Gardner in *Mafeking*, pp. 65, 137, asserts: 'Baden-Powell had followed Cecil's careful training of the Cadet Corps boys . . . but he considered that Cecil was "not much use". Cecil was often ill, when Panzera took his place.' This is the opposite of what Pakenham – who cites Gardner – says. Pakenham's account of the Mafeking Siege and of Baden-Powell's role in particular has been challenged by Tim Jeal, in his balanced and scholarly biography, *Baden-Powell*, ch.7.

The photograph of the Court of Summary Jurisdiction: the most often published, perhaps the only, photograph of the court in session shows Charles Bell and EC presiding when a man is on trial for his life. In Pakenham and Gardner's books, the crime is alleged to be the theft of a goat, but according the papers of Colonel Vyvyan, who attended many of these courts, the offence on this occasion was spying. The Weil Papers, 46855, reveal that a death sentence was indeed imposed for the theft of a goat, but this was on 29 March when EC and Bell were not presiding. Copies of this photograph captioned as the trial of a spy, are also in: HH/Muniments; Brenthurst library, Vyvyan Papers; John Comaroff, *The Boer War Diary of Sol T. Plaatje,* facing p.41; *Siege Views, Mafeking, From Original Photos by E.J. Ross During the Siege*; Brian Willan, *Sol Plaatje, South African Nationalist,* facing p.116; H.W. Wilson, *With the Flag to Pretoria*, Vol. 2, p. 623. In Iain R. Smith, ed., *The Siege of Mafeking* (pub. 2001), the same picture illustrates the article which Pakenham has contributed, the caption being corrected to 'a black man accused of spying for the enemy'.

Chapter 12
The Countess of Airlie, *The Happy Warrior*; Deneys Reitz, *Commando*; MPG; Thomas Pakenham, *Boer War,* ch. 31; A.J.P. Taylor, *Bismarck*; Sir Frederick Treves, *Tales of a Field Hospital*; Ian R. Whitehead, *Doctors in the Great War*, ch.1; John Wilson, *A Life of Sir Henry Campbell-Bannerman*.
AS, private collection, 8th Countess of Airlie to AS. BOD, AM Diaries; VM4, 5, Diaries; VM8, unpublished memoir by VM; VM17, VM to Olive; VM18, Admiral to VM; VM23, EC to VM, letters from Mafeking 16 Nov 1899–19 Feb. 1900; VM35, Brodrick to VM; VM44, Dr L.S. Jameson to VM; VM55 (Boer War letters). COR,

Weir Diary. HH/3M, VM to 3M; HH/GW, VM to GW; HH/3MCH, VM to 3MCH. WSRO, Leo.

Chapter 13
Published siege diaries as for ch.11; L.S. Amery, ed.*, The Times History of the War in South Africa*, Vol. 2; Creswicke, *op. cit.*, IV, V, VI; *Daily Chronicle*, 20 Dec.1900; F.P. Fletcher-Vane, *Pax Britannica in South Africa*; MPG, chs. 28 & 29; Iain R. Smith, ed., *op.cit*; H.W. Wilson, *After Pretoria: the Guerrilla War,* Vol.1. For the quote from the poem 'Bobs', see *Rudyard Kipling's Verse, Inclusive Edition 1885–1926*, London, Hodder & Stoughton, 1927, p.388: 'Oh 'e's little but 'e's wise/'E's a terror for 'is size,/An' – 'e – does – not – advertise –/Do yer, Bobs?'
BL, Weil Papers 46852, 46848, 46854. BOD, AM Diary; Iwan-Müller Journal; VM23, EC to VM; VM35, Brodrick to VM; VM55, Cissie Bentinck to VM; VM66, Jem Cranborne to EC. COR, Shimwell, Weir and Bell Papers, 30 March 1900. HH/3M, EC to 3M; HH/GW, VM to GW; EC to GW. PRO, WO 105/7 126/95, Baden-Powell, Mafeking despatch; WO 105/10 despatches and reports re Zeerust by Gen. Carrington and Col. E.B. Herbert, Sept. 1900. WSRO, Alice Salisbury to Kitty Maxse.

Chapter 14
Clara Boyle, *Boyle of Cairo*; The Earl of Cromer, *Modern Egypt*; A.B. de Guerville, *La Nouvelle Égypte*; Stephen Gwynn, ed., *The Letters and Friendships of Sir Cecil Spring Rice*, Vol. 1; Peter Mansfield, *The British in Egypt*; Douglas Sladen, *Egypt and the English*. BOD, AM Diary; VM8, unpublished memoir by VM. HH/CHE, GW & EC to Lord & Lady Robert Cecil, GW and Maud Selborne;/GW. WSRO, Maxse Papers, EC to Kitty Maxse.

Chapter 15
Country Life, May 1922; Gollin*, op.cit.*; Alfred M.Gollin, *Balfour's Burden*; Norman & Jean MacKenzie, eds., *The Diary of Beatrice Webb,* Vol. 3; G. B. Pyrah, *Imperial Policy and South Africa, 1902–1910*; Brian Roberts, *Those Bloody Women*; Alan Sykes, *Tariff Reform and English Politics*; Arnold Toynbee, *Acquaintances*; Rhodri Williams, *Defending the Empire*; John Wilson*, A Life of Sir Henry Campbell-Bannerman*; J.E. Wrench, *Alfred Lord Milner.*
BOD, AM Diary. BLJ, AM to Joseph Chamberlain.
Information the late Lord David Cecil .

Chapter 16
See Rudyard Kipling, in *Actions and Reactions*, 'An Habitation Enforced', a story supposedly inspired by the restoration of Wigsell; Rudyard Kipling, 'Weland's Sword' in *Puck of Pook's Hill.*
BOD, AM Diaries; VM25, Nelly to VM; VM27, 65, George to VM and EC; VM44, Kiplings to VM; VM60, VM to EC; VM68-71, VM to George; VM72, letters to George from various. HH/GW, letters.
Conversations with the Davies family, owners of Wigsell 1960s–1990s, with Hardinge family and with Jocelyn Thorne, former tenant of Wigsell.

Chapter 17

Clara Boyle, *Boyle of Cairo*; Lord Edward Cecil, *The Leisure of an Egyptian Official*; Gollin, *Proconsul in Politics*; Stephen Gwynn, ed., *op.cit.*; David Lloyd George, *War Memoirs*; Roy Jenkins, *Asquith*; Peter Mansfield, *The British in Egypt*; Priscilla Napier, *A Late Beginner*. BOD, AM Diary; VM8, unpublished memoir by VM; VM23, EC to VM; VM65, Cromer to EC. Helen Hardinge, private papers, Helen diary 1914. HH/CHE, GW to Lord and Lady Robert Cecil; HH/GW, GW to Maud Selborne. WSRO, Maxse Papers, EC to Kitty Maxse.

Chapter 18

J.M. Craster, *Fifteen Rounds a Minute*; Burton J. Hendrick, *The Life and Letters of Walter Hines Page*; *A King's Story: the Memoirs of HRH The Duke of Windsor*. BOD, AM diary; VM48, Angela Manners (Hore-Ruthven) to VM; VM60, VM to EC; Helen Hardinge, private papers, Helen Diary 1914.

Chapter 19

David Cecil, *The Cecils of Hatfield*; Cecil, ATW; Craster, *op.cit.*; Ethel Desborough, ed., *Pages from a Family Journal, 1888–1915*; Burton J. Hendrick, *op.cit.*; Tonie & Valmai Holt, *My Boy Jack?*; Thomas Pinney, ed., *The Letters of Rudyard Kipling*, vol. 4; Jane Ridley, Clayre Percy, eds., *The Letters of Arthur Balfour and Lady Elcho*. AS, private collection. BOD, AM Diaries; VM24, Jem to VM; VM25, Lord Robert Cecil to VM; VM27, re death of George; VM30, AM to VM; VM44, Kipling to VM; VM48, Angela Manners to VM ; VM60, 61, VM to EC; VM66, Lord Robert Cecil to EC. Helen Hardinge, private papers, Helen Diary 1914; WSRO, Clemenceau and Kipling to Leo.

Chapter 20

Lord Edward Cecil, *The Leisure of an Egyptian Official*; Cecil, ATW; M.W. Daly, *The Sirdar: Sir Reginald Wingate and the British Empire in the Middle East*; DNB, Lord Edward Cecil; Gollin, *Proconsul in Politics*; *Hertfordshire Advertiser*, 8 Jan.1919; David Lloyd George, *War Memoirs*; Peter Mansfield, *The British in Egypt*; Priscilla Napier, *op.cit.*; Andrew Wood, 'The Duke of Westminster's Favourite Rolls-Royce', in *Despatches, The Magazine of The Friends of the Imperial War Museum*, Dec. 2000. BOD, AM Diary; VM23, EC to VM; VM24, Alice Salisbury to EC; VM30, AM to VM; VM60, VM to EC; VM66, 67, letters to EC; Helen Hardinge, private papers, Helen Diary 1916; PRO, FO 407/183, 185, papers re Egypt in war, role of Colonial and Foreign Offices. SAD, Wingate, EC, letters. PEM, Ronald Storrs Papers.

Chapter 21

Robert Blake, ed., *The Private Papers of Douglas Haig 1914–1919*; Lord Edward Cecil, *op.cit.*; Joseph McPherson, *Bimbashi McPherson: a Life in Egypt*; Kenneth Rose, *The Later Cecils*, ch. 7. BOD, AM Diary; VM3, papers re estate of EC 1917–1919; VM12, papers re EC's book; VM23, EC to VM; VM60, VM to EC. HH/CHE, Nelly Cecil. Conversations with Angelo Hornak about Egyptian reaction to EC's book, and with the late Lord David Cecil.

Chapter 22
John Baynes, *Far From a Donkey, The Life of General Sir Ivor Maxse*; Georges Clemenceau, *Grandeurs et Misères d'une Victoire*; Michael De-la-Noy, *Eddy, The Life of Edward Sackville-West*; Wilfrid Ewart, *Scots Guard*; Peter Mansfield, *The British in Egypt*; Sir Frederick Ponsonby, *Recollections of Three Reigns*; J.P.R. Wallis, *Fitz, The Life of Sir Percy FitzPatrick*.
BOD, AM Diary. HH/CHE, Lord Robert Cecil's Diary of the Peace Conference. NAS, Betty Balfour Diary, 1919.

Chapter 23
Clough Williams Ellis, *Britain and the Beast*; John Marlowe, *Milner, Apostle of Empire*; *National Review*.
BOD, AM Diary; VM4, Diary; VM11, press cuttings; VM17, VM to Olive.

Chapter 24
Viscount Cecil of Chelwood, *The Great Experiment*; John Charmley, *Lord Lloyd and The Decline of the British Empire*; *National Review*; F.A. Voigt, *Unto Caesar*.
BOD, VM4, 5, Diaries.
Conversations with Iverach McDonald and the late 5th Marquess of Salisbury.

Chapter 25
James Lees-Milne, *Ancestral Voices*; *National Review*.
BOD, VM5, 6, Diaries.
Conversations with Iverach McDonald and the 6th Marquess of Salisbury.

Chapter 26
Cecil Headlam, ed., *The Milner Papers*; MPG. Keith Jeffery, ed., *The Military Correspondence of Field Marshal Sir Henry Wilson*.
AS, private collection. BOD, VM4, 5, 6, Diaries; VM8, 9, typescripts for MPG and 'Material for Vols.I & II'; VM47, letters to VM.
Conversations with the late Lord David Cecil, John Grigg, Viscount Hardinge, Hugh Hardinge, Sir John Johnston, Iverach McDonald and the Hon. Lady Murray.

Bibliography

All books were published in London unless otherwise stated.

Adams, R.J.Q. and Poirier, Philip P., *The Conscription Controversy in Great Britain, 1900–16*, Macmillan, 1987

Addison, Paul, *Churchill on the Home Front, 1900–1955*, Jonathan Cape, 1992

Airlie, Countess of, *The Happy Warrior: a Short Account of the Life of David 9th Earl of Airlie*, printed for private circulation, Winchester, Jacob & Johnson 'Hampshire Chronicle' Office, 1901

Amery, The Right Honourable L.S., *My Political Life, Vol. 1: England before the Storm, 1896–1914*, Hutchinson, 1953

——*The Times History of The War in South Africa 1899–1902*, Vols I & II, Marston, Samson Low, 1902

Arthur, Sir George, ed., *The Letters of Lord & Lady Wolseley 1870–1911*, Heinemann, 1922

Bacon's Road-Atlas for South-East England, for Cyclists and Motorists, G.W. Bacon, 1908

Baillie, Major F.D., *Mafeking, A Diary of the Siege*, Archibald Constable, 1900

Balfour, Lady Elizabeth, ed., 'Hatfield Letters, 1883–1903', unpublished, Hatfield House

Balfour, Lady Frances, *Ne Obliviscaris ('Dinna Forget')*, 2 vols, The Camelot Press, 1930

Barnett, Correlli, *The Collapse of British Power*, 2nd ed., Gloucester, Alan Sutton, 1984

Baynes, John, *Far from a Donkey: the Life of General Sir Ivor Maxse KCB, CVO, DSO*, Brassey's, 1995

Beaverbrook, Lord, *Men and Power, 1917–1918*, Hutchinson, 1956

——*Politicians and the War, 1914–1916*, Oldbourne Book Co., 1959

Belfield, Eversley, *The Boer War*, Leo Cooper, 1975

Bennett, Ernest N., 'After Omdurman', in *Contemporary Review 75*, Jan. 1899

Birkenhead, Lord, *Rudyard Kipling*, Weidenfeld & Nicolson, 1978

Black and White Budget, Vols 2 & 3, Jan.–June 1900

Black and White, Vols 18–20, Oct.1899–Sep. 1900

Blake, Robert, ed., *The Private Papers of Douglas Haig 1914–1919*, Eyre & Spottiswoode, 1952

——and Cecil, Hugh, *Salisbury, the Man and his Policies*, Macmillan, 1987

Blanchart, P., *Henry Becque*, Paris, NRC, 1931

Bloem, Walter, *The Advance from Mons, 1914*, Davies, 1930

Bottomley, John, ed., 'Underground Soldiers and All, A Diary of the Mafeking Siege', by T.W.P. Hayes, District Surgeon, *New Contree* no. 41, June 1997, Mafikeng, Occasional/Centenary Publication, University of the North-West

Boyle, Clara, *Boyle of Cairo*, Kendal, Titus Wilson, 1965

Briggs, Martin S., *Through Egypt in War-Time*, T. Fisher Unwin, 1918

Brock, Michael and Eleanor, eds, *H.H. Asquith Letters to Venetia Stanley*, Oxford, Oxford University Press, 1982

Brooke Simons, Phillida, photographs by Proust, Alain, *Groote Schuur: Great Granary to Stately Home*, Johannesburg, Fernwood Press, 1996

Bryce, James, *Impressions of South Africa*, 3rd edn, Macmillan, 1899

Buchan, John, *Memory-Hold-the-Door*, Hodder & Stoughton, 1940

Butler, Lieut.-General The Rt. Hon. Sir W.F., GCB, *Sir William Butler, an Autobiography*, Constable, 1911

Cannadine, David, *Ornamentalism*, Harmondsworth, Allen Lane, The Penguin Press, 2001

Carrington, Charles, *Rudyard Kipling*, Macmillan, 1955

Cartwright, Paddy, ed., *The Forthright Man: Vere Stent, Reuter's Correspondent*, Cape Town, Howard Timmins, 1972

Cassar, George H., *Kitchener: Architect of Victory*, William Kimber, 1977

Cassell's History of the Boer War 1899–1902, Vol.1, Cassell, 1903

Cawood, Samuel, *The Defence of Ladysmith & Mafeking*, part II: 'The Siege of Mafeking, Diary of Samuel Cawood, Subcommandant', Brenthurst Library Press, Johannesburg, 1983

Cecil, David, *The Cecils of Hatfield House*, Constable, 1973

Cecil, Lord Edward, KCMG, DSO, *The Leisure of an Egyptian Official*, 2nd edn, Hodder & Stoughton, 1921

Cecil, Evelyn, MP, *On the Eve of the War*, John Murray, 1900

Cecil, Lady Gwendolen, *The Life of Robert, Marquis of Salisbury*, 4 vols, Hodder & Stoughton, 1921–1932

Cecil of Chelwood, Viscount, *All the Way*, Hodder & Stoughton, 1949

——*The Great Experiment*, Jonathan Cape, 1941

Chandos, Viscount, *From Peace to War–A Study in Contrast, 1857–1918*, The Bodley Head, 1968

Charmley, John, *Lord Lloyd and the Decline of the British Empire*, Weidenfeld & Nicolson, 1987

Churchill, Randolph S., *Winston S. Churchill, Vol. 1, 1896–1900*, Heinemann, 1967

Churchill, Winston S., *My Early Life, a Roving Commission*, The Reprint Society, 1930

——*The River War, an Historical Account of The Reconquest of the Soudan*, Longmans Green, 1902

Clark, Alan, ed., *'A Good Innings': the Private Papers of Viscount Lee of Fareham*, John Murray, 1974

Clemenceau, Georges, *Georges Clemenceau à son ami Claude Monet, correspondence*, Paris, Editions de la Réunion des Musées Nationaux, 1993

——*Claude Monet*, Paris, Perrin, 1928

——*Grandeurs and Miseries of Victory*, George Harrap, 1930

Cobban, Alfred, *A History of Modern France, Vol. 2: From the First Empire to the Fourth Republic 1799–1945*, Harmondsworth, Penguin Books, 1961

Cohen, Morton, ed., *Rudyard Kipling to Rider Haggard, the Record of a Friendship*, Hutchinson, 1965

Comaroff, John L., *The Boer War Diary of Sol T. Plaatje: An African at Mafeking*, Macmillan, 1973

Conan Doyle, A., *The Great Boer War*, 3rd impression, Smith, Elder, 1900

——*The British Campaigns in France and Flanders, 1914*, Hodder & Stoughton, 1916

Cook, Edward T., *Rights and Wrongs of the Transvaal War*, Edward Arnold, 1901.

Cook, Col. H.C.B, OBE, ed., 'Letters from South Africa, 1899–1902', *Journal of the Society for Army Historical Research, Vols LXVIII & LXIX*, nos. 278–9, Granby, Grillford, 1991

Crankshaw, Edward, *The Forsaken Idea, a Study of Viscount Milner*, Longmans Green, 1952

Craster, J.M., *'Fifteen Rounds a Minute': the Grenadiers at War, August to December 1914, edited from the diaries and letters of Major 'Ma' Jeffreys and others*, Macmillan, 1968

Creswicke, Louis, *South Africa and the Transvaal War, and after*, 6 vols, The Caxton Publishing Co., 1902

Cromer, the Earl of, *Modern Egypt*, 2 vols, London, Macmillan, 1908 (2nd edn, Macmillan, 1911)

Curzon of Kedleston, The Marchioness, *Reminiscences*, Hutchinson, 1955

Dallas, Gregor, *At the Heart of a Tiger, Clemenceau and his World, 1841–1929*, New York, Carroll & Graf, 1993

Daly, M.W., *The Sirdar: Sir Reginald Wingate and the British Empire in the Middle East*, Philadelphia, The American Philosophical Society, 1997

De-la-Noy, Michael, *Eddy, The Life of Edward Sackville-West*, 1st edn (withdrawn), The Bodley Head, 1988

Desborough, Ethel, ed., *Pages from a Family Journal, 1888–1915*, Eton College, Spottiswoode Ballantyne, 1916

Dugdale, Blanche, *Family Homespun*, John Murray, 1940

——*Arthur James Balfour, First Earl of Balfour KG OM FRS, 1906–1930*, 2 vols, Hutchinson, 1936

Earle, Sir Lionel, *Turn Over The Page*, Hutchinson, 1935

Egremont, Max, *Balfour*, Collins, 1980

Emden, Paul H., *Randlords*, Hodder & Stoughton, 1935

Evans, Howard, *Our Old Nobility*, Manchester, *The Daily News & Leader*, 1913

Evans, Martin Marix, *The Boer War, South Africa 1899–1902*, Oxford, Osprey, 1999

Ewart, Wilfrid, *Scots Guard*, Rich & Cowan, 1934

Fingall, Elizabeth Countess of, *Seventy Years Young*, Collins, 1937

Fitzpatrick J.P., *The Transvaal from Within: a Private Record of Public Affairs*, Heinemann, 1899

Fletcher-Vane, F.P., *Pax Britannica in South Africa*, Archibald Constable, 1906

Gardner, Brian, *Mafeking: a Victorian Legend*, Cassell, 1966

Garland, Madge, *The Changing Face of Beauty*, Weidenfeld & Nicolson, 1957

Garvin, J.L., *The Life of Joseph Chamberlain, Vol. 3, 1895–1900: Empire and World Policy*, Macmillan, 1934

Gilmour, David, *Curzon*, John Murray, 1994

Gleichen, Major-General Lord Edward (Count Gleichen), *A Guardsman's Memories*, Blackwood, 1932

——*With the Mission to Menelik, 1897*, Edward Arnold, 1898

Gollin, A.M., *Balfour's Burden*, Anthony Blond, 1965

——*Proconsul in Politics: a Study of Lord Milner in Opposition and in Power*, Anthony Blond, 1964

Graham, Stephen, *A Private in The Guards*, Macmillan, 1919

Grenville, J.A.S., *Lord Salisbury and Foreign Policy*, revised edn, Athlone Press, 1970

Grigg, John, *Lloyd George, the People's Champion, 1902–1911*, Methuen, 1978

Guerville, A.B. de, *La Nouvelle Égypte*, Paris, La Librairie Universelle, 1909

Gwynn, Stephen, ed., *The Letters and Friendships of Sir Cecil Spring Rice, A Record, Vol.1*, Constable, 1929

Hancock, W.K., *Smuts, Vol. 1, The Sanguine Years 1870–1919*, Cambridge, Cambridge University Press, 1962

Harcourt Williams, Robin, ed., introduction by Hugh Cecil, *The Salisbury–Balfour Correspondence, 1869–1892*, Linton, Cambridge, The Hertfordshire Record Society, 1988

Headlam, Cecil, ed., *The Milner Papers: South Africa 1897–1905*, 2 vols, Cassell, 1931–3

Hendrick, Burton J., *The Life and Letters of Walter H. Page*, 3 vols, New York, Doubleday Page, 1922, 1925

Higgins, D.S., ed., *The Private Diaries of Sir H. Rider Haggard, 1914–1925*, London, Cassell, 1980

Holt, Tonie & Valmai, *My Boy Jack? The Search for Kipling's Only Son*, Barnsley, South Yorkshire, Leo Cooper/Pen & Sword, 1998

Horner, Frances, *Time Remembered*, Heinemann, 1933

——*The Household Brigade Magazine*, Vol. III, no. 26, 1900

Hunter, Archie, *Kitchener's Sword-Arm: the Life and Campaigns of General Sir Archibald Hunter GCB, GCVO, DSO*, Staplehurst, Spellmount, 1996

Hurst, Sir Arthur, *Medical Diseases of War*, Edward Arnold, 1916

Hutcheson, John A., *Leopold Maxse and the National Review, 1893–1914: Right-Wing Politics and Journalism in the Edwardian Era*, New York & London, Garland, 1989

Iwan-Müller, E.B., *Lord Milner and South Africa*, Heinemann, 1902

James, Robert Rhodes, *The British Revolution, Vol. I: 1880–1914*, Hamish Hamilton, 1976

Jeal, Tim, *Baden-Powell*, Hutchinson, 1989

Jefferey, Keith, ed., *The Military Correspondence of Field Marshal Sir Henry Wilson, 1918–1922*, The Bodley Head, for the Army Records Society, 1985

Jeffries, J.M.N., *Front Everywhere*, Hutchinson, 1934

Jenkins, Roy, *Asquith*, Collins, 1964

Jones, Mervyn, *The Amazing Victorian, A Life of George Meredith*, Constable, 1999

Kedourie, Elie, *The Anglo-Arab Labyrinth*, 2nd edn, Frank Cass, 2000

Kelly, R. Talbot, *Egypt Painted and described by . . .*, A. & C. Black, 1912

Keown-Boyd, Henry, *Soldiers of the Nile, a Biographical History of the British Officers of the Egyptian Army 1882–1925*, Herefordshire, Thornbury Publications, 1996

Kiernan, R.H., *Baden-Powell*, Harrap, 1939

Kipling, Rudyard, *Actions and Reactions*, Macmillan, 1909

——*Puck of Pook's Hill*, Macmillan, 1917 (1ˢᵗ edition1906)

——*Rewards and Fairies*, Macmillan, 1910

——*Rudyard Kipling's Verse Inclusive Edition 1885–1926*, Hodder & Stoughton, 1927

——*The Day's Work*, Macmillan, 1904

——*Something of Myself: for My Friends Known and Unknown*, New York, Doubleday Doran, 1937

Knight, E F., *South Africa after the War: a Narrative of Recent Travel*, Longmans Green, 1903

Koss, Stephen, *The Pro-Boers: the Anatomy of an Antiwar Movement*, Chicago, University of Chicago Press, 1973

Kusel, Baron de, *An Englishman's Recollections of Egypt 1863 to 1887*, John Lane, The Bodley Head, 1895

Lamb, Richard, *The Drift To War 1922–1939*, W.H. Allen, 1989

Lee, Emanoel, *To The Bitter End: a Photographic History of the Boer War 1899–1902*, Harmondsworth, Penguin Books, 1986

Le May, G.H.L., *British Supremacy in South Africa 1899–1907*, Oxford, Oxford University Press, 1965

Lees-Milne, James, *Ancestral Voices*, Faber & Faber, 1975

Leslie, Shane, *The End of a Chapter*, Constable, 1916

Lloyd-George, David, *War Memoirs*, Nicholson & Watson, 2 vols, 1933

Lockhart, J.G. & Woodhouse, The Hon. C.M., *Rhodes*, Hodder & Stoughton, 1963

Lucas, E.V., *Highways & Byways in Sussex*, Macmillan, 1950

Lutyens, Lady Emily, *A Blessed Girl: Memoirs of a Victorian Girlhood Chronicled in an Exchange of Letters, 1887–1896*, Rupert Hart-Davis, 1953

Lycett, Andrew, *Rudyard Kipling*, Weidenfeld & Nicolson, 1999

Lyttelton, General Sir Neville, *Eighty Years*, Hodder & Stoughton, 1927

McFee, William, *North of Suez*, Heinemann, 1930

Mackay, Ruddock, *Balfour, Intellectual Statesman*, Oxford, Oxford University Press, 1985

MacKenzie, John M., *Propaganda and Empire: the Manipulation of British Public Opinion, 1880–1960*, Manchester, Manchester University Press, 1984

MacKenzie, Norman & Jean, eds, *The Diary Of Beatrice Webb, Vol. 3: 1905–1924: The Power To Alter Things*, Virago, 1984

McPherson, Joseph, *Bimbashi McPherson: a Life in Egypt*, BBC, 1983

Magnus, Philip, *Kitchener: Portrait of an Imperialist*, John Murray, 1958

Mahfouz, Naguib, *Palace Walk, The Cairo Trilogy, Vol. 1*, Black Swan edn, 1994 (1st edn 1956)

Mansfield, Peter, *The British in Egypt*, Weidenfeld & Nicolson, 1971

Marling, Colonel Sir Percival, BT VC CB, *Rifleman and Hussar*, John Murray, 1931

Marlowe, John, *Milner, Apostle of Empire*, Hamish Hamilton, 1976

Martet, Jean, *Clemenceau*, Longmans, 1930

Maxse, Colonel F.I., CB DSO, *Seymour Vandeleur: the Story of a British Officer*, Heinemann, 1906

Maxse, Major & Mrs J.H., *Catalogue of the Maxse Family Papers Deposited in the West Sussex Record Office*, Chichester County Record Office, 1957

Mary Maxse, 1870–1941, A Record Compiled by her Family, privately printed, 1948

Medlicott, W.N., *Contemporary England 1914–1964*, Longmans Green, 1967

Menpes, Mortimer, *War Impressions – Being a Record in Colour*, A. & C. Black, 1901

Meredith, George, *Beauchamp's Career*, Archibald Constable, 1909

Middlemas, Keith & Barnes, John, *Baldwin: A Biography*, Weidenfeld & Nicolson, 1969

Midleton, The Earl of, *Records and Reactions 1856–1939*, John Murray, 1939

Millet, Philippe, *En Liaison avec Les Anglais, Souvenirs de Campagne*, Paris, Librairie Académique, Perrin, 1916

Millin, Sarah Gertrude, *Rhodes*, Chatto & Windus, 1952

Milner, Alfred, *England in Egypt*, Edward Arnold, 1894 edn

Milner, Viscountess, *My Picture Gallery*, John Murray, 1951

Mordacq, Général, *Le Ministère Clemenceau, Vols I & II*, Paris, Librairie Plon, 1930

Morris, James, *Vol. 1: Heaven's Command – An Imperial Progress*; *Vol. 2: Pax Britannica*; *Vol. 3: the Climax of an Empire*; *Farewell the Trumpets – An Imperial Retreat*, Penguin Books, 1979

Murphy, Dervla, *South from the Limpopo, Travels through South Africa*, John Murray, 1997

Napier, Priscilla, *A Late Beginner*, Michael Joseph, 1966

Officers died in the Great War 1914–1919, Polstead, Suffolk, J.B. Hayward, 1988

Pakenham, Thomas, *The Boer War*, Weidenfeld & Nicolson, 1979

Paterson, A.B., *Happy Dispatches*, Australia, Angus & Robertson, 1934

Perkin, Harold, *The Rise of Professional Society, England Since 1880*, Routledge, 1989

Pinney, Thomas, ed., *The Letters of Rudyard Kipling, 1911–1919*, vol. 4, Iowa City, University of Iowa Press, 1999

Ponsonby, Sir Frederick, *Recollections of Three Reigns*, Eyre & Spottiswoode, 1951

Porter, A.N., *The Origins of the South African War: Joseph Chamberlain and the Diplomacy of Imperialism 1895–99*, Manchester, Manchester University Press, 1980

Pretorius, Fransjohan, *Life On Commando During The Anglo-Boer War 1899–1902*, Cape Town, Human & Rousseau, 1999

Pyrah, G.B., *Imperial Policy and South Africa 1902–1910*, Oxford, Oxford University Press, 1955

Read, Donald, *England 1868–1914*, Longmans, 1979

Reitz, Deneys, *Commando: a Boer Journal of the Boer War*, Faber & Faber, 1929

——*No Outspan*, Faber & Faber, 1943

Lord Riddell's Intimate Diary of the Peace Conference and After, 1918–1923, Gollancz, 1933

Ridley, Jane, & Percy, Clayre, eds, *The Letters of Arthur Balfour and Lady Elcho*, Hamish Hamilton, 1992

Robbins, Keith, *A Biography of Lord Grey of Fallodon*, Cassell, 1971

Roberts, Andrew, *Salisbury, Victorian Titan*, Weidenfeld & Nicolson, 1999

Roberts, Brian, *Cecil Rhodes and the Princess*, Hamish Hamilton, 1969

——*Those Bloody Women: Three Heroines of the Boer War*, John Murray, 1991

Rose, Kenneth, *The Later Cecils*, Weidenfeld & Nicolson, 1975

Rose, Norman, *The Cliveden Set: Portrait of an Exclusive Fraternity*, Jonathan Cape, 2000

Ross, E.J., *Siege Views, Mafeking, From Original Photos During the Siege*, Eyre & Spottiswoode, 1900

Royle, Trevor, *The Kitchener Enigma*, London, Michael Joseph, 1985

Salehurst, The Parish Church of Saint Mary the Virgin, A Short History and Guide, Hastings, 1996

Salmond, Monica, *Bright Armour*, Faber & Faber, 1935

Sassoon, Siegfried, *Meredith*, Constable, 1948

Semmel, Bernard, *Imperialism and Social Reform: English Social-Imperial Thought 1895–1914*, George Allen & Unwin, 1960

Shannon, R., *The Age of Salisbury 1881–1902*, Longman, 1996

Sladen, Douglas, *Egypt and the English*, Hurst & Blackett, 1908

Smith, Iain R., ed., *The Siege of Mafeking*, 2 vols, Johannesburg, The Brenthurst Press, 2001

Smith-Dorrien, General Sir Horace, GCB, GCMG, DSO, *Memories of Forty-Eight Years' Service*, John Murray, 1925

Sparks, Alister, *The Mind of South Africa: the Story of the Rise and Fall of Apartheid*, Heinemann, 1990

Spiers, Edward M. (ed.), *Sudan: the Reconquest Reappraised*, Frank Cass, 1998

Spink, Sale Catalogue, London Wednesday 20 & Thursday 21 October, 1999: *The Anglo-Boer War Anniversary 1899–1999, Orders, Decorations and Campaign Medals Militaria and Memorabilia*, pub. Christie's Media Division, 1999

Stansky, Peter, *Ambitions and Strategies*, Oxford, Oxford University Press, 1964

Steele, E.D., *Lord Salisbury: a Political Biography*, University College London Press, 1999

Steevens, G.W., *With Kitchener to Khartum*, 13th edn, Edinburgh & London, Blackwood, 1898

——*From Capetown to Ladysmith*, 2nd edn, Edinburgh & London, Blackwood, 1900

Storrs, Ronald, *Orientations*, Ivor Nicholson & Watson, 1937

Sykes, Alan, *Tariff Reform in British Politics, 1903–1913*, Oxford, Oxford University Press, 1979

Taylor, A.J.P., *The Struggle for Mastery in Europe 1848–1918*, Oxford, Oxford University Press, 1943

——*Bismarck: The Man and Statesman*, New York, Knopf, 1955

Toynbee, Arnold J., *Acquaintances*, Oxford, Oxford University Press, 1967

Treves, Sir Frederick, *Tales of a Field Hospital*, Cassell, 1901

Viney, Graham and Proust, Alain, *Colonial Houses of South Africa*, Cape Town, Struik-Winchester, 1987

Voigt, F.A., *Unto Caesar*, Constable, 1938

Wallace, J.P.R., *Fitz: the Story of Sir Percy FitzPatrick*, Macmillan, 1955

Warburg, Gabriel, *The Sudan Under Wingate: Administration in the Anglo-Egyptian Sudan (1899–1916)*, Frank Cass, 1971

Wedgwood, Rt. Hon. Josiah C., *A Fighting Life*, Hutchinson, 1941

Weir, Charles James, Accountant at the Standard Bank, Mafeking, *The Boer War: a Diary of the Siege of Mafeking*, Spence & Phimister, 1901

Wells, H.G., *The Wheels of Chance*, J.M, Dent, 1896

Wheatcroft, Geoffrey, *The Randlords: the Men Who Made South Africa*, Weidenfeld & Nicolson, 1985

Whitehead, Ian R., *Doctors in the Great War*, London/Barnsley, Leo Cooper/Pen & Sword, 1999

Willan, Brian P., ed., *Diary of the Siege of Mafeking, October 1899 to May 1900, by Edward Ross*, Cape Town, van Riebeck Society, 1980

——'The Siege of Mafeking', in Warwick, Peter and Spies, S.B., eds, *The South African War: the Anglo-Boer War 1899–1902*, Longman-Trewin Copplestone Books, 1980

——*Sol Plaatje, South African Nationalist, 1876–1932*, Heinemann, 1984

Williams, A. Susan, *Ladies of Influence, Women of the Elite in Interwar Britain*, Allen Lane, The Penguin Press, 2000

Williams, Rhodri, *Defending the Empire: the Conservative Party and British Defence Policy 1899–1915*, New Haven, Yale University Press, 1991

Williams Ellis, Clough, *Britain and the Beast*, J.M. Dent, 1937

Williamson, Henry, *How Dear is Life*, Macdonald, 1954

Wilson, Angus, *The Strange Ride of Rudyard Kipling: His Life and Works*, Book Club Associates, 1977

Wilson, H.W., *With the Flag to Pretoria: A History of the Boer War of 1899–1900, Vol. 1*, Harmsworth Brothers, 1900

Wilson, H.W., *After Pretoria: the Guerrilla War*, Vol.1, Harmsworth Brothers, 1902

Wilson, John, C.B., *A Life of Sir Henry Campbell-Bannerman*, Constable, 1973

Wilson, Lady Sarah, *South African Memories*, Edward Arnold, 1909

Wilson, Trevor, ed., *The Political Diaries of C.P. Scott, 1911–1928*, Collins, 1970

Windsor, HRH The Duke of, *A King's Story: the Memoirs of HRH The Duke of Windsor*, Cassell, 1951

Wingate, Major F.R., RA, *Ten Years Captivity in the Mahdi's Camp 1882–1892, from the Original Manuscripts of Father Joseph Ohrwalder*, 13th edn, Sampson, Low, Marston, 1892

Wood, Andrew, 'The Duke of Westminster's Favourite Rolls-Royce', in *Despatches, The Magazine of the Friends of the Imperial War Museum*, Dec. 2000, Lambeth

Wormser, Georges, *Clemenceau vu de près*, Paris, Hachette, 1979

——*La république de Clemenceau*, Paris, Presses Universitaires de France, 1961

Wrench, J.E., *Alfred Lord Milner: the Man of No Illusions, 1854–1925*, Eyre & Spottiswoode, 1958

Young, K., *Balfour*, Bell, 1963

Zetland, The Marquis of, *Lord Cromer: being the authorized life of Evelyn Baring, First Earl of Cromer GCB, OM, GCMG, KCSI*, Hodder & Stoughton, 1932

Photographic Acknowledgements

We would like to thank Angelo Hornak for the majority of the photographic copyright work; the Marquess and Marchioness of Salisbury for the loan of photographs for the illustrations on pp. 3, 4, 9, 18, 19, 21, 59, 77, 79, 139, 191 and 328, and the front endpaper, and for permission to use the Hatfield House photographic archive; and Robin Harcourt Williams, the Hatfield House Librarian and Archivist, for his help in selecting illustrations.

We would also like to thank Hugh Hardinge and the Hardinge family for permission to use, from their family albums and Violet's autobiography, the illustrations on pp. 30, 33, 35, 40, 45, 48, 51, 81, 86, 100, 113, 126, 131, 137, 142, 151, 157, 159, 164, 189, 200, 211, 215, 217, 237, 239, 257, 259, 299, 305, 313, 318 and 321, and the rear endpaper, and, from the Violet Milner Papers in the Bodleian Library, that on p. 121. For the use of photographs and portraits in their possession, we thank the Hon. Lady Murray (pp. 226, 253 and 331), Sir John Johnston and Joanna Johnston (frontispiece and p. 52); the Mafikeng Museum (p. 112); Amanda Clements for the loan of her grandfather's 1918 album (p. 295); and Richard Davies for the preservation and generous gift of the album of Alfred Milner's early years in Germany, London and Oxford, from which the illustrations on pp. 54 and 55 are taken. Count Gleichen, *With the Mission to Menelik*, is the source for the illustration on p. 101. 'Breamore Down' on p. 261 is from Heywood Sumner, *Ancient Earthworks of Cranborne Chase*, and those on pp. 91 and 96 are from Guerville, *La Nouvelle Égypte*. The remaining illustrations are in the possession of the authors.

Index

Page numbers in *italic* indicate illustrations